A HIGHER FORM OF KILLING

A Higher Form of Killing

Six Weeks in World War I That Forever
Changed the Nature of Warfare

DIANA PRESTON

BLOOMSBURY PRESS
NEW YORK · LONDON · NEW DELHI · SYDNEY

Bloomsbury Press
An imprint of Bloomsbury Publishing Plc

1385 Broadway   50 Bedford Square
New York   London
NY 10018   WC1B 3DP
USA   UK

www.bloomsbury.com

BLOOMSBURY and the Diana logo are trademarks of Bloomsbury Publishing Plc

First published 2015

© Diana Preston 2015
Maps © Jeffrey L. Ward 2015

ISBN: HB 978-1-62040-212-2
PB: 978-1-62040-214-6
ePub: 978-1-62040-213-9

LIBRARY OF CONGRESS CATALOGING-IN-PUBLICATION DATA

Preston, Diana, 1952–
A higher form of killing : six weeks in world war I that forever changed the nature of warfare / Diana
Preston. —First U.S. edition.
pages cm
Includes bibliographical references and index.
ISBN 978-1-62040-212-2 (hardback) 978-1-62040-214-6 (paperback) 978-1-62040-213-9 (ebook)
1. Germany—Armed Forces—Weapons systems—History—20th century. 2. Weapons of mass
destruction—Germany—History—20th century. 3. Ypres, 2nd Battle of, Ieper, Belgium, 1915. 4. World
War, 1914-1918—Chemical warfare. 5. Lusitania (Steamship) 6. World War, 1914-1918—Naval
operations—Submarine. 7. Bombing, Aerial—England—London—History—20th century. 8. Airships—
Germany—History—20th century. 9. Just war doctrine—History—20th century. 10. War
(Philosophy)—History—20th century. I. Title.
UF505.G3P74 2015
940.4'21—dc23
2014019999

2 4 6 8 10 9 7 5 3 1

Typeset by Hewer Text UK Ltd, Edinburgh
Printed and bound in the U.S.A. by Thomson-Shore Inc., Dexter, Michigan

To find out more about our authors and books visit www.bloomsbury.com.
Here you will find extracts, author interviews, details of forthcoming events and the option
to sign up for our newsletters.

Bloomsbury books may be purchased for business or promotional use.
For information on bulk purchases please contact Macmillan Corporate and
Premium Sales Department at specialmarkets@macmillan.com..

CONTENTS

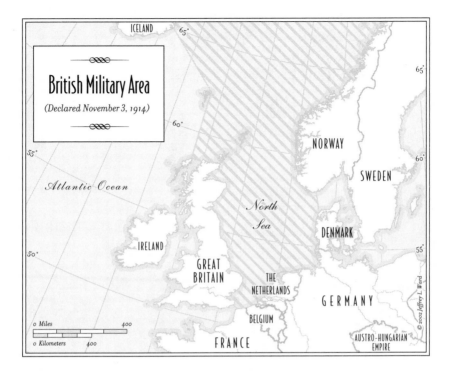

British Military Area
(Declared November 3, 1914)

ICELAND

Atlantic Ocean

NORWAY

SWEDEN

North Sea

DENMARK

IRELAND

GREAT BRITAIN

THE NETHERLANDS

GERMANY

BELGIUM

FRANCE

AUSTRO-HUNGARIAN EMPIRE

© 2002 Jeffrey L. Ward

Miles 400
Kilometers 400

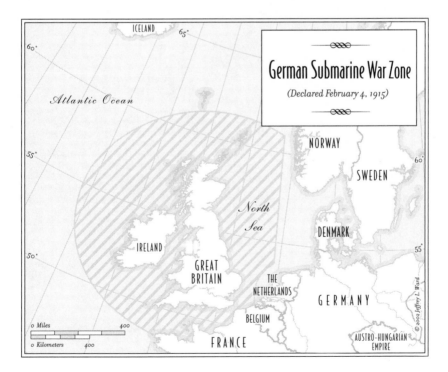

German Submarine War Zone
(Declared February 4, 1915)

ICELAND

Atlantic Ocean

NORWAY

SWEDEN

North Sea

DENMARK

IRELAND

GREAT BRITAIN

THE NETHERLANDS

GERMANY

BELGIUM

FRANCE

AUSTRO-HUNGARIAN EMPIRE

© 2002 Jeffrey L. Ward

Miles 400
Kilometers 400

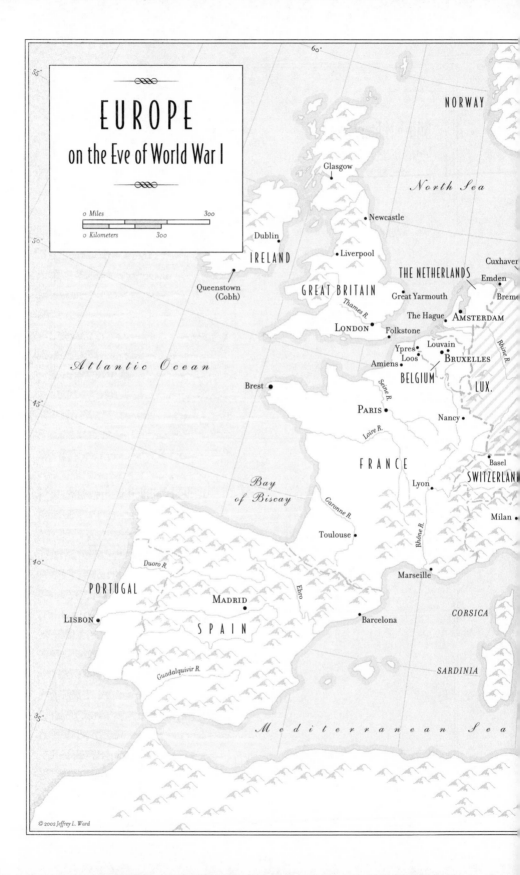

EUROPE
on the Eve of World War I

0 Miles 300
0 Kilometers 300

NORWAY

North Sea

Glasgow

Newcastle

Dublin

Liverpool

IRELAND

Cuxhaven

THE NETHERLANDS

Emden

Queenstown
(Cobh)

GREAT BRITAIN

Great Yarmouth

Bremen

Thames R.

The Hague

AMSTERDAM

LONDON

Folkstone

Ypres

Louvain

Atlantic Ocean

Loos

BRUXELLES

Amiens

BELGIUM

Rhine R.

Brest

Seine R.

LUX.

PARIS

Nancy

Loire R.

FRANCE

Basel

SWITZERLAND

Lyon

Bay
of Biscay

Garonne R.

Milan

Toulouse

Rhône R.

Duoro R.

Marseille

PORTUGAL

CORSICA

LISBON

MADRID

Barcelona

Ebro

SPAIN

Guadalquivir R.

SARDINIA

Mediterranean Sea

© 2002 Jeffrey L. Ward

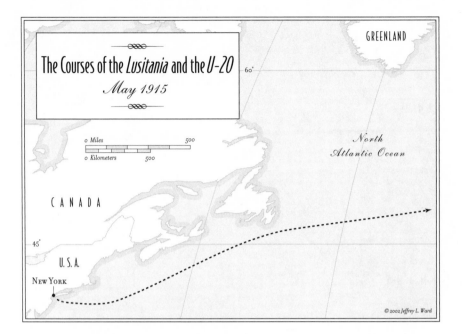

The Courses of the *Lusitania* and the *U-20*

May 1915

0 Miles   500
0 Kilometers   500

GREENLAND

60°

North Atlantic Ocean

CANADA

45°

U.S.A.

NEW YORK

© 2002 Jeffrey L. Ward

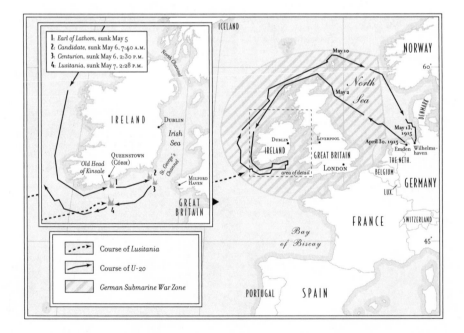

1: *Earl of Lathom*, sunk May 5
2: *Candidate*, sunk May 6, 7:40 A.M.
3: *Centurion*, sunk May 6, 2:30 P.M.
4: *Lusitania*, sunk May 7, 2:28 P.M.

ICELAND

NORWAY

60°

North Channel

IRELAND

DUBLIN

Irish Sea

QUEENSTOWN (CÓBH)

Old Head of Kinsale

St. George's Channel

MILFORD HAVEN

GREAT BRITAIN

May 10

North Sea

May 2

DENMARK

May 13, 1915

April 30, 1915

Emden   Wilhelms-haven

THE NETH.

DUBLIN

LIVERPOOL

IRELAND

GREAT BRITAIN

LONDON

BELGIUM

LUX.

GERMANY

area of detail

FRANCE

SWITZERLAND

45°

Bay of Biscay

PORTUGAL   SPAIN

Course of *Lusitania*

Course of *U-20*

German Submarine War Zone

Spring 1915—The Legacy

During peacetime a scientist belongs to the world but during wartime he belongs to his country.

—The words of Fritz Haber, the Nobel Prize–winning German chemist who developed poison gas as a weapon and personally supervised the world's first use of it on April 22, 1915, in a chlorine gas attack by the German army against French and Canadian troops at Ypres. Haber is later said to have commented: "In no future war will the military be able to ignore poison gas. It is a higher form of killing."

Lusitania. Missing a baby girl, fifteen months old. Very fair curly hair and rosy complexion. In white woollen jersey and white woollen leggings. Tries to walk and talk. Please send any information to Miss Browne,
Queens House, Queenstown.

—Notice in a shop window in Queenstown (Cobh), Ireland, seeking information about a child lost in the torpedoing without warning on May 7, 1915, by the German submarine *U-20* of the British Cunard liner *Lusitania* with the loss of 1,198 people including 128 citizens of the then-neutral United States.

> The principal objective is extremely simple and thoroughly German. They wish to kill as many people and to destroy as much property as they possibly can.

—Editorial in the *Times*, June 2, 1915, commenting on the first aerial bombing raid on London on May 31, 1915, by a German zeppelin.

THESE QUOTATIONS ENCAPSULATE three milestone events that occurred in a single six-week period during the initial year of the First World War and forever changed the nature of warfare. Each of the three was important in its own right. By the end of the war nearly 30 percent of German artillery shells contained poison gas, and gas was a major component of all belligerents' armories and strategies arousing particular fear and aversion as it still does today. The sinking of the *Lusitania* highlighted the potency of the submerged submarine as a commerce raider capable of destroying large tonnages of merchant shipping. This would be demonstrated both later in the First World War and in the Battle of the Atlantic in the Second World War when U-boats came close to cutting off imports of food and war matériel to Britain. In geopolitical tems the *Lusitania* was described as failing to bring two hundred U.S. civilians to Liverpool in 1915 but in 1917 bringing two million U.S. soldiers to France. This was because it provoked a long-running dispute between the United States and Germany about the latter's submarine tactics that led to the U.S. declaration of war in April 1917, and consequently and inexorably to Germany's defeat. The bombing raids on London's civilians were the precursor to the Second World War German blitz on London and the Allied destruction by area bombing of Hamburg, Dresden, and Tokyo.

However, viewed together, the three attacks acquire even greater significance and resonance. They represent a cataclysmic clash between the laws on the conduct of warfare laid down in the Hague Conventions of 1899 and 1907 under which all three were illegal and the new weapons developed by technology under the impetus of war. In doing so they epitomized the sharper edge science had given to the eternal dilemma as to how far the ends can ever justify the means. They also posed the question how the laws of war could be universally rather than unilaterally enforced, particularly given that in agreeing the Hague Conventions, politicians had felt compelled to ignore the pragmatic reservations of men such as British admiral "Jacky" Fisher, American admiral Alfred Mahan, and German admiral Alfred von Tirpitz. Fisher, the father of the Dreadnought battleship and a delegate at the first Hague Conference, summed up such views: "The humanising of war, you might as well talk about humanising hell! The essence of war is violence!"

The British and their allies had been forewarned of each attack. German army deserters and Allied agents clearly indicated the imminent probability of a gas attack on the western front near Ypres, providing considerable and—as it turned out—accurate detail. Indeed, the prospect of the use of gas was so widely discussed that the *Times* reported it thirteen days before it was deployed. The German embassy in Washington placed an advertisement in the American newspapers on the day the *Lusitania* sailed from New York warning passengers against traveling on British ships. In the *New York Times* it appeared next to Cunard's announcement of the *Lusitania's* schedule. The British Admiralty knew separately from decoded German targeting information that the *Lusitania* was at risk. The British authorities had recognized the potential for zeppelin raids on London from the beginning of the war.

Nevertheless, the authorities took little action to forestall these known threats. In part this was due to the relatively few defensive measures available at this stage in the war (no gas masks, no depth charges, no sonar, no fast-climbing fighters) and in part due to complacency. Even more significantly, those in high positions refused to believe in the face of all the evidence that Germany's political leaders and its military commanders would countenance the unleashing of attacks that in addition to being illegal would shatter long-cherished concepts of honor, decency, and "civilized" behavior in warfare.

Thus each attack was condemned roundly not only by the Allies but by most neutral opinion. In the press, banner headlines and editorials accused Germany of barbarism and "frightfulness." The latter—a translation of the German word *Schrecklichkeit* and often placed in quotation marks—was rapidly becoming shorthand for what were perceived as Germany's brutal methods of waging war. Reporting the gas attack at Ypres, the *Observer* deplored the use of "a poison-mixture patented by German frightfulness." On the sinking of the *Lusitania* it commented that "while the Germans think there is the least possibility that superiority in 'frightfulness' may save them, 'frightfulness' will continue to rage with increasing and extending virulence." The *Washington Herald* ruled that the Germans who were guilty of the "frightfulness against Belgium were the same who sank the *Lusitania*" while the *New York Nation* denounced the sinking as Germany's "latest display of frightfulness." In a similar vein, the *Guardian* called the first air raid on London "a piece of 'frightfulness.' "

The motivation for the attacks was the desire by the German government under Kaiser Wilhelm II to break the stalemate in the war and to achieve a quick victory before their enemies could fully mobilize their greater economic and military resources. Part of the attraction of the new weapons to the German authorities was indeed the potential of their "frightfulness" to cause mass panic not only among troops but also civilians, thus forcing their opponents to make peace. Although they failed in this aim, the attacks did indeed have an immense psychological effect disproportionate to the initial casualties incurred. Henceforth no one—whether a member of the armed forces or a civilian or even a neutral—could feel or be safe from attack without warning from air, land, or sea, however far they were from the battlefield, whatever they were doing, day or night.

As a consequence of these six weeks in 1915 no technology thereafter would be considered too indiscriminate to deploy in warfare. When Fritz Haber oversaw the release of gas over enemy trenches, science lost any innocence it had retained. Using the childhood argument "They started it!" the Allies swiftly followed their enemies in the use of poison gas, pursuing military victory at the price of legitimacy. The age of weapons of mass destruction had dawned when a single attacker or a small group in comparative safety, at a distance and often unseen, could launch at the press of a firing button or the touch of a bomb release a weapon that could kill thousands.

Hitherto-held concepts of morality had clashed with technology and political and military expediency and lost. We still feel the consequences today as the international community struggles to protect civilians in war-fare and to regulate the use of weapons such as poison gas still deemed too "frightful" or "barbaric" to be deployed. A 2013 article in the *Wall Street Journal* about the civil war in Syria headlined SYRIA'S GAS ATTACK ON CIVILIZATION affirmed that "it takes a barbarian to employ poison gas." It could have been written in 1915 with the simple substitution of "Germany" for "Syria."

CHAPTER ONE

"A Flash of Lightning
from the North"

IN EARLY TIMES warfare was total, constrained only by limits of weapons technology, transport, and communication. No distinction was made between combatants and civilians. Defeated enemies might be sacrificed to gods or enslaved, women raped and/or forced into marriage. Captured cities were looted and destroyed. Territory was taken by right of conquest. Scorched-earth policies where countryside and dwellings were razed were common, for example, in the long Peloponnesian Wars between Athens and Sparta in the late fifth century B.C.E.

However, as societies developed, they began to think about regulating the conduct of war. Several verses from chapter 20 of the Old Testament Book of Deuteronomy show the beginning of such thinking:

> When thou comest nigh unto a city to fight against it, then proclaim peace unto it . . . If it makes thee answer of peace, and open unto thee, then it shall be, that all the people that is found therein shall be tributaries unto thee, and they shall serve thee. And if it will make no peace with thee, but will make war against thee, then thou shalt besiege it. And when the Lord thy God hath delivered it into thine hands, thou shalt smite every male thereof with the edge of the sword. But the women, and the little ones, and the cattle, and all that is in the city, even all the spoil thereof, shalt thou take unto thyself; and thou shalt eat the spoil of thine enemies . . .

> When thou shalt besiege a city a long time, in making war against it
> to take it, thou shalt not destroy the trees thereof by forcing an axe
> against them: for thou mayest eat of them and thou shalt not cut them
> down (for the tree of the field is man's life) to employ them in the siege.

The next chapter of Deuteronomy stipulates that a victor may take a "beautiful" captive woman if he has "a desire unto her" but thereafter "if you
have no delight in her, then thou shalt let her go whither she will; but thou
shalt not sell her at all for money, thou shalt not make merchandise of her,
because thou hast humbled her."

In the sixth century B.C.E., in chapter 2 of his classic book on the art
of war, Sun Tzu advises that captive warriors must be kindly treated and
kept but suggests that the taking of booty should be permitted to maintain
the morale of troops. In the first century B.C.E. the Roman orator, lawyer,
and politician Cicero praised the conduct of wars that was "mild and
marked with no unnecessary cruelty" while again allowing the destruction
or seizure of enemy property.

In time, Christian thinkers began to discuss the justification for and
conduct of wars at least when they were between Christians. Both Saint
Augustine of Hippo (354–430 C.E.) and Saint Thomas Aquinas (1225–1274
C.E.) considered what constituted a "just" war. Saint Augustine thought
that war was a crime if fought "with a malicious intent to destroy, a desire
to dominate, with fierce hatred and furious vengeance." Conversely, it
became a moral duty if fought "in a just cause" to turn wrong into right.
Saint Thomas Aquinas believed war could be justified provided three conditions were satisfied: that there was a just cause, that it was begun on
proper authority, and that it was waged with the right intention for "the
advancement of good or the avoidance of evil"—conditions sufficiently
general to leave considerable room for debate.

In the Islamic tradition the first caliph, Abu Bakr, suggested "rules for
guidance on the battlefield" including: "Do not commit treachery . . . Do
not mutilate dead bodies . . . Do not kill women or children or an aged
infirm person . . . Do not cut down fruit-bearing trees . . . Do not slaughter
[your enemy's] sheep or camels except for food . . . Do not destroy an
inhabited place." This guidance amplified the Koran itself which requires

that in combat Muslims only strike back in self-defense against those who strike against them and, once the enemy ceases to attack, Muslims also should stop fighting.

Over centuries in Europe a system of uncoded customs and traditions concerning war evolved covering matters such as the status of treaties and ambassadors, and arrangements for the safe conduct of the latter together with heralds and other envoys. However, they did little to mitigate the horrors of warfare for the individual soldier or civilian. These reached a peak in the Thirty Years War starting in 1618 between the Catholics of the Holy Roman Empire and their neighboring Protestant states, with other countries such as Sweden and France also intervening. Armies routinely lived off the land, killing, raping, and looting, even digging up graveyards for the jewels buried with the dead. After the capture of Magdeburg, a center of Lutheranism, by the Catholic general Count Tilly, the city was destroyed and some twenty-five thousand of its thirty thousand inhabitants killed, the majority of the survivors being women who had been taken to the enemy camp to be raped. Even when order was restored the few surviving males were forced to buy back their womenfolk and ransom themselves. Those unable to do so had to march with their captors as forced laborers.

Writing during this period the Dutch jurist and diplomat Hugo Grotius (1583–1645) published a series of works that make him usually considered "the father of international law." One of his early works, *De Mare Liberum*, dealt with the freedom of the seas, suggesting they were open to all to conduct their trade—a proposition adopted by the Dutch but opposed by other thinkers and indeed nations, such as the British, who argued that the sea could be annexed by a state just as land could be. Disputes about free trade and freedom of the seas led to two Anglo-Dutch wars in the mid-seventeenth century after the English forbade any goods from entering their country except on an English ship. States reached a compromise in the early eighteenth century that the extent of the sea to which a nation could lay claim was the distance that a cannon shot could travel to protect it, which in turn evolved into the three-mile territorial limit. Nevertheless, the freedom of the seas and the ability of belligerents and others to impose restrictions on it remained a subject of controversy through the Napoleonic Wars and into the First World War, being among other things a prime cause of the Anglo-American War of 1812 and a source of tension between the Union side and Britain in the American Civil War.

Grotius's major work was, however, *De jure belli ac pacis* (About the law of war and peace) published in 1625, and prompted Grotius said by his belief "that there is a common law among nations which is valid alike for war and in war . . . Throughout the Christian world I observed a lack of restraint in relation to war . . . I observed that men rush to war for slight causes, or no cause at all, and that when arms have once been taken up there is no longer any respect for law divine or human; it is as if in accordance with a general decree, frenzy had openly been let loose by the committing of all crimes." His work was in three volumes; the first two looked at the justification for war, the third at its conduct. Grotius quoted a comment from Cicero that "people are apt to call lawful what they can do with impunity" and then argued that what they should think about is not the rigor of the law but what is "becoming to one's character." He maintained that humanity and morality are as crucial to the declaration and conduct of war as to any other sphere of life and he recognized three "just causes" for war—self-defense, reparation of injury, and punishment—and argued that once war has begun all parties should act humanely and are bound to do so whether or not their cause is just.

Over the next two centuries debates continued about the legitimacy of the causes and conduct of war, interacting toward the end of that period with the concept of the "civilized" nation as opposed to the barbarian one, which had developed in discussions about the United States Constitution as well as in Europe. (The earliest use of the word "civilization" in its modern sense dates from the late 1750s.) By the mid-nineteenth century a fairly general consensus had emerged about the justification for wars between civilized nations. Much more latitude was at least tacitly given to the treatment of "barbarian" states and individuals.

Few would have dissented from the definition of a just war quoted by an Englishman, Henry Lushington, in opposing his country's first (and disastrous) intervention in Afghanistan in 1838–42:

> The received code of international morality is not even in the nineteenth century very strict. One principle, however, seems to be admitted

in the theory, if not the practice of civilized men, that an aggressive war—a war undertaken against unoffending parties with a view to our own benefit only—is unjust, and conversely that a war to be just must partake the character of a defensive war. It may be defensive in various ways . . . either preventing an injury which it is attempted to inflict, or of exacting reparation for one inflicted, and taking the necessary security against its future infliction but in one way or other defensive it must be.

Another major step in the codification of laws about war followed what was intended to be a business trip by thirty-one-year-old Henry Dunant, a chubby banker from Geneva, to visit Emperor Napoléon III of France. At the time Napoléon was leading his army with that of his Piedmontese allies against the forces of Austro-Hungary commanded by their emperor Franz Ferdinand. On June 24, 1859, the two armies clashed at Solferino on the north Italian plains in the last major battle in Europe fought under the direct and personal command of reigning monarchs. The French and their allies were the victors but more than thirty-five thousand men from both sides lay dead or wounded when Dunant arrived that evening. At sunrise the next day, Dunant went to the battlefield and was appalled: "Corpses were strewn over roads, ditches, ravines, thickets and fields; the approaches to Solferino were literally thick with dead . . . The wounded . . . were ghostly pale . . . The most badly hurt had a stupefied look . . . Others were shaken by spasmodic trembling . . . Some had gaping wounds already beginning to show infection [and] begged to be put out of their misery . . . Many were disfigured, limbs stiffened, their bodies blotched with ghastly spots, their hands clawing at the ground." (The French had four veterinary surgeons for every one thousand horses but only one doctor for every one thousand men.) Dunant put aside all thoughts of business and began organizing help for the wounded, irrespective of nationality, with the assistance of some local people and four English tourists, a Parisian journalist, a French count, an ex-naval officer, and a chocolate manufacturer called Philippe Suchard.

On his return to Geneva Dunant wrote *A Memory of Solferino* and paid for the book's publication. In it he proposed societies of volunteers to help the wounded of all sides in war and "some international principles, conventional and sacred, which once agreed and ratified would form the basis for these national societies to help the wounded." His book was widely praised throughout Europe and beyond. Subsequently Dunant and four other prominent citizens of Geneva established an international committee for the relief of the wounded. The committee oversaw the establishment of kindred national organizations and then persuaded the Swiss government to sponsor an international governmental conference to draw up a convention on the treatment of the wounded.

The conference met in Geneva's town hall in August 1864. Within a fortnight the members had agreed to a convention requiring the care of all wounded irrespective of nationality, and neutrality for medical staff, hospitals, and ambulances. To ensure that humanitarian helpers and facilities were recognized, the delegates agreed on the use of a red cross on a white background (the Swiss flag's symbol with its colors reversed) to distinguish them. Quickly thereafter the national and international organizations became known as the Red Cross.

Although Britain and the United States were among the sixteen states represented at the conference, they were not among the first to sign up to the new convention. Florence Nightingale, who had done so much to improve the treatment of the wounded during Britain's war in the Crimea a few years previously, wrote that it would be "quite harmless for our government to sign . . . It amounts to nothing more than a declaration that humanity to the wounded is a good thing. It is like an opera chorus. And if the principal European characters sing,

> We never will be cruel more,
> I am sure, if England likes to sing too,
> I never will be cruel more,
> I see no objection.

But it is like vows. People who keep a vow would do the thing without the vow. And if people will not do it without the vow they will not do it with."

Britain signed the convention in 1865. Clara Barton, who had performed a similar role to Florence Nightingale and emerged with equal heroine status from the Union side in the American Civil War, was an avid supporter and her advocacy was a major factor leading to the United States' ratification of the convention though not until March 1882. It is symptomatic either of the slow speed and extent of communication or the chauvinism of the inhabitants of Geneva and quite probably both that in their deliberations the five founding members of the International Committee claimed not to have known the details of either Nightingale's or Barton's work. They professed themselves similarly unaware of the "Sanitary Commission" that on the Union side in the U.S. Civil War had much improved the care of the wounded, establishing convalescent homes and a corps of stretcher bearers as well as regular inspection of hospitals.

The Union side also issued guidance to troops on the conduct of warfare, developed by Francis Lieber, a German-born university professor who had emigrated to the United States after being wounded at the Battle of Waterloo. He concluded that the destruction of people and property was acceptable if essential to victory; however, cruelty to prisoners of war, torture, use of poison, and wanton destruction as well as "any act of hostility which makes the return to peace unnecessarily difficult" were not. "Men who take up arms against one another in public war do not cease on this account to be moral beings responsible to one another, and to God."

The Civil War established another milestone in the law of war by the conviction and execution of Captain Henry Wirz, the Confederate commandant of the Andersonville, Georgia, prisoner of war camp who was judged responsible for the death of Union soldiers in the camp "in violation of the laws and customs of war." The court set a precedent for future such trials by refusing to accept the validity of the defendant's plea that he was only following orders.

When in June 1866 Austro-Hungary and Prussia went to war, Louis Appia, one of the original five founding members of the International Committee wore the first Red Cross armband in Schleswig. By that time Henry Dunant had left the organization he had done so much to establish. He was never astute in commercial matters and probably distracted by the demands of his humanitarian work on his time and attention. In autumn 1865 one of his businesses—a bank called Credit Genevois—went into liquidation with large debts, and the bankruptcy court declared that Dunant had "knowingly swindled" shareholders. Dunant resigned from the Red

Cross and departed Geneva forever, pursued by the malice of his creditors and more surprisingly by that of another of the five founding members, Gustave Moynier. Now the president of the organization, he had long felt animosity to Dunant, partly at least due to jealousy of his charisma and celebrity. Moynier did his best to rewrite the history of the Red Cross, expunging Dunant's name and contribution wherever he could and warning any who would listen against further involvement with him.

After the agreement of a humanitarian approach to those involved in war when it broke out, as the nineteenth century drew toward its close, public attention began to turn toward preventing wars or at the very least regulating the methods used in their conduct to comply with the concept of what civilized values permitted. Peace unions sprang up in industrial-ized countries and international peace congresses were held where individuals and groups such as the Quakers urged alternatives to war such as the use of arbitration to resolve disputes between nations. As early as 1874 a nongovernmental conference of experts held in Brussels produced a draft code of laws on war and in 1894 the campaigning British journalist William Thomas ("W. T.") Stead proposed that the great powers should jointly pledge not to increase their military budgets until the end of the century.

Nevertheless, what the French newspaper *Le Temps* called "a flash of lightning from the north" shocked governments on August 24, 1898, when entirely unexpectedly at his weekly meeting with foreign ambassadors in Saint Petersburg, the Russian foreign secretary Count Mikhail Muraviev handed to them a call on behalf of Czar Nicholas II for the convening of an international conference to consider "the grave problem" of the devel-opment of "military forces to proportions hitherto unknown." His note stated:

> The intellectual and physical strength of the nations, labour and capital are for the major part diverted from their natural application and unpro-ductively consumed. Hundreds of millions are devoted to acquiring terrible engines of destruction, which though today regarded as the last word of science, are destined tomorrow to lose all value in consequence of some fresh discovery in this field. National culture, economic

progress and the production of wealth are either paralysed or checked in their development. Moreover, in proportion as the armaments of each power increase, so do they less and less fulfil the object which the government has set before themselves.

Many were surprised that such an initiative should come from autocratic, backward Russia. Some welcomed it as "an omen for the coming new century" or, as an American journalist wrote, possibly "the most momentous and beneficent movement in modern history—in all history." W. T. Stead brought out a new weekly, *War Against War*, launched an international peace crusade, and toured European capitals urging support for the proposal. Most, however, looked cynically for the motive, agreeing with Britain's Prince of Wales that it was "some new dodge of that sly dog M[uraviev] who put it into the Tsar's head." The ailing Russian economy could not in their view finance the latest weapons and therefore Russia had decided on the initiative.

Germany, only united since 1871 following its victory over France in the 1870 Franco-Prussian War in which it had seized from its defeated enemy the provinces of Alsace and Lorraine, had none of Russia's economic worries but great political and imperial ambitions. The thirty-nine-year-old mercurial, sometimes vacillating, sometimes impulsively unreasoning Kaiser Wilhelm II, among whose titles was that of "Supreme War Lord," was stunned that Nicholas had "put a brilliant weapon into the hands of our democrats and opposition. Imagine a monarch dissolving his regiments and handing over his towns to anarchists and democracy." He compared the invitation to the conference to a Spartan proposal during the Peloponnesian War that Athens agree not to rebuild its city walls and asked, "what will Krupp pay his workers with?" (Friedrich Alfred Krupp's company was then Europe's biggest business and at the forefront of artillery development.) Inclined as often to see issues between nations as personal ones between their rulers, Wilhelm alleged Nicholas was trying to steal the limelight from his own planned visit to Jerusalem. As a confidant of the kaiser put it, "he [Wilhelm] simply cannot stand someone else coming to the front of the stage."

However, with vibrant peace unions in many countries and with no desire to appear enemies of peace, all invited nations felt compelled to accept the czar's invitation even if many privately sympathized with the kaiser when he said, "I'll go along with the conference comedy but I'll keep my dagger at my side during the waltz."

CHAPTER TWO

"Humanising War"

ONE HUNDRED AND eight delegates from twenty-six countries assembled in May 1899 in a red brick Dutch royal chateau—"the House in the Woods"—just outside The Hague, which as the capital of the Netherlands, a neutral country, the nations had chosen as the venue. Thus began the city's association with the laws of war, just as the conference in Geneva began that city's association with the Red Cross. The head of the American delegation, Andrew White, was not alone in thinking that no similar group had ever met "in a spirit of more hopeless scepticism as to any good result."

The agenda had two main components—how to avoid war by the use of arbitration and the limitation of armaments, and how war should be conducted if it did break out. Each delegation had strict guidance from its government on how best to protect its interests. The British, for example, were told prohibiting or restricting innovations in weaponry would "favour the interests of savage nations and be against those of the more highly civilised."

Members of the press, soon to be considerably annoyed by being excluded from the formal sessions of the conference, and what would now be called "lobbyists" of all sorts thronged The Hague. The head of the German delegation, Count Munster, complained to his foreign minister, "The conference has brought here the political riffraff of the entire world, journalists of the worst type, baptised Jews like Bloch and female peace fanatics." In Munster's mind journalists "of the worst type" would have included W. T. Stead who was in The Hague to chronicle the conference and to campaign for his views. Ivan Bloch was a Russian railway magnate who believed that any future wars would be "suicide" and who was author of a newly published peace-promoting treatise in six volumes. Said to have influenced the czar, it prophesied the stalemate of trench warfare leading to a prolonged conflict whose intolerable human and economic costs would exhaust the belligerents or plunge them into social revolution. On the eve of the conference an international women's movement had organized demonstrations for peace in many of the countries involved and some of its members were in The Hague. Among the foremost female peace campaigners was the Czech Bertha von Suttner who considered peace "a condition that the progress of civilisation will bring about by necessity." The hotel in which she stayed for the conference flew a white flag in honor of her and her views.

Even mild-mannered Andrew White complained that "the queer letters and crankish proposals which come in every day are amazing . . . The Quakers are out in full force . . . The number of people with plans, schemes, notions, nostrums, whimsies of all sorts who press upon us and try to take our time, is enormous and when this is added to the pest of interviewers and photographers, life becomes serious indeed." To his regret the pressure of work imposed by the conference required that "for the first time in my life I have made Sunday a day of work."

White and the head of the British delegation, Sir Julian Pauncefote, both had members of their teams who were difficult to control and whose views were often at variance with their governmental instructions. Both the chief mavericks represented their country's navy. The Briton was fifty-eight-year-old Admiral Jacky Fisher, destined to play an important part in the events of spring 1915. From relatively humble beginnings—his father was a failed coffee planter—he had made a spectacular rise through the navy for which he advocated less bureaucracy, less ship painting, and far fewer time-wasting drills and in their place far more training, far better gunnery, heavier armaments, a broader officer-recruitment base, and a new emphasis on torpedoes and defenses against them.

Both charismatic and tactless, Fisher made friends and enemies equally quickly. He stood out at The Hague not only for his opinions but also for his white top hat and tireless skills on the dance floor. His language was colorful and exaggerated. The existence of politicians had "deepened his faith in Providence. How else could one explain Britain's continued existence as a nation?" His bold scrawl, usually in green ink, was full of exclamation marks, and double and triple underlinings, and he frequently admonished his addressee to burn his letters after reading to protect his confidences. He signed letters "Yours till hell freezes" and "Yours till charcoal sprouts."

At every opportunity Fisher derided the objective of humanizing war as naive:

> The humanising of war? You might as well talk about humanising Hell! The essence of war is violence! Moderation in war is imbecility! . . . I am not for war, I am for peace. That is why I am for a supreme Navy. The supremacy of the British Navy is the best security for the peace of the world . . . If you rub it in both at home and abroad that you are ready for instant war . . . and intend to be first in and hit your enemy in the belly and kick him when he is down and boil your prisoners in oil (if you take any) . . . and torture his women and children, then people will keep clear of you.

He believed all nations wanted peace "but a peace that suits them." An enemy's realization of the horrors of war coupled with conviction about Britain's readiness to fight were the best deterrents of all. It was his duty, Fisher said, to see that his country, and in particular its navy, were prepared.

He was similarly dismissive of the delegates' debate about the freedom of the seas and the rights of "neutral shipping":

> Suppose that war breaks out, and I am expecting to fight a new Trafalgar on the morrow. Some neutral colliers try to steam past us into the enemy's waters. If the enemy gets their coal into his bunkers, it may make all the difference in the coming fight. You tell me I must not seize these colliers. I tell you that nothing that you, or any power on earth, can say will stop me from sending them to the bottom, if I can in no other way keep their coal out of the enemy's hands; for to-morrow I am to fight the battle which will save or wreck the Empire. If I win it, I shall be far

too big a man to be effected by protests about the neutral colliers; if I lose it, I shall go down with my ship . . . and then protests will effect me still less.

Fisher was seconded in such opinions by another fifty-eight-year-old, the American naval delegate Captain Alfred Thayer Mahan, already a renowned naval strategist. An admirer of Admiral Horatio Nelson, he had propounded in his 1890 book *The Influence of Sea Power Upon History* and subsequent works that "control of the sea, by maritime commerce and naval supremacy means predominant influence in the world . . . [and] is the chief among the merely material elements in the power and prosperity of nations."

Andrew White in his summary of the conference observed that Mahan "prevented any lapses into sentimentality . . . When he speaks the millennium fades and this stern severe actual world appears." Mahan reiterated that "the object of war was to smite the enemy incessantly and remorselessly and crush him by depriving him of the use of the sea," strangling the enemy into submission by cutting off his trade, including the neutral's right to trade with him. With such powerful opposing voices as Mahan and Fisher arguing against the conference's generally pacific purpose of introducing restrictions on warfare, the delegates thought it better to leave unaltered the by now time-honored body of custom and practice relating to war at sea known as the "Cruiser Rules," the origins of some parts of which dated back even beyond Grotius to the time of Henry VIII. Other parts, such as a ban on privateering, were more recent.° The consensus embodied in these "rules" prohibited enemy warships sinking on sight merchant vessels of whatever nationality. They had to be stopped and searched for "contraband" and only if contraband were found could they either be sunk—after their crews had been given time to take to the boats—or seized as prizes. To effect such searches warships were allowed to blockade their enemies' ports.

The delegates made no headway either on disarmament against broad

---

° The delegates acknowledged the importance of Grotius's contribution to their task when they visited his grave in nearby Delft one day to lay wreaths on his tomb.

and implacable opposition vociferously led by Germany, satisfying themselves with the platitudinous resolution "that the restriction of military
budgets, which are at present a heavy burden on the world, is extremely
desirable for the increase of the material and moral welfare of mankind."
When the Russian delegation proposed that all states should agree "not to
transform radically their guns nor to increase their calibres for a certain
fixed period" the British objected that effective verification would be
impossible since new armaments could easily be concealed. Captain Mahan
opposed international control and verification in principle because they
would breach national sovereignty.

During the long debates about arbitration Mahan stated his belief that
"the great danger of undiscriminating advocacy of arbitration, which
threatens even the cause it seeks to maintain, is that it may lead men to
tamper with equity, soothing their conscience with the belief that war is so
entirely wrong that beside it no other tolerated evil is wrong." Despite such
objections, although no state would commit itself to put every dispute in
which it became involved to arbitration, none wanted to be seen as war-
mongering. Consequently, the conference in its resolutions encouraged the
use of arbitration and established at The Hague a permanent Court of
Arbitration ready and willing to consider all cases submitted to it by those
involved. Even the kaiser, who considered arbitration "a hoax" that a state
could use to gain time to build up its forces to improve its position before
war eventually began, felt forced to agree to the arbitration provision.
However, in doing so he wrote in the margin of one of the relevant documents, "I consented to all this nonsense only in order that the Tsar should
not lose face before Europe, in practice however I shall rely on God and
my sharp sword! And I shit on all their decisions."

The conference did however make major progress in codifying the
conduct of war once it broke out, agreeing to a convention on the laws of
war on land. Among the key prohibitions were those against "poison or
poisoned weapons"; killing or wounding "treacherously individuals
belonging to the hostile nation or army"; declaring that "no quarter will be
given"; employing "arms, projectiles, or material calculated to cause unnecessary suffering"; destroying or seizing "the enemy's property, unless such
destruction or seizure be imperatively demanded by the necessities of

war"; . . . "the attack or bombardment, by whatever means, of towns, villages, dwellings or buildings which are undefended; the pillage of a town or place even when taken by assault."

Neither these rules nor any other part of the Hague agreements spelled out specifically the position of civilians but rather relied on the consensus and the custom and usage evolved over the centuries as to their inviolability. Civilians were, however, implicitly covered by the catchall phrase that placed all caught up in warfare "under the protection and the rule of the principles of the law of nations, as they result from the usages established among civilised peoples, from the laws of humanity and the dictates of public conscience." Some of the other prohibitions, in particular that against bombardment of undefended places, provided them extra protection.

THE HAGUE CONFERENCE also considered banning certain weapons. At least since the Roman siege of the port of Syracuse in Sicily in the third century B.C.E. when Archimedes, one of the defenders, developed a crane-like claw designed to grapple Roman ships and a focused mirror system to blind their sailors and even burn their vessels, war has accelerated the pace of scientific and engineering development. The speed of innovation grew with the Industrial Revolution. At the beginning of the nineteenth century the Napoleonic Wars saw the introduction of the shrapnel shell and the Congreve black-powder-fueled artillery rocket. By the middle of the century warships were becoming steam powered and iron clad; breech-loading rifles were replacing muzzle-loading muskets; while the rifling of gun barrels was improving artillery. The U.S. Civil War brought innovations such as mechanical-fused land mines, machine guns and improved hand grenades, and the sinking of a Union warship by a man-propelled Confederate submarine. Alfred Nobel's inventions of dynamite and of smokeless powder—the latter patented by him during the decade before the Hague Conference—were among the latest developments to have a major effect on warfare. Smokeless powder, for example, allowed much greater visibility across the battlefield as well as permitting the concealment of artillery and increasing the range and accuracy of weapons.

Throughout history some weapons such as poison, which could be thought underhand or against the spirit of a fair or manly fight, have attracted popular revulsion. The Laws of Manu, the greatest of the ancient Hindu codes, prohibited Hindus from using poisoned arrows. Greeks and Romans customarily refrained from using poison or poisoned weapons, considering them abominable violations of nature and contrary to the laws of the gods. Often when new weapons were introduced, they too generated an outcry against their inhumanity. In 1132, the Lateran Council declared the crossbow and arbalest "un-Christian weapons." In 1139 Pope Innocent II again tried to ban the crossbow as too "murderous for Christian warfare." Nearly three hundred years later the French Chevalier Bayard, usually considered the epitome of the fearless and faultless chivalrous knight, valiant, honorable, and merciful to all, was so incensed by the introduction of the unchivalrous musket that he ordered no quarter to be given to captured musketeers.

The Hague Conference considered in detail three potentially inhumane weapons—the Dum-Dum bullet, asphyxiating or poison gas, and air-launched projectiles, that is, bombs. The prohibition of the use of the submarine in warfare had been proposed by Count Muraviev on behalf of Russia during the advance discussion of the agenda and was also debated on the sidelines of the conference but was not taken further.

The Dum-Dum or expanding bullet was the only one of the three that had actually been used effectively in warfare. Developed at and named after the British Dum-Dum arsenal near Calcutta, the bullets exploded and expanded within the body of the victim, considerably increasing the damage to surrounding tissue and bone. All nations at the conference were content to ban such bullets except Britain and the United States. The British army delegate, General Sir John Ardagh, told in his instructions from London "you have a difficult hand to play," underlined the distinction still then drawn between "civilised nations" and "barbarians."

> The civilised soldier when shot recognises that he is wounded and knows that the sooner he is attended to the sooner he will recover. He lies down on his stretcher and is taken off the field to his ambulance where he is dressed . . . by his doctor or his Red Cross Society according to the . . . rules of the game as laid down in the Geneva Convention.

Your fanatical barbarian, similarly wounded, continues to rush on, spear or sword in hand; and before you have had time to represent to him that his conduct is a flagrant violation of the understanding relative to the proper course for the wounded man to follow—he may have cut off your head.

Hence the requirement for the Dum-Dum bullet to knock down the "barbarian" immediately and once and for all. Despite British and American reservations, the other conference members agreed to ban expanding bullets.

Poison gas had never been used effectively in battle although the ancient world had experimented with what might be called "chemical warfare." The Spartans used sulfur fumes while besieging Plataea during the Peloponnesian Wars while in the third century C.E. Sassanian soldiers burned bitumen and sulfur in an attempt to asphyxiate their Roman adversaries. In 1456 the Christian defenders of Belgrade used a toxic cloud said to contain arsenic to repulse the Muslim Ottoman Turks. A commentator writing about it a century later described the event as "a sad business. Christians must never use so murderous a weapon against other Christians. Still it is quite in place against Turks and other miscreants." Leonardo da Vinci suggested throwing "chalk, fine sulphide of arsenic, and powdered verdigris . . . among enemy ships by means of small mangonels" so that "all those who . . . inhale the powder . . . will become asphyxiated." The Taino Indians of Hispaniola hurled gourds filled with ashes and ground chili peppers at the invading Spanish conquistadores to create a stinging smoke screen.

In Britain during the Napoleonic Wars, Thomas Cochrane, naval captain later to be admiral, first proposed the use of poison gas. While visiting Sicily—then the world's major sulfur producer—he noticed how, as sulfur was heated to separate it from the earth from which it had been dug, hot, toxic gases—in fact sulfur dioxide—were created which destroyed surrounding vegetation. People were forbidden to sleep within three miles of the sulfur works. Cochrane speculated about loading "stink ships" with sulfur and coal, anchoring them close to enemy positions and setting them alight to create fumes that would annihilate "every animal function."

The Admiralty eventually dismissed his proposals as impracticable. Many years later, after falling out with the Admiralty, a conviction for fraud, and a remarkable career commanding successively the fleets of Greece, Brazil, and Chile, culminating in a pardon and reinstatement in the British navy, Cochrane returned to the idea of poison gas. In 1846 the Admiralty this time responded that using sulfur gas would not "accord with the feelings and principles of civilised warfare," Furthermore, if Britain deployed it others would surely follow.

In 1854 during the Crimean War, the now near-octogenarian Cochrane tried again, proposing the use of stink ships to expel the Russians from the Baltic port of Kronstadt. Anticipating counterarguments about "civilized war," he put forward an argument often to be used to defend highly destructive new weapons: "No conduct that brought to a speedy termination a war which might otherwise last for years, and be attended by terrible bloodshed . . . could be called inhuman." As others would do, he also suggested that advanced weapons such as poison gas would have a deterrent effect: "The most powerful means of averting all future war would be the introduction of a method of fighting which, rendering all vigorous defence impossible, would frighten every nation from running the risk of warfare at all." A secret committee rejected his ideas, some members calling them "so horrible" that "no honourable combatant" could resort to them.

Undaunted, the following year Cochrane urged the use of his "secret weapons" to dislodge the Russians from the Crimean port of Sevastopol and asked for: "Four or five hundred tons of sulphur and two thousand tons of coke" to vaporize it as well as "a couple of thousand barrels" of tar and a large amount of straw, hay, and firewood to create smoke. He also suggested floating naphtha near Sevastopol and then "igniting it by means of a ball of potassium." By these means, he assured Prime Minister Lord Palmerston, Sevastopol's outer defenses would be "smoked, sulphured and blown up" and "thousands of lives" saved. Sevastopol fell soon afterward without chemical intervention.

While the Crimean War was still under way, British chemist Lyon Playfair [sic] recommended firing shells filled with toxic cacodyl cyanide at Russian ships since "such a shell going between the decks of a ship would render the atmosphere irrespirable and poison the men if they remained at their guns." When the government suggested this was a low trick akin to poisoning the enemy's water supply Playfair responded with another argument often to be used to defend poison gas: "It is considered a legitimate mode of warfare to fire shells with molten metal which scatters among the enemy, and produces the most frightful modes of death. Why a poisonous vapour which would kill men without suffering is to be considered illegitimate is incomprehensible."

The American Civil War saw several proposals for the use of poison gas but again none were taken up. Chemist William C. Tilden contacted Union general Ulysses S. Grant with "a scheme for producing chemically a means of settling wars quickly by making them terribly destructive." Grant responded, as the British Admiralty had to Cochrane, that "such a terrific agency for destroying human life should not be permitted . . . by the civilized nations of the world." In 1862, New Yorker John Doughty sent the U.S. War Department his proposal for a projectile to clear Confederate troops from fortified positions. For the first time it suggested the use of the chlorine gas that was to be used so destructively on April 22, 1915: "Chlorine is a gas so irritating in its effects upon the respiratory system, that a small quantity diffused in the atmosphere produces incessant and uncontrollably violent coughing—It is 2 ½ times heavier than the atmosphere and when subjected to a pressure of 60 pounds to the inch it is condensed into a liquid, its volume being reduced many hundred times. A shell holding two or three quarts would therefore contain many cubic feet of the gas."

The Hague Conference agreed to a ban on asphyxiating gases that in its detailed clauses was framed against projectiles containing them. The only dissent came from the United States at the urging of Captain Mahan who argued that not enough was known about the potential use of gas as a weapon to ban it and thus to place restrictions on the "genius" of U.S. citizens "in inventing and producing new weapons of war" was not justified. Besides, he said, being asphyxiated by gas could be no worse than four or five hundred sailors choking on seawater with only the remotest chance of rescue after their ships had been torpedoed by a submarine.

The proposal to ban projectiles or explosives launched from the air also proved contentious. As early as the seventeenth century an Italian Jesuit, Francesco Lana de Terzi, had imagined a diabolical air machine that would fly over helpless civilian populations, lobbing flaming and explosive weapons upon their heads. A century later, in his book *The History of Rasselas, Prince of Abissinia*, the lexicographer Dr. Samuel Johnson asked: "What would be the security of the good, if the bad could at pleasure invade them from the sky? Against an army sailing through the clouds neither walls, nor mountains, nor sea, could afford security. A flight of northern savages might hover in the wind, and light with irrepressible violence upon the capital of a fruitful region."

The first major breakthrough in making such flying machines reality came in 1783 when a fashionable crowd in France watched a manned hot air balloon, built by the Montgolfier brothers and powered by a wood fire, take off and fly some five miles. Among the spectators was Benjamin Franklin who, when a French officer derided the balloon as a mere toy, amusing but useless, replied, "Of what use is a new-born baby?" The same year, another Frenchman, Jacques Charles, piloted the world's first manned hydrogen-filled balloon which traveled over twenty miles in two hours. A few years later, during the Napoleonic Wars, people in southern England scanned the skies, alarmed by rumors of giant balloons crossing the Channel to deposit French soldiers, guns, and even horses on British soil.

That never happened, but balloons found uses in warfare. During the American Civil War, a Union army Balloon Corps used tethered balloons for observation. A young German officer, Count Ferdinand von Zeppelin, took his first flight in a balloon in 1863, courtesy of the Union army. During the Franco-Prussian War (1870–71) the French used balloons to convey people and mail out of a besieged Paris. By the time of the Hague Conference a more sophisticated "lighter than air" flying machine—the powered airship—was under development, pioneered by von Zeppelin who would give his name to it. By 1874 he had already decided that his craft "must have the dimensions of a big ship. The gas-chambers so calculated as to carry the machine . . . Elevation will then be obtained by starting the engine."

Von Zeppelin regarded war "as the main study of [his] life" and had pleaded with the German army to help fund his research into "dirigible balloons" as "a very important instrument in modern warfare" but had no success until 1896 when the endorsement of the Union of German

Engineers persuaded the authorities to finance his building of a prototype on the shores of Lake Constance. On July 2, 1900—barely nine months after the end of the Hague Conference—the "mad count," as the locals called him, would reveal his gargantuan creation to the world.

Though delegates at the first Hague Conference were mostly skeptical about airships—and the even more embryonic airplanes—many were reluctant to restrict their countries' options by agreeing to a ban on launching projectiles from the skies. Captain William Crozier, the U.S. Army's representative, on Mahan's advice objected to a prohibition unlimited by time, arguing that such weapons were untried and that the further development of dirigible airships or aircraft might make them valuable in warfare and in the long run shorten conflicts and spare lives. As a result, the conference agreed unanimously to ban the launching of weapons from the air but for five years only.

As they concluded their ten weeks of discussions, The Hague delegates expressed a wish that a further conference should be held in due course.

CHAPTER THREE

"The Law of Facts"

THE AGREEMENTS AT The Hague had little immediate practical effect. Shortly after the conference, in October 1899 the Boer War broke out between the British and the Boer republics of South Africa. The cause was partly rights for non-Boers in the Boer republics but perhaps more about the control over the diamond fields of the Rand. When the British in due course won, *Life* summed up, "A small boy with diamonds is no match for a large burglar with experience." The British initially suffered a series of heavy defeats but eventually began to win set-piece battles, causing the Boers to adopt guerrilla tactics. To combat these and prevent supplies and assistance reaching the Boer fighters, the British burned down Boer farms, confiscated their flocks and crops, and interned Boer women, children, and old men in what were to become known as "concentration camps." Although the intention of the camps was only to isolate the Boer guerrilla fighters from the support of their families, conditions were poor and disease was rampant so that twenty-five thousand internees died.

Reports on the conditions by an Englishwoman, Emily Hobhouse, prompted an outcry in Britain. Although one British civil servant described Hobhouse's campaign as "agitation . . . raised by a few unsexed and hysterical women . . . prepared to sacrifice everything for notoriety," the British parliamentary opposition led by the Liberal Henry Campbell-Bannerman took up the cause. "When," he asked, "is a war not a war?" "When it is carried out by methods of barbarism," he answered himself. Conditions in the camps were quickly improved. Nevertheless at home and abroad the British continued to be accused of imprisoning and ill-treating civilians contrary to the customs and usages of war. What the camps showed for certain was the difficulty of deciding who was a civilian and true noncombatant, rather than an active guerrilla (the Boers did not wear uniforms) or supplier of assistance to the fighting Boers, as well as the limits on the means of stopping such supplies.

The United States was then fighting its own war in the Philippines against a guerrilla rebellion demanding independence after the recent American seizure of the country from the Spanish. The Americans faced the same difficulties in distinguishing insurgents from civilians. Both sides committed atrocities. The Americans used expanding bullets. On occasion, in direct contravention of the Hague principles, they gave orders that no quarter should be given. When an American soldier was found with his throat cut villages were burned down and every inhabitant killed. American troops used the "water cure" and other torture to secure information. Although the United States, like Britain in South Africa, emerged victorious, neither country could look with any satisfaction on the conduct of their campaigns, their fiercest critics coming from within. Among the leaders of the opposition in the United States to the Philippine war, and an unsuccessful presidential candidate in 1900, was William Jennings Bryan, who would be American secretary of state when the First World War broke out in 1914.

In 1900, the world had also seen the assembly of its first international force. In some ways a forerunner of UN and NATO police actions, its purpose was to relieve the foreign legations besieged in Beijing by Boxer rebels enjoying the support, at least for a time, of the Chinese court and the Empress Dowager Tzu Hsi. The force consisted of contingents from the United States, the United Kingdom, Russia, France, Japan, and Germany under a German commander. When the kaiser addressed his own troops leaving for China he departed from his prepared text: "My men, you are about to meet a crafty, well-armed foe! Meet him and beat him! Give him no quarter! Take no prisoners! Kill him when he falls into your hands! Even as a thousand years ago the Huns under their King Attila made such a name for themselves as still resounds in terror through legend and fable, so may the name of Germany resound through Chinese history . . . that never again will a Chinese dare to so much as look askance at a German." As a consequence, his future opponents would frequently dub German troops "Huns."

When the international army eventually relieved the Beijing legations and captured the city, the majority of the foreigners indulged in an orgy of looting. But that was not the worst. A British officer described how "Every Chinaman . . . was treated as a Boxer by the Russian and French troops and the slaughter of men women and children . . . was revolting." The French commander, General Henri Frey, when challenged about "the frequent occurrence of disgraceful outrages upon women" by his men, responded dismissively: "It is impossible to restrain the gallantry of the French soldier."

In February 1904, without any declaration of war Japan attacked Russia in a dispute over their competing ambitions in Korea and Chinese Manchuria. In the fighting that followed, the Japanese navy, with its modern guns, torpedoes, and mines, first destroyed the Russian Far East Fleet and then at Tsushima—the greatest sea battle since Trafalgar in 1805—the Russian Baltic Fleet, which had sailed halfway around the world to its doom. Early in its voyage to the Far East, the Baltic Fleet had at the Dogger Bank in the North Sea fired on British trawlers, sinking one of them and killing two fishermen under the fanciful impression that the Japanese were confronting them. The incident produced a major crisis with Britain, only resolved when the two countries put the dispute to arbitration in The Hague. On land, in fighting that saw the first extensive use of barbed wire to defend positions, the Japanese defeated the Russians and captured Port Arthur in Manchuria—Russia's prized and recently occupied only eastern warm-water port. Captured Russian soldiers suffered greatly at Japanese hands.

In July 1905 U.S. president Theodore Roosevelt offered to mediate between the Russians and the Japanese, both of whom were nearly exhausted militarily and economically. At a meeting under his chairmanship at Portsmouth, New Hampshire, they agreed to a peace treaty. Soon afterward the United States also played a leading role in persuading the kaiser to agree to a peace conference to resolve a crisis between Germany and France over Morocco. In 1906 Roosevelt, the advocate of speaking softly but carrying a big stick, was awarded the fifth Nobel Peace Prize.

Although his inventions had produced major advances in weapons technology, Alfred Nobel had been an advocate of arbitration and deeply interested in the peace movement. (The peace activist Bertha von Suttner had briefly been his secretary.) On his death in 1896 he left most of his fortune to establish five prizes to be awarded irrespective of nationality or sex for eminence in physics, chemistry, medicine, literature, and peace promotion. The first peace prize in 1901 had gone to Henry Dunant, the founder of the Red Cross, rehabilitating his reputation.*

Politics were also changing in Europe. Shaken by its poor military performance in the Boer War and feeling threatened by the pace of German armament, Britain in 1904 concluded an informal alliance or "entente" with the French. King Edward VII had prepared the ground for the alliance by a royal visit to Paris. As Prince of Wales he had always been a lover of all things French, in particular the food and the women. A Parisian brothel owner proudly displayed the chair where he had habitually sat to select his woman for the evening. Now, as king, he showed himself a tactful diplomat. Following the entente with France, Britain moved toward a similar understanding with Russia, allied with France since 1892 in a marriage of convenience between autocracy and republicanism. The negotiations were protracted, fraught with long-standing suspicions and antagonisms on both sides, particularly about conflicting ambitions in Persia, Afghanistan, and Central Asia, but in 1907 an entente was finally agreed.

In 1904, the new Conservative British prime minister, Arthur Balfour, appointed Admiral Jacky Fisher as First Sea Lord, the professional head of the Royal Navy. The following year Fisher revolutionized the naval arms race by ordering the first of a new generation of battleships, the steam-turbine-driven, eighteen-thousand-ton HMS *Dreadnought*, which carried ten twelve-inch guns and rendered all other battleships obsolete at a stroke.

---

* In 1906 the winner of the physics prize was J. J. Thomson, discoverer of the electron. Marie Curie, her husband Pierre, Henri Becquerel, and Wilhelm Röntgen had all earlier received prizes for their work on radiation. Then considered pure science with its results openly published and internationally discussed, it would lead to the development of the atomic bomb—a weapon many times more powerful than any contemplated at The Hague.

Germany immediately set out to build similar ships of its own and to widen the Kiel Canal to allow them a swift and secure transit from their Baltic bases to the North Sea. Whether by coincidence or not, the work on the canal was finally completed on July 23, 1914, barely two weeks before the outbreak of war with Britain.

In the midst of these developments Theodore Roosevelt, pressed by U.S. peace campaigners, used his and the United States' emerging prestige to promote the convening of a second Hague Conference. Although none of the nations rushed to accept Roosevelt's proposal, just as in the case of the first conference none felt able to refuse and so on June 15, 1907, delegates assembled again at The Hague. This time 256 men represented forty-four countries.

By then Great Britain had a new Liberal government led by Henry Campbell-Bannerman. Roosevelt, becoming convinced that "aggressive" Germany "despises the Hague Conference and the whole Hague idea," was concerned lest Campbell-Bannerman and his colleagues be "carried away by sentimental ideas" and so "go to any maudlin extreme at the Hague Conference." He need not have worried. Although to please their Liberal supporters Campbell-Bannerman's government proposed placing disarmament on the agenda, supported by Roosevelt for the sake of U.S. public opinion, Germany, Austro-Hungary, and this time Russia protested. When the British did raise disarmament at the conference itself, they did so very briefly and the topic was quickly disposed of, all agreeing that it was for the future when it would merit "further serious study."

The Hague Arbitration Tribunal had since 1899 successfully resolved a number of international disputes voluntarily submitted to it, the first being between the United States and Mexico over church property and another the Anglo-Russian dispute over the sinking of the British trawlers in the North Sea. During the 1907 conference, Andrew Carnegie laid the foundation stone for the new Peace Palace, which was to house Hague arbitration proceedings and for whose construction he had donated $1,250,000. Although at the conference every delegation expressed support for arbitration, they could not agree about what should appear on a list defining subjects to be compulsorily submitted to the process.

With gas not having been used as a weapon and no significant

research done on such use, the agreement prohibiting the use of asphyxiating gases remained in force with little debate. The development of
airships and airplanes had, however, progressed considerably since the
earlier conference. On July 2, 1900, spectators at Friedrichshafen on the
shore of Lake Constance in southern Germany watched Count von
Zeppelin's cylindrical 420-foot-long *Luftschiff 1 (LZ1)*—the world's first
rigid dirigible airship with a frame of aluminum girders encased by
fabric—as it was moved from the floating shed on the lake in which it had
been built and ascended into the air where seventeen gas bags holding
four hundred thousand cubic feet of hydrogen and contained within the
fabric envelope held it aloft. Two gondolas suspended beneath the keel
each held one of the two 850-pound Daimler petrol engines that powered
her two four-bladed propellers. Each engine only produced fifteen horsepower, driving the airship forward at a mere sixteen miles per hour. In
1906, a year before the second Hague Conference, von Zeppelin produced the larger, stronger, speedier *LZ2*, however a storm destroyed the
craft at its moorings after its second flight. Using the last of his personal
fortune he constructed a third airship—the *LZ3*—capable of eight hours
of sustained flight, which he would soon demonstrate to a hitherto skeptical kaiser.

On December 17, 1903, American brothers Orville and Wilbur Wright
became the first to solve the technical problems of constructing and operating a heavier-than-air flying machine. Taking turns as pilot they completed
four flights aboard their biplane *Flyer I* from the sandy beach near Kitty
Hawk on one of the barrier islands off North Carolina. The brothers, who
had developed the craft at their own expense, saw the military forces of "a
great government" as the only market for their invention.

Recognizing the airplane's potential, which the U.S. government
then did not, the British War Office dispatched Lieutenant Colonel John
Capper to meet them at their new base at Dayton, Ohio. They demonstrated to him their new plane, *Flyer II*, capable of flying at thirty-five
miles per hour for more than three miles. Impressed by this "wonderful
advance," after a series of discussions over the next year Capper invited
the Wrights to Britain. However, when they asked for twenty thousand
pounds for four years work including supplying an airplane, training a

pilot, and granting the British government a license to build its own craft, the British balked, partly because the brothers, doubtless fearing industrial espionage, would not allow their planes to be inspected, partly because they were beginning to believe they could develop their own machines as the French were said to be doing. The Wrights therefore remained in America, refining their designs and setting new records. Unsure of where the next developments in aircraft and airships might lead, the Hague delegates, after some discussion, felt it prudent only to renew the prohibition on launching projectiles and explosives from the air for another five years.

Japan had opened its war against Russia in 1904 by surprise attack, and the second Hague Conference agreed to a prohibition against countries acting in this way in the future. Instead they were required first to issue an ultimatum or a declaration of war. Another convention, agreed to unanimously with strong support from Belgium, concerned neutral rights. The first of its twenty-five articles stated that "the territory of neutral Powers is inviolable," the second that, "Belligerents are forbidden to move troops or convoys of either munitions of war or supplies across the territory of a neutral Power." The convention on land warfare was revised while maintaining the key principles such as that in Article 23 which began "In addition to the prohibitions provided by special Conventions, it is especially forbidden: a. To employ poison or poisoned weapons"; or in Article 25 forbidding "the attack or bombardment by whatever means" of "undefended" areas. Article 3 of the same convention made belligerent states responsible for the acts of their armed forces and "liable to pay compensation" for violations. However neither of the Hague Conferences gave any thought to an international court either to punish those who broke the rules of the various conventions or to set the level of compensation.

Discussions on maritime matters were for the most part inconclusive. The chief German delegate, Baron Marschall, warned against the stupidity of making laws for naval combat that might be rendered useless "by the law of facts." Although the delegates agreed to ban the use of unanchored submarine contact mines that remained armed for more than an hour after release, the major issues of Cruiser Rules, contraband, and neutral rights were deferred to a meeting of naval powers to be held in London the following year, 1908.

Ironically, the second Hague Conference ended by adopting a resolution calling for a third in 1915.

CHAPTER FOUR

"A Scrap of Paper"

WHEN THE CONFERENCE on marine matters convened in London in 1908, Britain was the dominant maritime power in both naval and commercial terms. Engaged in a naval race with Germany, Britain's philosophy was that its navy should be equal in strength to any two others. (The U.S. Navy was omitted from such calculations indicating the growing closeness between the two countries and the consequent improbability of war between them.) Britain's merchant fleet made up 48 percent of the world's shipping and transported more than half the world's total seaborne trade.

Despite Jacky Fisher's introduction of the dreadnought battleship, some naval strategists saw the torpedo-armed submarine as the greatest threat to Britain's maritime hegemony. Fisher himself called them "the battleships of the future." The concept of underwater warfare was not new. Thucydides described divers acting as underwater saboteurs during the Roman siege of Syracuse. Leonardo da Vinci sketched a form of diving suit. In 1578 an Englishman, William Bourne, designed a submersible that could rise and sink by filling or emptying ballast tanks on either side—a key characteristic of modern submarines. Early next century Dutchman Cornelius Van Drebbel reputedly demonstrated a vessel based on Bourne's design on the river Thames.

David Bushnell produced the first documented precursor of the modern submarine when he launched his submersible *Turtle* against HMS *Eagle* during the American Revolution in New York harbor on September 6, 1776. The egg-shaped *Turtle* was a one-man wooden vessel, seven feet long and four feet wide with four portholes, three sleeved armholes, and an access hatch on top. She was propelled by two hand-operated screws—a horizontal one to propel her up and down and a vertical one to move her backward and forward. A foot-operated valve let water flow in to help her descend, while a foot pump pushed it out again to enable her to rise. Bushnell's plan for the *Turtle* to attach a 150-pound explosive charge to the *Eagle* failed because the operator, Sergeant Ezra Lee, could not get the drill bit designed to fit dynamite charges to penetrate the *Eagle's* metal-reinforced hull.

In May 1801 Robert Fulton of Pennsylvania followed up Bushnell's work, launching the copper-skinned *Nautilus*—the first submarine built of metal. He offered his designs first to France and then to Britain during the Napoleonic Wars. Both declined. British admiral Earl St. Vincent summed up the general view that they were "a mode of war which we who command the seas do not want, and which, if successful, would deprive us of it."

In February 1864, the USS *Housatonic*—a new 1,264-ton frigate serving with the Union squadron blockading the Confederate port of Charleston—was the first ship sunk by a submarine. On a clear, cold, moonlit night, the CSS *Hunley*, a slender submersible forty feet long but just forty-two inches in diameter and built of 3/8-inch boiler plate, slunk out of Charleston harbor. Commanded by Lieutenant George E. Dixon, she crept semi-submerged toward the Union fleet. The eight-man crew labored over the hand crank which, connected to the propeller, drove the *Hunley* forward at four knots. Dixon was standing up since the only way he could navigate was by peering out of the forward hatch.

Just before eight forty-five P.M., the master of the *Housatonic* saw something resembling a piece of driftwood heading straight for his ship. Realizing that a current or tide could not be propelling it, he took evasive action but too late. Dixon brought the *Hunley* alongside and detonated the 143 pounds of gunpowder supported on her projecting spar. The *Housatonic* was flung into the air, settled back, and slowly sank. The *Hunley's* crew vanished, probably sucked into the gash in the frigate's side.

An Irish emigrant to the United States, John P. Holland, undertook the next crucial developments. Beginning in the late 1870s, over successive prototypes he developed petrol-engine-driven designs with the streamlined porpoise shape of modern submarines. His designs did not ascend or descend by their own weight but tilted their hydroplanes in the appropriate direction and propelled themselves by their engine power.

Holland was not the only man developing submarines. Thorsten Nordenfelt in Sweden and British clergyman the Reverend George William Garrett were creating their own designs. Queen Victoria's chaplain endorsed Garrett's company's prospectus, reassuring investors with familiar arguments: "As to the invention being for murdering people—this is all nonsense. Every contribution made by science to improve instruments of war makes war shorter and, in the end, less terrible to human life and to human progress."

Although Garrett, and in particular Nordenfelt, had some success, Holland maintained his lead. His sixth prototype, the *Holland VI*, constructed in 1898 in New Jersey, was nearly fifty-four feet long. Powered by a forty-five horsepower petrol engine for surface cruising and for recharging the batteries of a fifty-horsepower electric motor that drove the craft when submerged, her main weapon was a torpedo launched from an eighteen-inch torpedo tube. She made her first successful dive off Staten Island on Saint Patrick's Day, March 17, 1898. Her formal trials ten days later so impressed then assistant secretary of the navy Theodore Roosevelt that he recommended that the navy purchase the vessel which on April 11, 1900, became the USS *Holland* (SS-1).

A powerful lobby within the British Admiralty continued to dismiss submersibles as "not our concern." In 1900 Lord Goschen, First Lord of the Admiralty, asserted that "submarines were a weapon for Maritime Powers on the defensive." His parliamentary secretary was categoric: "The Admiralty are not prepared to take any steps in regard to submarines because this vessel is only the weapon of the weaker nation." Rear Admiral Sir Arthur Wilson, VC, Controller of the Royal Navy, fulminated: "Underwater weapons, they call 'em. I call them underhand, unfair and damned un-English. They'll never be any use in war and I'll tell you why: I'm going to get the First Lord to announce that we intend to treat all submarines as pirate vessels in wartime and that we'll hang all the crews."

Nevertheless with the support of Admiral Jacky Fisher and his belief in "the immense impending revolution which the submarines will effect as offensive weapons of war," in 1901 the British Admiralty ordered five Holland boats to be built in England by Vickers under license. The first was launched at Barrow-in-Furness the same year. The British vessels first introduced the periscope to the submarine—the U.S. Holland boats had had to surface so that men could look through the glass ports in the conning tower.

In 1901 German secretary of state for the navy Admiral Tirpitz declared that Germany had no need of submarines. In spring 1904 he was still lecturing the Reichstag about his contempt for submarine warfare but that July, reacting to Britain's program, he announced the building of a submarine. The German navy's first Unterseeboot—the *U-1*—was completed in 1906 at Krupp's plant in Kiel.

The torpedoes which armed all submarines were named after the crampfish or electric ray and pioneered by British engineer Robert Whitehead. While working in Austria for a company supplying the Austro-Hungarian navy, he developed in strict secrecy an "automobile device" driven by compressed air which could travel at eight knots and carry dynamite. Soon after he perfected a depth-keeping mechanism. The Royal Navy invited him home to demonstrate the new weapon and in 1870 concluded that "any maritime nation failing to provide itself with submarine locomotive torpedoes would be neglecting a great source of power both for offence and defence"and paid fifteen thousand pounds for the right to manufacture his torpedoes. Other nations quickly followed suit.

The first torpedoes were designed to be fired from surface vessels and had spectacular success in the Russo-Japanese War. Admiral Fisher predicted the weapon "would play a most important part in future wars" since ships as currently constructed were powerless against them and "the constant dread of sudden destruction" would demoralize seamen. By 1904 the British Holland submarines had a one in two chance of hitting a destroyer from a range of three hundred to four hundred feet with their improved torpedoes.

Perhaps the area where Britain's commercial as distinct from naval maritime supremacy was at the greatest risk as the delegates to the London Maritime Conference assembled was the transatlantic passenger trade—just as now for airlines one of the most profitable sources of revenue.

American Moses Rogers pioneered steam propulsion across the Atlantic when in 1819 he captained the paddle steamer *Savannah* to Liverpool, although the vessel used steam for only eighty-five hours of the twenty-seven-day voyage and sailed for the rest of the time. The first ship to steam continuously across the Atlantic was the British *Sirius* in 1838. She was fitted with the recently invented marine surface condensers which prevented her boilers from becoming clogged with salt.

Born in Halifax, Nova Scotia, in 1787, Samuel Cunard was already a successful businessman when in 1838 the British government invited tenders to carry transatlantic mail by steamer. He hurried to London where he won a contract to carry the mail to and from America twice a month for a fee of fifty-five thousand pounds. In July 1840 the first of Cunard's fleet, the paddle steamer *Britannia*, made her maiden voyage from Liverpool, reaching Boston in fourteen days.

Charles Dickens never forgot his voyage to America on the *Britannia* in 1842. He derided his cabin as "an utterly impracticable, thoroughly hopeless, and profoundly preposterous box." The only thing conceivably smaller for sleeping in would be "a coffin" and the flat quilt that covered him was "like a surgical plaster [bandage]." Furthermore, there was as much chance of accommodating his wife's luggage as of persuading a giraffe "into a flower pot." Bad weather forced him to spend a great deal of time in the cabin and he felt seasick. "Read in bed (but to this hour I don't know what) . . . ; and reeled on deck a little; drank cold brandy and water with unspeakable disgust and ate hard biscuits perseveringly," he wrote. "Not ill, but going to be."

British and American lines dominated the transatlantic route, using more and more sophisticated ships, until in 1889 the kaiser, impressed by a new British White Star Line vessel he saw at a British naval review, decided "we must have some of these." By 1897, the year of Queen Victoria's Diamond Jubilee, the huge 14,350-ton *Kaiser Wilhelm der Grosse* was the fastest liner on the Atlantic with a top speed of over twenty-one knots, taking the Blue Riband for the Atlantic crossing on her maiden voyage. By 1903, German companies owned the four fastest ships crossing the Atlantic.

In 1902 the American banker John Pierpont Morgan bought the White Star Line for twenty-five million dollars for the new shipping conglomerate he was building—International Mercantile Marine (IMM). Having negotiated an alliance with the two main German lines, Hamburg-Amerika and North German Lloyd, he approached Cunard, the only major line still in British ownership, with an offer for the company's shares at 80 percent above the market value.

The British press railed against the " 'Morganization' of the Atlantic" and warned of the consequences of losing "the great north Atlantic trade, the only trade which can support ships of great speed and tonnage so essential as cruisers in time of war." The British government feared that Germany would soon have a fleet of nine liners, all of which could outstrip the fastest British steamers. Its stark choice lay between acquiescing in the acquisition of Cunard by IMM or rescuing Cunard "for the nation" through a large government subsidy. While the debate ebbed and flowed an aging Cunard liner broke down in mid-Atlantic and had to be towed to the Azores by an IMM tramp steamer. The press highlighted the disturbing symbolism.

In July 1903 the British government agreed to lend Cunard £2,600,000 to build two new ships, subsequently named the *Lusitania* and the *Mauretania*, that with a top speed of at least twenty-four-and-a-half knots could outstrip the upstart German liners and whose specifications the Admiralty would approve. It also agreed to pay Cunard an annual subsidy of £150,000 for maintaining both vessels in a state of war readiness, together with £68,000 for carrying the mail. In return, the Admiralty had the right to commandeer the ships for use as auxiliary merchant cruisers, troopships, or hospital ships.

The *Lusitania* was the first of the two ships to enter service, making her maiden transatlantic voyage in September 1907 during the second Hague Conference. She was half the size again of any vessel yet built, and three quarters more powerful. Novel features included high-tensile steel in her hull for additional strength and electric controls for steering, for closing her 175 watertight compartments, and for detecting fire. On her first arrival in New York the American newspapers hailed the luxury of a ship that was "more beautiful than Solomon's Temple and big enough to hold all his wives." On her second westbound crossing she won back the Blue Riband.

At the conference of the ten leading maritime nations in London in 1908, Britain's commercial interests as a supplier and transporter of much of the world's trade dominated the policy of Campbell-Bannerman and his Liberal Party government rather than what might become its naval interests if it became involved in a war. Other delegations too emphasized the importance of trade and freedom of the seas. Consequently, no change was made to the old Cruiser Rules to allow for new, modern technologies such as the submarine. Merchant ships still could not be sunk without warning; rather, they had to be stopped and searched for contraband and, if it was found, the crew given the time to take to the boats before the vessel was sunk or seized as a prize. Tight definitions were drawn up of what constituted "contraband," differentiating between goods clearly intended for military use such as weapons and those for civilian use. Some goods such as blankets or cloth were defined as "conditional contraband," which could be used for either military or civil purposes. Before they could be seized and destroyed their use and destination had to be established. Close blockades of an enemy's ports by warships at the edge of territorial waters remained acceptable.

Mahan—now an admiral—was a frustrated American delegate at the conference, unable to make his sterner views on the need to allow greater freedom of action by navies toward their enemies prevail even within his own U.S. delegation. However, after the conference ended he continued to voice his concerns. They were taken up by some of his followers in Britain who argued that by ratifying the conference decisions, Britain would forfeit its naval supremacy. A heated debate followed in Britain further fueled by the 1909 "naval scare" resulting from a German decision to accelerate its battleship-building program. As a consequence, Britain never ratified the revised rules agreed to in London. Neither, under renewed pressure from Mahan, did the United States. Without the signature of two of the leading maritime nations the new provisions never came into force. First Sea Lord Jacky Fisher took little part in the debates about the British attitude, either cynically content to disregard the rules if Britain ever went to war or more likely too preoccupied with the feuding over new training procedures and gunnery practice with more hidebound colleagues which would soon precipitate his retirement in January 1910.

BY NOW THE Balkans were the most likely source of conflict. In 1908–9, a prolonged confrontation stopping short of war flared up between Serbia—backed by Russia—and Austro-Hungary after the latter took Bosnia-Herzegovina from the crumbling Ottoman Turkish Empire. In 1912–13, the independent Balkan states, Serbia, Montenegro, Bulgaria, and Greece, first combined to defeat the Ottoman Turks and seize from them nearly all their remaining European territory and then fell out among themselves about the division of the spoils. Serbia was the principal winner, emerging with a doubling of its territory and increased national self-confidence. Austro-Hungary, since 1879 bound in tight alliance to Germany, felt it had lost out by not intervening in the 1912–13 conflicts and saw inherent problems for its diverse empire if pan-Slavism, and with it Russian influence, grew further.

Many observers comforted themselves that the Balkan conflicts had been confined to that region. Nevertheless the European arms buildup continued. In 1911, thirty-six-year-old Winston Churchill, then a member of the Liberal Party, had been appointed First Lord of the Admiralty—the overall head of the organization to whom the professional head, the First Sea Lord, reported. The First Lord of the Admiralty in turn reported to Parliament and the cabinet, and was a member of both. Churchill, described in his early years in Parliament by an opponent as "restless, egotistical, bumptious, shallow-minded and reactionary but with a certain personal magnetism, great pluck and some originality," had in 1911–12 headed inconclusive discussions with Germany about a pause in the naval arms race. The British naval budget, with its emphasis on high technology had, at more than forty-five million pounds, quadrupled over the last quarter of a century and was taking an increasing proportion of the rising national defense budget. Churchill tried again in 1913, contacting the German naval attaché in London, but he was thwarted by the response of Admiral Alfred von Tirpitz who suggested that the approach was a mere ploy to delay Germany's naval program.

The kaiser had appointed Tirpitz—then still to earn his ennobling 'von'— Germany's secretary of state for the navy in June 1897. Nine days later, Tirpitz had written in a memorandum: "For Germany at the moment the most dangerous naval enemy is England . . . The strategy against England demands battleships in as great a number as possible." Thereafter he had been the inspiration and architect for Germany's naval expansion, his views on naval matters mirroring those of Fisher and Mahan. Just as the latter two could not always effectively control their changing political masters, he could never be certain of the febrile, inconsistent kaiser's reactions, writing: "I could never discover how to ward off the frequent interference of the Emperor whose imagination, once it had fixed on shipbuilding, was fed by all manner of impressions . . . Suggestions are cheap in the Navy and change like a kaleidoscope."

Despite the troubles in the Balkans and the continuing arms race, in the golden summer of 1914 few saw reason to worry unduly about an impending war. Then the assassination of Archduke Franz Ferdinand, the heir to the Austro-Hungarian throne, and his morganatic wife Sophie, in the Bosnian-Herzegovinan city of Sarajevo, changed everything. It happened on June 28, their wedding anniversary, and also the day Serbs commemorated the anniversary of the Battle of Kosovo in 1389 when their troops had been heavily defeated by the Ottoman Turks but a single Serb had penetrated Ottoman lines and killed their sultan. Austro-Hungarian interrogation of captured members of the assassination team revealed that although subjects of the Austro-Hungarian Empire they had been trained and armed in Serbia and were part of an organization that wanted to incorporate Bosnia-Herzegovina into Serbia. The Austro-Hungarian authorities demanded but failed to secure guarantees from the Serbian government that it would move against anti-Austrian nationalist and terrorist groups in its territory and accept on-the-spot Austro-Hungarian oversight of its compliance. Therefore, having satisfied itself of German support, Austro-Hungary declared war on Serbia on July 28.

Governments across Europe ordered the mobilization of their armies to ensure they were not disadvantaged should a more general war break out. The German general staff alone time-tabled eleven thousand train movements. Despite further diplomatic maneuverings during which, for a brief period, arbitration to solve the conflict seemed possible, Germany—concerned to preserve the advantage its speed of mobilization gave—declared war on August 1 on Russia and on August 3 on France in the latter case with only the most sketchy pretense of justification. The day before, Germany had sent an ultimatum to neutral Belgium demanding to use its territory in operations against France and stating that if Belgium resisted it would be considered an enemy. Britain had previously refused to commit itself in the buildup to war. However, the intended violation of neutral Belgium's rights in direct contravention of the 1907 Hague Convention on neutral rights, and even more specifically of the Treaty of London signed by the European powers, including Prussia, in 1839 guaranteeing Belgian neutrality, left Britain no room for maneuver.

At three P.M. on August 4, 1914, the tall distinguished-looking German chancellor Theobald von Bethmann Hollweg rose to address a packed Reichstag. German troops, he announced, were advancing on France, had occupied Luxembourg, and were "already in Belgium." "Our invasion of Belgium is contrary to international law but the wrong—I speak openly—that we are committing we will make good as soon as our military goal has been reached." His words handed the Allies the moral high ground and an unassailable propaganda advantage.

That evening the British ambassador to Berlin, Sir Edward Goschen, called on von Bethmann Hollweg to present a British ultimatum: leave Belgium or face Britain's entry into the war. Germany had until midnight to decide. Goschen found the chancellor, a habitual chain smoker, "excited" and "very agitated"; he complained that Britain was committing an "unthinkable" act, "like striking a man from behind while he was fighting for his life against two assailants." Britain, the chancellor said, would be responsible for everything dreadful that must follow "just for a word—neutrality," a word which in war time had so often been disregarded—all just for a scrap of paper Great Britain was going to make war on a kindred nation." Sir Edward replied stiffly that if it was strategically a matter of life or death for Germany to advance through Belgium, it was equally a matter of life or death for Britain to keep its solemn compact.

Some hours before midnight and the expiry of the ultimatum, according to a British diplomat within, a mob "of quite well-dressed individuals, including a number of women," stoned the British embassy, smashing many windows. The crowd "seemed mad with rage . . . howling 'Death to the English pedlar nation!' " "that was guilty of Rassen-verrat!"— "race treason."

Von Bethmann Hollweg later complained: "My blood boiled at his [Goschen's] hypocritical harping on Belgian neutrality, which was not the thing that had driven England into the war." British hypocrisy would soon become a familiar German charge. The kaiser too was nonplussed at Britain's decision. His relationship with Great Britain had always been one of his most complex, emotional, and ambiguous. Her first grandchild, he adored his grandmother Queen Victoria and is said to have held her in his arms as she died in 1901. He had cordially loathed her successor, his uncle Edward VII. After one of Edward's royal visits to France to cement the Anglo-French entente, the kaiser told three hundred guests at a Berlin dinner "He is Satan. You can hardly believe what a Satan he is." When Edward died in 1910, the kaiser advised Theodore Roosevelt that the forty-five-year-old George V was "a very nice boy . . . He is a thorough Englishman and hates all foreigners but I do not mind that as long as he does not hate Germans more than other foreigners."

As an autocrat the kaiser overestimated the power of the monarchy in the British democracy. In late July 1914, on the eve of war, he placed great credence in an account from his brother Henry, then yachting in England, of a conversation with George V in which the latter said that Britain would remain neutral. He told a skeptical von Tirpitz that "I have the word of a King and that is sufficient for me." When Britain declared war he complained, "to think that Nicholas [the czar of Russia] and Georgie should have played me false! If my grandmother had been alive she would never have allowed it . . . Only among the ruins of London will I forgive Georgie."

The ambiguity of the kaiser's feelings toward Britain extended far beyond its royal family. He admired much about the country and its culture, including its capital's fine architecture. His enthusiasm for battleships and Atlantic liners had been roused in British ports. He was proud not only of being a Knight of the Garter but also an honorary British Admiral of the Fleet and Field Marshal. Initially he had wanted an alliance between what he thought of as "the two Teutonic nations," commenting in 1901 that "with such an alliance not a mouse could stir in Europe without our permission and the nations would in time come to see the necessity of reducing their armaments." Such an alliance would be a defense against the encirclement of Germany, which he feared.

Subsequently, he had simply wanted Britain to stand aside and allow Germany a free hand in Europe and in so doing recognize in political terms its real and rising economic strength. Germany had become the dominant force in European steel and chemical production as well as coal mining. In 1870 Britain had 32 percent of the world's manufacturing capacity, but by 1910 its share had fallen to less than 15 percent, while Germany's had risen to 16 percent. (The United States by then had 35 percent.)* Thereafter the kaiser had come to believe that Britain still treated Germany too lightly, undervaluing both him and his nation, and to share his mentor Bismarck's view of the British: "I have had all through my life sympathy for England and its inhabitants but these people do not want to let themselves be liked by us."

It is easy to portray the kaiser—sensitive about his withered arm, early at odds with his parents, and alternately looking for love or bullying to gain attention—as a sad, somewhat comic, deluded figure. However, his ambitions and his views of Britain reflected those of most of his cabinet and much of his nation as is evident from von Bethmann Hollweg's comments to Goschen about a "kindred nation" and shouts of "race treason" by the mob attacking the British embassy. Von Tirpitz too had been something of an Anglophile, speaking fluent English and reading English books like the kaiser, sending his daughters to Cheltenham Ladies' College and admiring the British navy wholeheartedly. But he too had come to feel slighted and patronized, complaining that "the English believed that they could treat us like Portugal." Nevertheless, when von Bethmann Hollweg told the German cabinet on August 3 that with the German invasion of Belgium Britain's entry into the war was inevitable, von Tirpitz cried out,

---

* Key population statistics in 1914 were approximately: United Kingdom, 46 million; Germany, 68 million; United States, 99 million; France, 40 million; Austro-Hungary, 51 million; Russia, 166 million.

"All is then lost." James Gerard, U.S. ambassador to Berlin, described how: "The army and all Germany believed . . . that Great Britain would remain neutral, and that Germany would consequently become, if not the actual owner, at least dictator of the world."

The kaiser would have happily included the United States in a Teutonic alliance between Germany and Britain. In January 1914, he told Colonel Edward Mandell House, U.S. president Woodrow Wilson's main confidant and frequent envoy to Europe, that the Russians as Slavs and the French as Latins would never be suitable allies for the English. Only an English, American, and German alliance based on their common Anglo-Saxon racial heritage would withstand the challenges of the new century. As Gerard later remarked as the war progressed, Germany and its people would be even more ready to include the United States with Britain in their charges of hypocrisy.

The war had popular support in each of the belligerent countries. In France an officer described how as his troop train left a Paris station at six A.M. he saw a huge crowd and "quite spontaneously, like a smouldering fire suddenly erupted into roaring flames, an immense clamour arose as the *Marsellaise* burst from a thousand throats. All the men were standing at the train's windows waving their kepis . . . The women were throwing kisses and heaped flowers on our convoy." In Saint Petersburg the French ambassador saw an enormous crowd in front of the Winter Palace "with flags, banners, icons and portraits of the Tsar. The Emperor appeared on the balcony. The entire crowd at once knelt and sang the Russian national anthem. To those thousands of men on their knees . . . the Tsar was really the autocrat appointed of God, the military, political and religious leader of his people, the absolute master of their bodies and souls."

In Munich, an Austrian eking out a living as a painter—Adolf Hitler— witnessed a vast crowd gathered in the Odeonsplatz acclaim the proclamation of mobilization. He was "not ashamed to acknowledge that I was carried away by the enthusiasm of the moment . . . and . . . sank down upon my knees and thanked heaven out of the fullness of my heart for the favour of having been permitted to live in such times." Almost immediately he petitioned for permission to join a Bavarian regiment even though he was an Austrian subject. It was speedily given.

Religious leaders backed their countries. In Berlin, the kaiser's pastor led a vast congregation in its prayers for victory while at the Oranienstrasse synagogue the rabbi prayed for a German triumph. A German newspaper proclaimed this is "a holy war: Germany cannot and is not allowed to lose . . . if she loses so, too, does the world lose its light, its home of justice." On the opposing side, the bishop of London insisted, "The Church can best help the nation first of all by making it realise that it is engaged in a holy war."

On a much more personal level, a British girl, then seven years old, recalled how her grandmother summoned her from the garden telling her, " 'I have got something very serious to tell you. The Germans are fighting the British, there is a war on and all sorts of people will be killed by these wicked Germans. And therefore there must be no playing, no singing and no running about.' And then she took from us all our toys that were made in Germany, amongst them a camel of which I was very fond."

Soldiers marching off to the conflict believed it would not last long. A Russian officer worried about packing his dress uniform for a triumphal entry into Berlin. German officers talked of being in Paris in a few weeks. The crowds waving French troops off called *"Au revoir. A bientot,"* expecting to see them again soon. In Britain a Cambridge University under-graduate enlisted with some friends, recalling, "We were quite clear that Germany would be defeated by the 7th of October when we would go back to Cambridge [for the beginning of term]." The kaiser told his departing troops, "You will be home before the leaves have fallen from the trees."

CHAPTER FIVE

"The Worst of Contrabands"

BUT THE TROOPS were not even home by Christmas. In the first few days and weeks of the war, Germany's armies advanced through most of Belgium and into France, despite stronger resistance by the Belgian army than expected that allowed the leading elements of the British Expeditionary Force time to join the fighting. The German advance deprived France of 10 percent of its territory and a third of its industrial capacity.

On September 9 the usually cautious von Bethmann Hollweg, elated by the speed and scale of Germany's advance, listed extravagant war aims for Germany. The overall goal was "Security for the German Reich in west and east for all imaginable time. For this purpose France must be so weakened as to make its revival as a great power impossible for all time. Russia must be thrust back as far as possible from Germany's eastern frontier." More specifically, France should be forced to give up the iron ore fields of Briey "which is necessary for the supply of our industry" and pay a large war indemnity. A treaty should make France economically dependent on Germany, excluding British commerce from French markets. Belgium, if allowed "to continue to exist" should be a "vassal state" with Germany taking military control over the Belgian coastal ports, perhaps with the French ports of Dunkirk, Calais, and Boulogne being added to the vassal state. Luxembourg should become part of Germany. Colonial concessions should be forced from the defeated. Germany should be dominant in "a central European economic association through common customs treaties to include France, Belgium, Holland, Denmark, Austro-Hungary, Poland, and perhaps Italy, Sweden, and Norway . . . All its members would be formally equal but in practice would be under German leadership and [this will] stabilise Germany's economic dominance over Mitteleuropa."

Other influential German leaders proposed even more far-reaching war aims, demanding greater territorial concessions by France and land seizures from Russia. One politician demonstrated Germany's detestation of being patronized by Britain by including among his principal war aims "elimination of the intolerable tutelage exercised by Britain over Germany in all questions of world politics." In a memorandum submitted to government on the same day as von Bethmann Hollweg dispatched his war aims, the powerful German industrialist August Thyssen demanded the annexation of Belgium, much of northern France including the Pas de Calais, and in the northeast the territories on which stood the French frontier fortresses. To the east he demanded the Baltic states and perhaps the Don Basin, the Caucasus, and the Crimea for Germany. His prime justification was to secure "Germany's supply of raw materials." Noteworthily, none of these various submissions spelled out what would be the strategy toward Britain, merely implying it should be humble toward Germany and as a result of other changes commercially and militarily less powerful.

Von Bethmann Hollweg and the others were to be disappointed in their dreams of a speedy victory. The German armies in the west were held and in places pushed back at the battles of Mons, the Marne, and the first battle of Ypres. Thereafter the front lines quickly began to stabilize even if at Ypres the British were left in an exposed salient. By New Year's Day 1915, a line of trenches 450 miles long stretched from Switzerland to the North Sea, across which 110 Allied divisions—as yet only ten of them British—faced 100 German ones. Over three hundred thousand Frenchmen and nearly a quarter of a million Germans were already dead. Britain had lost some thirty thousand men, nearly one fifth of its small regular army. The war of movement on the western front was over. Stalemate had begun. In the east too stalemate was approaching. The Austro-Hungarian army had lost over a million and a quarter men and the Russians one and a half million.

Across the Atlantic the world's other emerging great power had watched Europe's disintegration into war with both alarm and a degree of detachment and disbelief. The *North Dakota Daily Herald* said of Franz

Ferdinand's assassination, "One archduke more or less makes little difference." The *Philadelphia Public Ledger* quipped in addressing
Austro-Hungary: "If the Serbs defeat you it will 'Servia right'!" The *Dallas
News* joined many in Europe in thinking the war would soon be over, suggesting it would be "long before the cotton season is." A more serious
commentator considered that the great safeguard "against the armies and
navies Europe has gathered for war is that Europe is not rich enough to
use them and is too human and humane to want to use them." However,
Germany's invasion of neutral Belgium turned sympathy toward the Allies.
"As if by a lightning flash," wrote a columnist, "the issue was made plain;
the issue of the sacredness of law; the rule of the soldier or the rule of the
citizen; the rule of fear or of law."

Such emphasis on the rule of law chimed well with the views of
fifty-seven-year-old Woodrow Wilson, then in the second year of his first
term. He had been a student of law and history, and subsequently a professor at Princeton and then president of the university. His secretary of
state, William Jennings Bryan, defeated three times for the presidency, had
been essential to Wilson securing the Democratic presidential nomination.
Like Wilson a lawyer, but also a lifelong fundamentalist Christian and teetotaler and more radical than Wilson, he championed labor rights against
big business.

A strong supporter of the Hague Treaties and of arbitration, Bryan
saw the United States as a "republic . . . becoming the supreme moral factor
in disputes." One of his first acts as secretary of state in 1913 was to persuade most of the major powers (including Great Britain and France but
not Germany) to agree to treaties committing themselves, to some extent
at least, to the use of cooling-off periods and of arbitration to settle international disputes. At the signing ceremony he presented the diplomats with
paperweights cast in the symbolic form of ploughshares from old swords
from Washington Naval Yard. He supplemented his income by frequent
performances on the lecture circuit. His audiences' response convinced
him they shared his love of peace, but many American commentators
doubted whether Bryan's intellect and political acumen matched his elo-
quence and undoubted sincerity—a view shared by diplomats with whom
he came into contact. British ambassador Sir Cecil Spring-Rice thought

talking to Bryan was "like writing on ice" and Bryan himself "a jellyfish . . . incapable of forming a settled judgement on anything outside party politics." Continental Europeans gagged when served nonalcoholic grape juice by the teetotaler as a substitute for wine at his diplomatic receptions.

Immediately before the outbreak of war Wilson was preoccupied with the illness of his wife Ellen, who was dying of kidney disease. They were a devoted couple—he referred to them as "wedded sweethearts." When he first heard of Austro-Hungary's declaration of war on Serbia, Wilson put his hands to his face and said: "I can think of nothing, nothing when my dear one is suffering." Ellen died on August 6. When the British foreign secretary Sir Edward Grey, who had lost his own wife in a carriage accident a few years before, wrote him a letter of condolence, Wilson replied, "My hope is that you will regard me as your friend. I feel that we are bound together by common principle and purpose." One of Grey's main aims in the early years of the war would be to maintain that sense of shared understanding and empathy with Wilson.

Nevertheless, Wilson was as committed as Bryan to maintaining U.S. neutrality and, if possible, to mediating peace. On August 3 he told a press conference that America stood ready to help the rest of the world resolve their differences peacefully and to "reap a permanent glory out of doing it." On August 18 he asked his people to be "neutral in fact as well as in name during these days that are to try men's souls . . . impartial in thought as well as in action" so that the United States could "speak the counsels of peace" and "play the impartial mediator." Early in September he would make his first tentative offer to Germany to mediate, which would be rebuffed on the grounds that Germany had had war forced on it and that accepting mediation at this stage would be "interpreted as a sign of weakness and not understood by our people."

Even before war had begun, Wilson had shown his determination to ensure neutrality among his officers and officials by muzzling the now retired Admiral Mahan, who had long warned Britain through the press of the need to thwart German commercial and colonial ambitions before it was too late. On August 3 he advised the British navy to strike at once, or Germany would defeat France and Russia and turn on Britain. He also suggested that Britain should immediately make a preemptive attack on

Italy, then teetering on the brink of joining Germany and Austro-Hungary because of a previous alliance. Under pressure from public opinion, not least from Italian Americans, Wilson initiated a special order on August 6 that prohibited officers of the navy and army of the United States, active or retired, from commenting publicly on the military or political situation in Europe. Mahan asked to be exempted from the order and was refused. He died less than four months later on December 1, 1914, before he could see many of his ideas on sea power vindicated.

Sharing a language and increasingly a common popular culture, the American public with the exception of nearly all German Americans and some Irish Americans were generally sympathetic to Britain. The kaiser would complain in early October, "England has managed to make the whole world believe that we are the guilty party." However, in reality the actions of his troops were mainly responsible for increased anti-German sentiment in the United States and elsewhere as reports emerged of war crimes committed by them during the early days of the German invasion of Belgium and France. Fearing or believing they were under attack by "citizen guerrillas," German troops routinely took hostages to ensure good behavior. They shot at least 110 citizens at Andenne Seilles near Namur and burned the town down. At Leffe on the outskirts of Dinant, German soldiers lined up hostages—men, women, and children—in the town square and executed them by firing squad. The dead exceeded six hundred.

The most well-publicized atrocity was at Louvain in Belgium. After German troops had occupied the city, the Belgian army launched a counter-attack on August 25. The German soldiers panicked and over the next five days burned down much of the city including its world-famous ancient library with its 230,000 precious volumes, killed more than two hundred civilians, and ejected the remaining forty-two thousand inhabitants by force including sixteen hundred men, women, and children they deported to Germany. A German officer told an American diplomat who visited Louvain on August 28: "We shall wipe [Louvain] out, not one stone will stand upon another! Not one, I tell you. We will teach them to respect Germans. For generations people will come here to see what we have done!"

Such actions were of course in direct breach of the laws of war agreed to internationally at The Hague. British prime minister Herbert Asquith claimed it was "the greatest crime against civilisation and culture since the Thirty Years War—the sack of Louvain . . . a shameless holocaust . . . lit up by blind barbarian vengeance." Many in Britain called for an announcement that when the war was won the kaiser would be exiled to Saint Helena as Napoleon had been after his defeat at Waterloo. Others called for those responsible to be tried as war criminals. The dean of Peterborough Cathedral in England encapsulated this view: "We may be far still from the final abolition of war, but we should not be far from the end of atrocities in war if those responsible for them in whatever rank had the risk before their eyes that they might have to suffer just penalties as 'common felons.' "

Unwilling for their nation to be seen as book burners and murderers, ninety-three German academics, scientists, and intellectuals, including the Nobel Prize winner Wilhelm Röntgen and future winner Max Planck, as well as the composer Engelbert Humperdinck and the theater director Max Reinhardt, signed a "Proclamation to the Civilised World" protesting Germany's right to have carried out reprisals and claiming that "if it had not been for German soldiers, German culture would long have been swept away."

The most likely source of friction between the Allies and the United States and other neutrals early in the war was action by the British navy to enforce a blockade against goods being shipped to Germany. On August 6 the U.S. government asked all belligerents to commit themselves to following the rules laid down for the conduct of maritime warfare in the Declaration of London which—though not ratified by either the United States or the United Kingdom—represented in their view the consensus of world opinion. In line with Grey's wish to do all that he could to preserve friendly relations with the United States, Britain responded on behalf of the Allies with a note that seemed on the surface an affirmative until, in what could be construed as "small print," it reserved rights "essential to the conduct of naval operations."

On the second day of the war, August 5, the German navy sent out a requisitioned excursion steamer, the *Königin Luise*, crudely disguised as a British North Sea ferry. In direct contravention of the agreement at the Second Hague Conference which prohibited the use of unattached mines that would not become harmless after being in the sea for an hour, she began laying her cargo of 180 mines in the North Sea. HMS *Amphion*, a British light cruiser, caught up with and sank her but as she was returning to port hit one of the floating mines the *Königin Luise* had laid and herself sank with considerable loss of life including most of the survivors she had picked up from the *Königin Luise*.

In the years immediately before the war German engineers had achieved a breakthrough in submarine design. Beginning with the Danzig-built *U-19* class, all German submarines were fitted with diesel engines. Diesel was cleaner than the petrol or paraffin that fueled earlier U-boats and had made them, when running on the surface, "almost as visible as a smoke-belching steamer." It also had a higher flashpoint which made it safer. However, the major advantage was the reliability, power, and endurance of the new engines. Designed by MAN of Augsburg, they gave the submarines the best range—some five thousand miles—and depth performance in the world, meaning they could now be exploited as independent, offensive, strategic weapons rather than primarily defensively. The German navy began the war with twelve such newly built diesel-powered craft.

An event on September 22, 1914, revealed the potential of even its older submarines. Otto Weddigen, captain of the *U-9* patrolling off the Dutch coast, spotted three four-funneled British cruisers steaming line abreast straight toward him at a modest ten knots. They were the obsolescent British cruiser HMS *Cressy* and her sister ships, the *Aboukir* and the *Hogue*. Weddigen immediately attacked. Hit by a single torpedo, the *Aboukir* began to list as water flowed into the longitudinal coal bunkers running the length of the ship which had been designed to withstand shells not torpedoes. She capsized within twenty-five minutes. The *Hogue*, believing a mine had caused the explosion, approached to pick up survivors only to be hit by two torpedoes and sink in ten minutes. The *Cressy* then also tried to rescue the drowning and was torpedoed in turn. Within barely an hour, a single unseen enemy—an old German submarine—had destroyed three cruisers and killed 1,459 British sailors, about a thousand more than the number Nelson lost at Trafalgar.

Since in 1914 few effective devices existed to prevent either submarine or mine attacks, the British navy early recognized the impracticality of maintaining the close blockades of enemy ports to interrupt trade in contraband generally accepted as legal. Strangling seaborne trade into Germany, however, remained crucial to the navy's war strategy and the British quickly instituted what was in effect a distant blockade by patrolling the exits from the North Sea and in particular the two hundred miles between the Shetland Islands and the Norwegian coast. The patrol squadron initially comprised twelve old cruisers. After sighting a merchant ship the cruiser dispatched a boarding party to look for contraband. If they found anything suspicious they escorted the merchant vessel into a British port for more thorough examination. Commercial passenger liners requisitioned into the navy as armed merchant cruisers, given naval crews, repainted with camouflage paint, and fitted with a couple of four- or six-inch guns soon replaced the old cruisers.

On November 2 Britain issued a declaration that the whole of the North Sea must henceforth be considered "a British military area" and that as a consequence of previous and continuing illegal German mining, Britain would mine parts of this zone. This would be the first but not the last time in the war that one country claimed "necessity" forced it to follow its enemy into conduct or the use of weapons banned by international law. If neutral shipping vessels wished to avoid the perils of mines they should approach the military area through the English Channel, where they would be stopped and searched for contraband and then escorted safely through British minefields to resume their journeys.

Even before November 2, the distant blockade together with British unilateral expansions of the definition of "contraband"—for example, by including goods judged by Britain to be going to Germany through neutral countries in "a continuous voyage"—had caused friction with neutral maritime nations. One American paper claimed that Britain not only ruled the waves but waived the rules. However, Foreign Secretary Grey's determination to restrict the blockade to "the maximum that could be enforced without a rupture with the United States" had resulted in soothing responses from Britain which, helped by Britain's willingness to pay top prices for any goods brought into its ports whatever their original intended destination, meant relations were not too heavily strained. At the same time as declaring the military zone, Britain wrote to the U.S. State Department explaining that only recently Germany had illegally scattered mines in the northern sea route from New York to Liverpool and that the White Star liner *Olympic* had "escaped disaster" only by "pure good luck." Therefore, the Admiralty had concluded that it was "necessary to adopt exceptional measures appropriate to the novel conditions under which this war is being waged." The United States did not even formally protest to Britain about the declaration despite being pressed to do so by Norway and Sweden, two of the other leading neutral maritime nations.

Just a few days before the declaration of the military zone another issue had been delicately solved between the United States and the Allies using the niceties of language and legal drafting. In August 1914 the French government had attempted to raise loans through J. P. Morgan and Company to finance its arms purchases. However, Secretary of State Bryan, believing money to be "the worst of contrabands . . . it commands all other things," persuaded President Wilson that for American banks to lend money to governments at war would be "inconsistent with the true spirit of neutrality." J. P. Morgan Jr., the head of the company following his father's death in 1913, determined to overturn this ruling by an administration that he despised: "A greater lot of perfectly incompetent and apparently thoroughly crooked people has never, as far as I know, run or attempted to run a first-class country."

He approached Robert Lansing, the fifty-year-old New York–born legal counselor to the State Department. An anglophile and ambitious right-wing Democrat, Lansing was unkindly described by a colleague as "meticulous, metallic and mousy." Nevertheless, many found him easier and more clearheaded to deal with than Bryan. Morgan and a fellow New York banker, Samuel McRoberts of National City Bank, soon persuaded Lansing of the advantages to U.S. commerce of a more flexible approach toward the financing of Allied purchases, warning that without it the Allies might buy elsewhere leaving the United States in its present economic depression. On October 23, 1914, McRoberts provided Lansing with a helpful note on the subject. In Bryan's absence from Washington, Lansing quickly copied the phraseology into a memorandum, only inserting a few first-person pronouns to claim the ideas as his own, then rushed with his memo to the White House at eight thirty the same evening and easily secured Wilson's approval. Henceforth, American banks would not make loans to warring governments; they would extend them credit.

The hairsplitting distinction between credits and loans was typical of lawyers like Wilson and Lansing. "An arrangement as to credits has to do with a commercial debt rather than with a loan of money" and therefore was "not a matter for Government," they concluded. Lansing's stock rose with both Wilson and Wall Street. The Allies quickly agreed to large credits with American banks, who in turn eagerly advanced money to fund contracts with American munitions manufacturers. The *New York Sun* rejoiced, "All talk of stagnation in our export trade has ceased." J. P. Morgan and Company was soon playing a pivotal and highly profitable role in keeping Britain and its allies supplied with American munitions. In 1915, Britain's imports of £238 million from America were 68 percent greater by volume and 75 percent greater by value than in 1913. French imports rose similarly.

Appalled by the growing trade between the United States and the Allies, the kaiser refused to see the American ambassador, James Gerard: "I have nothing against Mr. Gerard personally, but I will not see the Ambassador of a country which furnishes arms and ammunition to the enemies of Germany." Von Tirpitz thought the United States "contrary to the whole spirit of neutrality . . . an enemy arsenal." The German government continued to press the Wilson administration but it remained unsympathetic. By January 1915, Germany was pursuing another and illegal method of redressing what it perceived as an unfair balance—sabotage. A German Foreign Office telegram to its Washington embassy stated, "The sabotage in the United States can extend to all kinds of factories for war matériel" and named several contacts who could suggest "suitable people for sabotage." German agents quickly infiltrated the New York docks and manufactured novel cigar-shaped fire bombs designed to be smuggled about merchant ships and to explode when the vessel was at sea. Elsewhere agents plotted the sabotage of infrastructure and munitions plants such as the "Black Tom" facility in New Jersey, destroyed in 1916.

At the end of October 1914, Winston Churchill had called seventy-three-year-old Sir Jacky Fisher out of retirement and appointed him First Sea Lord once more. "Lord Fisher can only think on a Turkish rug," a subordinate claimed after Fisher on his return demanded improvements to his Admiralty offices. Fisher began firing off his characteristic scrawled, heavily underlined memos in green ink designed to shake up the navy. "I'm *exceeding* busy!" he wrote. "I've just told Garvin that war is 'Great Conceptions' and 'Quick Decisions'! 'Think in Oceans,' 'Shoot at Sight.' I'm stirring up accordingly." However, Fisher knew that in practice, he could do little to defend against the submarine threat.

One area where Britain and, in particular the intelligence unit head-quartered in Room 40 of the Admiralty building, was making progress was in reading German codes. On August 11 the Royal Australian Navy captured the German merchant shipping codebook and soon after the Russians took the signal book of the Imperial Navy from a grounded German cruiser in the Baltic. Both were sent to London. On November 30 a British trawler fishing off the Dutch coast hauled up a lead-lined chest in its nets. Inside was the Imperial German Naval codebook—the so-called Traffic Book used to communicate with overseas naval attachés and warships. The captain of a German destroyer had jettisoned the chest in desperation while under attack by British ships. Room 40's personnel called the discovery "The Miraculous Draught of Fishes" since it provided the last remaining information they needed to decode messages between German warships, submarines, and their bases—an invaluable asset in thwarting German plans to disrupt Britain's mastery of the seas.

CHAPTER SIX

"England Will Burn"

AS WELL AS the control of the seas Churchill and Fisher were battling with another issue, which had, perhaps surprisingly, become part of the Admiralty's remit—the control of British airspace. Developments in both zeppelin and airplane technology had been rapid. In November 1908, the kaiser traveled to Lake Constance to see for himself what Count von Zeppelin's *LZ3* airship was capable of. Though with true Prussian hauteur he privately considered von Zeppelin "the greatest donkey" of all southern Germans, his airship's performance so impressed the kaiser that he awarded him the Order of the Black Eagle and hailed him as "the greatest German of the twentieth century" and "the Conqueror of the Air."

That same year the German army ordered the 450-foot-long *LZ4* from von Zeppelin, but after only her second flight she broke her moorings and burst into flames. David Lloyd George, then Britain's chancellor of the exchequer, visiting Germany shortly after the incident, recalled how "disappointment was a totally inadequate word for the grief and dismay" that swept Germany. "There was no loss of life to account for it. Hopes and ambitions far wider than those concerned with a scientific and mechanical success appeared to have shared the wreck of the dirigible . . . What spearpoint of Imperial advance did the airship portend?" A public appeal launched in the aftermath of the disaster raised six million marks to allow the now impoverished von Zeppelin to continue his work.

The army purchased further zeppelins—by the outbreak of war it had seven—as well as airships from the Schütte-Lanz company, established in 1909, whose machines had plywood rather than aluminum frames. The army believed airships' chief value in wartime would be in scouting and observation. However, the Naval Airship Division, set up in 1912, foresaw a more attacking role. A naval officer invited his Kiel audience to "imagine a war with England, which from time immemorial has had an unwarlike population. If we could only succeed in throwing some bombs on their docks, they would speak with us in quite different terms. With airships we have . . . the means of carrying the war into Britain." British planes—unlike zeppelins—could not fly at night and thus could "afford no protection against airships."

The Naval Airship Division suffered several early disasters. In the first fatal zeppelin accident, its inaugural airship plunged into the North Sea in bad weather in September 1913, taking the first head of the Naval Airship Division with it, though six crewmen survived. Five weeks later another exploded: "We could recognise the men looking out of the cars," an eyewitness described. "At about fifteen hundred feet up, one of the crew tried to climb from the catwalk into the forward engine car . . . Then our blood ran cold. A long thin tongue of flame leapt from the forward gondola and ran along the catwalk. There was a terrific explosion, the whole earth seemed to echo and re-echo with it. In the twinkling of an eye the airship . . . was a mass of flames." There were no survivors and the Naval Airship Division's very future seemed uncertain until its new head, naval captain Peter Strasser, a neat, dapper man with a goatee, convinced his superiors of the airship's military potential.*

Airplanes also achieved success. On October 16, 1908, Samuel Cody, an American who had come to Britain with a Wild West show before being employed by the British army, flew fourteen hundred feet in a biplane over Farnborough Common in Britain's first successful heavier-than-air flight. The plane crashed on landing but Cody survived to become such an iconic public figure that when he died in another flying accident in 1913, one hundred thousand people lined the route of his funeral procession.

On July 25, 1909, a Frenchman, Louis Blériot, nursed his monoplane

---

* Meanwhile, Count von Zeppelin had set up a company—the Deutsche Luftschiffahrt Aktiengesellschaft, known as DELAG—to operate what was effectively the world's first commercial airline. By July 1914 DELAG zeppelins had carried more than ten thousand passengers and flown some one hundred thousand miles between Germany's largest cities.

in a thirty-seven-minute dawn flight across the English Channel to land behind Dover Castle. The following day the author H. G. Wells warned the *Daily Mail*'s readers that "within a year we shall have—or rather they will have—aeroplanes capable of starting from Calais . . . circling over London, dropping a hundredweight or so of explosive upon the printing machines of *The Daily Mail* and returning securely to Calais." The previous year his *The War in the Air* had conjured a nightmare vision of "the little island set in the silver sea . . . at the end of its immunity" as planes and giant airships battled in the skies above.

One hundred twenty thousand people queued for a glimpse of Blériot's plane when it went on display in Selfridges department store in London. Yet despite such popular enthusiasm on the one hand and Wells's apocalyptic warnings on the other, the British government remained cautious about airplanes. Sir William Nicholson, chief of the general staff, dismissed them as "a useless and expensive fad." A government committee concluded that planes posed no serious threat but endorsed the Royal Navy's proposal to acquire an airship to explore its military potential. The craft—named *Mayfly*—had a short life. As she was being readied for her maiden flight, crosswinds ripped her apart and British interest in airships waned.

However, on November 1, 1911, an Italian pilot demonstrated the airplane's potential. In the world's first bombing raid Lieutenant Giulio Gavotti dropped four five-pound bombs over Turkish lines near Tripoli in Libya during an Italo-Turkish conflict. The next day, patriotic Italian papers rejoiced in exaggerated headlines such as AVIATOR LIEUTENANT GAVOTTI THROWS BOMB ON ENEMY CAMP. TERRORISED TURKS SCATTER UPON UNEXPECTED CELESTIAL ASSAULT. The Turks claimed wrongly that the bomb hit a hospital. Italian pilots went on to conduct the world's first night bombing. In Morocco in 1912 the French dropped bombs from airplanes as did pilots during the 1912–13 Balkan conflicts. Aware of the limited effects of such bombings and planes' obvious vulnerability to ground fire, Britain concentrated on building large, slow-flying, stable craft suited to the reconnaissance role that they and most other governments, including Germany's, saw as their most promising application. In 1914, General Douglas Haig, who at the end of 1915 would become commander in chief of British forces in France, was still unconvinced airplanes were even useful for reconnaissance: "There is only one way for a commander to get information . . . and that is by the use of cavalry."

Churchill worried about Britain's vulnerability to air attack and supported the Aerial League of the British Empire set up by those who believed that, just as Britannia ruled the waves, so it must rule the skies. League members, who included H. G. Wells, highlighted the potential risk to London from enemy aircraft, identifying the Houses of Parliament as a likely target. Lurid German publications depicting airships laden with explosives crossing the North Sea to hover menacingly above the capital fed public fears. In June 1914, an author claiming to be a former member of "the German Secret Service" described a fleet of zeppelins waiting to attack England: "huge cigar-shaped engines of death . . . ready to drop explosives to the ground." "Picture the havoc a dozen such vultures could create attacking . . . London. They don't have to aim. They are not like aviators trying to drop a bomb on the deck of a warship. They simply dump overboard some of the new explosives of the German government, these new chemicals having the property of setting on fire anything that they hit . . . They do not have to worry about hitting the mark . . . If they do not hit Buckingham Palace they are apt to hit Knightsbridge."

As Churchill later wrote, at the time he did not rate airships highly: "I believed this enormous bladder of combustible and explosive gas would prove to be easily destructible. I was sure the fighting airplane . . . would harry, rout and burn these gaseous monsters." He did his best "to restrict expenditure upon airships and to concentrate [Britain's] narrow and stinted resources upon airplanes." Nevertheless, recognizing that even if Britain was wise not to invest in airships it needed to guard against the zeppelin threat, he encouraged experiments with devices like the "Fiery Grapnel"—a four-pronged grappling hook loaded with explosives to be swung by airplane pilots against the sides of airships—and "flaming bullets." Test flights were made with a semiautomatic cannon mounted on a plane. However, the gun's powerful recoil when fired caused the plane to stall and plunge five hundred feet. Dropping small explosive or incendiary bombs on airships seemed more promising.

As the war began, Britain's meager air power was divided between the

Royal Naval Air Service (RNAS) for which Churchill and Fisher were responsible, and the army's Royal Flying Corps (RFC). (The two air arms would not combine into the Royal Air Force until April 1918.) The RNAS had more than 90 planes, 53 of them seaplanes, and 7 small airships. The RFC possessed 190 planes. However, many of the planes of both services were unairworthy.

With all the RFC's serviceable airplanes dispatched to France, on September 3, 1914, Churchill and the Admiralty accepted responsibility for the air defense of Britain from the army. Two days later Churchill announced his strategy. The RNAS would establish a forward line of defense in France and a second line somewhere between Dover and London. Other measures included ordering and siting antiaircraft guns and searchlights and laying out floodlit landing strips in London's parks for British fighters. By the end of 1914, Churchill's plans had crystallized into a two-tier system; aircraft stationed inland should receive sufficient warning of zeppelins approaching London to get airborne to intercept them while planes nearer the coast would be waiting to attack returning zeppelins. In practice, however, he knew that all planes then available would struggle to reach the height at which zeppelins flew.

From October 1 the government imposed a blackout—limited at first but soon extended. The tops and sides of streetlamps were painted black to mask their radiance from above and people were asked to draw their curtains tight. In these early weeks anxious Londoners scanned the night skies but no zeppelins came. During the first days of the war the German army lost three zeppelins on the western front. French shell fire brought down the first two while the third was fired on initially by German soldiers in error, then by Allied troops who shot off its rudder leaving it to drift helplessly before plummeting into a forest. However, any hopes that airships might not be as menacing or effective as feared were extinguished when zeppelin attacks in August and early September on Liège and Antwerp in support of the German advance killed a number of civilians.

Believing the best place to attack a zeppelin was on the ground, Churchill ordered an RNAS raid on zeppelin sheds in Cologne and Düsseldorf. On October 8, 1914, two British pilots took off from Antwerp just as British troops were about to pull out of the city in the face of a

German advance. One headed for Cologne where he was unable to find the sheds. However, Flight Lieutenant Reggie Marix in a Sopwith Tabloid reached Düsseldorf and finally located a shed further outside the city than his map indicated. Swooping low, he released his two bombs: "As I pulled out of my dive, I looked over my shoulder and was rewarded with the sight of enormous sheets of flame pouring out of the shed." After landing his bullet-riddled plane north of Antwerp because his fuel was running out and finally catching up with the retreating British forces by means of train and bicycle, he learned that he had destroyed a brand-new airship.

Encouraged by what was Britain's first successful bombing raid on Germany and learning from intelligence reports that two zeppelins had almost been completed at the zeppelin plant in Friedrichshafen, Churchill ordered a further RNAS raid. On November 21 four new Avro 504 biplanes, each armed with four twenty-pound bombs, took off from Belfort in eastern France. Three reached Friedrichshafen and dropped nine bombs but failed to destroy the zeppelins. Two of the pilots returned to base but the third was forced to land near the burning zeppelin sheds where local people attacked him. German soldiers intervened and took him to a hospital. The German government at once accused the British of barbarously dropping bombs on the "innocent civilians" of Friedrichshafen despite knowing the only casualties had been mechanics and crewmen.

In December the RNAS targeted zeppelin sheds at Nordholz on the German North Sea coast. Since Nordholz was beyond the range of any British plane flying from Britain, France, or unoccupied Belgium, the navy converted three Channel passenger steamers into carriers from which sea-planes could be lowered into the water for takeoff. On Christmas Day 1914, seven RNAS seaplanes launched the raid which in foggy conditions failed to locate and destroy any zeppelins but provoked the word's first air-sea battle as zeppelins and German seaplanes attacked the British seaplane carriers and their naval escort.

The German army and navy both hoped for the glory of being the first to bomb the British mainland. Von Tirpitz wrote in mid-November 1914 of his conviction that "the English are now in terror of Zeppelins, perhaps not without reason." Though "not in favour of 'frightfulness' " and considering indiscriminate bombing "repulsive" when it "killed an old woman," he saw the potential that "if one could set fire to London in thirty places then the repulsiveness would be lost sight of," later adding that "all that flies . . . should be concentrated on that city." Admiral Gustav Bachmann, shortly to become chief of the naval staff, agreed, arguing that Germany "should leave no means untried to crush England, and that successful raids on London, in view of the already existing nervousness of the people, would prove a valuable means to this end." However, the army and navy high commands had to contend with the kaiser, who hesitated over what the zeppelin targets should be and in particular whether zeppelins should be allowed to bomb London, where his royal relations lived and of which he had sentimental memories. Chancellor von Bethmann Hollweg, a habitual opponent of von Tirpitz's aggressive policies, whom the admiral would accuse of "lukewarm flabbiness," was also reluctant.

While the kaiser pondered, German planes conducted three small air raids on England. On December 21, 1914, an Albatross seaplane dropped two twenty-pound bombs that fell into the sea near Dover pier. In the days that followed, a second plane dropped the first bomb to fall on British soil. It landed near Dover Castle, shattering several windows. A third dropped two bombs on the village of Cliffe on the Thames estuary.

Churchill believed from intelligence sources that raids on London itself could not be far away. On New Year's Day 1915 he told the British cabinet that Germany had approximately twenty airships capable of reaching London "carrying each a ton of high explosives. They could traverse the English part of the journey, coming and going, in the dark hours . . . There is no known means of preventing the airships coming, and not much chance of punishing them on their return. The un-avenged destruction of non-combatant life may therefore be very considerable." So perturbed was Admiral Jacky Fisher that he suggested Britain inform Germany that any captured zeppelin men would be shot as pirates. When Churchill disagreed with him he threatened to resign but Churchill deftly dissuaded him.

Early in January 1915, the kaiser agreed that zeppelins could attack England but insisted their targets be limited to naval shipyards, arsenals, docks, and other military establishments in the Thames estuary and on the east coast, and that "London itself was not to be bombed." On January 19 three naval zeppelins took off, aiming to inflict the damage so ardently demanded in a popular German song:

Zeppelin, flieg,	*Fly Zeppelin*
Hilf uns in Krieg,	*Help us in war,*
Fliege nach England,	*Fly to England,*
England wird abgebrannt,	*England will burn,*
Zeppelin, flieg!	*Fly Zeppelin!*

L6 was only halfway across the North Sea when engine trouble forced it back but *L3* and *L4* continued and despite rain, fog, and sleet reached the Norfolk coast. A young man on the ground spotted "two bright stars moving, apparently thirty yards apart"—the navigation lights of the *L3* and *L4*. Once over land, the two zeppelins separated. At eight thirty P.M. that evening *L3* dropped nine high-explosive bombs onto Great Yarmouth—the first zeppelin raid on British soil—killing a fifty-three-year-old cobbler and a seventy-two-year-old woman, injuring three people, and wrecking several houses. The *L4* meanwhile headed for King's Lynn, dropping bombs as it went, killing two and wounding thirteen. A woman who watched it drift overhead called it "the biggest sausage I ever saw in my life" and another witness thought it resembled "a church steeple sideways."

King's Lynn was close to the royal estate at Sandringham, which King George V and Queen Mary had left earlier the very day of the attack. The British press speculated whether the *L4* had been sent specifically to attack them and raged against German "frightfulness." The raid left many Britons fearful and angry about why no advance warning had been given or efforts made to down the airship. Though the *L4*'s commander reported having been heavily shelled and pinpointed by searchlights, the guns existed only in his imagination and the "searchlights" had been the lights of King's Lynn penetrating the misty skies.

Neutrals like the United States, Holland, Switzerland, and the Scandinavian countries condemned the attacks as a clear violation of the Hague prohibition on the bombardment of undefended places. The *New York Herald* wondered whether "the madness of despair or just plain everyday madness" had prompted Germany to attack quiet English coastal resorts and asked "What can Germany hope to gain by these wanton attacks on undefended places and this slaughter of innocents?" adding that such behavior was no way to win the good opinion of neutrals.

In Germany the raids were greeted with exultation as confirmation that Britain could no longer look to the sea to keep out the enemy. In their wake, the kaiser agreed, albeit reluctantly, that the London docks be included on the list of targets. While the German army and navy awaited the imminent delivery of a new generation of airships capable of reliably reaching the city, naval zeppelins again attacked England's east coast, raiding from Tyneside to East Anglia.

In mid-March 1915, Ernst Lehmann, the commander of the army airship *Sachsen*, diverted from an attack on Britain's east coast by fog, turned toward Calais where he decided to test his invention of a tiny observation car that could be lowered on steel cables. Its purpose to enable airships to survey their targets while remaining hidden in the clouds—in other words to provide airships with the aerial equivalent of a submarine's periscope. As the *Sachsen* hovered in clouds above Calais, Lehmann ordered a crewman to descend into clear air in his prototype observation car whence he telephoned precise guidance for bombing Calais. Lehmann described the "shattering" effect: "The anti-aircraft batteries could hear us, but they couldn't see us. They fired blindly into the air with no effect whatever. We planted our bombs nicely, but the bombs seemed to cause less panic than the fact that we were invisible." Learning of Lehmann's experiment, a week later Peter Strasser tested the observation car for himself and was so impressed he ordered new naval airships to be equipped with them.

CHAPTER SEVEN

"A Most Effective Weapon"

BY JANUARY 1915, only four months into the war, both the British and German governments were developing strategies to break the stalemate that had already ensued. The British War Cabinet, with Winston Churchill playing a prominent role, saw the solution in a naval expedition to the eastern Mediterranean. Their plan was to control the Dardanelles, the heavily guarded strait leading from the Aegean through the Sea of Marmara to the Black Sea, so that, at a minimum, they could get supplies through to Russia and, at best, force Ottoman Turkey, which had joined the Austro-German alliance at the end of October 1914, quickly out of the war. Success might draw Greece and perhaps Bulgaria and Rumania into the Allied camp. Churchill believed that "at the summit true politics and strategy are one. The manoeuvre which brings an ally into the field is as serviceable as that which wins a great battle." To that end he was also taking a leading role in the wooing of Italy to join the Allies. Conscious of the need for new weapons to break the deadlock in the trenches, in February he gave the Admiralty's support and funding to the development of "land ships." Under their code name of "tanks" they would make their first appearance on the battlefield in September 1916 and first be used en masse at the Battle of Cambrai in 1917 and become one of the lasting major advances in weaponry of the First World War.

Perhaps surprisingly for a nation whose power was historically land based, one of the principal areas to which Germany was looking to break the deadlock was the sea and the submarine. At the beginning of the war, Germany's U-boats had been used to attack enemy warships like the *Cressy* and troop transports, leaving surface vessels to do the commerce raiding. However, on October 20, 1914, a U-boat captain demonstrated the U-boat's potential as a commerce raider. Captain Johannes Feldkirchner in *U-17* forced the British merchant ship *Glitra* to stop in waters off Norway. He briefly searched her cargo of whisky and sewing machines and ordered her crew into their boats. The *U-17* then sank the *Glitra* but obligingly towed her laden lifeboats for a quarter of an hour toward the shore. The *Glitra* was the first British merchant ship to be sunk by a U-boat and, as he sailed home to Germany, Feldkirchner worried how his superiors would react. According to a fellow U-boatman his action was "entirely unexpected. Attacks on commercial steamers had not been foreseen. The possibilities . . . had not been anticipated." Feldkirchner need not have been concerned. He was commended for his attack.

Lack of a single head of the navy bedeviled German naval policy. Although the inspiration of Germany's naval buildup and preeminent in naval matters before 1914— instantly recognizable by his great domed bald head and forked white beard—Secretary of the Navy von Tirpitz was formally only head of the Imperial Naval Office, responsible for finance and political affairs, including new construction and budgets. Admiral Friedrich von Ingenohl commanded the High Seas Fleet. Separate from both was the Admiralty Staff headed in January 1915 by Hugo von Pohl, responsible for planning and directing operations in war in a way analogous to a land army's general staff. Finally, there was the kaiser's naval cabinet under Georg von Müller. All reported direct to the kaiser and policy decisions rested with him alone.

In October Hermann Bauer, commander of one of Germany's submarine flotillas, had, unknown to his crews, already suggested to his superior von Ingenohl using submarines as commerce raiders. Feldkirchner's success confirmed the practicability of the idea. Von Ingenohl circulated the proposal to von Pohl and others, writing, "From a purely military point of view a campaign of submarines against commercial traffic on the British coasts will strike the enemy at his weakest point and will make it evident . . . that his power at sea is insufficient to protect his imports." Von Pohl worried about the restrictions of international law since submarines would find it extremely difficult to follow the Cruiser Rules—U-boat commanders were already complaining how hard it was to distinguish enemy shipping from neutral vessels. He knew too that surfacing to stop and search would expose fragile submarines to enemy attack.

However, von Pohl changed his mind after what he saw as Britain's attempt to starve Germany when Britain in November 1914 declared the "military area" and made all food contraband—the latter on the grounds that one could not be sure whether food was for military or civilian use and that in case of shortage military requirements would take priority over civilian. When he saw the proposal Chancellor von Bethmann Hollweg was concerned about the effect on neutrals such as the United States. The kaiser too worried about neutrals but also about killing and wounding women and children, and would not endorse the action. Von Pohl persisted. Von Tirpitz, often opposed to von Pohl in the maneuvering for support in the German naval hierarchy, then threw his authority behind the use of the submarine, convinced it was Germany's "most effective weapon." A young naval officer admired how von Tirpitz "fought, with a doggedness which can hardly be described . . . for the inauguration of intensified U-boat warfare."

At the end of November von Tirpitz gave an interview to a German-born American journalist in which he criticized the United States for not protesting against the British military zone and asked, "Now what will America say if Germany institutes a submarine blockade of England to stop all traffic?" When the journalist asked whether Germany was going to do so, von Tirpitz responded, "Why not? . . . England is endeavouring to starve us. We can do the same, cut off England and sink every vessel that attempts to break the blockade." The article when published in Germany received great support from naval officers, and von Pohl and von Tirpitz pressed hard for a submarine campaign. In mid-January von Tirpitz told the kaiser that if Germany did not use the submarine "to get our knife into the English . . . we should accomplish nothing."

On February 4, his last day as chief of the naval staff before he succeeded von Ingenohl as commander of the High Seas Fleet and was himself succeeded by Admiral Gustav Bachmann, von Pohl accompanied the kaiser to some naval exercises at Wilhelmshaven. While the emperor was preoccupied with the maneuvers, von Pohl secured his signature on a declaration agreeing the launch of a campaign of unrestricted submarine warfare whereby enemy merchant vessels would be sunk without search or even warning and citing as justification Britain's blockade of Germany. From February 18, the waters around Great Britain, except for a designated route north of Scotland from the Atlantic to Scandinavia, would be a war zone in which all enemy ships "would be destroyed even if it is not possible to avoid thereby the dangers which threaten the crews and passengers . . . It may not always be possible to prevent the attacks meant for hostile ships from being directed against neutral ships." In a telegram to its Washington embassy, Berlin was even more specific, advising that "neutral vessels will not in most cases be recognizable as such in the war zone and will therefore be destroyed without more ado." The embassy was instructed to use the press to warn American vessels to keep clear of the war zone "to avoid dangerous complications."

Not long afterward, Berlin dispatched another telegram to Washington containing the draft of a notice to be inserted by Ambassador Count Johann von Bernstorff in the American press, warning Americans against traveling through the war zone on British ships or those of its allies. "Thinking it a great mistake," von Bernstorff threw it into his desk drawer and "hoped Berlin would forget about it."

U-boats were now equipped with machine guns, grenades, and formal instructions about contraband. Shipping schedules were distributed and scarce copies of the British-produced *Lloyd's Register* listing every ship in the world became a highly prized aid to identifying targets for German submariners.

Despite the German declaration of unrestricted U-boat warfare, the British navy continued throughout the war to follow Cruiser Rules in any attacks their submarines made against merchant vessels—a decision made easier not only by the need to retain the good will of neutral governments like the United States, but also by the limited number of German merchant vessels still operating— almost exclusively in the Baltic or coastal waters.

When the war began the British and German governments requisitioned passenger liners and converted them for war duties as armed merchant cruisers. The British Admiralty reminded Cunard of its agreement to hand over the *Lusitania* and the *Mauretania* but then decided neither was suitable as an auxiliary cruiser—they simply consumed too much coal. The *Mauretania* was dazzle-painted to camouflage her for duty as a troop transport and hospital ship. Although having had four six-inch gun rings fitted in 1913 to her deck to allow guns to be mounted quickly in wartime, the *Lusitania* was left unarmed with Cunard to continue the commercial transatlantic run, but under strict conditions. The Admiralty would inform her master of the course she was to follow; any contact between Cunard and the ship, while at sea, must be through the Admiralty; her cargo space must be at the Admiralty's disposal.

By the beginning of 1915 the *Lusitania* was the only one of the great prewar liners of any nation still plying the Atlantic although some smaller British, U.S., and other neutral vessels were also making the crossing. The British Admiralty's Room 40—using improved instruments developed by Guglielmo Marconi—was able to pick up German transmissions to and from U-boats for the day or two after they left port before they were out of range of radio contact with their base. Among some of the early targeting information they intercepted and decoded was: FAST STEAMER LUSI-TANIA COMING FROM NEW YORK EXPECTED AT LIVERPOOL 4TH OR 5TH MARCH. The purpose of the communication was clear especially compared with another sent to U-boats: AMERICAN SS PHILADELPHIA AND WEST HAVERFORD WILL PROBABLY ARRIVE IN THE IRISH SEA BOUND FOR LIVERPOOL. BOTH STEAMERS ARE TO BE SPARED. Obviously the *Lusitania* was not.

On March 2 *U-27* lay submerged on the approaches to Liverpool. In his war diary, her captain recorded letting several tempting targets pass close by because "the *Lusitania* was expected to arrive in English waters on 4 March and in my present position I believed I had a good chance of attacking her." On March 5, he turned reluctantly homeward. The *Lusitania* arrived a few hours later. On this occasion the British Admiralty had tried to provide her with a naval escort but it failed to rendezvous with the liner due to a comic opera series of communication failures.

WOODROW WILSON HAD recognized early in 1915 that the stalemate in the war offered a good opportunity for America to lead arbitration to secure a peace settlement before casualties rose too high and both military and political positions became too entrenched to allow concessions. He sent Colonel House on a secret mission to investigate the prospects for a brokered peace. The small, softly spoken, slightly frail House, whose rank was an honorary one, was throughout the war Wilson's most trusted adviser. Wilson wrote of him "Mr. House is my second personality. He is my independent self. His thoughts and mine are one." Surprisingly, given his neutral status, House sailed to Britain not on an American ship but on the *Lusitania*.

Nearing the Irish coast in early February the *Lusitania* raised the U.S. flag. The press pursued House about the incident as soon as he landed. He wrote in his diary: "Every newspaper in London has asked me about it, but fortunately, I was not an eye witness to it and have been able to say that I only knew it from hearsay." The incident caused fury in Germany, which insisted that it was illegal for British shipping to hide behind neutral flags. In the United States fears were roused that U-boats would attack American vessels suspecting they were disguised as enemy ships. President Wilson protested to London that using neutral flags would create intolerable risks for neutral countries, while failing to protect British vessels. The British government responded blandly that the flag had been flown at the request of the *Lusitania*'s American passengers to indicate that there were neutral Americans on board. Germany's declaration that it would sink British merchant ships on sight made such actions necessary and legitimate.

The U.S. government's reaction to the German promulgation of unrestricted submarine warfare was much harsher than exchanges with Britain about the blockade or the use of neutral flags. On February 10 President Wilson declared that Germany's action violated the rights of neutral countries and that it would be held "to a strict accountability" for any consequent loss of American life and any deprivation of American citizens' "full enjoyment of their acknowledged rights on the high seas." The two words "strict accountability" would achieve great significance in the months ahead. However, von Pohl expected Britain to be brought to its knees by the submarine campaign within a few weeks and von Tirpitz was soon rejoicing in the "magnificent" work of the German submarines, thinking their war diaries "as exciting as novels."

The U.S. threat to hold Germany to account was quickly tested when, on March 28, 1915, the *U-28* sank the SS *Falaba*, an unarmed British passenger-cargo ship of five thousand tons, in the recently declared war zone off the southern Irish coast. More than one hundred people died including one American, mining engineer Leon Thresher, bound for West Africa from Liverpool. The *Falaba* was given some warning by the *U-28*'s commander, who had surfaced. However, he did not allow many minutes— twenty-three according to the U-boat war diary, seven according to British accounts—for evacuation before firing a single torpedo. The American press called the sinking "a massacre" and "piracy" but President Wilson avoided invoking the doctrine of "strict accountability" or reacting formally in any way.

Churchill thought the U-boat campaign was in fact having little impact. By the end of its first week, out of 1,381 vessels arriving or departing from British ports only eleven had been attacked and seven sunk. During the second week, only three ships were attacked and all escaped. By April the British press was rejoicing that inward and outward sailings were now running above fifteen hundred a week. Churchill even believed certain political advantages could be found in the new situation. On February 12, he had written to the president of the Board of Trade, Walter Runciman, that it was "most important to attract neutral shipping to our shores, in the hope especially of embroiling the United States with Germany . . . For our part we want the traffic—the more the better; and if some of it gets into trouble, better still."

Churchill had, however, on February 10 issued instructions to merchant captains to avoid headlands, steer a mid-channel course, operate at full speed off harbors, and post extra lookouts. If attacked by a submarine they should do their "utmost to escape" but if they could not they should steer for the submarine "at utmost speed" to force it to dive. The word "ram" was not used but ramming was clearly what was meant. When the Germans discovered these instructions they protested, saying any merchant captain who attempted to ram would, if captured, be treated as a criminal. On July 27, 1916, the German authorities would execute Captain Charles Fryatt, a British merchant captain who in March 1915 had saved his ship from a U-boat by attempting to ram it but had been captured on a subsequent occasion. Prime Minister Asquith would describe their action as "terrorism," continuing: "It is impossible to guess to what further atrocities [the Germans] may proceed. His Majesty's Government therefore desire to repeat emphatically that they are resolved that such crimes shall not . . . go unpunished . . . They are determined to bring to justice the criminals, whoever they may be and whatever their station . . . The man who authorises the system under which such crimes are committed may well be the most guilty of all."

Although he had not accepted Fisher's intemperate proposal to promulgate that captured zeppelin crews would be shot, Churchill ordered that in the future any captured U-boat crewmen should not be treated as ordinary prisoners of war but segregated for possible trial as pirates at the conclusion of hostilities. In retaliation, the German authorities placed in solitary confinement thirty-nine captured British officers, picking those whom they supposed related to the most prominent families in Great Britain. Among them was one of Sir Edward Grey's relations. An outraged British press demanded that any special privileges given to von Tirpitz's son, a naval officer captured earlier in the war, should be removed.

CHAPTER EIGHT

"Something That Makes People Permanently Incapable of Fighting"

As well as considering new strategies to secure a quick victory, the German high command had begun to consider new weapons to achieve the same end. As early as September 1914, General Erich von Falkenhayn, minister of war at the war's start but since mid-September chief of the general staff succeeding General Helmuth von Moltke, whom the kaiser had ordered to report sick following what he thought of as his mistakes at the Battle of the Marne, concluded that "the ordinary weapons of attack had often failed completely . . . A weapon had, therefore, to be found which was superior to them but would not excessively tax the limited capacity of the German war industry . . . Such a weapon existed in gas." He turned to Germany's industrialists and scientists to provide it.

Among those who responded was a bespectacled, shaven-headed, forty-six-year-old Prussian chemist and future Nobel Prize winner, Fritz Haber, the director of the newly established Kaiser Wilhelm Institute for Physical Chemistry and Electrochemistry in the Berlin suburb of Dahlem. Haber's path to prominence had not been straightforward. Born in 1868 into a wealthy Jewish family in Breslau (now Polish Wroclaw), his mother had died three weeks later, a loss from which his father, Siegfried, took many years to recover. Siegfried Haber was a businessman trading primarily in dyes. Since he had started his business the nature of dyes had been changing—formerly they were made from mainly organic substances but now most were synthetic dyes of which Germany had become the world's leading producer, as with so many other chemicals.

The nineteenth century is often said to be the century of chemistry, just as the twentieth is that of physics. To the young Haber, as to many, chemistry seemed the key to Germany's economic advance. In 1886, restless and with little interest in the family business, he convinced his father to allow him to study chemistry at Berlin University. Finding the work less than stimulating he moved to Heidelberg to study under Robert Bunsen— inventor of the eponymous burner—only to find him a dull teacher and return to Berlin. When he reached twenty, the one year's military service that was the minimum obligation for all German males intervened and he was posted to an artillery regiment in his hometown of Breslau—his first contact with the military. He enjoyed the army, became a noncommissioned officer, and aspired unsuccessfully to be an officer.

Military service over, Haber returned to Berlin again where in 1891 he completed his doctorate. By now interested in physical chemistry, a new subject combining the two sciences, he applied to join the Leipzig laboratory of the leading exponent but was rejected. Using his business contacts and still hoping his son would join the family firm, Siegfried Haber then arranged three short apprenticeships in chemical companies for him to gain industrial experience. Perhaps despite himself the young Haber found industrial processes stimulating, supplementing as they did his academic knowledge. At a Budapest distillery he saw how potash was extracted from residues left over from distilling molasses. At a chemical plant northwest of Kracòw he first became acquainted with the new Solvay process using ammonia to produce sodium carbonate, a key component in the production of glass and soap. Although he dismissed the neighboring countryside as a monotonous "wasteland of sand, swamp, and fever"—(it would become the site of Auschwitz)—he thought the plant was dominated by "a splendid and energetic intelligence" and was grateful to visit. His third apprenticeship was at a cellulose factory.

Shortly afterward at his father's urging he reluctantly joined the family business. Six months of tension and argument followed, culminating in a major dispute over a business venture in which the young Haber purchased a large amount of chloride of lime for use as a disinfectant during a cholera outbreak in Hamburg, only to be left with it when the outbreak subsided unexpectedly quickly. As a result of the argument, he left Breslau and his father's business to work as an unpaid laboratory assistant in Jena while studying chemistry again. He also converted to Christianity—a gesture that friends and family interpreted as underlining his rift with his father but behind which other factors may also have lain. Although there was no overt or legal religious discrimination in the newly unified Germany, the position of Jews within German society—especially their commitment to the newly formed nation—remained an issue, debated in the press and by right-wing political parties and in the military. Conversion symbolized his loyalty and commitment to Germany and might have made it easier for him to obtain an academic post.

In 1894 Haber did get a junior position in the chemical institute of Karlsruhe's Technical University. There he specialized in the physical chemistry that had roused his interest in Berlin. Publishing papers on electrochemistry and working ferociously hard and successfully—though frequently bemoaning the state of his "nerves"—within four years he was close to becoming a full professor. His rapid thinking and fast talking as well as his energy impressed many. However, he could also appear combative, aggressive even. Viennese physicist Lise Meitner, later the discoverer with Otto Hahn and Fritz Strassmann of nuclear fission, admired his intellect but observed that "his immediate reactions could be very violent and therefore not always objective." She also said that sometimes Haber wanted to be "both your best friend and God at the same time." When in 1900 Haber applied for the newly created chair in physical chemistry at the Karlsruhe chemical institute and it went to a rival, he vented his disappointment in even harder work, robustly challenging the successful candidate's theories. In doing so he drove himself to near nervous breakdown as he had done on earlier occasions in his life—from 1898 he had been a regular visitor to sanatoriums. In 1906 when the holder of the chair of physical chemistry moved on, Haber was at last appointed to it.

To supplement his academic income, Haber was already acting as a consultant to the chemical industry. Germany's rapidly expanding population meant that one of the great challenges was producing enough food and that required more fertilizers. The German chemical industry was therefore focusing on producing artificial fertilizers containing potassium, phosphorous, and vitally nitrogen. A major source of nitrogen was saltpeter imported from Chile. However, estimates that Chile's saltpeter deposits would be exhausted by 1930 led to pressure to discover a way of extracting gaseous nitrogen from the air and bonding or "fixing" it in another form.

Haber became one of several scientists investigating whether nitrogen could be combined with hydrogen before being "fixed" in the form of ammonia and then used for conversion into fertilizer. While other scientists abandoned the idea as unfeasible on an industrial scale, Haber persisted. In 1908 the industrial giant Badische Anilin—& Soda-Fabrik (BASF) became his sponsor and the following year he succeeded in synthesizing ammonia, excitedly shouting to a colleague, "You have to see how the liquid ammonia is pouring out." He reported to BASF the success of his process which involved heating nitrogen and hydrogen with an osmium catalyst under pressure of around 175 atmospheres to between 500 degrees Celsius and 550 degrees Celsius. The company was doubtful whether such a technology could safely be applied on an industrial scale but a member of the staff, the future Nobel Prize winner and industrialist Carl Bosch, convinced his colleagues that the technical obstacles to large scale production could be overcome and that "we should risk it." On the eve of war, BASF was profitably producing thirty thousand tons of sulfate of ammonia fertilizer a year.

In the summer of 1911, Haber took up his new directorship at the Kaiser Wilhelm Institute for Physical Chemistry and Electrochemistry. Among the scientists who accepted his invitation to join him there was Albert Einstein, nine years his junior, who in 1905 had published his theory of special relativity and the ideas expressed in the world's most famous equation: $E = mc^2$. Einstein thought Haber a "splendid man" but one suffering from "personal vanity." Other colleagues would recall his "hunger for power" though also his generosity, loyalty, and personal courage.

When the war began, Walther Rathenau, a prominent industrialist and head of the major German electrical company AEG and an adviser to von Bethmann Hollweg among others, was already concerned that if the short war implicit in all German planning had to be prolonged, Germany would run short of imported raw materials. The inevitable British naval blockade would, for example, deprive the country of both Chilean copper and saltpeter, the latter essential for explosives production as well as fertilizer. On August 9, 1914, Rathenau approached von Falkenhayn, then minister of war, and finding his concerns chimed with those of some of the military, persuaded von Falkenhayn to found the Kriegsrohstoffsamt (KRA)—the Wartime Raw Materials Office—within the Ministry of War with himself as its head. KRA's purpose was to put German industry on a war footing and find substitutes for scarce strategically important materials.

Soon afterward, Rathenau approached Haber to lead the KRA's chemistry department. A proud patriot, Haber accepted with alacrity. As early as 1909 Haber had spoken of "the relationship of chemistry to war" and in 1912 unsuccessfully sought to link his institute with the Prussian Ministry of War. Haber would soon, like Röntgen and Planck, be one of the ninety-three "representatives of German science and arts" to sign the "Proclamation to the Civilised World" denying that Germany was responsible for the war and had committed atrocities at Louvain and refuting the accusation "that our warfare pays no respect to international laws." Einstein, now a professor at Berlin University, saw matters differently, shortly afterward being one of the few to sign a counter-manifesto arguing for an end to the war and calling on Europe to unite. In 1917 Einstein would liken Germany's "much-praised technological progress and civilization" to "an axe in the hand of a pathological criminal."

The KRA chemistry department soon became known as the "Bureau Haber" and Haber himself became involved in the debate about the best way to synthesize nitrates to replace saltpeter. Haber and Carl Bosch argued for a massive expansion of the ammonia synthesis program to produce the essential ammonia feedstuff. After much debate, not only with other scientists proposing competing technologies but also with other industrialists keen to promote and protect their financial and commercial interests, the KRA agreed to expand the Haber-Bosch process plant at the BASF factory, eventually increasing its capacity thirtyfold.

Meanwhile, in September 1914 Haber had been one of several chemists invited by von Falkenhayn to consider the viability of "developing shells that contained solid, gaseous, or liquid chemicals that would damage the enemy or render him unable to fight." The idea had originated with Major Max Bauer, an artillery expert who was acquainted with Haber as well as with some of Germany's leading industrialists. Von Falkenhayn was attracted to the idea of the new weapon, both as a way to gain the desired quick victory and also to provide an alternative to the high explosive-shells of which Germany was running short. At one stage in mid-November, von Falkenhayn would calculate he had only enough for four more days of fighting in Flanders.

In addition to Haber, the chemical weapons group included chemists Walther Nernst and Carl Duisberg, the latter an "imperious Prussian who would not tolerate dissent in either his personal or his business life" and an enthusiastic advocate of chemical warfare—a fact some thought not unrelated to his position as head of the Bayer chemical company.* As Duisberg knew, Germany's chemical industry was exceptionally well placed to conduct chemical weapons research. The techniques and equipment developed by companies like his own to gain their prewar dominance in world trade could be readily turned to the bulk production of toxic gases just as that of BASF could be to the production of fixed ammonia for nitrates.

Tests of such gases began quickly. Duisberg and Nernst experimented with dianisidine chlorosulphate—a compound used in the synthetic dyes familiar to Haber—which caused sneezing fits. The German army fired shrapnel shells filled with this powder at the Battle of Neuve Chapelle in France in late 1914 but to no noticeable effect. German scientists also experimented with xylyl bromide—a liquid that vaporized on contact with air to form a variety of tear gas. Shells specially designed to hold liquid— known as "T-shells" after their creator Dr. Hans von Tappen—were filled with the xylyl bromide and used against the Russians on the eastern front at the end of January 1915, again with little effect. The scientists pondered why, then realized that the extreme cold might have inhibited the chemical's vaporization. Hoping T-shells would perform better in the warmer

---

* After the war Duisberg showed an Allied officer a giant mural in Bayer's offices, celebrating the company's contribution to the war effort and depicting the manufacture of gas and shells being filled with it.

climate of the western front, scientists oversaw the manufacture of a further batch of shells, this time mixing xylyl bromide with bromacetone. However, these new shells, fired at Nieuwpoort in Flanders, in March 1915 again had no obvious effect on the enemy. German scientists concluded for such irritant gases to succeed in temporarily incapacitating the enemy, they would need to be deployed in greater concentration and quantity.

In the interim, however, General von Falkenhayn's views on the use of gas had hardened. He no longer wanted weapons that would merely incapacitate but "something that makes people permanently incapable of fighting"—a step that, even more than the deployment of irritant gases, was entirely illegal under the provisions of the Hague Conventions prohibiting the use of poison, poison weapons, and asphyxiating gases. Duisberg thought the production of such a weapon would require an immense effort by "all suitable forces in the German Empire" and might indeed be beyond their capability. However, Emil Fischer, a leading organic chemist, suggested the possibility of using phosgene, which could kill "even in extraordinarily great dilution" and Duisberg began experimenting with it.

Haber too explored toxic gases at his institute where, an employee recalled, "the work was pushed day and night." Every morning members of the military arrived in "steel-grey cars" to inquire about progress. The exhausting pace was not conducive to safety. On December 17, Haber was called away just as two colleagues were about to combine two chemicals—dichloromethylamine and cacodyl chloride—in a test tube. Moments later he heard a tremendous explosion and ran back to find one of the scientists dying and the other with his hand blown off. Within two weeks of learning of von Falkenhayn's changed and lethal requirement, Haber suggested deploying liquid chlorine which, on coming into contact with the air, would immediately gasify and form a low, heavy cloud that would roll over the enemy trenches, suffocating or driving out the enemy and clearing the way for German troops to advance. Chlorine gas had first been characterized in 1774, then in 1810 established as a pure element by scientist Sir Humphry Davy who, because of its distinctive color, named it from the ancient Greek *khloros* meaning "pale green."

Having witnessed some of the early T-shells trials, Haber was convinced that "owing to the small area affected by each shell it would be necessary to fire a large number simultaneously to produce any technical effect." The remedy, he suggested, was "the use of a large number of mortars." Told that such a quantity could never be provided in time, he proposed storing the chlorine in liquid form in pressurized steel canisters, each large enough to hold twenty kilograms. The canisters would be buried in the ground a meter apart in a long line. Inserted in the top of each would be a lead pipe which could be raised above the trench and directed toward the enemy. When the wind was in the right direction, they would be opened simultaneously to release the vaporizing chlorine. He asked for some of Germany's existing stock of twelve thousand gas canisters in which liquid chlorine used as an industrial bleaching agent was stored to be put at his disposal.

In mid-January 1915, von Falkenhayn endorsed Haber's proposals. Although it seems inconceivable that the use of gas would not have been discussed with the kaiser, no record of this appears to have survived either in the official sources or elsewhere. Haber began his preparations. Unlike Duisberg whose progress was being hindered by the scarcity of phosgene, Haber had no shortage of chlorine—another by-product of the dye industry. Even before war broke out the group of chemical companies including Bayer and BASF (who in 1916 would combine their relevant activities to form the Interessengemeinschaft [IG]) had been producing forty tons a day. However, he had quickly to assemble a suitable scientific team, as well as recruit and train five hundred soldiers in the delicate task of handling the gas canisters.

The scientists whom Haber—who retained his rank of noncommissioned officer (NCO) in the army reserve dating from his military service in Breslau—assembled into what became Pioneer Regiments 35 and 36 included future Nobel laureates James Franck, Gustav Hertz, and Otto Hahn as well as Hans Geiger, inventor of the Geiger counter for radiation monitoring. Hahn was summoned by Haber to a meeting at a hotel in Brussels in January 1915 to find him "lying in bed." Haber told him "how the war had now become frozen" so that "the fronts were immobile." Because of this "the war now had to be fought by other means . . . He then gave me a lecture on chlorine gas clouds which had to blow over the enemy trenches in order to force the enemy to come out of them." When Hahn objected that this surely violated the Hague Convention, Haber responded that the French had already started it "by using rifle ammunition filled with gas." (In fact, the French had not done so at this time but there is some evidence that they would in March experiment in battle with non-lethal tear gas cartridges and grenades.) Haber also argued that "it was a way of saving countless lives, if it meant that the war could be brought to an end sooner."

Hahn and the other chosen scientists received special training in Berlin in the handling of poisonous gases and also in observing wind and weather conditions. Some, like Hahn, were then deployed to regiments on the western front as "gas pioneers"—soon to be nicknamed "Stinkpioneere" by other German troops— tasked with selecting positions from which gas might be deployed and instructing officers "in the nature of the new weapon" as well as actually releasing the gas.

The problem for von Falkenhayn was where to launch the chlorine attack. Most of his commanders refused outright to have anything to do with the indisputably illegal poison gas, ignoring his arguments that its use was essentially humane because by shortening the war it would save lives. Colonel-General Karl von Einem denounced gas as dishonorable and claimed its use would provoke a worldwide reaction that could only damage Germany's reputation. Crown Prince Rupprecht of Bavaria agreed that poison gas was unchivalrous and also pointed out that except for a brief period in the spring, the prevailing winds along the western front blew toward the German lines not away from them. He also predicted that if gas proved a success, the Allies would swiftly follow suit and deploy it against German troops.

Von Falkenhayn found a more receptive ear in fifty-year-old Albrecht, Grand Duke of Württemberg, commander of the Fourth Army in Flanders. In October 1914, the Grand Duke had almost succeeded in taking the moated fourteenth-century city of Ypres, a quiet backwater in the western corner of Belgium—the only significant portion of the country the Germans had failed to occupy and one that blocked the route to the strategically important Channel ports whose capture was a key German war aim. Ypres and its outlying villages and farms lay in a fertile basin intersected by canals, including the Yser Canal, and surrounded to the north, northeast, and south by wooded hills.

However, by mid-November 1914 in the First Battle of Ypres the British Expeditionary Force had halted the German army's advance in three weeks of fighting that had almost exhausted stocks of shells in both armies and produced casualties of eighty thousand killed and wounded on the German side and fifty-four thousand on the British. Consequently, German troops were now occupying a network of trenches they had dug for themselves east of Ypres. Facing them were British, Canadian, and French divisions, similarly dug into the Ypres Salient, an elongated tongue of land projecting eastward into German-held territory from the village of Steenstraat, five miles north of Ypres, to St. Eloi some three miles to the south.

The Grand Duke hoped poison gas might deliver the breakthrough that had so far eluded him. Satisfied that he had finally identified a suitable place to deploy chlorine, von Falkenhayn ordered Haber to make the necessary preparations. Haber decided the gas should be transported in liquid form to a railhead in German-occupied territory, then poured into the metal canisters ready to be brought up to the front. By February 1915 he was ready to travel to the German front lines near Ypres to oversee the arrangements in person. His wife Clara—herself a scientist, the first woman to obtain a doctorate from Breslau University and according to James Franck a gifted woman "with outspoken views that often contradicted her husband's"—was fundamentally opposed to chemical weapons and tried to dissuade him. Haber ignored her pleas and by March had settled into lodgings in the small German-held town of Geluveld east of Ypres.

The senior German officer who would actually superintend the attack was Major General Berthold von Deimling. By his own account, "when von Falkenhayn informed us that a new weapon, poison gas, was to be deployed for the first time in my sector" he was shocked. "I must admit that the task of poisoning the enemy as if they were rats went against the grain with me as it would with any decent sentient soldier." What convinced him to continue was the thought that "using poison gas might perhaps lead to the fall of Ypres, perhaps even make the entire campaign victorious. With such an important goal, all inner doubts had to be silenced. We had to go on, come what may. War is self-defence and knows no law. That will always be so as long as war exists."

Haber decided to position his gas cylinders on Hill 60, a German-held sixty-meter-high heap of spoil dug out during construction of a new railway cutting in the nineteenth century, which faced the southeast sector of the Ypres Salient. Before the war locals called the hill "Lover's Knoll." Working at night to avoid being spotted, his soldiers dug some six thousand of the heavy, unwieldy steel canisters requisitioned from civilian use into the earth. Otto Hahn, who was assisting, found himself so close to the British lines that "at times we could only talk in whispers. We were not very well entrenched and we were constantly under enemy fire so the installation of the gas cylinders for the proposed attack was very difficult indeed. [To protect] against enemy hand grenades we used wire netting that catapulted the grenades back into the enemy lines."

In early March, British shells by chance ruptured two chlorine cylinders, gassing several German soldiers including one who died coughing up blood. Not long after, similarly random Allied rifle fire damaged further cylinders, releasing chlorine gas which injured fifty German soldiers and killed three. Deimling, who visited the wounded, wrote, "They suffered terribly. These incidents severely shook the troops' confidence in the horrible devices." By March 10, all six thousand cylinders were in place but the required wind from the east refused to blow steadily and consistently enough. Deimling rode over to Haber's command post to yell at the "pale and exhausted" scientist. An officer who was present recounted how Deimling called him "a charlatan and a lot else besides for making false claims to the high command about the utility of poison gas." Deimling's accusations left Haber "extremely unhappy."

On March 25 the Grand Duke—under relentless pressure from von Falkenhayn to launch the attack "at the first possible favourable opportunity"—ordered Haber to set up an "alternate gas front" facing the northern curve of the Ypres Salient. On April 5, shortly after Haber himself suffered the effects of gas after riding too close to some fumes during a test, the work began. Six days later 5,730 chlorine canisters—some new, some dragged laboriously from the earlier position on Hill 60 and containing 168 tons of chlorine gas—were in place.

As timescales continued to extend, the German commanders worried that their plans would be discovered. They might have been if the Allies had taken a slew of warnings more seriously. Toward midnight on April 13, 1915, twenty-four-year-old German private August Jaeger deserted, crossing the several hundred yards of scarred ground that separated the German and French lines to surrender to soldiers of the Fourth Battalion of Chasseurs. Taken to the headquarters of the French Eleventh Division, he startled his interrogators by reporting that "an attack is planned for the near future against the French trenches . . . Four batteries have been placed in position in the first line trenches; these batteries each have 20 bottles of asphyxiating gas . . . At a given signal—3 red rockets fired by the artillery—the bottles are uncorked, and the gas on escaping, is carried by a favourable wind towards the French trenches. This gas is intended to asphyxiate the men who occupy the trenches and to allow the Germans to occupy them without losses." He added that German troops would use wads of chemically treated cotton to protect themselves from the fumes.

The Eleventh Division's commander, General Edmond Ferry, sensibly pulled some of his men back from the front lines to lessen casualties in the event of a gas attack and ordered his artillery to concentrate its fire on the area where, according to Jaeger, the gas cylinders were buried. He passed the deserter's information to the British Twenty-eighth Division positioned to the right of his own troops, urging them "to exercise the greatest vigilance and to seek suitable means to prevent inhalation of gas." Having also warned the Canadian troops who were about to relieve his own men, Ferry believed he had done all in his power "to avoid surprise, the effect of terror, and the heavy losses the Germans counted on inflicting with this new and abominable weapon of war." However, Ferry received no thanks for his timely actions from his seniors at French headquarters, who sent a liaison officer to reprimand him for breaking protocol by communicating directly with the British and the Canadians and to tell him that "all this gas business cannot be taken too seriously." This was despite the fact that French spy Charles Lucieto had also been warning for some time that BASF was manufacturing poison gas at its factories in Mannheim in the Ruhr.

When Ferry's report reached the headquarters of Lieutenant General Sir Herbert Plumer, commander of the three British divisions defending the Salient, it was greeted with similar skepticism and the suspicion that Private Jaeger's confession was in fact part of some dastardly German plot to mislead and confuse the Allies. However, like the French commanders, the British had also received earlier warnings that the Germans were planning a chemical attack. In late March a captured German officer had told a British sergeant of the Leicestershire Regiment that gas cylinders were being buried ready for an attack "at the first favourable wind." The sergeant had gone out with a small patrol and found "cylinders in dozens" but although his report "was passed to headquarters" no action was taken. On April 9, the *Times* carried a statement from a war correspondent that "it has been reported that in the Argonne [northeastern France], where the trenches are very close, the Germans have on several occasions pumped blazing oil or pitch on to the French, but, according to the statements of our prisoners, they are preparing a more novel reception for us in front of parts of our line. They propose to asphyxiate our men if they advance by means of poisonous gas. The gas is contained under pressure in steel cylinders, and, being of a heavy nature, will spread along the ground without being dissipated quickly."

Further evidence that something was being planned continued to reach the British and French lines. A more detailed report from Jaeger describing exactly how the gas cylinders worked and enclosing a wad of cotton from his own gas mask reached Plumer on April 15. The same day, explicit intelligence Plumer received from the headquarters of his senior, General Sir Horace Smith-Dorrien. Based on information from a Belgian agent it warned of an imminent gas attack: "Passages have been prepared across old trenches to facilitate bringing up of artillery. Germans intend making use of tubes with asphyxiating gas. They are placed in batteries of 20 tubes per 4 metres . . . A favourable wind necessary." However, more attention was paid to the statement of a second German deserter, NCO Julius Rapsahl of the Fifty-second Reserve Division, that there were no gas cylinders in the German front lines and that the cotton mask found in his own kit was for protection should the Allies use chemical grenades.

Senior British officers met at Plumer's headquarters to discuss how to cope with any casualties from an attack with asphyxiating gas. However, the war diary of one of those present which refers merely to "a rumour" of a gas attack shows that, though such an attack was not ruled out, it was considered a fairly remote possibility—a view confirmed when aerial reconnaissance by Royal Flying Corps aircraft flying slowly over the German lines failed to spot anything untoward. The night of April 15 duly came and went. A young Canadian officer wrote, "Last night [April 15] we got ready to receive a German attack . . . with tubes of poisonous gas; but it didn't materialise . . . Today is quite normal." A British report stated: "We were aware of the fact that the Germans were making preparations for the discharge of gas for several days previously . . . Nobody seems to have realised the great danger that was threatening, it being considered that the enemy's attempt would certainly fail and that whatever gas reached our line could be easily fanned away. No one felt in the slightest degree uneasy."

The date set by Grand Duke Albrecht for the first gas attack had indeed been April 15 but the conditions noted by the young Canadian had again frustrated it. Without a wind—and one blowing steadily from the right direction—a gas attack was impossible. On April 17 on orders from von Falkenhayn, German reserve troops began to pull back from the Salient and elsewhere to begin their long journey to Galicia to strike against the Russian armies on the eastern front to which von Falkenhayn was now shifting his focus—so much so that he refused the Grand Duke's request for a division to remain in reserve to exploit a German breakthrough should the gas attack succeed. Von Falkenhayn was, however, still committed to the use of poison gas around Ypres to test its effectiveness on the battlefield.

That same day, Germany issued a communiqué accusing the British of using "shells and bombs with asphyxiating gas" near Ypres. Again that might have given the Allies some pause for thought. The British Official History later described the communiqué as typical of "the German mentality"—intending to do something themselves they "were putting the blame on their opponents in advance." (In fact, the British authorities had looked very briefly at the possible use of tear gas but dropped work on it as they considered even the use of such a nonlethal gas breached the Hague Convention.)

Another action that began that day, April 17, should also have provided clues. British tunnelers detonated five mines beneath Hill 60 and as the mines exploded they observed that the enemy seemed more panic-stricken than usual, even seeming to turn their bayonets against their comrades in their desperation to scramble out of the trenches. The British moved in to occupy the hill before the Germans launched a counterattack in which James Franck joined with several of the other gas pioneers, winning a medal for bravery. Eventually after attack and counterattack British troops finally took and held the hill. They did not, however, find any of Haber's gas cylinders that remained. Though some among the first wave of attackers reported a smell of gas, and that their eyes suddenly started streaming and they felt nauseous and weak, their commanders assumed they must have encountered some sort of tear gas.

Meanwhile, worried that the British might indeed have discovered the gas cylinders remaining on Hill 60, Grand Duke Albrecht set Tuesday, April 20 as the new day for a gas attack on the northern sector of the Salient. Its code name was "Disinfection" and its objectives were twofold. Two divisions of General Otto von Hügel's XXVI Reserve Corps were to overwhelm French troops and seize Pilckem Ridge, high ground just two and a half miles north of Ypres which—according to the official German history— commanders assumed would render the Allied position in the remainder of the Salient untenable, allowing German troops to take the city. Meanwhile, soldiers of General Hugo von Kathen's XXIII Reserve Corps, advancing on von Hügel's right, were to dash westward to seize crossings over the Yser Canal. The day before—April 19—the Grand Duke ordered one of his giant seventeen-inch guns—a so-called Big Bertha—to start pounding Ypres with its one-ton shells to distract the Allies from observing his final preparations, which included bringing up one of his Fourth Army's own reserve divisions to the front lines to await the attack. Their officers told the infantrymen who would lead the attack simply to await the order to follow the gas cloud that would knock out the opposition. There was no need to load rifles—steel bayonets were all that would be needed to dispose of the choking survivors.

Through the early hours of April 20, the men crouched in their trenches. However, at four A.M. the wind suddenly died. The next day a frustrated von Falkenhayn called on the Grand Duke at his headquarters at Thielt to insist on an attack as soon as even a "halfway favourable opportunity" offered. With predictions of strong winds gusting from the northeast on the following day, German troops were again put on alert. Infantry officer Leutnant Becker recalled how they "spent the night in the front line brimming with confidence. The pioneers came and checked the locking valves on the steel cylinders. The gas was trapped inside the cylinders under high pressure. Harmlessly the cylinders sat there in the Flanders mud. The pipes through which it would be released nestled in amongst the breastworks, hidden from view."

However, April 22 dawned without a breath of wind. Not until late afternoon did a light breeze finally begin gusting toward the southwest. German commanders passed down the line the code words that would launch the attack "*Gott strafe England!*" (May God Punish England!). The German artillery opened up against the northern edge of the Salient held by French and Canadian troops. An hour later at five P.M., as the three red flares Private Jaeger had warned of shot into the sky from an observation balloon, Haber was told to order his "Stinkpioneere" to open the valves on the canisters.

CHAPTER NINE

"Operation Disinfection"

THE TWO FRENCH divisions dug in along the Ypres Salient's northern front line around the village of Langemarck were about to experience the world's first chlorine gas attack. The men of the Eighty-seventh Territorial Division were veterans recalled to military service at the outbreak of the war. Stationed to their right was the Forty-fifth Infantry Division—known informally as the Forty-fifth "Algerian" Division—which had served in France's North African colonies. It included three Zouave regiments. Originally recruited from North African Berbers, the Zouaves by 1914 were conscripted Frenchmen who at this early stage in the war still wore the traditional Zouave uniform of baggy red pantaloons, braided blue jackets, and red fezzes.

The Forty-fifth also included a regiment of Tirailleurs or "sharp-shooters"—native North Africans with French officers also wearing Zouave-style uniforms. In addition, two battalions of the Infanterie Légère d'Afrique (African Light Infantry) had recently joined it. The latter were composed of French convicts whose offenses ranged from vagrancy and pimping to theft and assault, and soldiers transferred from other regiments as punishment for deserting or disobeying orders. The members of the African Light Infantry had long ironically dubbed themselves "Les Joyeux" (The Happy Ones).

The Forty-fifth had only taken over their positions eight days earlier on the night of April 14. Captain Louis Botti of the Seventh Zouaves despaired at the problems of digging trenches in ground more resembling a cemetery than a defensive position: "In certain places shod feet stick out of the soil and at a place we pass a hundred times a day, red trousers appear. Everywhere, however little we seek them, the eye falls on out-stretched corpses . . . anonymous, not meaning anything to anyone." Living conditions for all Allied soldiers around Ypres were indeed atrocious. The high water table and low elevation—barely above sea level—meant trenches flooded easily. Newcomers thought those already there "looked like tramps, all plastered with filth and dirt, and unshaven."

One of the few consolations was smoking—sometimes, despite their "vile taste," the tobacco leaves they found hanging in the lofts of farmhouses. But smoking required caution since as one soldier recalled, "if Jerry saw any smoke he would send a grenade over because he knew there was someone there." The belief in the trenches that to light three cigarettes from one match was unlucky was not superstition but well founded— lighting up the first revealed your presence to the enemy, lighting the second allowed him to take aim, lighting the third gave him time to fire.[*] Then there were the rats. Some thought there was no point in killing them since "they would putrefy and it would be worse than if you left them alive. I think they lived in corpses, because they were . . . big as cats . . . horrible great things."

It was not much better for the German troops although occupying as they did more of the higher ground their trenches were somewhat drier. A commander of a cavalry troop, Rudolf Binding, thought

> the battlefield . . . fearful. One is overcome by a peculiar sour, heavy and penetrating smell of corpses. Rising over a plank bridge you find that its middle is supported only by the body of a long-dead horse. Men that were killed last October lie half in swamp and half in the yellow-sprouting beet-fields. The legs of an Englishman, still encased in puttees, stick out into a trench, the corpse being built into the parapet; a soldier hangs his rifle on them. A little brook runs through the trench and everyone uses the water for drinking and washing; it is the

---

[*] The writer H. H. Munro, better known as "Saki," was shot dead by a German sniper in France in November 1916 while as a lance sergeant sheltering with his men in a shell crater. His last words reputedly were "Put that bloody cigarette out."

only water they have. Nobody minds the pale Englishman who is rotting away a few steps farther up . . . At one point I saw twenty-two dead horses still harnessed, accompanied by a few dead drivers. Cattle and pigs lie about half-rotten; broken trees . . . crater upon crater in the roads and in the fields. Such is a six month's old battlefield.

To the right of the Forty-fifth and Eighty-seventh French divisions and holding a forty-five-hundred-yard front were four battalions of the Second and Third Canadian Infantry Brigades that had recently replaced French general Ferry's Eleventh Division. During the handover some Canadians had gotten lost in the cratered terrain. Sergeant Raymond MacIlree described to his parents in Victoria, British Columbia, how "a Frenchman found us, for it was a French Regt. we were relieving and he steered us over all kinds of obstacles, shell holes polka dot the whole place, some so big that a Frenchy drowned in one, also there were dykes and ditches galore." A further eight Canadian battalions were in reserve behind the lines and some of the men were playing football in the sunshine on the afternoon of the attack.

The Canadian troops belonged to the First Canadian Division. Since Canada was a British dominion, the division was part of the British army. Its British commander, Lieutenant General Edwin Alderson, reported to General Sir Horace Smith-Dorrien, commander of the British Second Army. When Britain entered the war, many Canadians and especially the dominion's numerous British immigrants had greeted the news with patriotic enthusiasm. The *Toronto Globe* related how people came out onto the streets, stood for a few moments in silence, then broke into a cheer. "It was not for the war, but for the King, Britain, and—please God—victory . . . Heads were bowed and the crowd began to sing 'God Save the King.'" In towns and cities including Vancouver and Regina mobs attacked property thought to belong to Germans. In Berlin, Ontario, a metal statue of the first kaiser was thrown in a lake, then fished out and melted down.

As soon as recruiting offices opened, men converged on them in such overwhelming numbers it was clear there was no need yet for conscription. At one office in Toronto, guards with fixed bayonets had to restrain eager volunteers. By early September 1914 nearly thirty-three thousand men were in training at a specially constructed camp in Quebec and a month later the first Canadian troops were disembarking in England. Churchill, never concerned about straying outside his naval brief, sent them a rousing cable: CANADA SENDS HER AID AT A TIMELY MOMENT. THE CONFLICT MOVES FORWARD AND FIERCER STRUGGLES LIE BEFORE US THAN ANY WHICH HAVE YET BEEN FOUGHT. The *London Times* remarked that "nothing like the Canadian contingent has been landed in this country since the time of William the Conqueror."

In February 1915, after rigorous training on Salisbury Plain, the Canadian Division embarked in stormy weather for Saint-Nazaire at the mouth of the Loire where they boarded trains for the five-hundred-mile journey to the front in Flanders. Once arrived they accustomed themselves to their muddy, dangerous environment, suffering the constant itching and scratching caused by lice. One soldier recalled it as "enough to make a saint swear . . . We did not notice the lice so much when standing, perished with cold on look-out. But when we got in our tiny dug-outs, and our bodies began to get warm, then out would come the lice from their hiding places in our clothing, forming up in columns of fours, [they] would start route marching over our flesh . . . There have been times when utterly worn out, both mentally and physically, yet unable to sleep because of the lice, I have known men to actually cry." Meals were of bully beef so solid that the soldiers sometimes used the unopened tins as bricks to line their trenches. The Canadians also quickly developed respect for the German snipers who, an officer commented, "are the very deuce. They pick off our men whenever they get a chance."

The brigade commanders of the Canadian troops settling into their new positions at Ypres were tall, heavyset, thirty-nine-year-old Brigadier General Arthur Currie, whose prewar career had included teaching, selling insurance, and speculating on property on Vancouver Island, in charge of the Second Brigade; and forty-three-year-old Brigadier General Richard Turner, a Quebec wholesale merchant who had won Britain's highest military decoration, the Victoria Cross, during the Boer War, in charge of the Third Brigade. Many of their soldiers were of Scottish stock or recent emigrants from Scotland. Turner's Third Brigade included the Canadian Scottish, Royal Highlander, and Forty-eighth Highlanders of Canada regiments who fought in kilts. Other Canadians were in the khaki uniforms adopted by their British counterparts in the Boer War when in their red coats they proved all too easy for Boers to pick out and pick off.

Since relieving the French, the Canadians had worked under cover of darkness, when the risk of being sniped was less, to improve the trenches the French had bequeathed them. To their dismay, they found that these trenches were shallow, badly connected, and inadequately protected by barbed wire. To give proper cover, entrenchments needed to run in long, continuous lines that zigzagged to prevent an infiltrating enemy firing down the length of them. They also had to be protected by high bulletproof parapets to the front and further parapets behind to provide some shelter from shell bursts. Instead Sergeant MacIlree found his position had only "a mere breastwork, bullet proof for about two feet up, no cover behind." The Canadians also discovered, as another sergeant complained, that "the French have used the trenches as latrines." Even worse, bits of body protruded through the earthworks like the hand dangling through a parapet that some men "used to shake hands with."

To the Canadians' right the British Twenty-seventh and Twenty-eighth Divisions held the rest of the British army's ten-mile portion of the Salient's front line, including its easternmost point. Major Cuthbert Lawson described in a letter to a friend how the British were situated: "The position round Ypres has always been like a horseshoe—Ypres is in the centre of the heels and we are right in the toe."

For all these Allied troops, April 22 had passed much as usual except for exceptionally beautiful weather. A Canadian officer recalled how "we spent the time basking in the sun and writing letters" before enjoying "a glorious tea of Scotch shortbread and chocolate biscuits." To another officer it seemed "the very essence of spring . . . when the spring feeling suddenly gets into the blood, when one throws work to the winds and takes to the woods in search of the first violets." For most of the day German artillery had continued pounding Ypres with its masterpieces of Gothic architecture—the Guild Hall of the Cloth Merchants and Saint Martin's Cathedral—so that, as a soldier noted, "a dark red pall of dust and smoke" hung over it. Many of its once seventeen-thousand strong population were streaming out of the city, "in scattered groups . . . in Sunday black or rags;

old men sweating between the shafts of handcarts piled high with house-hold treasures; deep-chested dogs harnessed underneath and straining at the axle with lolling tongue; aged women on wagons stacked with bedding or in wheel-barrows trundled by the family in turn, bewildered children and anxious mothers, all hastening in stricken flight before the breaking storm."

Allied troops observed little untoward except that British aerial recon-naissance reported an unusual amount of activity to the rear of the enemy lines, including the forming up of long lines of troops. However, at four P.M., as the revised time set by the German command for the gas attack approached, the German artillery shortened its range and began bom-barding not Ypres but the French and Canadian lines. Then shortly before five P.M. their guns fell silent.

Soon afterward, French sentries saw the three red rockets shoot across the sky followed by puffs of white smoke rising from the German trenches. The smoke was the chlorine that began to condense as it absorbed moisture from the atmosphere. As its volume increased it changed color; the pale wisps were soon a grubby-looking yellow-green cloud rolling across no man's land toward the French trenches. Haber's "Stinkpioneere" had taken only five minutes to release the 150 tons of compressed chlorine gas bil-lowing forward along a front nearly four miles wide to engulf the soldiers of the Forty-fifth "Algerian" Division. A German airman observing the advancing gas from above was struck by "how extraordinary it looked when the clouds came up to the enemy trenches, then rose, and after as it were peering curiously for a moment over the edge of the trenches, sank down into them like some living thing."

The war diary of the First Battalion of the African Light Infantry relates how "the north wind that blew that cloud towards our lines . . . brought on our companies asphyxiating vapours of chlorine and nitrous products." A French medical officer saw troops suddenly scrambling from the trenches on all sides. Wondering what had caused "this panic" he looked around to find "the sky totally obscured by a yellow-green cloud." Moments later the vapor enveloped him so that he felt he was peering "through green glasses." At once he experienced effects on his respiratory system: "throat burning, chest pains, choking and spitting of blood, dizziness. We believed we were all lost." An officer beside him turned purple and no longer had the strength to walk.

Canadian troops stationed to the right saw "a heavy greenish cloud hanging over the French lines" and "the French running back." However, at five ten P.M. German field guns, ordered to hold fire while the gas had been released for fear that shells might disperse the chlorine before it could form a cloud, opened up once more. As the barrage descended again, for the moment the Canadians "could find out nothing more." By now German infantry in their uniforms of *feld grau* (field gray) were advancing cautiously in the wake of the cloud, many wearing crude face masks of dampened cotton and gauze. Skeptical whether the gas would indeed immediately knock out the enemy as their officers had promised, many had ignored the order not to load their rifles, only to fix bayonets. As cautiously they approached the shallow trenches of the Forty-fifth Division; some defenders, coughing and choking though they were, managed for a short while to return fire before being quickly overrun or fleeing. On entering the French trenches the German troops found them crammed with the dead and the dying, some of the latter vomiting green phlegm. The official German account of the attack records how "even before [the gas] reached them the enemy could be seen to waver."

Capitaine Tremsal of the African Light Infantry had been resting in a cellar when the sounds of heavy machine gun fire brought him rushing toward his front line. Running the opposite way was one of his men shouting that he and his fellows had been poisoned. Looking beyond the soldier, the captain saw "an enormous cloud several meters high, yellow in the centre and green on the edge masking and discolouring the landscape." As more of his men staggered choking toward him from the now gas-enshrouded trenches he tried to rally them, shouting, "The Joyeux have never lost a trench!" However, within moments "the asphyxiating cloud" overwhelmed both him and them. He experienced "a horrible sensation of burning" in his throat as his lungs "refused to receive that poisoned air" while blood-tinged mucous ran from his nose and mouth. Some men of the Forty-fifth rushed toward the Eighty-seventh Territorials on their left to collapse in their trenches. Soon the Eighty-seventh too were fleeing, clogging the roads as they made for the bridges over the Yser Canal hoping to cross to the west bank, or heading for the Canadian lines. A Canadian Royal Highlander watched French troops "pouring into our trench, coughing, bleeding and dying all over the place."

At around six P.M. French gunners of the Eighty-seventh Division east of the canal spotted the gas cloud and the advancing Germans. Spared the worst effects of the gas by a shift in the wind, they trained their sixteen modern seventy-five-millimeter "quick-firers" and twenty-nine older ninety-millimeter guns, brought out of "retirement" for the war, on the enemy, claiming heavy casualties. However, they quickly exhausted their limited ammunition. Soon, as an artillery officer related, "we distinctly heard the cries of their officers, 'Vorwaerts!' 'Vorwaerts!' and the rolling artillery barrage which preceded them intensified more and more. Finally groups of the enemy surged to the right and to the left. We had to extricate the guns as quickly as possible or abandon them. A great many of the gunners were unable to escape in time and were taken prisoner." By seven P.M. most of the forty-five guns were also in enemy hands.

The first that Colonel Jean Mordacq, commander of the Forty-fifth Division's Ninetieth Brigade, knew of the attack was when, some twenty minutes after the arrival of the gas cloud, Major Villevaleix of the First Tirailleurs telephoned him and "in a gasping voice, punctuated, barely distinct . . . announced to me that he was being violently attacked, that immense columns of yellow smoke issuing from the German trenches were now extending across his entire front," that the Tirailleurs were starting to evacuate their trenches and beating a retreat—"many falling asphyxiated." Mordacq's first reaction was to ask himself whether the major "had not lost his head a little or suffered one of those shocks to the brain I'd seen so often since the start of the campaign . . . In any case a gas attack was far from my thoughts, having never entertained the possibility or heard it being discussed since my arrival in Belgium." However, a subsequent call from a hoarse-voiced other officer, of the First Tirailleurs, told a similar story and reported that "he was being forced to abandon his command position" since he could not breathe and the situation was untenable. Whole groups of Tirailleurs were collapsing all around him due to the gas and German shelling. Moments later Villevaleix rang again: "Everyone around me is falling, I am leaving my position." Then the line went dead.

No longer doubting some catastrophe had happened, Mordacq hurried outside, mounted his horse, and made for the Yser Canal, which he could no longer see because of drifts of yellow smoke. Approaching the village of Boesinghe on the canal's west bank, his nose and throat began to tingle violently, his ears buzzed, and his breathing was becoming labored. An "unbearable stench of chlorine" hung over everything. With his horse refusing to go on, Mordacq dismounted and walked into Boesinghe to a sight "worse than lamentable, it was tragic. Men who had fled their positions were everywhere: territorials, 'Joyeux,' zouaves, artillerymen without their guns, haggard, greatcoats thrown away or hanging open . . . running hither and thither like madmen, crying loudly for water, spitting blood, some even rolling on the ground in a desperate struggle to breathe." One "Joyeux" called out to Mordacq, "Those [bastards] have poisoned us." Meanwhile, "a mass of crazed unfortunates" crowded the canal banks hoping water would relieve "their horrible sufferings." Mordacq—one of several to liken the sights of that day to scenes from Dante's *Inferno*—decided there was no point trying to prevent those who could still walk from fleeing since they were "no longer soldiers . . . but poor beings who had suddenly turned mad."

By six forty-five P.M.—less than two hours after the start of the gas attack—German advance troops were approaching the east bank of the Yser Canal and would soon establish a bridgehead over it at Het Sas, north of Boesinghe. So far, the gas had done its work. Haber had chosen to release a mixture of one thousand parts chlorine to one million parts air—a level that burned the throat, distended the chest, and destroyed the lining of the lungs which, engorged with liquid, swelled to twice their normal size. An Allied soldier described how the victim drowned in his own body fluids: "It produces a flooding in the lungs . . . the coughing-up of a greenish froth off the stomach and lungs, ending finally in insensibility and death. The colour of the skin turns a greenish-black and yellow, the tongue protrudes and the eyes assume a glassy stare."

Another soldier saw several hundred men in an orchard "wriggling and writhing . . . their faces black . . . tearing at their throats" watched by a medical officer who lamented, "Look at the poor bastards and we can't do anything for them." Lieutenant Colonel Edward Morrison, a Canadian officer who had been a journalist in Ottawa before the war, described demoralized French troops "absolutely in rout" and "ambulances loaded with unwounded men, ammunition wagons, transport vehicles crowded with infantry . . . galloping across country through hedges, ditches, and barbed wire . . . After this rabble came men on foot, without arms [weapons], singly and in groups, alternately running and walking, and only intent on getting away" and men "tearing madly through the crush of fugitives with staring eyes and their faces flecked with blood and froth. Frequently these men would fall down under the feet of the mob, and roll about like mad dogs in their death agonies." Another Canadian officer commanding a battery one thousand yards south of Saint-Julien, a village northeast of Ypres, saw Algerians "running back as if the devil was after them, their eyeballs showing white, and coughing their lungs out—they literally were coughing their lungs out: glue was coming out of their mouths. It was . . . very disturbing, very distressing."

In the initial chaos and with many field telephone lines—the principal means of communication—severed by shell fire, Allied commanders found it hard to gauge what had happened, beyond that the Germans appeared to have used some type of poison gas and that French troops had fled their position along the northern edge of the Ypres Salient. In fact, the French flight had created a breach to the left of the Canadians of four to five miles between the Poelcapelle to Ypres road and Steenstraat on the Yser Canal. No organized French units remained east of the canal. Therefore, the Canadian front line, despite still holding firm, was in imminent and grave danger of being outflanked. Until reserves could be called up, only five hundred Canadian troops in Saint-Julien, a Canadian battery of four eighteen-pounder field guns protecting the approach to the village, a British battery in Kitcheners Wood west of Saint-Julien, and some scattered French troops stood in the way of the German advance.

The most imminent danger was to the Canadian Royal Highlanders in the trenches immediately adjoining the abandoned French lines. Major D. Rykert McCuaig at once pulled men out of the front line to establish a protective flank while Major Edward Norsworthy, together with two platoons and some French troops he had gathered up, for a while succeeded in holding up the German infantry as they tried to cross the

Ypres-Poelcapelle road to outflank the Canadian front line. Norsworthy's entire force was either captured or, like him, killed.

Advancing German troops attempted to capture the guns of the Canadian battery blocking their path to Saint-Julien but machine gunner Lance Corporal Frederick Fisher of the Royal Highlanders, who had come out from Saint-Julien with his crew, held them off, winning time for the guns to be loaded on their limbers and dragged off to safety. Like Norsworthy and his men, Fisher and his team paid with their lives. Fisher was awarded a posthumous Victoria Cross—the first to a Canadian soldier in the war. Meanwhile, the two Canadian frontline brigades were doing what they could to plug the gaps the French had left in the trenches adjoining theirs while Canadian reserves were rushed up. As night fell, the German troops had met enough resistance to convince them to halt for the night and dig in.

At eight o'clock that evening, a French liaison officer told Lieutenant General Edwin Alderson, commander of the First Canadian Division, that the French Forty-fifth Division was about to counterattack toward Pilckem and asked for help in clearing the Germans from Kitcheners Wood. Unaware that as a fighting force the Forty-fifth no longer really existed and had anyway lost most of its artillery, Alderson agreed. At eleven forty-eight P.M. the order to advance was issued (by whisper rather than by whistle to avoid alerting the enemy) and fifteen hundred soldiers from two battalions (the kilted Sixteenth Canadian Scottish and the Tenth Calgary-Winnipeg) went forward, bayonets fixed, toward the south side of the woods, five hundred yards away. In the bright moonshine a subaltern reflected "what a picture the flashing bayonets made."

When they were still two hundred yards from the wood, the leading men found their way obstructed by a high hedge of twigs, branches, and barbed wire. As they forced their way through, the noise alerted the German troops ahead of them in the woods. A German flare lit the sky and the Canadians dropped to the ground. Then urged on by a company commander they stood and charged forward to be met by small-arms fire so intense it sounded "like hailstones on a zinc roof." Many fell but those who could crossed a shallow trench the German defenders had dug to engage in what a survivor called "dreadful hand-to-hand conflict." "We fought in clumps and batches, and the living struggled over the bodies of the dead and dying . . . All who resisted were bayoneted; those who yielded were sent to the rear."

As the Canadian troops pushed deeper into the trees, German machine gunners fired at them from the protection of banks of sandbags. Nevertheless, by two A.M. the Canadians had flushed the Germans from most of Kitcheners Wood, driving one thousand yards north into enemy lines. However, in doing so they exposed themselves to fire from all sides. After attempts to reinforce them failed, they were ordered to pull back to the wood's southern edge. Of the original Canadian force, less than one third was still standing.

That same morning of April 23—Saint George's Day—commander in chief of the British forces, Sir John French, visited General Ferdinand Foch at his headquarters in the hilltop town of Cassel twenty miles west of Ypres. Commander of the northern wing of the French armies, Foch was also responsible to the French commander in chief, Marshal Joseph Joffre, for liaising with the British and Belgian forces. Sir John French intended to inform Foch that the defense of the current positions within the Salient was unsustainable and that he was going to pull back his troops. Foch, however, told French that he had called up fresh divisions. Once they were in position, his troops would counterattack and regain their lost ground. He asked for British support. Persuaded by Foch's passion, French agreed to maintain his present line within the Salient and even to cooperate in a counterattack later that day. Returning to his headquarters at Hazebrouck, he duly ordered troops he had already placed on standby to move up to the front.

The counterattack was to begin at three P.M. and German positions on Mauser Ridge, directly north of Ypres, were the initial target. However, congestion on the roads delayed the arrival of British reserve troops so that the assault did not start until an hour and a half later. Even so there had been little time to reconnoiter. Worse still, because of poor communications the British and Canadian batteries ordered to launch a preliminary bombardment of the ridge were not informed that the attack had been postponed. They therefore wasted ammunition by firing their guns too early. When eight British and two Canadian battalions finally did advance on the ridge, first German artillery, then rifle and machine gun fire cut them down. The only significant assistance from the French troops promised by Foch came from a few hundred men of the Forty-fifth on the east bank of the Yser Canal, and even this was only brief as they soon fell back. By seven P.M. the counterattack was over with the loss of more than half the British and Canadian troops and the majority of their officers. The British Official History records: "No ground was gained that could not have been secured . . . by a simple advance after dark, to which the openness of the country lent itself."

As darkness fell on April 23, the Allies' consolation was that most of the German troops had remained in the positions they had dug the previous night and shown no sign of launching an all-out infantry assault. The only significant German push was in the north of the Salient where troops were extending their bridgehead over the Yser Canal at Het Sas and advancing toward the village of Lizerne, on the canal's west bank.

The German behavior puzzled the Allies. However, just as confused intelligence had hindered their decision taking, so it had clouded the judgment of the German high command. Their troops had met greater resistance than anticipated and suffered higher casualties. Therefore, German commanders were convinced they had insufficient reserves to advance further at present. The result was orders to one division (the Fifty-second Reserve) "not to go beyond the southern slope of Pilckem Ridge" and lukewarm instructions to another (the Fifty-first) to take Saint-Julien "if possible." An official German war diary attributed the German failure to capitalize on their advantage to low morale, declaring that "the infantry . . . had lost its daring and indifference to heavy losses." Whatever the case, the result was that instead of pushing on, the Germans concentrated on bringing up field guns and trench mortars to their new front line while waiting for supplies. They did, however, have more than enough stocks of their new weapon— chlorine gas—and of containers from which to release it.

CHAPTER TEN

"This Filthy Loathsome Pestilence"

ON THE NIGHT of April 23–24 German troops hauled further cylinders into place so gas could be released on the still unbroken Canadian lines facing them to the east. This time the attack was not so unexpected. Lieutenant Colonel Louis Lipsett, commander of the Eighth Battalion of the First Canadian Division, had received reports of German activity "in the ditch in front of his trench." Suspecting this meant an assault was imminent he ordered shelling of the positions where the Germans seemed to be massing, though this apparently did not destroy or damage the gas canisters. Lipsett also devised a special SOS signal to be used in the event of a gas attack and ordered more telephone wires to be laid to improve communications with the artillery batteries supporting his battalion.

In addition, though only thirty-six hours had passed since the first attack, some general precautions against gas, albeit primitive, had already been devised. Reporting to London the previous day that the Germans had used "powerful asphyxiating gases very extensively in attack on French yesterday with serious effect," Sir John French had noted that "as a temporary measure, [I] am arranging for troops in trenches to be supplied with solutions of bicarbonate of soda in which to soak handkerchiefs." If no sodium bicarbonate was within reach, men were to moisten a piece of fabric with any liquid "to hand"—a euphemism for their own urine. Private Alfred Bromfield recalled, "I don't mind admitting that I didn't think much of the urinating on handkerchiefs. I didn't think it was sufficient protection, so I went to one of the trench latrines, you know just a bucket stuck in a hole, and I stuck my head in the bucket . . . I stopped down long enough till I couldn't hold my breath any more, came up, took a good breath of air, down again!"

The attack came at four o'clock in the morning of Saturday, April 24. Captain George McLaren of the Fifteenth Battalion's Forty-eighth Highlanders watched scarlet flares drop from a balloon tethered behind the German line. Then in the dim predawn light he saw "men (perhaps 2 or 3) appear over the German parapet." They seemed to be wearing helmets "much like those worn by divers, with hoses in their hands from which came a heavy green gas." One of his subalterns, Lieutenant Herbert Maxwell-Scott, a descendant of the novelist Sir Walter Scott, thought the flares, resembling "red stars," made "quite a pretty sight" but recalled how "our gaze must have lingered on this sight a little too long, for when I turned the men were leaving the trenches on our right and a great wall of green gas, about 15 to 20 feet high was on top of us." To battalion commander George Tuxford the gas looked like "a heavy Scotch mist, swallowing up the landscape as it came."

Wafted by a steady northeasterly wind, the gas engulfed the Forty-eighth Highlanders. Lieutenant Maxwell-Scott recalled how "Captain McLaren gave an order to get handkerchiefs, soak them and tie round our mouths and noses. Some managed to do this, others, myself included, didn't owing to a scarcity of the necessary articles . . . It was hopeless to try to stand up against the stuff . . . We just lay in bundles at the bottom of the trench, choking and gasping for breath." McLaren's company was forced back to its reserve trenches, many too weak even to hold let alone fire a rifle. Maxwell-Scott himself, by now "barely conscious," was saved by two of his men who "coaxed, dragged and pushed" him to the rear.

By now German shells were ripping into the Canadian parapets and dugouts. Lance Corporal Jim Keddie of the Forty-eighth Highlanders had "managed to get a mouthful of rum" before the attack began but no sooner had he swallowed it than "the enemy started an attack, beginning with gas. They then began to shell the reserve trenches . . . You could hardly get breath for the concussion!"

Lieutenant Colonel Lipsett, gasping from the gas fumes that had rolled over his headquarters, got off an SOS message to brigade artillery, which began firing on the German lines but could not halt the mass of advancing German troops. The immediate danger was to the Canadians' left flank where a one-hundred-yard gap had opened between the Eighth and Fifteenth Battalions. Lipsett ordered his only reserve—two platoons— to secure the exposed flank. Private Tom Drummond was among them. With the German guns pounding, he thought "all hell" had been let loose: "high explosive, shrapnel, coal boxes, whizz bangs, machine gun fire. Men went down like ninepins and looking around, I found myself and one other man to be the only ones still standing of our platoon . . . We both dived into shell holes and then the nature of the greenish cloud became apparent. Gas! I wet my scarf and wound it about my face, but this did not seem to have much effect, although there is no doubt that it helped." Moving to another shell hole Drummond found two soldiers with "strings of sticky saliva" drooling from their mouths. Peering over the edge he saw other men leaving the line, throwing away their rifles and ripping off clothing as they ran. "Some managed to get halfway to where they were going only to fall writhing to the ground, clutching at their throats, tearing open their shirts in a last struggle for air, and after a while ceasing to struggle and lying still while a greenish foam formed over their mouths and lips."

Five hours after the attack started, German troops had penetrated one thousand yards on a half-mile front to the far right of the Canadian lines and were fanning out to threaten both the Canadians' right and left flank. The history of the German Reussner regiment likened the German advance in which they took part to that of "a fiery steed that can be reined in only with difficulty." A day of ferocious fighting and at times considerable con- fusion followed during which Canadian and British reinforcements were rushed to the front line, Colonel Mordacq's French troops launched an abortive counterattack, and the Germans took Saint-Julien in desperate hand-to-hand fighting, only to be pushed out again. It was also a day during which a significant number of German atrocities were reported. Private Thurgood described how when he and his colleagues surrendered the Germans "started to wipe us out. Three of our men were bayoneted before an officer arrived and saved the rest of us." Even so, Thurgood's captors kicked and beat him with their rifle butts. A major described German troops firing on wounded men "with some sort of projectile that set fire to their clothing." This day too a Canadian sergeant was said to have been found crucified with bayonets on a barn door.

Yet except for those caught in the heart of the chlorine cloud, the effects of the gas had not been as devastating as in the attack of April 22. Only one part of the Canadian line had been forced back and as the gas had begun to disperse most of the Canadian troops had held their ground, allowing time for reinforcements to reach them. By the day's end the Germans had been fought to a standstill and had made only a modest dent in the Allied line. As the official German account acknowledged, their troops had "encountered strong opposition and progressed but slowly."

By now, the city of Ypres and the surrounding countryside "beggared description" according to a seventeen-year-old British private who had enlisted under age in hopes of "adventure": "The Cloth Hall in Ypres itself . . . burning . . . and all the little farms around . . . alight" so that "around the Salient . . . it made as awful a picture of warfare as anyone could imagine." Another soldier marching with British reinforcements to the Salient on the night of April 24–25 as German artillery shelled the city saw the sky become "a whirling and twisting mass of red and yellow flames, and enormous volumes of black smoke. A truly grand and awful spectacle. The tall ruins of the Cloth Hall and the Cathedral were alternately silhouetted or brightly illuminated in the yellow glare of the flames." Another soldier marched through the narrow cobbled streets of a city burning so ferociously "that the men on the flanks had to creep in to the middle to avoid the blistering heat." Elsewhere food rotted on the counters of abandoned cafés, dogs howled, and the stink of burning horse carcasses filled the nostrils. The scenes filled the soldiers with "a terrible sense of decay and desolation." A Canadian officer reflected that "Dante lacked imagination when he wrote *Inferno*. He ought to have ridden with me through Ypres." Gas had blighted the landscape, yellowing grass, shriveling the leaves on the trees and destroying wildlife—birds, rabbits, mice, and hares—and farm animals.

With fragile Allied frontline positions suffering further heavy bombardment as well as infantry attacks, General Smith-Dorrien, commander of the British Second Army, was contemplating an orderly withdrawal within the Salient. However, Sir John French, who was still trying to discover how or whether the French intended to reinforce their positions, ordered him to stay put. The result was two days of futile and exhausting fighting, including on April 26, when French troops arrived to assist yet a further attempt to retake Mauser Ridge by the British whose forces now included reinforcements from the Lahore Division of the British Indian Army—Pathans and Gurkhas among them— recently arrived from India via Hong Kong. As the Allied troops approached the wire protecting the enemy positions, the Germans released gas that was blown by the wind toward them, turning the attack into a scrambled retreat as men fled the engulfing vapor.

German—as well as Allied troops—were becoming increasingly exhausted. Since the first gas attack, von Hügel's men had advanced to within three miles north of Ypres itself while von Kathen's troops had gotten across to the west bank of the Yser Canal. However, though the Germans had taken a large bite out of the northern part of the Salient, "Operation Disinfection" had not delivered the hoped-for breakthrough. In particular, the most recent gas attack had failed to dislodge the Canadians, and Ypres remained in Allied hands. A British soldier summed up the current position nicely. German troops had made

> a huge effort to cut across the Salient and so capture Ypres and probably capture a big slice of the British Army and the situation was desperate. Reinforcements were sent to fill the gap and the effects of the gas gradually wore off. The Canadians distinguished themselves and were largely responsible for holding the line. The Germans did not succeed in gaining their objective but they advanced several kilometres, closing in and making the Salient round Ypres smaller and our positions more hazardous. They could concentrate fire from three sides and some of our positions could be infiltrated and at times we appeared to be shelled from the rear.

Many German officers remained unconvinced about the new weapon. Cavalry commander Rudolf Binding thought "the effects of the successful gas attack were horrible. I am not pleased with the idea of poisoning men.

Of course, the entire world will rage about it first and then imitate us. All the dead lie on their backs with clenched fists; the whole field is yellow."

Though the German army would soon launch further gas attacks around Ypres, toward the end of April Haber returned to Berlin, himself a disappointed man. He would later recall his frustration with the German high command which, focused on its campaign on the eastern front, had treated the gas attacks at Ypres as a sideshow and a "*Versuch*"—experiment. They had failed to provide enough troops to capitalize on the gas attacks and thereby squandered the chance he had given them of making a major breakthrough in the west that could have carried them to the Channel ports. Major General Deimling agreed: "Had we had enough reserves to hand, our troops could have broken through the [Allied] front all the way to Ypres."

The kaiser, though, was delighted when von Falkenhayn told him the results of the first gas attack. He embraced the general three times and promised pink champagne to Colonel Gerhard Tappen, von Falkenhayn's chief of operations and brother of the creator of T-shells. Haber was promoted from sergeant of the reserves to the rank of captain. Though the exact date is unclear, Otto Hahn recalled attending a meal shortly after the Ypres gas attack to celebrate Haber's new status. Another member of the gas fraternity recalled him "proudly appearing among us in his new uniform instead of . . . the military official's uniform that we called his 'pest controller's outfit.' "

On the night of May 1, soon after Haber's return to Berlin, Clara Haber took her husband's army pistol into their garden in Dahlem and shot herself. She left no suicide note; however, she had deplored the idea of using poison gas. James Franck, Haber's collaborator and friend, thought that "the fact that her husband was involved in gas warfare definitely played a part in her suicide." Furthermore, a family friend of the Habers' revealed many years later that shortly before her death Clara had told his own wife of her "despair over the horrible consequences of gas warfare, for which she'd seen the preparations, along with the tests on animals."

Haber himself certainly felt some guilt for Clara's death, writing on June 12, 1915, that he could still hear "the words the poor woman once spoke, and in my weariness I see her head appear between orders and telegrams and I suffer." However, within hours of the discovery of her body, he had boarded a train to the eastern front to superintend the deployment of poison gas against Russian troops west of Warsaw, and he did not attend her funeral.

MEANWHILE, IN THE aftermath of the first attacks, the psychological as well as the physical effects of poison gas were becoming yet clearer. Canadian major Harold Mathews thought it impossible "to give a real idea of the terror and horror spread among us by this filthy loathsome pestilence. Not, I think, the fear of death or anything supernatural but the great dread that we could not stand the fearful suffocation . . . Many of the physically strongest men were more affected than their apparently weaker comrades."

Haber always believed the chief value of gas lay in its ability to inspire fear and uncertainty, undermining the enemy's power to resist by causing him "to imagine defeat." By manipulating "psychological imponderables," gas turned soldiers "from being a sword in the hand of their commander into a heap of despairing people." Compared with weapons like artillery, poison gas caused "more fright and less destruction."

The Allies were considering urgently what else they could do to protect their troops against Haber's new weapon. After the first attack officers were dispatched to Paris to buy gauze, flannel, and elastic to make masks like "mouth protectors" found on captured German soldiers, and Allied medical staff appealed to women in the small towns around Ypres—like the nuns of Poperinghe Convent—to start sewing masks. Gas casualties were evacuated to hospitals in and around Boulogne and their symptoms closely studied. In London, the British War Office asked eminent Scottish physiologist Dr. John Haldane to assess the gas's effects. By April 27 he was at a casualty station at Bailleul in France, near the Belgium border, where he saw "men . . . struggling for breath and blue in the face . . . There was nothing to account for the blueness (cyanosis) and struggle for air, but the one fact that they were suffering from acute bronchitis, such as is caused by the inhalation of an irritant gas." A postmortem confirmed that that one victim had died from "acute bronchitis" and "accompanying slow asphyxiation" caused by an "irritant gas." Having reviewed the available evidence—including examining brass buttons that the gas had turned green—Haldane concluded that the Germans had probably used chlorine or bromine "for the purposes of asphyxiation."

While Dr. Haldane was still preparing his report, which was published on April 29, the gas attacks were, as Rudolf Binding predicted, already being condemned around the world. On April 25, Will Irwin of the *New York Tribune* pointed out that the Hague Conferences had positively banned poison gas—prohibitions that "have prevented the more civilised nations of Europe from going far with experiments in this line." He added that "the gaseous vapour which the Germans used against the French division near Ypres . . . introduces a new element into warfare."

Such opinions were in the majority, but a few U.S. publications suggested gas was a humane weapon. In doing so they followed the line taken in German papers like the *Frankfurter Zeitung* of April 26 which questioned "the serious difference" between conventional explosives "which break to atoms everything living" and gas "which takes effect over a wider area, produces a rapid end and spares the torn bodies the tortures and pains of death." The *Chicago Tribune* of April 28, 1915, carried a cartoon titled "Anaesthetics in Military Operations," depicting marching German troops of the "Chloroform Brigade," "Ether Battalion," and "Twilight Sleep Reserves" and asked "will trenches be taken without casualties on either side . . . ?" The *New York Evening Sun* concluded that Germany's success in developing gas derived from its scientific ingenuity, especially in applied chemistry, and predicted a new type of warfare, "the chemist's battle."

In Ontario, Canada, the *Windsor Evening Record*, spoke of "the terrors of gas" and "the seeming chaos of a new fog of battle" while insisting Canadian troops would fight on "coldly determined and undismayed." A headline in another Canadian paper spoke of "Prehistoric Methods." In France *Le Matin* reminded its readers that deploying poison gas was a breach of the Hague Convention but suggested that, considering German troops had already "burned down villages, shot civilians, slaughtered children and torpedoed merchant vessels without warning," their resort to using gas was only to be expected. Furthermore, the "effects" of poison gas were not as "murderous" as the Germans hoped and less to be feared than machine guns and artillery. Though gas had taken French troops by surprise and caused them to fall back, the Germans would meet stiffer resistance in the future. The newspaper *La Croix* urged "the whole world to combine" to wipe out people who defied international law and "turned war into an unspeakable barbarity." It also asked whether the Germans believed they "had the monopoly" on such weapons of destruction and asserted French scientists could easily outdo their German counterparts except that France "respected the treaties we have signed."

In Britain, Sir John French's account of the first gas attack was published on April 24. He related how the enemy had used "a large number of appliances for the production of asphyxiating gases. The quantity produced indicates long and deliberate preparations for the employment of devices contrary to the terms of the Hague Convention to which the enemy subscribe. The false statements made by the Germans a week ago to the effect that we were using such gases is now explained. It was obviously an effort to diminish neutral criticism in advance." Also on April 24, the *Times* (London) published an official German statement received the previous day: "The [Allied] appeal to the laws of warfare is not to the point. The German troops do not fire any shells the sole purpose of which is the spreading of asphyxiating or poisonous gases, and the gases which do develop on the explosion of German shells are not as dangerous as the gases of the ordinary French, Russian and English artillery shells. Also the smoke-developing contrivances used by us in hand to hand fighting are in no manner contrary to the laws of warfare."

In making this statement the German authorities were arguing that because the Hague Convention on asphyxiating gases was worded as if to ban only projectiles containing them and the chlorine had been released from canisters, their poison gas attack was technically, if not morally, outside the convention's scope. However, in so doing they were ignoring Article 23 of the Hague Convention on land warfare that explicitly supplemented that on asphyxiating gases by banning all "poison or poisoned weapons."

On April 26, a *Times* editorial told readers that

the enemy are fighting with desperation . . . the wholesale employment of asphyxiating gases against the French is a fresh indication of the temper in which the Germans are now waging war. It is to the use of these gases in a manner forbidden by the Hague Convention, which Germany signed, that the retirement of the French on Thursday is attributed. Sir John French speaks of "the large number of appliances for the production of asphyxiating gases" . . . The Germans are thus violating one more of the conventions of civilised warfare upon land, and continuing with ostentation to violate them by the drowning of non-combatants and the sinking of merchant ships without notice at sea.

On April 26 another paper called the gas attacks "but one more instance of the contempt for international law to which the Germans have accustomed the world and in which they persist as long as it is profitable."

The *Times'* medical correspondent who visited gas victims in France wrote, "The Germans are a scientific people. These gases were chosen carefully, tested carefully, and their effects determined by means of experiments upon animals. The terrible sufferings about to be inflicted upon our men were fully understood and had been measured beforehand." Gas was an "atrocious method of warfare . . . This diabolical contrivance will fill all races with a horror of the German name." A letter from a British regular soldier to his sister in April 1915, published in his local paper, stated: "I had a good experience of warfare, so called, but this is not warfare, it is science against science, or deliberate murder."

Such condemnation—and the shock that science could be put to such uses—of course ran counter to Haber's thinking. He believed people criticized gas merely because it challenged orthodox thinking: "The disapproval felt by the knight for the man with a firearm is the same as that of the soldier who fires steel bullets towards the man who adopts chemical weapons." The invention of chemical weapons was a logical step along the path of technological discovery to overcome new challenges such as the evolution of trench warfare, which had made devising ways of driving enemy soldiers from those defenses essential. He was proud that he and Germany—through its preeminence in the chemical industry—had gotten there first. Yet he also argued that the German gas attacks at Ypres were not a new phenomenon but a renewal of an ancient military tradition dating back as far as the Peloponnesian Wars in the fifth century B.C.E. between Athens and Sparta when "smoke and sulphuric acid" were used.

Reporting to Lord Kitchener in London on the first gas attack, Sir John French had written, "Apparently these gases are either chlorine or bromine . . . [I] strongly urge immediate steps to be taken to supply similar means of most effective kind for use by our troops." The war minister had responded that since the use of poison gases was "contrary to the rules and usages of war," before Britain stooped to the level "of the degraded Germans" he must consult his government colleagues. Prime Minister Asquith's cabinet discussed the matter on April 26 during which some members expressed ethical reservations. However, Asquith's handwritten note to the king reporting the cabinet discussion "on the recent resort by the enemy to the use of asphyxiating gases" hinted at the path Britain would follow: "As the gases are apparently stored in and drawn from cylinders, and not projectiles, the employment of them is not perhaps an infraction of the literal terms of the Hague Convention." He was also aware that—as an official had pointed out—"the normally prevailing wind in France is westerly, so that if this form of warfare is to be introduced we, in the long run, shall have an enormous advantage."

As Asquith well knew, in deciding whether to use chemical weapons, Britain faced practical as well as moral and legal problems. In April 1915 the country was producing barely one ton of liquid chlorine a day. Manufacturing an amount equivalent to that the Germans released at Ypres would take months. Therefore, government officials immediately consulted Britain's leading chemical industrialists and scientists to see whether and how quickly production could be stepped up.

On April 28 the War Office appealed in the national press to British women to produce five hundred thousand gas masks, hoping to dispatch the first one hundred thousand to British troops on the western front within the week. Harrods department store displayed samples in their windows and set up counters selling the necessary materials to make masks conforming to War Office requirements:

A face piece (to cover mouth and nostrils) formed of an oblong pad of bleached absorbent cotton-wool . . . covered with three layers of bleached cotton gauze and fitted with a band, to fit round the head and keep the pad in position, consisting of a piece of ½in. cotton elastic 16in. long, attached to the narrow end of the face pad, so as to form a loop with the pad.

Meanwhile, the situation around Ypres remained critical as Allied troops faced further gas attacks. On April 26, during fighting around Saint-Julien Lieutenant Corporal Jack Dorgan of the Northumberland Fusiliers found a group of Canadian soldiers huddled in a reserve trench who told him: "You can't go any further . . . The Germans have released gas and we've had to retire." Crossing the trench Dorgan and his men got no more than a hundred yards when he found himself enveloped in gas: "We'd had no training . . . never heard of the gas business. Our eyes were streaming with water and pain, and all we had was a roll of bandages in the first aid kit . . . So we bandaged each other's eyes and anyone who could see would lead a line of half a dozen or so men, each with his hand on the shoulder of the one in front. In this way lines and lines of British soldiers moved along . . . back towards Ypres."

The next day General Smith-Dorrien reported to Sir John French's chief of staff the recent heavy losses sustained by the Lahore Division and other British troops and his view that unless the French would "make a big push" to regain the ground they had lost "the area East of Ypres will be very difficult to hold, chiefly because the roads approaching it from the west are swept by shell-fire." If no French push was forthcoming he proposed withdrawing his troops to defend a shorter perimeter within the northeastern portion of the Salient. French, long a critic of Smith-Dorrien, informed him he "had abundance of troops" and should act "vigorously with the full means available in cooperation with and assisting the French." Within hours he ordered Smith-Dorrien to relinquish "command of all troops engaged in the present operations about Ypres" to General Herbert Plumer, commander of V Corps.

However, Plumer was, as he wrote to his wife, "in absolute agreement" with Smith-Dorrien "as to what should be done." Furthermore, Sir John

French began to come round to the view that little was to be expected from French troops, and the British should fall back from what had become an untenable position. On April 30, Sir John consulted his subordinate General Sir Douglas Haig, commander of the British First Army, who agreed with him that it was his duty as commander in chief to remove his men from "what was really a death trap."

At eight o'clock on the evening of May 1 the first British troops began to withdraw from their forward positions in the Salient. Meanwhile, men of the British Dorsetshire Regiment dug in around Hill 60 and saw the German troops pulling back from their front lines barely forty yards away. Moments later they came under heavy German bombardment, then saw gas billow from projector pipes. Uncertain what to do, some men huddled in the bottoms of their trenches. Quick thinkers who realized that gas was heavier than air, leaped onto the fire steps. Meeting heavy rifle fire from the Dorsets, German troops advancing behind the gas faltered, allowing British support troops to rush forward. At the same time, British planes dropped improvised "bombs" like jam tins filled with nails and gun cotton on the enemy.

During the intense and bloody fighting, Private Edward Warner of the Bedfordshire Regiment, despite being gassed, cleared a trench of infiltrating Germans and then succeeded in holding it almost single-handedly to win the Victoria Cross. For the first time a German gas attack failed to capture any new ground. The British would hold on to Hill 60 until May 6, though at a cost, including Private Warner, who died from the effects of the chlorine. "Clean killing is at least comprehensible" wrote an officer, "but this murder by slow agony absolutely knocks me. The whole civilized world ought to rise up and exterminate those swine across the hill."

CHAPTER ELEVEN

"Solomon's Temple"

THE MORNING OF May 1, the day of the German gas attacks on Hill 60 in Flanders, dawned gray and drizzly in New York. When over breakfast people opened their copies of the *New York Times* they found—on the very page where Cunard was announcing the departure that day of "The Fastest and Largest Steamer Now in Atlantic Service" (the *Lusitania*)—a small insert, framed in black:

NOTICE!

Travellers intending to embark on the
Atlantic voyage are reminded that a state of war
exists between Germany and her allies and Great
Britain and her allies; that the zone of war
includes the waters adjacent to the British Isles;
that, in accordance with formal notice given by
the Imperial German Government, vessels flying
the flag of Great Britain, or of any of her allies,
are liable to destruction in those waters and that
travellers sailing in the war zone on ships of Great
Britain or her allies do so at their own risk.

IMPERIAL GERMAN EMBASSY
Washington D. C. April 21 1915

This was the warning that some weeks earlier his government had instructed German ambassador Count von Bernstorff to place in the American press. Although it did not refer to the *Lusitania* specifically, the threat to the pride of Britain's merchant fleet seemed obvious and those due to sail on her wondered what to do. With the ship scheduled to depart at ten A.M., many passengers were already on their way to Cunard's Pier 54 at the foot of Fourteenth Street when they learned of the warning. Together with newspapermen they clustered around Cunard's general manager, Bostonian Charles Sumner, on the pier. He assured them there was no danger: "The fact is that the *Lusitania* . . . is too fast for any submarine. No German vessel of war can get near her."

With four boiler rooms containing a total of twenty-five boilers providing steam to four giant steam turbines, the *Lusitania* was indeed fast. At full power, her turbine blades produced seventy thousand horsepower to turn four quadruple screw propellers that pushed her through the water at a top speed of twenty-five knots. What Sumner failed to mention was that on this next voyage the six boilers of boiler room number four would not be operating, reducing her maximum speed to twenty-one knots. This was a wartime economy measure since when running at top speed the *Lusitania* consumed nearly twenty trainloads of coal—six thousand tons— in a single Atlantic crossing and required sixty-five thousand gallons of water per minute to cool her engines.

However, at this stage in the war no ship traveling at faster than fourteen knots had been torpedoed and Sumner assured anxious passengers that the British Admiralty would take "mighty good care" of the *Lusitania* and "there was absolutely nothing to fear." Most believed him and only a few altered their bookings to ships belonging to neutral countries. The American Line's *New York*, with actress Ellen Terry and avant-garde dancer Isadora Duncan aboard, and Holland-Amerika's *Rotterdam* were both sailing that day for England. However, neither could match the *Lusitania* for comfort or speed. When the *Lusitania* sailed she would be carrying 1,257 passengers—her largest eastbound complement since the start of the war—including 198 citizens of the neutral United States.

The warning also unsettled the 702-strong crew. A superstitious sailor seized the peacock-feathered hat of a newly wed passenger as she came aboard and flung it into the sea, telling her that peacock feathers spelled bad luck. The news of the warning soon spread below decks to the stewards and stewardesses preparing the cabins; the cooks and scullions like sixteen-year-old George Wynne from Liverpool and his semi-invalid father Joseph, cutting up vegetables in the galley, and the bellboys, like fifteen-year-old Ben Holton, who had amused themselves the previous night electrocuting rats in the hold but were now hurrying around the ship in their brass-buttoned uniforms delivering messages. It also reached the trimmers and firemen of the "black gang" who had been laboring all night to raise steam—the trimmers bringing coal from the huge longitudinal bunkers that, like those of the elderly cruisers *Aboukir*, *Hogue*, and *Cressy* sunk by the *U-9* in the early days of the war, ran the length of the ship and the firemen, working stripped to the waist and wearing clogs to protect their feet from the showers of hot ash, as they stoked the boiler furnaces. Now, sweaty and grimy though they were, some of the "black gang" left their posts seven decks below the bridge to come up and see what was happening.

The *Lusitania*'s captain, fifty-eight-year-old Liverpool-born William Turner, was phlegmatic—talk of torpedoing his ship was "the best joke I've heard in many days." He had some experience. Earlier that year while captaining the Cunarder *Transylvania*, he had escaped a pursuing U-boat and believed he had outrun another on the *Lusitania*'s last voyage to New York.

As the time for departure approached the quayside became a jostling mass of passengers and porters as well as reporters eager for a good story and photographers ready to snatch a good shot of departing celebrities. Among the latter was rakish millionaire Alfred Gwynne Vanderbilt, who was traveling to England to attend a board meeting of the International Horse Show Association and to donate a fleet of vehicles to the British Red Cross. Four years earlier the tall, elegant Vanderbilt had married his second wife, heiress Margaret Emerson McKim, after settling out of court with her then husband who had threatened to sue him for alienation of affection.

Security men also mingled with the crowds, not just because of the warning but because the U.S. and British authorities suspected that New

York's docks, from which 80 percent of ships bound from the United States to Britain departed, had been infiltrated by German agents planning to sabotage ships carrying American-manufactured war matériel to Britain. Despite their efforts, in all the upheaval at least three German spies slipped aboard the *Lusitania* that morning and concealed themselves.

Just after twelve twenty P.M., because of delays caused by last-minute arrivals of forty extra passengers and their baggage from the Anchor Line's *Cameronia*, which was to be requisitioned by the British Admiralty—and according to press speculation was to sail to Halifax, Nova Scotia, to take on troops and supplies for England—and a last-minute visit to the ship by Captain Turner's actress niece, tugs at last backed the *Lusitania* out into the Hudson. The earlier rain had cleared and in bright sunshine spectators on the quayside waved, flung confetti, and then covered their ears as the "Big Lusy's" foghorn sounded three mighty blasts. At one end of the deck the ship's band played "Tipperary" while at the other a Welsh male voice choir sang "The Star-Spangled Banner." Photographs taken as the *Lusitania* slipped away show a group of young women, thought to be volunteer Red Cross nurses on their way to the western front, crowding the rail clutching American flags.

As the ship nosed past Sandy Hook out into the Atlantic, those on deck saw the three camouflage-painted British warships hovering just outside American territorial waters to keep watch on marine traffic arriving in and leaving New York and in particular to ensure that German liners interned there did not escape. Two of the three were purpose-built warships. However the third—the *Caronia*—had been a Cunard passenger vessel until the start of the war when the Admiralty requisitioned her into the navy and mounted guns on her deck to make her an armed merchant cruiser. Some seamen rowed from the *Caronia* with mailbags for the *Lusitania* to carry to England. A sailor on the *Caronia*'s deck took a last photo of the departing liner.

FIVE DAYS EARLIER, a German intelligence report had been issued from Berlin detailing the movements of enemy merchant ships for the information of U-boat crews and other naval staff. One entry read:

1 May: Lusitania (Cunard), English, 30,396 tons, in passage to Liverpool, expected around 8 May

On the day before the *Lusitania* sailed, the submarine *U-20* left the German naval base of Emden near Wilhelmshaven on the North Sea. The *U-20* belonged to the Third U-boat Half-Flotilla together with two other submarines—the *U-27*—due to sail several days later, and the *U-30*, which had already departed. In addition to intelligence reports, the formal orders to all three from their commander, Hermann Bauer, read: "Large English troop transports expected starting from Liverpool, Bristol Channel, Dartmouth . . . Get to station on fastest possible route around Scotland. Hold as long as supplies permit . . . attack transport ships, merchant ships and warships." More specifically, the *U-27* was to head for the Bristol Channel, the *U-30* for Dartmouth, while the *U-20*, under her commander Kapitän-Leutnant Walther Schwieger, was to make for the approaches to Liverpool, the *Lusitania*'s home port.

The thirty-year-old Berlin-born Schwieger had commanded the *U-20* since the previous December and had become much respected by his men for his competence, courage, and concern for their safety. His submarine was one of the new generation powered by MAN of Augsburg's advanced diesel engines and commissioned in 1913. She could travel at fifteen knots on the surface and nine knots when submerged. Her armaments were one three-and-a-half-inch deck gun and four eighteen-inch torpedo tubes, two fore and two aft. She carried seven torpedoes, each with a 350-pound charge of trotyl—a newly developed TNT-type explosive.

Despite her technical sophistication, living conditions for the *U-20*'s crew of four officers and thirty-one men as well as for Schwieger's dachshund were cramped. The submarine was only 210 feet long while the width between her ribs was a mere 20 feet. Supplies packed every spare space, with sausages wedged next to grenades. Most of the crew slept in hammocks—only a few had bunks. Even then, the bunk was not necessarily all their own since crewmen took turns using them depending on their duty rosters. Sometimes they had to share with equipment too. A submariner on the *U-20* recalled how "when the boat was fully loaded there was one torpedo more than there was place for. I accommodated it in my bunk. I slept beside it. I had it lashed in place at the outside of the narrow bunk, and it kept me from falling out of bed when the boat did some of its fancy rolling. At first I was kept awake a bit by the thought of having so much TNT in bed with me. Then I got used to it."

Living in such confined conditions sometimes for months at a time was stressful. The air grew foul—"enough to give you a headache that you would never get over." With little water to spare for washing, men stank of sweat and oil fumes. They wore the same leather clothes, sometimes for weeks, and hardly shaved, becoming in the words of one submariner as bearded and shaggy-haired as "the real pirates of old days." Lack of fresh food, fresh air, and exercise wore them down. Constipation was a particular problem. Officers doled out castor oil to sufferers who then had to negotiate the U-boat's complicated WCs, or "internal heads." These operated on a system of valves and levers that blew the contents back in the user's face if he made a mistake. "Getting your own back," submariners called it.

The crew were also often damp. Bilge water slopped about while, since the internal temperature of a U-boat exceeded that of the seawater outside, "the moisture in the air condensed on the steel plates and formed drops which had a very disconcerting way of dripping on the face of a sleeper." The men protected themselves with waterproof clothing or rubber sheets, but "it was really like living in a damp cellar." Sailors woke up choking "with considerable mucus in the nose and frequently a so-called 'oil-head.'"

Claus Bergen, a German war artist seconded to the U-boat service, described what happened on the order to dive, *"Alarm! Tauchen!"* The deck emptied immediately as men rushed for the open hatchway to hurl themselves down the steel ladder. The captain stood in the conning tower as the heavy hatch was swung shut over his head. As soon as a bell signaled that the hatch was sealed, crewmen spun the wheels and levers to open vents, allowing seawater to pour into the diving tanks and the boat's pumps to expel the air from them. Gradually the boat tipped forward and the interior took on a spectral quality. "In the dim glow of the electric light, a mystic modulation of various shades of grey, stands a figure enclosed in a narrow iron space, surrounded by all manner of levers and wheels, on a sort of pedestal, connected with the periscope that can be raised and lowered like a lift . . . . the commander."

Peering through the glass of a small side porthole men saw "foaming masses of water crashing over our bows . . . Then a confusion of bright foam and clear water, inaudible, fantastic, outside the glass: light grey, dark grey, the deep water grows ever darker and more calm." They were enchanted by "the magical green light" and the air bubbles sparkling over the hull. If a U-boat came to rest on the ocean floor, shoals of fish, ordinarily frightened away by the noise of the propellers, were lured by the electric lights and would "stare at us with goggling eyes close to the windows in the turret."

To surface, the chief engineer blew out the diving tanks with compressed air and the boat rose to an "infernal din of hissing, roaring water." The bow and the gun emerged first but soon the whole deck was clear, dripping with seawater. Strips of golden yellow seaweed dangled from the steel hawsers. At the welcome opening of the hatch fresh sea air streamed in and very soon the diesel engines began to throb. Surfacing was a relief but also essential. The batteries that powered a submerged U-boat's electric motors needed frequent recharging which was only possible on the surface using the power of the main diesel (or petrol) engine to do so.

U-boatmen never forgot the "peculiar thrill and nervous sensation" of standing for the first time in the conning tower as the submarine submerged, or the anxiety of wondering whether all the valves and hatches had been properly closed and whether the U-boat's steel hull could withstand the pressure. They found it hard to escape the feeling of being caught in "a gigantic mouse-trap." Running beneath the surface, the crew were blind to "advancing ships, derelicts or projecting rocks." They had to trust their commander at the periscope. If he did sight a ship he had only moments to decide whether to dive or to attack, knowing that his periscope could easily be spotted by a ship's lookout in the crow's nest. If the submarine hit a mine or was rammed, death was almost inevitable. A German submariner described opening a U-boat salvaged after striking a mine: "A burst of choking poisonous air poured out, and the sight of the corpses was terrible . . . What scenes of horror and madness had been enacted in that narrow cabin! The scratches on the steel walls, the corpses' torn finger-nails, the blood-stains on their clothes and on the walls, bore all too dreadful witness." What he saw brought home that "death in a plunging submarine was as evil a fate as the imagination could conjure."

On April 30, as the *U-20* put out into the North Sea, one issue Schwieger knew he would face was which route to take to the Irish Sea and Liverpool. British naval patrols, mines, and wire nets had made the shortest, and therefore fastest, route via the Dover Straits too hazardous. Consequently, as his orders required, he would first have to sail around the coast of northern Scotland, then decide between taking the faster but riskier North Channel between Britain and Ireland or the longer but safer route down and around the west coast of Ireland. As the *U-20* passed the Borkum Reef Lightship, Schwieger's radio officer Otto Rikowski tested his equipment by sending two messages and found the signal quality good. The *U-20* was able to remain in contact up to five hundred miles from its base. However, Schwieger and his crew could not know that in the Admiralty's Room 40 the British, using the captured German naval codes, were reading every message.

ABOARD THE *LUSITANIA*, passengers settled down to what promised to be a crossing in perfect weather. The suites and cabins of those fortunate enough to be traveling first class —only 290 compared to the ship's 540 capacity—were located amidships where least movement was felt in rough seas. The suites were in every style from Georgian to Empire and fitted out in gleaming walnut, sycamore, satinwood, and mahogany. Their open fire-places and curtained windows in place of portholes conveyed the impression that guests were not at sea at all but in a grand country house—or even a palace. The private drawing room of one of the two Regal Suites was mod-eled on a salon in the French château of Fontainebleau while its white-and-gold-paneled dining room evoked Marie Antoinette's Petit Trianon at Versailles.

Occupants of the suites included Alfred Vanderbilt, who the night before sailing had been in the audience of *A Celebrated Case* on Broadway—a coproduction of David Belasco and impresario Charles Frohman, also aboard the *Lusitania*. Unlike Vanderbilt, Frohman pre-ferred to keep to his suite, which he had equipped with a portable gramophone so he could listen to his favorite song, "Alexander's Ragtime Band." He relied on a walking stick and when he did venture around the ship he could use the first-class elevators decorated with Renaissance-style gilded rosettes and medallions rather than have to climb the stairs.

Also traveling in first class were Lady Mackworth—a former militant suffragette— and her Welsh coal magnate father David Thomas; Marie de Page, the king and queen of Belgium's special envoy to the United States, where she had raised more than one hundred thousand dollars for the Belgian Red Cross; spiritualist and architect Theodate Pope from Connecticut; Boston bookseller Charles Lauriat and Surgeon Major Warren Pearl, who had served as a United States Army surgeon during the Spanish-American War. Pearl had been instructed to report to the American embassy in London and was accompanied by his wife, four children, and two nurses. Marie de Page's husband, Antoine, was the medical director of a nurse-training hospital in occupied Brussels where the matron was an Englishwoman named Edith Cavell. Together with the other first-class passengers she and the Pearls dined in a domed, double-tiered dining saloon decorated in white and gilt in the style of Louis XVI where glistening caviar, served with wafer-thin toast, juicy oysters on beds of crushed ice, and classic dishes like beef Wellington and Dover sole were offered. Lanson and Perrier Jouet champagnes were on the wine list, though the war had pushed up prices, but "enemy" drinks like German lager and Austrian wines and mineral water were no longer served. The Pearls and their fellow passengers read or wrote letters in the gray-and-cream silk brocade–hung Adam-style writing room and library while their children played in a well-equipped nursery and had their own dining parlor decorated in eighteenth-century French style "like the adults" but "advisedly simpler."

The *Lusitania's* spacious second-class cabins were toward the stern and equipped with mahogany washstands and soft woolen hangings that could be pulled around the berths for privacy. The second-class section was designed for a maximum of 460 but on this voyage some 600 passengers had been squeezed in, necessitating two sittings for every meal served in the sixty-foot-long Georgian-style dining room. A typical dinner menu featured dishes such as roast gosling Normande, braised ham with Madeira sauce, fillets of plaice in a white wine sauce followed by puddings, cheese, nuts, and fruit. Passengers like Professor Ian Holbourn, writer and laird of the tiny Scottish island of Foula, returning from a lecture tour in America, and young English medical student Dick Prichard relaxed in a gray-and-rose-hued Louis XVI–style saloon and promenaded open decks linked to those of first class by a gangway.

The third-class section toward the bows was, by contrast, relatively empty with only 367 occupying cabins designed to hold twelve hundred—Cunard had always made the bulk of its profits from the "steerage" passengers. Though plain and utilitarian, the cabins were better fitted and larger than on other ships, with crisply laundered sheets and toilets that flushed automatically—a precaution dreamed up by the *Lusitania*'s designers in case third-class passengers did not know how to flush. Plentiful meals were served in a large dining hall at long tables lined with steel-legged, wooden-backed chairs, ten to a side. Many traveling third class on *Lusitania* reckoned they had never eaten so well in their lives before with large cooked breakfasts, a substantial midday "dinner" of roasts, pies, and puddings and a "tea" with plates of mutton chops, sausages, and fish cakes.°

Among those now enjoying the meals in third class was fifty-two-year-old twice-widowed Elizabeth Duckworth. She had been employed as a weaver in a cotton mill in Taftville, Connecticut, but had felt a strong desire to return to her roots in Lancashire in the northwest of England. Also traveling in third class was Annie Williams, a recent emigrant from England to the United States whose husband John had deserted her and their six children immediately on arrival. She was returning home in hopes of tracking him down.

Regular transatlantic travelers like Theodate Pope sensed from the start that the atmosphere on board was unusually subdued. Reminders of the war were everywhere from the Red Cross collecting boxes around the ship to the *Cunard Daily Bulletin* reporting Germany's "lavish use of gases against the British." Tactfully it made no mention of U-boats but people

---

° On the *Lusitania*'s maiden voyage passengers in all classes and crew had consumed forty thousand eggs, four thousand pounds of fresh fish, two tons of bacon and ham, four thousand pounds of coffee, one thousand pineapples, five hundred pounds of grapes, one thousand lemons, twenty-five thousand pounds of meat, nearly three thousand gallons of milk, over five hundred gallons of cream, and thirty thousand loaves of bread.

could not forget the German warning. As soon as she came aboard, one young woman "looked about and mentally decided upon the place to make for in the event of any incident."

Twelve-year-old Avis Dolphin, traveling in second class to school in England in the care of two nurses, thought the *Lusitania* "like a floating palace" but was nervous about the German warning that she had heard the adults discussing. Professor Holbourn noticed her lying seasick and home-sick in a deck chair. Missing his own young family, he befriended her. When she confessed her fears about U-boats he promised that if any attack hap-pened he would find her wherever she was on the ship and rescue her.

Professor Holbourn was among the few passengers to consider prac-ticalities in the event of a U-boat attack. He thought it only common sense that people should know how to put on their life jackets, but when he suggested an exercise to other passengers, a deputation came to him asking him not to talk about the possibility of trouble for fear of upsetting the women. He nicknamed them "the Ostrich Club." Holbourn was also critical of Captain Turner's reluctance to hold a passenger lifeboat drill because it might "cause panic or worry." The passengers were not even assigned to specific lifeboats. The only drills were for the crew. Though held daily, they seemed to Holbourn to be a perfunctory formality. Eight crew members lined up in front of one of the heavy wooden lifeboats and after an officer inspected them "climbed up the davits into the boat; they then stood for a moment in the boat with oars dressed, and immediately sat down ready for the boat to be launched." At a further command they jumped back onto the deck.

Oliver Bernard, a young British theatrical designer traveling in first class, shared Holbourn's concerns about the cursory crew drills, noting that no attempt was made to lower the boats. He wondered what would happen if the lifeboats had to be launched fully loaded and in difficult conditions. However, unlike on the *Titanic* there were enough lifeboats for all, both crew and passengers, should the worst happen. The *Lusitania*'s twenty-two wooden clinker-built boats suspended from davits could hold 1,322 while her twenty-six wooden and canvas-sided collapsible boats, mostly stowed beneath them, could carry a further 1,283. There were also plenty of life jackets—bulky, fiber-filled "Boddy's Patent Jackets."

Some passengers were interested to know whether the ship was mounting guns and what she might be carrying. Michael Byrne, an American in first class, searched for guns on the first day at sea, inspecting every deck above the waterline, but could find none. The *Lusitania's* relatively limited cargo space, located near the bows on the orlop and lower decks, was of course off limits to passengers. When asked what the *Lusitania* had in the hold, crew members replied "general cargo." This was true according to the one-page manifest sworn by Captain Turner the day before the *Lusitania* sailed for submission to the New York customs authorities. However, four days after the *Lusitania* had left New York, Cunard staff handed to the New York customs authorities a twenty-four page hand-written "Supplemental Manifest." It detailed eighty consignments including cheese, beef, lard, and bacon as well as furs, confectionery, bales of leather, automobile parts, dental goods, crates of books, sewing machines, wool, beeswax, and a case of oil paintings belonging to first-class passenger Sir Hugh Lane, director of the National Gallery of Ireland. Although not specified in the manifest, the paintings reputedly included works by Rembrandt, Monet, and Rubens.

The Supplemental Manifest, a summary of which would be published in New York on May 8, also listed a significant amount of war matériel: 4,200 cases of Remington rifle cartrideges, packed one thousand to a box; 1,250 boxes of empty shrapnel shells—powder, propellant charge, and fuse were to be fitted in Britain—and eighteen cases of fuses (both shells and fuses supplied by the Bethlehem Steel Company); a large amount of aluminum powder and fifty cases of bronze powder. In monetary terms, over half the *Lusitania's* cargo consisted of munitions for the Allies' war effort. According to a U.S. Treasury official, "practically all of her cargo was contraband of some kind" in the sense that, had the ship been stopped by a German vessel and boarded, the Germans would have been entitled to impound or destroy most of the contents in her hold. However, the carriage of all the war matériel in the manifest, including small-arms ammunition and empty shell cases, was perfectly legal under U.S. law. Since May 1911, following extensive testing by both manufacturers and the military, including exposure to severe shock and direct flame, the Department of Commerce and Labor had permitted small-arms ammunition to be carried on passenger ships. The cases of small-arms ammunition and fuses now in the *Lusitania*'s hold were accordingly all stamped "non-explosive in bulk."

AS THE *LUSITANIA* sailed eastward, U-boats were making their presence felt in the war zone declared by Germany around the British Isles. On the day the liner left New York, a U-boat torpedoed the American oil tanker *Gulflight* off the Isles of Scilly near the southern entrance to the Irish Channel and in the waters for which the *Lusitania* was now making. However, the British authorities were taking the danger the *Lusitania* might be in rather lightly. Cunard chairman Sir Alfred Booth only learned of the German threat the day after the *Lusitania* had sailed and only then from his newspaper. Charles Sumner, his general manager in New York, had not bothered to send a cable to the Cunard headquarters. Booth's initial reaction was that there was no reason to believe "the ship was in any serious danger of being sunk." In mid-April Cunard had briefed its captains about how to respond to the submarine menace: within the danger zone watertight doors were to be closed, boats swung out, portholes closed, and the ship darkened. Ships bound for Liverpool were not to wait to take on a pilot at the Mersey Bar but to head straight in. In the event of any specific risk to the *Lusitania* on this voyage, Booth was certain the Admiralty would issue special instructions to Captain Turner and send a naval escort to bring the ship safely home.

The British and American press were similarly sanguine. The *Daily Telegraph* derided the German warning as "Berlin's latest bluff" which had been "Ridiculed in America." Beneath bold headlines: THE INEFFECTIVE BLOCKADE—NEW TRICKS TO FRIGHTEN AMERICANS—LUSITANIA WARNED, the *Times* (London) assured its readers that "the manoeuvre is simply an ill-timed and excessively impertinent effort, begotten probably of the failure of the submarine blockade, to advertise German frightfulness." The *American Tribune* of May 2 stated, "No big passenger steamer has yet been sunk."

Wesley Frost, U.S. consul in Queenstown (now Cobh) on the southeast coast of Ireland, where the *Lusitania* had in the past called in to pick up or deposit passengers and on one occasion when diverted there because of U-boat danger, also thought the warning hollow: "The reference to the *Lusitania* was obvious enough but personally it never entered my mind for a moment that the Germans would actually perpetrate an attack upon her. The culpability of such an act seemed too blatant and raw . . . In addition, I did not believe that the submarines had yet shown any striking power equal to the task of attacking and destroying a ship as huge, well-built and fast as the *Lusitania*."

Meanwhile, aboard the *Lusitania*, passengers learned that three men thought to be Germans had been found hiding in a steward's pantry during a routine check for stowaways. The ship's detective, Liverpudlian William Pierpoint, interrogated them through an interpreter. Finding that they were indeed German, he ordered them to be locked up in cells beneath the waterline so they could be questioned properly on arrival in Liverpool. The rumor among the passengers was that the trio were spies or saboteurs. Otherwise why travel clandestinely to a country with whom their nation was at war?

By May 5, with the *Lusitania* nearing the war zone, the *U-20* was rounding the southern tip of Ireland after Schwieger had decided not to take the North Channel but to sail down the west coast of Ireland. The previous days had proved eventful for the *U-20*. On May 2, forty miles off Peterhead on Britain's northeast coast, Schwieger had dived to avoid six British destroyers sailing toward him "in a broad searching line." By May 3 the *U-20* was in the North Atlantic where in fading light, Schwieger spotted a small steamer. The British ruse of disguising their ships as neutrals was now well known. His experienced pilot Lanz was convinced it was a British vessel from Leith despite the neutral flag—that of Denmark—she was flying. Schwieger ordered an attack but the torpedo stuck in its tube, a common problem. From February to September 1915 nearly two thirds of German torpedo attacks failed through faulty triggers, defective steering mechanisms, or dud warheads with the risk that a torpedo that failed to launch might explode in its tube.

On May 4, off Black Rock Light on Ireland's northwestern point, Schwieger spotted another ship—"Swedish. *Hibernia* with neutral markings, no flag." He ordered the *U-20* to dive but the *Hibernia* passed too close for him to launch "a clean bow shot." On May 5, hoping for better luck he entered the Irish Channel to find thick fog and gave the order to dive. When he surfaced some hours later, he was relieved to discover the weather better, though still a little misty. Toward evening, nearing the Old Head of Kinsale, a small schooner, the *Earl of Lathom*, came in view. At 132 tons she was too small to be any danger so, obeying the Cruiser Rules, Schwieger challenged and stopped her, then allowed her crew to abandon ship before sinking her. However, later that same evening he attacked without warning a much larger three-thousand-ton steamer he again suspected was British despite her neutral markings. His torpedo missed, and fearing its trail of bubbles would betray the submarine's presence, Schwieger "ran away to avoid the danger of being fired upon."

By now, the *U-20* had been at sea for five days and provided the British Admiralty with ample evidence of her presence. They had intercepted all her early radio messages and at ten P.M. on May 5 learned of the attack on the *Earl of Lathom* from Vice Admiral Sir Charles Coke, naval commander in Queenstown near Kinsale. At ten thirty P.M. Coke began warning all ships at regular intervals: "Submarines active off south coast of Ireland."

The following day, May 6, Schwieger enjoyed further success. Off the Waterford coast the *U-20* sank the six-thousand-ton Liverpool steamer *Candidate*, whose name had been painted out and which was flying no flag, and later that day her sister ship the *Centurion*, torpedoing both ships without warning. He attempted to sink without warning a sixteen-thousand-ton passenger steamer, again with no visible markings, which he identified correctly as the White Star Liner the *Arabic*, but she was too quick for him. Then, according to the *U-20*'s war diary, Schwieger submerged and headed further out to sea while he considered what to do. He was some twenty miles south of the Coningbeg Lightship and his orders from his commander Hermann Bauer were to make for the approaches to Liverpool. He still had three of his original seven torpedoes but was under standing orders to save at least two for the return voyage.

The war diary records Schwieger making a momentous decision—not to sail to his "true field of operations," Liverpool. One stated reason was the weather. The fog of the past two days seemed unlikely to clear fully, which would force him to submerge often or risk being run down in these busy shipping lanes. Such conditions would make it difficult to attack troop transports which would be likely to slip out at night under cover of the fog, perhaps with a naval destroyer escort. Another reason the diary cites was that sailing to Liverpool would leave insufficient fuel to return to Germany around the south and west of Ireland, forcing the *U-20* to take the more hazardous North Channel between England and Ireland. Schwieger therefore decided to remain in the southern Irish Channel, attacking steamers until *U-20* had used up 40 percent of her fuel. Then he would begin his return journey to Emden, retracing his outbound route. That night he ordered his crew to make for the open sea where the *U-20* could surface and recharge her batteries unobserved.

At seven fifty-two that same evening bellboy Ben Holton handed the *Lusitania*'s Captain William Turner a message. It was one of the warnings of U-boat activity that Coke had been broadcasting for nearly twenty-four hours but the first that the *Lusitania* had received. The message—"Submarines active off south coast of Ireland"—seemed so terse and also so vague that Turner wondered whether part had been lost in transmission. He at once asked one of the ship's Marconi operators to tap out a request in Morse for the transmission to be repeated. A few minutes later, a message arrived identical to the first. However, soon after at eight thirty P.M. came a further message from the Admiralty, this time in code: "To all British ships 0005: Take Liverpool pilot at bar and avoid headlands. Pass harbours at full speed. Steer mid-channel course. Submarines off Fastnet."

Turner pondered the implications for his ship, now some 370 miles, or eighteen hours' sailing time, from the Fastnet Rock landfall. In the circumstances, he was even less in the mood than usual for socializing with his passengers whom he routinely if privately dismissed as a group of "bloody monkeys." However, the traditional passengers' talent concert in aid of the Seamen's Charities was taking place that night in the first-class saloon and his presence was expected. The concert was the last important social event of the voyage and, among the rich, a pretext for some final lavish entertaining. New York wine merchant George Kessler, known as the "Champagne King," was once again urging cocktails on his guests, including Boston bookseller Charles Lauriat, the formidable Theodate Pope, and Staff Captain John Anderson who undertook the main burden of the social responsibilities Turner so disliked. Charles Frohman was entertaining the theatrical set on board including his friend actress Rita Jolivet as well as Alfred Vanderbilt, who had just received an affectionate radio message from a woman named May Barwell in England: "Hope you have a safe crossing. Look forward very much to seeing you soon."

However, arriving at the concert, Oliver Bernard thought most passengers were still keeping to themselves and that "a submarine would have at least socialized the audience." During the interval Captain Turner stepped forward and told his passengers of the submarine warning, assuring them that "on entering the war zone tomorrow we shall be securely in the care of the Royal Navy" and that "of course there is no need for alarm." The next day he would steam at full speed so as to arrive at Liverpool in good time. He requested male passengers not to light their cigarettes or cigars on deck that night.

The concert continued, but as soon as the small ship's orchestra wound up with "God Save the King" and "America," passengers anxiously discussed the captain's news. Munitions manufacturer Isaac Lehmann decided not to go to bed but to remain "dressed all night" in his stateroom on the upper deck. Some passengers, too nervous to spend the night in their cabins at all, slept in the public rooms. Others walked on deck to calm their nerves. That night in Scotland, Professor Holbourn's wife had what she described as "a waking vision." Going to bed about eleven, she was not yet asleep when she saw "a large vessel sinking with a big list from side to side and also from stem to stern. There was a crush of frightened people, some of them slipping and sliding down the sloping decks. I thought it strange that I could be seeing this while I was wide awake, and I stretched my arms out of bed and clenched and unclenched my fingers to make sure that I was not dreaming!"

CHAPTER TWELVE

"They Got Us This Time,
All Right"

PASSENGERS WOKE NEXT morning, May 7, to the mournful sounds of the *Lusitania*'s foghorn and to find the ship sailing slowly through dense mist. The noise worried some like Oliver Bernard who "could not understand the policy of announcing a liner's whereabouts to friend and foe alike." A few began planning what to do if a U-boat attacked. One group of men agreed that "in view of the number of women and children on board" no man could honorably get away by lifeboat. These should be left to the women. They themselves would meet on the poop deck below the boat deck to see how best they could save themselves. Surgeon Major Warren Pearl, concerned about his young family, ensured that his wife and their two nurses, Alice Lines and Greta Lorenson, "had been drilled as to what to do in an emergency."

However, by ten A.M. the fog was lifting and ship's lookouts saw "the loom of the land through the haze." By midday the sun was shining brightly and the visibility good enough for Captain Turner to identify familiar landmarks along the Irish coast. Having earlier dropped the ship's speed to fifteen knots, he ordered the engine room to bring it back up to eighteen knots.

The sight of the coast of Ireland "in the sunshine of an ideal early summer day" reassured some but not Charles Lauriat who reflected that "if a German submarine really meant business" the conditions—"light wind, a smooth sea, and bright sunshine"—could not have been more ideal.

Others worried about the ship's continuing slow speed. To Mabel Henshaw, an English emigrant who had settled in Saskatoon and was taking her baby Constance home to England to show her family, it was as if the *Lusitania* were saying to the enemy, "Here I am, do your darndest." Oliver Bernard also felt that Turner was calling the bluff of the German newspaper warnings. He noted how "the general feeling . . . that morning was . . . patient expectation, that when the fog lifted the *Lusitania* would at last give some demonstration of speed to meet the potential danger she now faced."

Yet as the *Lusitania* sailed on across a pancake-smooth, deep-cobalt sea nothing changed. Was Captain Turner "waiting for something to happen, perhaps for an escort?" wondered some, recalling how at the concert Turner had promised that on entering the war zone they would be safely in the care of the Royal Navy. Scanning the empty seas they saw no sign of warships. Turner, however, had a quite different reason for not running at full speed. He was planning to cross the final stretch of the Irish Sea in darkness, timing his arrival at the Mersey Bar for two or three hours before high tide at six fifty-three A.M. This would enable him to sail straight over the bar into the harbor without waiting for a pilot and thus avoid delaying in notoriously submarine-infested waters.

Shortly after eleven A.M. that morning, Turner received a message relayed by the Valentia station from naval headquarters in Queenstown in the Admiralty's Merchant Vessel (MV) code. It read simply: "QUESTOR". Meaning "Which edition of the MV code do you have?" The *Lusitania* replied "WESTRONA," meaning "I have the first edition of the MV code." Having established this, the Valentia station quickly transmitted a coded warning. "Submarines active in southern part Irish Channel; last heard of twenty miles south of Coningbeg Lightship." The Valentia station had been ordered to "make certain the *Lusitania* gets this."

On entering the war zone, in line with Admiralty guidance Turner had ordered the *Lusitania*'s portholes and all watertight doors not necessary for the operation of the ship to be closed. He sent stewards to check the portholes were indeed shut in all the suites and cabins but some passengers later opened theirs again. The hydraulically operated doors in the engine rooms had to be left open to allow the ship to function but could be quickly closed from the bridge in an emergency. As also suggested by the Admiralty, Turner had doubled the lookouts and posted two quartermasters on either side of the bridge "to look out for submarines." He had also ordered the engine room to be ready "to give her full speed" and "to keep the highest steam they could possibly get" on the nineteen operational boilers; however, he did not order the six boilers in the fourth engine room to be fired.

As the morning drew on, tension among the crew mounted. The ship's carpenter noticed how the chief engineer, though off duty, was watching through his binoculars "for ships or anything like that in the water" while Quartermaster Hugh Johnston, at the wheel, overheard officers discussing the danger: "You could catch words about the submarines and they were in the vicinity and all this stuff you know . . . Oh we knew there were submarines around." Meanwhile in Liverpool, company chairman Alfred Booth was also growing anxious, having just learned of the sinking of the Harrison Line's *Candidate* and *Centurion*. Having hitherto placed his faith in "the Admiralty and . . . Captain Turner's discretion" he decided he had to ensure that Turner was warned that "submarines were on his track." Since the Admiralty had forbidden Cunard to communicate direct with the *Lusitania*, Booth asked the senior naval officer in Liverpool, Admiral Stileman, to send a wireless message to the ship, and Stileman assured him he would see what he could do.

However, the minds of senior members of the Admiralty were not on the *Lusitania*. On May 5 Winston Churchill, the First Lord of the Admiralty and its overall head, had gone to Paris to join in the continuing negotiations with Italy, which had broken off diplomatic relations with Germany and Austro-Hungary the previous day, about its possible entry into the war on the Allied side. He was then intending to travel to Sir John French's headquarters on the western front. Churchill had left his immediate subordinate First Sea Lord Admiral Jacky Fisher, the navy's professional chief, in charge in London but their relationship was almost at breaking point because of their disagreement about the wisdom and conduct of the Dardanelles campaign. By March 22 the attempt by a fleet of twelve British and four French battleships, supported by cruisers, destroyers, and minesweepers, to force the Dardanelles had failed. On April 25 Allied troops had landed on the Gallipoli Peninsula but were being prevented by strong Turkish opposition from pushing inland. Several large naval ships had been lost in the course of the two operations and Churchill was arguing, against Fisher's wishes, for their replacement and the fleet's reinforcement. By early May the seventy-four-year-old admiral appeared to his staff to be both exhausted and in a high state of nervous tension.

Nevertheless, the *Lusitania* had not been forgotten in London's diplomatic circles. At ten A.M. on May 7 President Wilson's envoy and friend Colonel House, back in London, called on Foreign Secretary Sir Edward Grey. The two had been intending to spend the morning at the botanical gardens at Kew, but then House had been invited to see the king at eleven thirty which meant their visit to the gardens had to be curtailed. On their way, House and Sir Edward discussed how America could best assist the Allies if it came into the war and also "spoke of the probability of an ocean liner being sunk." House told Grey that "if this were done, a flame of indignation would sweep across America, which would, in itself, probably carry us into the war." Later that morning at Buckingham Palace, House and the king also "fell to talking, strangely enough, of the probability of Germany sinking a trans-Atlantic liner and of the consequences of that act" and the king remarked, "Suppose they should sink the *Lusitania* with American passengers aboard?"

Aboard the *Lusitania*, just before midday and with crew and passengers already starting to prepare for arrival in Liverpool the next morning, Turner made out the hazy smudge of land off his port bow. He decided it must be Brow Head, a promontory on the western tip of Ireland fifteen miles northwest of the Fastnet Rock, which fog had prevented him from seeing. He was surprised—by his calculations the *Lusitania* should have passed Fastnet well to seaward and should now be heading up the east coast toward Queenstown.

At around twelve forty P.M., he received a further coded warning: "Submarines 5 miles south of Cape Clear proceeding west when sighted at ten a.m."

Turner knew that if the land spied at noon had indeed been Brow Head, then the U-boats should now be many miles astern of his ship. However, shortly after one P.M., a further promontory came in view which Turner thought must be Galley Head. Yet Galley Head was forty miles from

Brow Head—a distance he could not possibly have sailed in an hour. Therefore, a perplexed Turner realized he must have identified one of the two landmarks wrongly.

Then at around one forty P.M. the unmistakable sight of the 256-feet-high Old Head of Kinsale topped by its lighthouse appeared and Turner at last knew for certain where he was. Concerned that the fog might close in again, he decided to fix his exact position by ordering his officers to take a four-point bearing on the Old Head. The process would take forty minutes and require the ship to sail a straight course at a constant speed. At one fifty P.M. with the *Lusitania* steaming at eighteen knots and holding a steady course some twelve miles from land, his officers began to take the bearing.

Turner's maneuverings had delivered the *Lusitania* to the submerged *U-20*, only some eleven miles away and racing to get into position to attack. Earlier that morning as the fog had dispersed, the *U-20*'s lookouts had sighted a small vessel approaching slowly from the Irish coast. Fearing it was a naval patrol vessel—it was in fact a trawler—Schwieger had given the order to dive. However, shortly before midday the *U-20* crew had heard what sounded like the chugging of powerful engines. Schwieger brought the submarine high enough for his pilot to see through the periscope what ship was passing. Lanz identified her correctly as an elderly English warship—the cruiser *Juno*, hurrying back to Queenstown after receiving U-boat warnings. Schwieger gave chase but the old ship, steaming at full speed and zigzagging, eluded him.

Schwieger ordered the *U-20* to surface to find "unusually good visibility, very beautiful weather." Then at one twenty P.M., a petty officer spotted something else and shouted to Schwieger to come and look. Staring through his binoculars, Schwieger saw "a forest of masts and stacks." At first he assumed "they must belong to several ships. Then I saw it was a great steamer coming over the horizon." According to his war diary, as he and his men continued to watch they made out the four funnels of a large passenger steamer directly ahead. Schwieger gave the order "diving stations." Leveling off at the periscope depth of thirty-five feet, Schwieger watched the *Lusitania*. At first he thought that, as with the *Juno*, he would not be able to catch her: "When the steamer was two miles away it changed its course. I had no hope now, even if we hurried at our best speed, of getting near enough to attack her." He had just summoned Lanz to the periscope but "at that instant . . . saw the steamer change her course again. She was coming directly at us. She could not have steered a more perfect course if she had deliberately tried to give us a dead shot. A short fast run and we waited."

With the *Lusitania* just twenty-three hundred feet away, Schwieger ordered his torpedo officer Raimund Weisbach to be ready to fire the fifth of his original seven torpedoes. Weisbach checked the position of rudder and hydroplanes and set the depth at ten feet. A young conscript electrician from Alsace, Charles Voegele, protested against attacking what was clearly a passenger liner but Schwieger ignored him and at two ten P.M. ordered Weisbach to fire. Released from a bow torpedo tube, the three-thousand-pound missile—twenty-feet long, with a diameter of twenty-one inches and carrying 350 pounds of TNT—sped through the water at over forty knots, ten feet beneath its surface, releasing a stream of bubbles in its wake.°

The *Lusitania*'s lookouts had been ordered to "report *anything* that appeared suspicious," even if it was just "a broom handle in the water." Seaman Leslie Morton had just taken up his position as "extra look-out, right up in the eyes of the ship on deck; my responsibility being the starboard side of the bow from ahead to the beam." To his horror he suddenly spotted "a turmoil, and what looked like a bubble on a large scale in the water, breaking surface some 800 to 1000 yards away. A few seconds later I saw two white streaks running along the top of the water like an invisible hand with a piece of chalk on a blackboard. They were heading straight across to intercept the course of *Lusitania*. I grabbed the megaphone which was provided for the look-outs' use and yelled towards the bridge: 'Torpedoes coming on the starboard side, Sir!' "

As other lookouts also yelled warnings, Second Officer Percy Hefford grabbed his binoculars and seeing something moving through the water ordered every watertight door to be closed. Captain Turner ran from his cabin up the narrow stairs to the bridge in time to see a foaming white line

---

° The German naval authorities later arrested and court-martialed Charles Voegele.

streaking straight for the ship but too late to order evasive action. He heard a sound "like the banging of a door on a windy day" followed by "a kind of a rumble" and thought a torpedo had struck between the second and third funnels on the starboard side. Quartermaster Hugh Johnston, at the wheel, and those on the bridge found themselves choking in coal dust so thick "we couldn't see each other for quite a while." Turner told Johnston to steer "hard-a-starboard the helm," intending to make for the shore twelve miles off.

Johnston obeyed and Turner then ordered him to hold the ship steady and "keep her head into Kinsale." However, Johnston found it impossible to steady the helm. Turner again gave the command "hard-a-starboard" and Johnston again put the wheel round only to find that this time there was no response at all—the steering mechanism had locked. Turner told him to "keep trying." With the *Lusitania* still plowing ahead, Turner ordered "full speed astern," intending to reduce her speed by reversing the engines. Down in the engine room Senior Third Engineer George Little heard the bell ring with the command but could not obey. The steam pressure had plunged from 195 pounds to 50. The engines were out of commission and the *Lusitania* out of control.°

Second Officer Hefford, scanning the list indicator beneath the compass, told Turner that the ship was listing 15 degrees to starboard. Turner muttered "My God" and ordered all boats to be lowered to the rail and his officers to their boat stations. Meanwhile, in the Marconi room radio officer Robert Leith was repeatedly tapping out an SOS message: COME AT ONCE, BIG LIST OFF SOUTH HEAD, OLD KINSALE. A coastal wireless station picked the distress call up almost immediately and Leith next transmitted the ship's precise position: 10 MILES SOUTH OF THE OLD HEAD OF KINSALE. Again the message was picked up.

In the first minutes after the attack, passengers' initial reactions were shock and uncertainty. One man noticed that "most of the people seemed transfixed where they stood." When the torpedo struck many had been finishing lunch, like bellboy Ben Holton, who was enjoying a "sweet boiled

---

° Had Schwieger launched the torpedo either five seconds earlier or twenty seconds later he would have missed his target altogether.

apple pudding" when he heard "a shattering roar" or, like first-class passengers Oliver Bernard and Theodate Pope, taking a stroll on deck in the afternoon sun. Bernard suddenly glimpsed what looked like "the tail of a fish," but he was convinced it must be a submarine periscope. Staring harder he made out "the fast-lengthening track of a newly-launched torpedo, itself a streak of froth." Though everyone aboard had been "thinking, dreaming, sleeping, and eating submarines" since leaving New York, he could scarcely believe that an attack had actually happened. When the torpedo hit, he felt "a slight shock through the deck," followed by "a terrific explosion" and "a sullen rumble in the bowels of the liner." Next a huge column of water shot about sixty feet into the air and debris rained down. Before long he noticed "on all hands a pell-mell scurry below to obtain lifejackets." People reappeared singly, in pairs or in groups with life jackets in their hands or with them "inadequately strapped on." Setting out to find a life jacket for a friend, on the port side of the promenade deck Bernard saw crewmen attempting to lower some of the boats. A seaman wielding an ax was holding back frantic passengers already trying to climb in. By the entrance to the first-class saloon Bernard nearly collided with Alfred Vanderbilt, who grinned at him. Another passenger heard Vanderbilt say quietly, "Well, they got us this time, all right."

While passengers poured on to the boat deck, dazed, confused, and often panic-stricken, the officers sent by Turner to superintend the lowering of the remaining lifeboats—the explosion had blown at least one, the third on the starboard side, into the sea—struggled to maintain order. Bellboy Ben Holton recalled "there were no loud speakers or public address [system] or anything like that, it had to be done by word of mouth." With the roar from "the steam escaping from the engine room and up the exhausts and black smoke from the funnel and the startling list to starboard, it wasn't conducive to running a well-organised exercise." All the while the ship's increasing list added to the terror. For a moment she seemed to right herself "in a rocking motion" but then to list more heavily than ever, going "over and over and over" so that passengers scrambled for a footing on the tilting decks.

At two fourteen P.M., just four minutes after the torpedo struck, the *Lusitania's* electricity failed. Some of the ship's butchers who had leaped into the lift used to bring meat up and down found themselves stuck between decks as power to the lift failed. A bellboy recalled how "we could hear their screams coming up—they knew they were trapped." Passenger lifts also stuck, their occupants futilely clawing at the elegant metal grilles. Meanwhile, without power and light in the engine and boiler rooms trimmers and firemen groped their way through choking dust and blinding steam to try to find a way out. "A rush of water" knocked Ian McDermott, a trimmer in the number-two boiler room, off his feet leaving him "struggling for two or three minutes" before washing him "out through the bottom of the ventilation shaft." Passengers thought the injured, bleeding black gang scrambling onto the decks through the ventilators looked like creatures from hell.

Parents searched frantically for their children, peering into baby carriages, some empty, others not, that were rolling wildly around. Major Pearl could only find one of his four children. Unknown to him, nursemaid Alice Lines, who had been below when the torpedo hit, had managed to get the two Pearl children in her care—baby Audrey, whom she had tied in a shawl around her neck, and five-year-old Stuart—out on deck. Some mothers tried to give their children to strangers in the hopes they could save them. Florence Padley was on deck when "one lady asked me to take her baby in arms . . . I told her I did not have a lifejacket, she could look after it better. I felt awful about it." Norah Bretherton, a baby in her arms, pleaded with a man to go to her cabin and fetch her little boy but he ignored her. Managing to reach her son herself, she struggled out on deck with him, appalled that "not one of the men who rushed by offered to help me . . . It was every man for himself."

According to his official war diary, watching through his periscope, Schwieger was convinced the ship was sinking:

> Clean bow shot . . . Torpedo hits starboardside right behind the bridge. An unusually strong explosion takes place . . . The explosion of the torpedo must have been accompanied by a second one (boiler or coal or powder?) The superstructure right above the point of the impact and the bridge are torn asunder, fire breaks out and smoke envelops the high bridge . . . The ship stops immediately and heels over to starboard

very quickly, immersing simultaneously at the bow. It looks as if the ship
is going to capsize very shortly by the bow.

As more and more people converged on the lifeboats, many crowding
the higher port side which felt safer, Captain Turner appeared on the
bridge and, rescinding his earlier orders, shouted: "Don't lower the boats.
Don't lower the boats. The ship can't sink. She's all right. The ship can't
sink." However, by two twenty-two P.M.—just twelve minutes after the
torpedo had hit and with water washing over the *Lusitania's* bows—Turner
finally accepted his ship was lost. He commanded the boats to be lowered
to the water as soon as the ship had slowed sufficiently for this to be done
safely. However, given the speed at which the ship was still moving this was
near impossible. Furthermore, the steep list to starboard meant that lifeboats on that side, released from their snubbing chains, were swinging
crazily out so that passengers had to leap seven or eight feet to get into
them.

Conversely, on the port side, the lifeboats were hanging in over the
deck. Even when seamen and passengers succeeded in pushing them out
over the rail, as they were lowered the sixty feet or so to the water, the angle
rivets protruding from the ship's hull ripped into their planking. At every
bump and jolt people tumbled from them into the sea. Widow Elizabeth
Duckworth saw her friend Alice Scott and her little son Arthur tossed out
of a lifeboat. She decided to await her fate and began to pray. Nearby she
heard three Irish girls singing "There Is a Green Hill Not Far Away" in
thin, frightened voices, twisting the words of the hymn to reassure themselves that land was near.

Fear rose with the water and several other attempts to get boats away
ended in disaster. On the port side Third Officer Albert Bestic and some
male passengers tried to push Boat No. 2, loaded with women and children,
over the side but lacked the strength to shift the weight of over two tons
so that the laden lifeboat slammed inward, crushing people against the
ship's superstructure. Another boat fell onto the tilting deck and careered
down it, smashing into people before they could fling themselves out of the
way. Only one port-side lifeboat got safely away without capsizing or
becoming waterlogged. Nurse Alice Lines, still with baby Audrey tied in a

shawl around her neck and five-year-old Stuart clinging to her skirts, had tried to climb into it. A crewman lifted the boy in but when Alice made to follow with Audrey, he told her the boat was now full. Watching it lowered to the water, Alice decided her only option was to jump. As she hit the water and went under, she had "a terrible sensation of being sucked under the ship" but then felt someone grab her long auburn hair and pull her into the lifeboat, still clutching the baby.

When the torpedo hit, Professor Holbourn kept his promise to school-girl Avis Dolphin. Guessing she must be at lunch in the second-class dining room, he pushed his way through the onrushing crowds of frightened people and found her there. Together they made for his cabin to find life jackets but the list was already so steep they struggled to get up the stair-case. Reaching the cabin at last, Holbourn and a fellow passenger fastened a life jacket on Avis. Then carrying his own jacket he managed to find the two nurses traveling with Avis. One already had a jacket on, but the other refused Holbourn's offer, saying, "he should have it as he had a wife and three children." They compromised. If he could place her in a boat he would keep the life jacket.

His first thought was to get Avis and the nurses into one of the port-side boats but the mass of crushed and bleeding people lying on the deck decided him to head for the starboard side. Forcing a way through he helped Avis and the two women across the gap into a swaying lifeboat. Convinced he himself would not survive, he asked Avis "to find his wife and children and kiss them goodbye from him" when she reached Britain. Glancing at his watch he realized less than fifteen minutes had passed since the *Lusitania* had been struck. Shocked by how low the ship now was in the water, he put on a life jacket, went to the rail, and leaped. As he did so he had "the horrible shock of seeing the child's boat swamp and capsize." Hitting the water, he tried to struggle through the mass of churning wreckage and threshing people to reach Avis only to see her sucked under.

Also on the starboard side, Charles Lauriat had been trying to free Boat No.7 which, "well filled with people, principally women and children," was still attached to the ship by its rope falls. However, looking up at "the tremendous smokestack" hanging out over them as the ship listed yet fur-ther he realized the futility and pleaded with the boat's occupants to jump.

Most refused. Plunging in himself and swimming as hard as he could to get away from the ship and avoid being dragged under by suction, he looked back to see the lifeboat and its occupants pulled under.

With the ship's screw propellers and rudders rising out of the water, children were being thrown from the decks to be caught by men in the lifeboats. Young Canadian mother Charlotte Pye, who had her baby in her arms and no life jacket, kept falling to the deck because of the list when a man said, "Don't cry. It's quite alright." As he tied his own life jacket on her and helped her into a boat, she recognized him as the man who had paid her five dollars for a concert program at the passenger concert—Alfred Vanderbilt. Despite owning one of the most beautiful swimming pools in America, Vanderbilt could not swim. In the *Lusitania*'s dying moments, the ship's barber, Lott Gadd, saw him still "trying to put lifejackets on women and children. The ship was going down fast. When the sea reached them, they were washed away. I never saw Vanderbilt after that. All I saw in the water was children—children everywhere." A Canadian passenger had heard Vanderbilt say to his valet, Ronald Denyer: "Find all the kiddies you can, boy." As Denyer brought them to Vanderbilt, he "dashed to the boats with two little ones in his arms at a time."

Some people slid down wires and ropes, including the log line which trailed astern to record the ship's run but which, being made of wire after the first six feet of rope, flayed people's hands and feet. Some stripped off their clothes, believing their chances of survival in the water would be better. An American veteran of the Mexican war tore the clothes from his wife so that "all she had on was her stockings and her lifejacket." Theodate Pope and her companion Edwin Friend decided to jump and together with her maid Emily Robinson chose what seemed a good spot on the port side. Friend found life jackets for them all and jumped first. Miss Pope, with a patrician instruction to her maid—"'Come, Robinson"—followed. Major Warren Pearl, who had found all his party except for nurse Alice Lines with Audrey and Stuart, felt the ship make a sudden plunge and saw foaming water rushing over the forecastle. He just had time to grab some pieces of wood to serve as supports for his family when the sea sucked them all off the ship. Charles Frohman, at the rail with some friends, remained calmly philosophical. One recalled how just before "a mighty green cliff of water came rushing up, bearing its tide of dead and debris" and washed them into the sea, he paraphrased a line from *Peter Pan*, the play he had been responsible for bringing to the London and New York stages: "Why fear death? It is the most beautiful adventure life gives us."

Up in the wheelhouse Quartermaster Johnston saw that "the starboard wing of the bridge was level with the sea and it was coming over the rail." Some minutes ago he had reported that the list to starboard had reached 25 degrees but had received no response from his captain. Now Turner shouted, "Quartermaster, save yourself." Just as the ship began her dive beneath the waves and Johnston was washed into the sea he glimpsed Turner climbing the ladder to the top bridge.

Captain Schwieger's war diary describes the *Lusitania*'s last moments:

2.10 p.m. Great confusion on board; boats are cleared away and some are lowered into the water. Apparently considerable panic; several boats, fully laden, are hurriedly lowered, bow or stern first and are swamped at once. Because of the list fewer boats can be cleared away on the port side . . . The ship blows off steam; the name Lusitania is visible in gold letters on the bows . . .

2.25 p.m. Since it seems as if the steamer can only remain afloat a short while longer, dive to 24 meters and head out to sea. Also it would have been impossible for me to fire a second torpedo into this crushing crowd of humanity trying to save their lives.

As the *Lusitania* went under, several people including clergyman's wife Margaret Gwyer were sucked into her cavernous funnels, only to be shot out again a few moments later like human cannonballs. Some were dragged under by the funnel stays or mauled by the ship's falling wireless aerials, both sharp as cheese wire. Professor Holbourn kicking out to free himself from a mess of tangled ropes glanced back to witness the *Lusitania*'s final moments. So did Oliver Bernard who had slid off the ship in her last moments into the sea with one of the radio operators and later wrote of the "picturesque grandeur even tho' we knew that many hundreds of help-less souls, caught like rats in a gilded trap, were in her."

Some lifeboats still dangled uselessly from their davits. A man hanging on to a rope over the stern screamed as a still revolving propeller sliced his leg off. The stern itself "was crowded with people who seemed to make for the last piece of the wreck left above water." The sea was full of the waving hands and arms of people making "agonizing efforts to keep afloat." Charles Lauriat heard "a long lingering moan" as if "they who were lost . . . [were] . . . calling from the very depths." In the final moments as the ship's bow hit the seabed some 340 feet below, it seemed to some that she nearly righted herself. Then "a mighty crescendo of screams and cries of fear . . . died away to a whisper" as the ship turned slowly onto her starboard side and disappeared. At two twenty-eight P.M., eighteen minutes after the U-20's torpedo had punched into her hull, the thirty-thousand-ton *Lusitania* was gone. As the U-20 turned away, Schwieger took a final look through his periscope. His war diary records: "Astern, in the distance, a number of lifeboats are drifting; the *Lusitania* is no more to be seen."

CHAPTER THIRTEEN

"Wilful and Wholesale Murder"

IN THE WATER, passengers and crew tried to help one another. Charles Lauriat and a friend scrambled onto a collapsible lifeboat and, finding their penknives, "went at a kind of can-opening operation" to try to raise the boat's canvas sides; however, terrified, half-drowning people were clinging to the rail to which the canvas was attached. Lauriat asked them to let go just for a moment and hold on to the life ropes instead, but many thought he meant to "push them off" and abandon them. Eventually he and his friend managed to raise the sides and loaded the boat with people "until it sunk flush with the water." Lauriat recalled when there were "about as many in our boat as we ought to take," he heard a woman say, "in just as natural a tone of voice as you would ask for another slice of bread and butter, 'Won't you take me next? I can't swim.' " Peering into the water he saw "a woman's head, with a piece of wreckage under her chin and with her hair streaming out . . . She was so jammed in she couldn't even get her arms out, and with it all she had a half smile on her face and was placidly chewing gum." Lauriat succeeded in dragging her in. He also rescued Margaret Gwyer, thoroughly coated in oil and soot from the funnel.

Elizabeth Duckworth had eventually found a place in one of the few lifeboats that had gotten away safely. Overwhelmed by the terrible sights and sounds, she had begun reciting the Twenty-third Psalm when she noticed "a man struggling in the water right near our boat and I said to the mate: 'can't we help him?' He said 'NO.' I said 'Yes, we can.' " After a hard struggle they pulled him on board.

Captain Turner was also saved. As the waters had risen around him on the bridge he had jumped into the sea where he clung first to an oar, then a chair, all the while fighting off seagulls which, he recalled—perhaps somewhat improbably—swooped "on the dazed and benumbed people floating helplessly on the surface and pecked their eyes out." Growing weak from exposure he "flung up a gold-braided arm" hoping to attract attention. A crewman spotted him and supported him in the water until rescue arrived.

Those shivering in lifeboats or clinging to pieces of wreckage like bellboy Ben Holton, keeping afloat by hanging on to an upturned dog kennel, looked hopefully toward the shore that was so tantalizingly close and wondered when help would come. Steward Robert Barnes, sharing an upturned collapsible lifeboat with ten others including a dead woman, could not understand the delay since they were "in sight of Queenstown all the time" and feared their frail craft was drifting out to sea.

Marconi Operator Bob Leith's distress calls, which had been picked up by stations along the Irish coast, had immediately been relayed to Vice Admiral Coke at naval headquarters in Queenstown. At two twenty P.M. he received the ship's own request for help and then a further forwarded message: LUSITANIA TEN MILES SOUTH EAST APPARENTLY SINKING. At two forty-one P.M. a message from the signal station at Kinsale told him simply: LUSITANIA SUNK. As Coke set about organizing a rescue fleet, in the town the cry went up "the *Lusy's* gone."

U.S. consul Wesley Frost was in his office above O'Reilly's bar in Queenstown when his assistant burst in to tell him of "a wildfire rumour about town that the *Lusitania* had been attacked." From his window Frost saw "a very unusual stir in the harbor" as "tugs, tenders and trawlers, some two dozen in all, began to steam past the town toward the harbor-mouth." Frost immediately rang the Cunard office, which "admitted . . . that it appeared probable that the vessel was sunk or sinking." Frost hurried to the bank to withdraw funds to enable him to help American passengers and cabled Secretary of State William Jennings Bryan in Washington: LUSITANIA SUNK 2.30 TODAY PROBABLY MANY SURVIVORS RESCUE WORK ENERGETICALLY PROCEEDING SHALL I CABLE LIST OF SURVIVORS.

The first telegram from Queenstown reporting the disaster only reached Cunard's headquarters in Liverpool at five P.M. because the Admiralty censor delayed it. By early evening rumors were spreading throughout the city, and crowds converged on Cunard's offices. In London, Lloyd's posted a bulletin announcing the disaster and at five fifteen P.M. the Foreign Office issued a statement. Admiral Jacky Fisher had learned of the sinking from Coke shortly before three P.M. but Churchill, still in France and now at Sir John French's headquarters, was not informed until later that day.

Meanwhile, the small flotilla of converted fishing trawlers, armed naval patrol craft, and elderly torpedo boats that Frost had seen was hurrying from Queenstown to the scene of the disaster. Fishing smacks and lifeboats from elsewhere along the coast joined them, including the Courtmacsherry lifeboat which set out at three P.M. with twelve men at the oars. Having no engine, it would take the men some three hours heavy pulling to reach the scene. As they rowed they prayed "as hard as men could pray, a prayer with every stroke. 'O God, keep them alive until we're there.' "

The first rescue vessel to arrive was an Isle of Man fishing boat, the *Wanderer*. Some four hundred yards from where the *Lusitania* had gone down the fishermen found the first lifeboats. Elizabeth Duckworth was rowing hard in one of them. As she was helped aboard she saw another lifeboat "tossing about in the water" with only three occupants. One of them stood up and shouted that he and his two companions were the only survivors from an entire boatload. He begged for help to row back and rescue "some of the drowning." The captain of the *Wanderer* refused, saying he could not spare the men. However, Elizabeth leaped the gap between the vessel and the lifeboat, seized an oar, and together with the men rescued "about forty of those struggling in the water" and brought them back to the *Wanderer*.

Charles Lauriat, aboard his heavily laden collapsible lifeboat, also reached the *Wanderer*. Margaret Gwyer was ecstatic to see the tall figure of her husband standing at the rail of the fishing boat but he looked at her with "a perfectly blank expression." She was in such a terrible state and he was in such shock that he did not recognize her until he seemed to pull himself together, leaned over the side, and looked her squarely in the face.

Lauriat recalled that although "it was positively slippery with fish scales and the usual dirt of fishermen . . . the deck of that boat, under our feet, felt as good as the front hall of our own homes." The fishermen were horrified at the state of the survivors—many naked and bleeding, some clutching fractured limbs or in the worst cases with broken bones protruding through torn flesh. They improvised bandages, pulled woolen blankets from their bunks, and brewed hot tea. When that ran out they handed round mugs of boiling water. Sips from the boat's one bottle of whiskey were rationed out to those most in need.

The *Wanderer* also picked up Professor Holbourn. He sat huddled and sodden in the tiny hold, which smelled strongly of fish, worrying about Avis. Next to him lay a man with a broken leg and an expectant mother with crushed ribs. The vessel was so crowded that some were forced to dangle their legs over the side. Fearing she might sink beneath the weight, the *Wanderer*'s captain took two further lifeboats in tow and set out for Queenstown.

Not until around six P.M.—three and a half hours after the sinking— did the main rescue fleet begin to arrive. Oliver Bernard had managed to reach a badly waterlogged lifeboat and had been baling and rowing hard for some time when "gradually smoke appeared on the horizon, east and west" and "all kinds of steamers heaved in sight . . . A woman moaned, 'Why didn't they come before?' "

The fishing boat *Bluebell* rescued Captain Turner and the unconscious and badly bruised former suffragette Margaret Mackworth. Sucked from the deck into the sea, she had found a thin piece of board two or three feet long to cling on to. A man with "a white face and yellow moustache" had also grabbed it and begun to inch toward her. Instinct had told her "he wanted to hold on to me" and she had asked him to go back to his own end which he did. After a while he had disappeared. She had continued to cling on, shivering with cold and only dimly aware of people around her praying out loud or calling, "Bo-at . . . bo-at . . . bo-at . . ." Bellboy Ben Holton, who had passed out in the water with the cold, woke to find himself lying on a ship's hatch among a pile of corpses. When he sat up an astonished sailor exclaimed, "Good gracious, are you alive? We put you amongst the dead ones."

At the Cunard Wharf in Queenstown, police erected a makeshift barrier to keep back onlookers as toward nightfall the rescue vessels began to return. Wesley Frost watched "the ghastly procession . . . as they landed the living and the dead that night under the flaring gas torches" with "bruised and shuddering women, crippled and half-clothed men, and a few wide-eyed little children" having to be helped or carried up the gangplank. Many grabbed at the sleeves of officials begging for news of their loved ones. One woman with a baby in her arms and a blanket given her by a sailor around her shoulders refused to leave the quayside "but waited until the last survivor had passed, searching each face as it went by, in the vain hope of finding her husband."

American shipowner Charles Bowring, hobbling ashore in his sodden Norfolk jacket, put his hand in his pocket to retrieve his glasses. He found that "they were all twisted in a piece of paper." Putting them on he found that the paper was the German warning that had appeared in the New York newspapers the day the *Lusitania* sailed. He reflected wryly that he had at least one souvenir of the day's events.

Those strong enough were ushered into the Cunard offices to register their names on a list of survivors that flustered company staff were trying to compile. Young cook George Wynne, who had been dragged half drowned aboard a trawler and revived by sailors who worked his arms to pump the water from his lungs, was among them. In the *Lusitania*'s last moments, his semi-invalid father Joseph, knowing George could not swim, had rushed off to find him a life jacket. He had not returned and George had not seen him since. Nevertheless, unable to bear the thought of causing his mother anxiety, he sent a telegram to her in Liverpool telling her they were both safe.

U.S. consul Wesley Frost had received a cable from Secretary of State Bryan: COMPANY REPORTS ALL PASSENGERS SAVED. IF REPORT UNTRUE CABLE NAMES OF AMERICANS LOST OR NOT ACCOUNTED FOR. In London U.S. ambassador Walter Hines Page was waiting for Frost's latest updates. During the afternoon Sir Edward Grey had called him to the Foreign Office to tell him that the *Lusitania* "had been torpedoed and sunk by German submarines off the Irish coast." The ambassador was giving a farewell dinner for Colonel House and his wife that night. Since the initial reports suggested there had been no fatalities, Page decided not to cancel it. However, returning home he learned that the first reports had been wrong and that there had been a massive loss of life. It was too late to cancel the dinner, but during the subdued affair Page read out to his guests the ever grimmer updates arriving from Frost and the Admiralty. Colonel House predicted: "We shall be at war with Germany within a month."

In Queenstown, as the night wore on, many arriving vessels now carried more dead than living. Wesley Frost watched as "piles of corpses like cordwood began to appear among the paint-kegs and coils of rope on the shadowy old wharves." Corpses were placed on stretchers and carried to the temporary mortuaries set up in a shed on the Cunard quay and then, as the numbers of dead rose, in the large town hall and in a disused ship's chandlery. Leslie Morton, the young seaman who had been the first to spot the torpedo and had later dived overboard after trying to help launch the lifeboats, went to one of the mortuaries looking for his brother John who had also been on board. Hesitantly, he reached out to twitch the sheet off a corpse when, as he later recalled, "by the most amazing coincidence a hand on the other side went to turn the sheet back and I looked up and there was my brother."

Professor Holbourn learned that night to his great relief that a rescue ship had picked up Avis Dolphin. Margaret Mackworth was helped off the *Bluebell* to find her father David Thomas, fortified with brandy given him by a Catholic priest, waiting on the quayside desperate for news of her. Not all were so fortunate. George Wynne soon learned that his father Joseph was among the dead. On his return to Liverpool he would wander the streets, postponing the moment when he had to tell his mother the truth. He only eventually managed to do so with the aid of another priest.° Charlotte Pye, whom Vanderbilt had helped, and

---

° As his mother's and siblings' almost only means of financial support, George Wynne was soon back at sea. He later joined the army only to be gassed but survived that as well, living into his eighties.

Mabel Henshaw both lost their babies. Major Pearl found that though his wife, baby Audrey, five-year-old Stuart, and their nurse Alice Lines were alive, the other nurse Greta Lorenson and the two daughters in her care were missing.

Notices began to appear in shop windows such as: LUSITANIA. MISSING A BABY GIRL FIFTEEN MONTHS OLD. VERY FAIR CURLY HAIR . . . IN WHITE WOOLLEN JERSEY . . . TRIES TO WALK AND TALK. PLEASE SEND ANY INFORMATION TO MISS BROWN, QUEEN'S HOUSE, QUEENSTOWN. Consul Wesley Frost quickly compiled a list of confirmed American dead which included Charles Frohman. However, many remained unaccounted for, such as Alfred Vanderbilt.

For most survivors their journey was not yet over. They still needed to get to England. Charles Lauriat was one of the first to depart, leaving on an Irish mail ship on May 8. However, the thought that other U-boats might yet be lurking made sleep difficult. Going to the saloon he saw that "every man who had been a passenger on the *Lusitania* was sitting by a table, or reclining on a couch, with a lifejacket strapped around him." Many were still wearing those from the *Lusitania*.

By May 10, solemn mass funerals were taking place. Led by a military band, the corteges wound up the steep hill past Saint Coleman's Cathedral to the small cemetery outside Queenstown where three large pits had been dug. However, even before the first burials, in fact on Saturday, May 8, the day after the sinking, county coroner John J. Horgan opened an inquest on five of the *Lusitania*'s victims at the old market house in the center of the nearby town of Kinsale. Captain Turner, the main witness, appeared on Monday, May 10, wearing "a badly fitting old suit" rather than his resplendent uniform.

Answering Horgan's questions he confirmed he had been "fully aware" of the German warning, that the *Lusitania* had been unarmed, and that, when entering the danger area, he had taken precautions including having the lifeboats swung out and the watertight bulkhead doors closed as well as doubling the lookouts. He had been in radio contact "all the way across to receive but not to send messages" and had received messages that submarines were off the Irish coast. He answered other questions about the weather and the ship's speed but was not prepared to discuss some issues in open court. He confirmed to Horgan that he had had "special instructions" but was "not at liberty to say what they were" although he had carried them out "to the best of [his] ability."

On the sinking itself he said that a single torpedo had struck the *Lusitania* between "the third and fourth funnels" and he had not been able "to stop the ship." There had been "headway" on the *Lusitania* "until the moment she went down." He had not been zigzagging when attacked. A member of the jury of twelve "shopkeepers and fishermen" inquired whether he had asked the Admiralty for an escort because of the warning. He said he had not. "I leave that to them, it is their business." Horgan's own last question was whether the submarine had given any warning. "None whatever, sir. It was straight and done with, and the whole lot went up in the air," Turner responded. The coroner said, "We all sympathise with you . . . in the terrible crime which has been committed against your vessel . . . We realise the deep feeling you must have in this matter," whereupon Turner, sitting head bowed, burst into tears.

Horgan told the jury "the warning in the American papers . . . had no more legal or valid effect than that of an assassin who sent an anonymous letter to his intended victim." He directed them to return a verdict placing the guilt on Germany: "We find that the deceased died from their prolonged immersion and exhaustion in the sea . . . owing to the sinking of the RMS *Lusitania* by a torpedo fired without warning from a German submarine. This appalling crime was contrary to international law and the convention of civilised nations, and we therefore charge the officers of the said submarine and the Emperor and government of Germany, under whose orders they acted, with the crime of wilful and wholesale murder."

As Horgan was about to leave Old Market House half an hour later, Harry Wynne, crown solicitor for Cork, arrived to announce that the Admiralty had told him to stop the inquest so that nothing should be said "as to instructions issued by Naval Authorities for guidance of merchant vessels in avoiding submarines." Captain Turner was ordered to remain silent until a formal Board of Trade inquiry into the sinking. Southern Ireland was then part of the United Kingdom and Horgan would have had to comply but—as he told Wynne—he was too late. The verdict was already with the world's press. Horgan later claimed that the Admiralty were "as belated on this occasion as they had been in protecting the *Lusitania* against attack."

CHAPTER FOURTEEN

"Too Proud to Fight"

THE FINAL OFFICIAL death toll from the sinking of the *Lusitania* was 1,198. (If the three German agents still locked in their cell when the ship went down are included, which they were not, the figure would rise to 1,201.) Of the 1,257 passengers, 785—including 128 Americans—had perished as had 413 members of the 702-strong crew. Compared with daily casualty figures at the front the *Lusitania* fatalities were tiny. But world reaction to what had occurred off the Irish coast on Friday, May 7, 1915, was enormous.

The German press saluted the "extraordinary success" of a justified attack on the *Lusitania*, an armed ship carrying both munitions and Canadian troops that had been warned before she sailed. One paper stated that "hundreds of non-participant passengers were victims, victims of the haughty greed of English shipping lines." Another accused Britain of cynically using "citizens from neutral nations as a shield." The *Koelnische Volkszeitung* "with joyful pride" called the sinking "a success of our submarines which must be placed beside the greatest achievement of this naval war" claiming it as "of moral significance" and a just response to British attempts to starve the German people to death through her blockade. The *Neueste Nachrichten* declared, "The torpedoing . . . fills us with satisfaction . . . Now finally the firm of Wilson and Grey will realise that we will no longer be deterred by anything . . . Should he [Wilson] crave action with us, just let him begin . . . We would willingly bear the American declaration of war along with the Italian. Of victory we are certain." Crown Prince Wilhelm, a firm supporter of unrestricted

U-boat warfare, telegrammed the kaiser from his headquarters in northern France telling his father of the "great joy" there at the sinking, and urging that the more determinedly the U-boat war was waged, the quicker the war would be won.

The German Admiralty learned for certain on May 12 which U-boat had sunk the *Lusitania*. Back in radio range, Walther Schwieger signalled: HAVE SUNK ONE SAILING VESSEL TWO STEAMERS AND LUSI-TANIA. Later he added that he had sunk the liner with one torpedo. The British Room 40 team intercepted both messages, immediately recognized their significance, and carefully checked them before forwarding them to Churchill, Fisher, and other senior figures in the Admiralty. Each recipient now knew that whatever else had caused the second explosion reported by so many *Lusitania* survivors, it was not a second torpedo.

The British press's reaction, meanwhile, had been predictably hostile, raging about the "Latest Achievements of German Frightfulness at Sea" and "The Hun's Most Ghastly Crime" perpetrated by "German pirates" and "Tirpitz's murderers." Images of confused, pale-faced orphans, bereaved women, and dead babies stared out from the pages. Several accounts pictured submarines circling as gloating U-boatmen leaned from their conning towers to taunt their victims. Some even described submariners machine-gunning people in the water.

Editorials suggested the sinking was a further case of a new unprincipled form of warfare. The *Daily Chronicle*, for example, believed: "Sowing of illegal mines, submarining of merchantmen, butchery of fishermen, the *Falaba* case, the *Lusitania* case—it is a long and terrible list. On land the sacking of towns, the massacres of non-combatants, the use of explosive bullets and asphyxiating gas." The *Times* demanded the whole world "join in branding . . . the renegade among the nations." The *Daily Mirror* believed "this cold bloodiest piece of murder was specifically planned to provoke the USA." The *Daily Express* hoped that President Wilson, "good man that he is," would do "something more than protest."°

° Just as today, the newspapers were eager for exclusive photographs and reports. The *Daily Mirror* of May 8 included the following: "*The Daily Mirror* pays the highest price for exclusive photographs and has always done so. Photographs of the sinking of the *Lusitania* and incidents aboard before the disaster should be sent to (the paper)."

Anti-German rioting erupted in many British cities. Some newspapers incited it with headlines like HUNT THEM DOWN, NOW FOR A VENDETTA, and DOWN WITH THE SWINE, and all reported violent unrest from "widespread havoc" to "pillage and fire." In London, German-owned businesses were looted from the East End to Kentish Town. A bystander described how "when the news . . . went round that the *Lusitania* had been sunk . . . all the women turned out furious, cursing the Germans, and suddenly began to talk about people who had German names . . . From nowhere came a great rush of women . . . outside this draper's shop shouting and shaking their fists." The women produced half bricks from beneath their shawls and threw them through the window. They made "a mad rush . . . into the shop elbowing one another, shoving, thumping, and . . . snatch[ed] at everything . . . Stock boxes were pulled out . . . things snatched from the shelves . . . boots, men's suits, socks, anything . . . Even those who couldn't get anything tried to thieve what the others had stolen."

The disturbances were particularly violent in Liverpool where mobs numbered up to two or three thousand. By May 13 forty thousand pounds worth of property had been destroyed in the city. Two Americans, newly arrived on the liner *New York*, joined in. One later told the *New York Times* how the mob attacked a cutlery shop:

> The crowd was muttering and growling and the shop was dark but there were people upstairs. So I just picked up a brick and heaved it through the window . . . Then everyone took to shying them, and in a few minutes the place was a wreck . . . Soon all the furniture, carpets and everything else were thrown out of the windows into the street. There were policemen at the corner . . . and they only grinned. The crowd then went on down the street and wrecked four German pork shops . . . I saw one young fellow going off with half a hog and an old woman was dancing in the middle of the street with strings of sausages all over her and flying in the wind."

There was also serious anti-German rioting in Britain's dominions. In Canada the capital of British Columbia, Victoria, had to be placed under martial law.

On May 13 Prime Minister Asquith announced the internment of all male enemy aliens of military age (seventeen to forty-five years old). The following day the kaiser's banner was unceremoniously hauled down from the Chapel Royal at Windsor Castle to mark his expulsion from the British Order of the Garter, bestowed on him thirty-eight years earlier by his adored grandmother, Queen Victoria.

Elsewhere, the French press declared "the German's divorce from civilisation is complete" and predicted that neutral countries would now join the Allies.

Many neutrals indeed condemned the attack. The Dutch *Telegraaf* thought, "Criminal is too mild a word to be applied to this outrage; it is devilish"; the Norwegian *Morgenblad* that "the news of the sinking of the *Lusitania* puts . . . all other events in the background and arouses the whole world to a feeling of horror. The Germans have meant to terrify. They have terrified their friends and terror breeds hate."

The British government quickly realized the sinking was a powerful weapon in the propaganda war and wished no portion of the blame for it to attach to them. When Churchill returned to London from France on May 10, three days after the sinking, he faced a barrage of questions in the House of Commons. Members of Parliament asked him how fast was *Lusitania* traveling when torpedoed? What were the captain's instructions? Why had the *Lusitania* not been escorted when submarines were known to be active in the area? What had been done in response to the newspaper warning in the United States?

Churchill's performance was not among his most distinguished. Insisting he was hampered by being unable to disclose classified information, he told the Commons that the Board of Trade had set up an independent inquiry into the sinking to be chaired by Lord Mersey, Britain's commissioner for wrecks, and that the *Lusitania* had received instructions and at least two warnings from the Admiralty. However, he could not discuss them since "it might appear I was trying to throw blame on the Captain of the *Lusitania* in regard to an affair which will be the subject of full investigation."

This was a mere hint of the "blame Turner" attitude prevalent within the Admiralty and being spun to the British and American press. Captain

Richard Webb, director of the Trade Division of the Admiralty and responsible for guidance to merchant shipping, had written a damning memorandum, the key paragraph of which read:

> In taking the course he did, the Master of the *Lusitania* acted directly contrary to the written general instructions received from the Admiralty and completely disregarded the telegraphic warnings received from Queenstown during the hours immediately preceding the attack. On the facts at present disclosed, the Master appears to have displayed an almost inconceivable negligence, and one is forced to conclude that he is either utterly incompetent or that he has been got at by the Germans. In considering this latter possibility it is not necessary to suppose that he had any conception of the loss of life which actually occurred and he might well have thought that being close to the shore there would be ample time to run his ship aground into a place of security before she foundered.

On receiving the note, Fisher had little doubt who to blame, scrawling "Fully concur" in his characteristic green ink against Webb's comment that Turner was either utterly incompetent or had been got at. He added: "As the Cunard Company would not have employed an incompetent man, the certainty is absolute that Captain Turner is not a fool but a knave. I hope that Captain Turner will be arrested immediately after the inquiry whatever the verdict." He then noted: "Ought not Lord Mersey to get a hint" and "I feel *absolutely* certain that Captain Turner of the *Lusitania* is a scoundrel and been bribed . . . No seaman in his senses could have acted as he did."

Churchill's reaction was only slightly more circumspect. He wrote in red ink, "Fully concur with DTD [Webb]. I consider the Admiralty case against the Captain should be pressed before Lord Mersey by a skilful counsel and that Captain Webb should attend as witness if not employed as assessor. We should pursue the captain without check." Having agreed this very clear government policy guidance for what should have been an independent and impartial inquiry, Churchill and Fisher now left the detail to their staffs. They turned instead to a topic both considered more important than the *Lusitania* but over which their disagreements were becoming ever more pointed—the Dardanelles.

CONVINCED BY INTERCEPTS from Room 40 that further German submarines were bound for the Mediterranean, Fisher insisted on May 12 that the navy's newest battleship, HMS *Queen Elizabeth*, be withdrawn from the Dardanelles back to the Home Fleet. He reluctantly agreed to Churchill's demand that older vessels should replace her. On Friday, May 14, Churchill urged additional reinforcements for the Dardanelles fleet and the two met that evening. Afterward Fisher believed that they had agreed to limit further deployments to a level he could accept. He went to bed early as usual but on rising before dawn discovered that Churchill had written again requiring additions "greatly in excess" of those they had agreed on. Around five A.M. Fisher penned his letter of resignation which finished "I am off to Scotland at once so as to avoid all questionings."

At first neither Prime Minister Asquith nor Churchill took his resignation seriously. He had, after all, threatened to resign at least nine times in the past four months. Then alarmed at his continued absence from the Admiralty, both attempted to persuade Fisher, who had not in fact left London, to relent but he would not.

At the same time Asquith and his administration were themselves under great pressure following an article in the *Times* of May 14 alleging a "scandalous shortage of shells on the Western Front." The rumor was that Churchill had leaked the story during his visit to France to further his own political ambitions. If so, the affair backfired on him badly. To avoid an onslaught from the Conservative opposition, by Monday, May 17, Asquith decided to seek a coalition government of national unity with the Conservatives. Eleven years previously Churchill had deserted the Conservatives to join the Liberals. The Conservatives were also critical of his conduct of the Dardanelles operation and of other naval matters, including the loss of the *Lusitania*. Therefore, part of their price for joining a coalition would be his removal from the Admiralty.

Fisher saw an opportunity and on May 19 wrote to Asquith graciously agreeing to return and "guarantee the successful termination of the War and the total abolition of the submarine menace" on strict conditions, including that "Mr. Winston Churchill is not in the Cabinet to be always circumventing me," that he himself should have "absolutely untrammelled sole command of all the sea forces whatsoever" and an equally free hand in all appointments. This "extraordinary ultimatum" angered Asquith who told the king that it "indicated signs of mental aberration." Fisher's resignation was accepted.

Churchill did not long survive him. Under the new coalition government he was indeed replaced, being moved on May 25 to be chancellor of the Duchy of Lancaster, a less important position with only a few ill-defined duties. (He would resign from the government entirely on November 12 to become a battalion commander on the western front.) The cool, languid, self-contained former Conservative prime minister, Arthur Balfour, succeeded him as First Lord of the Admiralty. Thus, in less than three weeks after the sinking of the *Lusitania* the two most senior figures had left the Admiralty. Soon after taking office and despite the outcry at the *Lusitania's* sinking, Balfour quickly announced, in a bid to avoid further German retaliation against British prisoners of war, that captured U-boat crewmen would be treated no differently from other prisoners.

IN LINE WITH Churchill's statement to the Commons, one of Captain Webb's first tasks in preparing the Admiralty's deposition for the forthcoming inquiry into the sinking of the *Lusitania* was to ensure nothing was said that might undermine national security. He therefore required the deletion from the list of questions proposed by the Board of Trade (the government department responsible for the inquiry) for answer in the published report, the simple question: What were Captain Turner's instructions from the owners or the Admiralty? He did, however, allow two other questions to stand. Had the captain had instructions? If so, had he carried them out? Both could be answered simply "yes" or "no."

Closed sessions would, however, discuss the nature of the instructions. Captain Webb therefore had to list those that were relevant and that Turner could be shown to have received. He included the detailed Admiralty note of February 10, 1915, with its instructions to avoid headlands; to steer a

Kaiser Wilhelm II

First Lord of the Admiralty Winston
Churchill, 1915

Admiral John Arbuthnot Fisher

Captain Alfred Thayer Mahan

President Woodrow Wilson

Secretary of State William Jennings Bryan

Secretary of State Robert Lansing

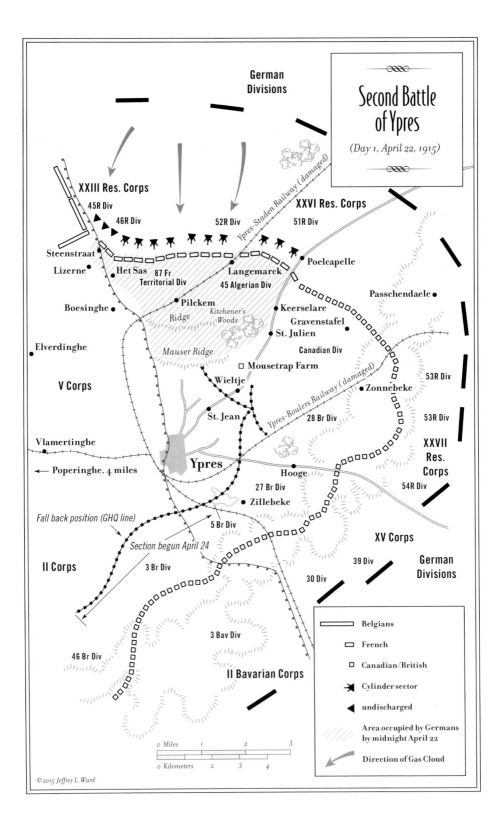

Second Battle of Ypres

(Day 1, April 22, 1915)

German Divisions

XXIII Res. Corps
45R Div
46R Div
52R Div

XXVI Res. Corps
51R Div

Ypres-Staden Railway (damaged)

Steenstraat
Lizerne
Het Sas
87 Fr Territorial Div
Langemarck
45 Algerian Div
Poelcapelle
Passchendaele

Boesinghe
Pilckem
Pilckem Ridge
Kitchener's Woods
Keerselare
Gravenstafel
St. Julien

Elverdinghe

V Corps

Mauser Ridge
Mousetrap Farm
Wieltje

Canadian Div

St. Jean
Ypres-Roulers Railway (damaged)
Zonnebeke
53R Div

28 Br Div
53R Div

Vlamertinghe
Ypres
Hooge
27 Br Div
Zillebeke

XXVII Res. Corps
54R Div

← Poperinghe, 4 miles

Fall back position (GHQ line)
5 Br Div

Section begun April 24

II Corps
3 Br Div

XV Corps

German Divisions

39 Div
30 Div

3 Bav Div

46 Br Div

II Bavarian Corps

	Belgians
	French
	Canadian/British
	Cylinder sector
	undischarged
	Area occupied by Germans by midnight April 22
	Direction of Gas Cloud

0 Miles   1   2   3
0 Kilometers   2   3   4

© 2015 Jeffrey L. Ward

Gassed British soldiers

Gas attack

Fritz Haber and Albert Einstein (Courtesy of the Fritz Haber Institute)

General Erich von Falkenhayn

The *Lusitania* in New York Harbor

Admiral Alfred von Tirpitz

A cross-section of the *Lusitania* (Mary Evans Picture Library)

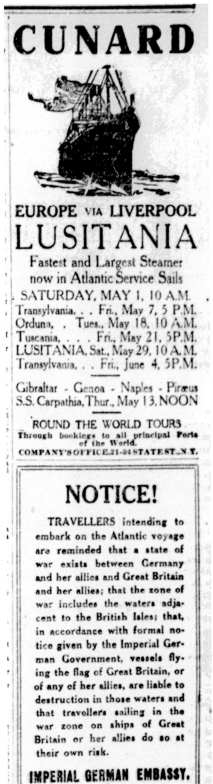

CUNARD

EUROPE VIA LIVERPOOL
LUSITANIA

Fastest and Largest Steamer
now in Atlantic Service Sails
SATURDAY, MAY 1, 10 A.M.
Transylvania, . . Fri., May 7, 5 P.M.
Orduna, . Tues., May 18, 10 A.M.
Tuscania, . . . Fri., May 21, 5P.M.
LUSITANIA, Sat., May 29, 10 A.M.
Transylvania, . . Fri., June 4, 5P.M.

Gibraltar - Genoa - Naples - Piræus
S.S. Carpathia, Thur., May 13, NOON

ROUND THE WORLD TOURS
Through bookings to all principal Ports
of the World.
COMPANY'S OFFICE. 21-24 STATE ST., N. Y.

NOTICE!

TRAVELLERS intending to
embark on the Atlantic voyage
are reminded that a state of
war exists between Germany
and her allies and Great Britain
and her allies; that the zone of
war includes the waters adjacent to the British Isles; that,
in accordance with formal notice given by the Imperial German Government, vessels flying the flag of Great Britain, or
of any of her allies, are liable to
destruction in those waters and
that travellers sailing in the
war zone on ships of Great
Britain or her allies do so at
their own risk.

IMPERIAL GERMAN EMBASSY.
WASHINGTON, D. C., APRIL 22, 1915.

A warning from the German government in the *New York Times* published on May 1, 1915

Alfred Vanderbilt

Captain William Turner

Kapitän-Leutnant Walther Schwieger

The German U-boat *U-20*, responsible for sinking the *Lusitania*, grounded on the Danish coast in 1916

A sketch by Oliver Bernard illustrating the moment a torpedo struck the *Lusitania* (© Illustrated London News Ltd/Mary Evans)

Passengers evacuate the ship (Mary Evans Picture Library)

Survivors of the *Lusitania* tragedy in Queenstown (Mary Evans/EpicTallandier)

Ferdinand von Zeppelin

L3 zeppelin

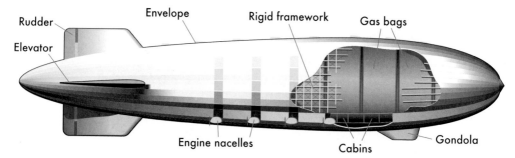

Diagram of the interior of a zeppelin (Wikimedia Creative Commons license, Korteenea)

L3 zeppelin taking flight

The skeletal remains of a crashed zeppelin

Peter Strasser, Head of Germany's
Naval Airship Division

Kapitän-Leutnant
Heinrich Mathy

Damage to homes in London caused by zeppelin bombing raids (Mary Evans
Robert Hunt Collection/Imperial War Museum)

mid-channel course; to operate at full speed off harbors; to post extra lookouts, and to ram any attacking submarines. He added another four, including some issued earlier and related mainly to avoiding attacks by surface vessels. His sixth and final choice was a dubious one—an instruction dated April 16 advising captains that "fast steamers can considerably reduce the chance of successful surprise attack by zig-zagging."

Webb knew that a more comprehensive version of the zigzagging note, including an illustrative diagram, had not been issued until May 13. However, he thought an initial three-paragraph note might have gone out on April 16. If so, and if Turner could be claimed to have received and ignored it, it would further demonstrate his incompetence. Webb asked Cunard to establish whether they had received and issued it. The answer was inconclusive but Webb decided to include it anyway, perhaps because he believed that if Turner could be shown to have ignored it—the *Lusitania* had not been zigzagging—it would focus criticism on Turner, which he, as well as Fisher and Churchill, considered both justified and expedient.

Captain Webb also had to determine what should be said to the inquiry about the signals sent to the *Lusitania* during her final voyage. He asked the various wireless stations to provide details of all transmissions. He then listed in his submission only general messages to all ships in the area, such as ones sent out nightly and based on the February guidance about avoiding headlands and steering a mid-channel course. He did not include the messages sent to the *Lusitania* alone during the two days before the sinking, for example, the QUESTOR/WESTRONA exchange about which code the *Lusitania* was using, or personal messages, such as that from May Barwell to Alfred Vanderbilt.

From gaps in the telegram sequence on Admiralty files and from informal statements made by the Ministry of Defence to previous historians, it is possible there may have been further official messages sent only to the *Lusitania*. Their content has been a matter of fervid speculation. If they indeed existed, Webb did not include them in any of his drafts. What he did include was criticism of Turner for not following some of the instructions he had listed. The captain had not only failed to zigzag but had also not kept a mid-channel course as well as tarrying at reduced speed in a danger zone. Webb's concluding sentence read: "He thus kept his valuable vessel for an unnecessary length of time in the area where she was most liable to attack, inviting disaster." The sensitivities were such that Webb produced at least two drafts of his note. The major change in the later version was to emphasize the trouble taken by the Admiralty to ensure that Captain Turner received the messages sent and to provide further details of some of them.

In addition to Webb's submission, statements were collected from every surviving crewmember and recorded in the same hand on partially preprinted forms but signed by the individual witness. Where witnesses like able seaman Hennessy, on lookout in the crow's nest when the torpedo was sighted, were illiterate each man marked them with his cross. All statements recorded in almost identical wording that the ship had been in good order, unarmed, and that boat drills had been carried out before departing New York. Hugh Johnston, the quartermaster who had remained at the wheel until told by Captain Turner to save himself, later recalled the pressure from Cunard to be loyal to the company. Despite the Admiralty knowing definitively that the U-20 had sunk the *Lusitania* with only one torpedo, in what seems to have been a concerted attempt by the authorities to cover up the possibility that the widely reported second explosion had been caused by the munitions the liner had been carrying, witnesses were also encouraged to testify that there had been two torpedo strikes. According to Hugh Johnston, "I was asked in Liverpool getting ready to go to London how many torpedoes struck the ship. I said one. Well I was told two would help the case. I said there was only one."

Passengers' statements were carefully sifted and five were initially invited to give evidence. A few more volunteered to do so and were accepted but Oliver Bernard's persistent offers were ignored despite the prominence given to his statements and drawings of the sinking in the press. He explained the reason in a letter to the grieving mother of the missing medical student Dick Prichard: "I have been prepared and am still ready to declare under oath that we were struck by only ONE torpedo . . . abaft the bridge."

IN THE UNITED States, the neutral country where Britain was most concerned to preserve the propaganda advantage, the press condemned the sinking as barbaric. Editors broke the news using banner headlines set in the enormous typeface they irreverently called "Second Coming type." The *Minneapolis Journal* declared: "Germany intends to become the outlaw of nations. Perhaps we are yet to witness savagery carried to its ultimate perfection." The *New York Nation* called the sinking "A deed for which a Hun would blush, a Turk be ashamed and a Barbary pirate apologize . . . The law of nations and the law of God have been alike trampled upon . . . The torpedo that sank the *Lusitania* also sank Germany in the opinion of mankind . . . It is at once a crime and a monumental folly . . . She has affronted the moral sense of the world." To the *Boston Post* the sinking was "a reversion to barbarism . . . the worst crime against civilization and humanity that the modern world has ever known" and to the *Boston Herald* it was "another and a most frightful illustration of the German official temper. It is the spirit of Attila the Hun, translated into the 20th century." The *Richmond Times-Dispatch*'s view was "Germany surely must have gone mad. The torpedoing and sinking evince a reckless disregard of the opinions of the world in general and of this country in particular." The *Los Angeles Times* wrote that Germany had placed itself "outside the pale of civilization."

Crowds booed and hissed German ambassador Count von Bernstorff in New York. As he got into a taxi for the station to return to Washington reporters jostled him. He shouted that he would not make a statement and when the driver did not move off yelled, "Go on, damn you, go on!" Reporters pursued him to Pennsylvania Station, down to the platform and on to the train demanding his reaction to claims that he had provoked the attack on the *Lusitania* by placing the warning in the papers, even that he was a murderer. Von Bernstorff responded angrily that he was indifferent to anything the papers might allege.

President Wilson received the news of the *Lusitania*'s sinking at the end of a cabinet meeting. When he spoke to his private secretary, Joe Tumulty, he had "tears in his eyes" and told him that if he dwelled on the personal tragedies reported in the newspapers he would "see red in everything . . . I am afraid that when I am called upon to act with reference to this situation I could not be just to anyone. I dare not act unjustly and cannot indulge my passionate feelings." After a pause, he added, "In God's name how could any nation calling itself civilised purpose so horrible a thing?"

On Wall Street, industrial stocks plunged on news of the sinking. Bethlehem Steel, the manufacturers of the empty shrapnel shells and fuses on board the *Lusitania*, dropped from 159 to 130 and Amalgamated Copper from 74¾ to 63. A message from Colonel House in London argued that "America has come to the parting of the ways when she must determine whether she stands for civilized or uncivilized warfare . . . We can no longer remain neutral spectators. Our action in this crisis will determine the part we will play when peace is made, and how far we may influence a settlement for the lasting good of humanity . . . Our intervention will save rather than increase the loss of lives." The American ambassador to Britain, Walter Hines Page telegrammed that "the sinking of the *Lusitania* following the use of poisonous gas . . . the English regard as the complete abandonment of war regulations and of humanity. The United States must declare war or forfeit European respect."

Ex-President Roosevelt, whose decision to run in the 1912 presidential election as a Progressive had split the Republican vote and handed the White House to Wilson, called the sinking "the greatest act of piracy in history" and demanded "immediate decision and vigour" from the president he damned as a coward and "as insincere and cold-blooded an opportunist as we have ever had in the Presidency" and a Secretary of State he thought a "human trombone." Ex-President Taft, the official Republican candidate in 1912, wrote in much more measured terms to Wilson suggesting that in the light of "the ruthless spirit in [Germany's] conduct of war which breaks every accepted law of war and every principle of international justice to neutrals" a diplomatic protest might not be sufficient. Severing diplomatic relations with Germany might be a sensible way forward.

However, Wilson told Tumulty he had to consider his first step carefully and cautiously "because once having taken it I cannot withdraw from it." He bided his time while gauging the public mood. Secretary of State William Jennings Bryan led the call for moderation, arguing that the Allies could not rely upon neutral passengers to shield ships carrying contraband. "It would be like putting women and children in front of an Army," he wrote to Wilson.

The British ambassador to Washington, Cecil Spring-Rice, gauged correctly that, although there was widespread indignation and hostility to Germany in the United States, there was little support for war. He was also, like the British government, well aware that if it joined the war, the United States would want a major say in the peace, and therefore it was more in Britain's interest to retain the United States as a supplier of munitions. He wrote to London on May 9 cautioning, "As our main interest is to preserve U.S. as a base for supplies I hope language of our press will be very guarded."

May 10 was a busy day for Wilson. He was now passionately in love with Edith Bolling Galt, a buxom Southern widow sixteen years younger than him. On May 4 she had refused his proposal of marriage saying she had not known him long enough and it was less than a year since his wife had died but she encouraged him to continue to hope. On May 10 he found time to meet her at least once as well as to write to her that "when I know that I am going to see you and am all a-quiver with the thought how can I use this stupid <u>pen</u> to tell you that I love you? . . . The greatest and the most delightful thing in the world [is] that I am permitted to <u>love you</u>." Later that day the president headed for Philadelphia where he had decided to test public opinion on the *Lusitania* before a crowd of fifteen thousand, including four thousand newly naturalized citizens, in the convention hall. He told them "the example of America must be the example not merely of peace because it will not fight but of peace because peace is the healing and elevating influence of the world and strife is not. There is such a thing as a man being too proud to fight. There is such a thing as a nation being so right that it does not need to convince others by force that it is right."

Wilson, for once, misjudged the nation's mood. Although few wanted war neither did they require intellectual theorizing that suggested principles might not be worth fighting for. The backlash was instant and not only from hawks like Theodore Roosevelt who proclaimed, "President Wilson's delightful statement about the nation being 'too proud to fight' seemed to me to reach the nadir of cowardly infamy." Wilson recognized his error and at a press conference the next day explained that he had been "expressing a personal attitude" and not giving "any intimation of policy on any special matter." He confessed to Edith Galt, "I just do not know what I said in

Philadelphia . . . because my heart was in such a whirl." Nevertheless, the phrase "too proud to fight" would dog Wilson for the rest of his career.

On May 10 Count von Bernstorff submitted a note to the U.S. administration from his government expressing "deepest sympathy at the loss of American lives" but placing all responsibility on the British government. The sinking was one of the retaliatory measures to which the British hunger blockade had forced Germany; British merchant ships were usually armed and had "repeatedly tried to ram submarines," thus preventing the use of "visit and search" procedures; what's more the *Lusitania* had been carrying contraband. The German government could only regret that the American passengers had relied on British promises rather than heeding German warnings.

During a three-hour discussion the U.S. cabinet worked through a draft response prepared by Robert Lansing, which the president later redrafted. Dispatched on May 13, it reminded Germany of the principle of "strict accountability" and that America had warned Germany not to kill American citizens on the high seas. Employing submarines humanely against merchant shipping was a "practical impossibility . . . No warning that an unlawful and inhumane act will be committed can possibly be accepted as an excuse or palliation for that act" or diminish "the responsibility for its commission." The German government should, the memorandum demanded, disown the sinking, offer reparation, and take immediate measures to prevent its reoccurrence.

Bryan had argued for a simultaneous protest to Britain about its blockade of Germany while reviving his previous suggestion that the United States government should warn its citizens of the danger of sailing on the ships of combatant nations. Wilson rejected both proposals, the latter after consulting Lansing, still Bryan's subordinate, because his own "strict accountability" statement in February could be construed as condoning U.S. citizens traveling on belligerent ships. To change policy now might cause people to question whether his previous position had been sound.

The more hawkish among Wilson's cabinet and advisers were now clearly dominant, perhaps not least because—despite his desire to keep the United States neutral so it could mediate a settlement—Wilson's private and deepest sympathies chimed with theirs, thinking as he did "England's violation of neutral rights is different from Germany's violation of the rights of humanity." The administration's firm note to the German government also resonated with most American opinion. To the *Baltimore Sun* it contained "all the red blood that a red-blooded nation can ask"; to the *New York Times* the president had "the united support of the American people." America's fellow neutrals approved too, *La Prensa* in Buenos Aires stating "If the principles laid down in the Note don't prevail, there will be an end to all neutrality and universal war will come."

American opinion against Germany grew even stronger with the publication in May of a British government report by a highly respected former British ambassador to Washington, Lord Bryce, which detailed German atrocities in Belgium. As well as such confirmed outrages as the burning of Dinant and Louvain and the cases of the indiscriminate killing and punishment shootings of civilians, it contained allegations of rape and baby murder of more dubious authenticity. Nevertheless, Bryce's prestige, and the outrage at the sinking of the *Lusitania*, ensured that they were readily believed. The *Washington Herald* commented that the Germans who were guilty of the "frightfulness against Belgium" were the same "who sank the *Lusitania* and murdered 115 [*sic*] Americans because England interfered with her commerce."

On May 15 the *Times* printed the horrific story that had been circulating widely among troops at the front for some time of how counterattacking Allied troops at Ypres had discovered the body of a Canadian sergeant crucified on a Belgian barn door, hands and neck pierced by German bayonets. Even though genuinely believed by the troops, no reliable evidence has ever been produced to substantiate the story and it is quite probably untrue. However, against the background of American revulsion at other German "frightfulness" it was immediately believed and made ever more difficult Bryan's effort to soften the president's approach.

In May, too, the first reports of the mass killing by Germany's allies, the Turks, of Armenians further increased feelings against Britain's enemies. Ultimately, the death of some seven hundred thousand men, women, and children would become the first modern genocide. On May 24 the British, French, and Russian governments accused the Turks of "deliberately exterminating" the Armenians and stated: "In view of these crimes of

Turkey against humanity and civilisation the Allied governments announce publicly . . . that they will hold personally responsible for these crimes all members of the Ottoman Government and those of their agents who are implicated in such massacres." This was one of the first uses of the phrase "crimes against humanity."

Meanwhile Colonel House had left Europe, abandoning his attempts to broker a peace settlement. He wrote to the president: "The sinking of the *Lusitania*, the use of poisonous gases and other breaches of international laws made it impossible for me to continue the discussion in England of the freedom of the seas or the tentative formation of a peace covenant. If these things had not happened, I could have gone along and by midsummer we would have had the belligerents discussing through you the peace terms."

THE GERMAN GOVERNMENT reacted angrily to the American note of May 13. The kaiser spoke of "the necessity of intensified submarine warfare, even against neutrals." Germany's uncompromising reply reached Washington on May 31. It stated simply that its previous note had already expressed "deep regret" for the deaths of neutral citizens and suggested the American government should order a "careful examination" of the circumstances of the sinking. Despite a definitive report to the contrary from the German Foreign Office's legal director, it repeated Germany's claims that the *Lusitania* was an armed auxiliary cruiser, adding that the British government allowed its ships to hide behind American flags, British merchantmen had orders to ram submarines, and the *Lusitania* had been carrying Canadian troops and munitions whose explosion had caused the sinking.

Despite this firm, formal response, German civilian officials such as Chancellor von Bethmann Hollweg and Foreign Minister Gottlieb von Jagow appreciated how badly the sinking had damaged Germany's reputation and began briefing their embassies abroad on how best to defend the position. Captain Schwieger of the *U-20*, summoned to Berlin on landing and expecting to be congratulated, was instead interrogated and according to von Tirpitz "treated very ungraciously." Now as he anxiously awaited a U.S. response, von Bethmann Hollweg understood just how much depended on there being no further such incidents. Conscious that the Allied strategy to bring Italy into the war on their side had succeeded when Italy had declared war on Germany's ally Austro-Hungary on May 23, and knowing that this would divert Austrian troops from the eastern front where they would have to be replaced by German divisions, he warned his colleagues that if the U-boat campaign continued as at present, it would provoke America to declare war, bringing even more forces to the Allied side. He asked the kaiser to convene a Crown Council of military and civil leaders. The kaiser agreed and the council met at the end of May.

The mood was tense. Von Falkenhayn stated that Germany's military position on land would be prejudiced if "more neutral powers joined our enemies as a result of the U-boat war." Von Tirpitz and Bachmann insisted that the safety of neutral ships could only be guaranteed by suspending the U-boat campaign, something they could not support. The kaiser sided with them, adding that the chancellor would have to bear the responsibility for stopping submarine warfare, a decision "which would be very unpopular among the people." Von Müller, head of the kaiser's naval cabinet, recommended a compromise—to issue orders to U-boat commanders "which would take the political situation into account" by telling them that when in doubt it was preferable to allow an enemy ship to escape than to sink a neutral. To his relief the kaiser agreed.

While the German high command bickered and sniped at one another, the American press condemned Germany's latest note. "Impudently trifling in spirit and flagrantly dishonest in matter," wrote the *Philadelphia North American*. The *New York World* called it "the answer of an outlaw who assumes no obligation to Society."

President Wilson immediately drafted a firm response on his Hammond typewriter, which he put to a cabinet meeting the next morning, June 1. To a fellow cabinet member, Bryan looked "under great strain." When his renewed proposal of a simultaneous protest to Britain about its blockade was rejected, he burst out "You people are not neutral—you are taking sides." President Wilson told him with a "steely glitter" in his eyes, "Mr. Bryan, you are not warranted in making such an assertion. There are none of us who can justly be accused of being unfair." Bryan apologized but continued to argue that "arbitration was the proper remedy."

Wilson's next draft of the reply stated that American customs officials had done their duty in verifying that the *Lusitania* was not a naval vessel, was not armed, was not serving as a troop transport, and that her cargo complied with the laws of the United States. If the Germans had evidence to the contrary they should produce it. In any case, questions of carrying contraband and of any contribution to the sinking from exploding munitions did not justify attacking the *Lusitania* without warning. Only if the *Lusitania* had resisted or refused to permit "visit and search" would the submarine commander have been justified in hazarding the ship.

Bryan believed he was losing any influence he retained and, deeply concerned by the latest draft's uncompromising tone, on Saturday, June 5, visited William McAdoo, the secretary of the treasury and an old friend. A "visibly nervous" Bryan told him this second note, as drafted, "would surely lead to war with Germany . . . His usefulness as Secretary of State was over" and he intended to resign.

McAdoo persuaded him to think it over during the weekend but was under no illusion that Bryan would change his mind. He went to the White House to warn Wilson who showed no surprise, observing that Bryan had been "growing more and more out of sympathy with the Administration in the controversy with Germany." In a letter to Edith Galt he put it more bluntly, indicating that Bryan "is a traitor, though I can say so as yet only to you."

Bryan spent a troubled weekend—his wife had to call a doctor to prescribe him sleeping pills. On June 8, he visited Wilson and tried for an hour to make him change his stance, but could not. He told the president that "Colonel House has been Secretary of State and I have never had your full confidence." Then he went back to his office and wrote out his resignation.

President Wilson immediately appointed Robert Lansing acting secretary of state and on June 9 he dispatched the final version of the United States' second protest to the German government. It stated Germany must accept the right of American citizens "bound on lawful errands" to travel on merchant ships of belligerent powers. The lives of noncombatants "cannot lawfully or rightfully be put in jeopardy by the capture or destruction of an unresisting merchantman." The German government should undertake the "measures necessary to put these principles into practice in respect of the safeguarding of American lives and American ships."

The press and his opponents vilified Bryan following his resignation. A sarcastic *New York Times* called it the wisest action of his political career. The *New York World* described it as "unspeakable treachery, not only to the President, but to the nation." The *New York Telegraph* thought that his "idea of an ultimatum seems to be that it should be addressed to the President of his own country."

Even many fellow Democrats rejoiced. Ambassador Page congratulated Wilson on being a fine "executioner," adding, "One American newspaper says truly: 'There always was a yellow streak in [Bryan], and now in this crisis he shows a white liver.' . . . Conscience he has about little things—grape juice, cigarettes, peace treaties, etc.—but about a big situation, such as embarrassing a President, he is fundamentally immoral. Well, cranks always do you a bad turn, sooner or later. Avoid 'em, son, avoid 'em!"

CHAPTER FIFTEEN

"The Very Earth Shook"

JUST OVER A week earlier, on May 31, as dusk was about to fall, between three and four hundred German army ground crew carefully guided the gray-painted zeppelin *LZ38*—secured by guylines to trolleys running along rails—out of its shed at Evere, north of German-occupied Brussels. The airship—536 feet long and 61 feet in diameter—was one of a new generation of zeppelins that both the German army and navy had been waiting for. *LZ38* could climb at one thousand feet a minute and its four six-cylinder 210-horsepower Maybach petrol engines gave it a top speed of fifty-five miles per hour. Its self-contained gas cells—secured by wire and netting within the latticed metal girders—held 1,126,400 cubic feet of hydrogen. *LZ38* could remain airborne for twenty-four hours.

The zeppelin was about to depart on the first ever air raid on London. The kaiser had sanctioned the mission only the day before, till then still reluctant to bomb any part of the city where his royal relations lived. A recent British raid on German headquarters at Charleville while he had been inspecting positions on the western front had prompted this change of heart. In the kaiser's mind, by their act the British had violated what von Tirpitz called his "quaint" concept of "tacit understanding" between monarchs not to attack one another personally. The only condition he had imposed was that German raids had to be east of the Tower of London.

Thirty-five-year-old Hauptmann Erich Linnarz, the army's most experienced pilot, was commanding *LZ38* on the mission that would launch Der Feuerplan (The Fire Plan) advocated by von Tirpitz when he had urged setting fire to London "in thirty places." His hope was that the mass dropping of incendiary bombs on London would cause such ferocious fire-storms that its citizens would demand an end to the war.

During the minutes before takeoff Linnarz and his men went through their final checks of the instruments—the compass, the inclinometer measuring the airship's upward or downward angle in flight, the altimeter showing the height above ground, the variometer for measuring the speed of ascent or descent, the electric thermometer recording the temperature of the gas cells—all the controls and dials painted with luminous radium so they could be read in the dark. While *LZ38* had still been in its shed, the effect of the "lift"—the amount by which, with its gas bags full of hydrogen, it was lighter than the air it was displacing—had been exactly counterbalanced. Everything from the crew themselves, the petrol and lubricating oil, the guns and bombs had been carefully weighed and water ballast added to achieve the "neutral buoyancy" required to counteract the airship's tendency either to rise or to rest too heavily on the ground.

In the hours ahead Linnarz and the rest of his twenty-strong crew would depend on each other as much as on *LZ38*'s technical sophistication for their safety and success. Being an airshipman required special qualities. Peter Strasser, commander of the German navy's Airship Division, defined them as "a keen pleasure in flying, a strong sense of duty, self-control, will-power, and the ability to form rapid decisions; good eyesight, physical dexterity, and a sound physique, particularly heart and nerves; no tendency to dizziness or sea-sickness; a well-developed sense of direction; a quick perception of tactical and strategic conditions; a knowledge of the principles of both open and trench warfare; familiarity with the science of gunnery . . . the ability to take aerial photographs and interpret them; a working knowledge of petrol engines, meteorology, field telegraphy and wireless telegraphy . . . and the use of carrier pigeons"—the latter to take information back to base giving the airship's last position in the event of mechanical or other problems.

Linnarz would command the mission from the fully-enclosed forward-control gondola slung beneath the airship's keel where the windows gave him good all round visibility, except toward the rear. With him was his second in command, responsible for operating the bombsight—a complex instrument manufactured by the company Carl Zeiss of Jena, renowned for its optical instruments. To get a fix on the target, the officer first consulted the altimeter, then checked the airship's speed over the ground using a stopwatch to time the passage of an object between two crosshairs representing a distance of three hundred meters. Also in the control car were the navigator and two warrant officers responsible for working the elevation and rudder controls. Immediately behind them, in a compartment soundproofed to cut out noise, were the two wireless operators who would use the radio equipment that for a while at least would keep Linnarz in touch with his base.

Linnarz's engineer and team of mechanics were in the small streamlined rear gondola with the airship's engines where the noise level made talking near impossible in the fume-laden air. Linnarz thought that "to exist for hours in this roaring devil's cauldron where glowing heat and biting cold alternated, required a stone constitution and iron nerves." However, it was nothing compared to "the demands made upon the mechanics when . . . the lives of the entire crew depended upon the repairing in mid-air of damage to the motor or propeller." *LZ38* was also carrying a skilled sailmaker ready to mend any tears in the exterior skin enclosing the airship's rigid duralumin frame or in the gas-tight fabric covering the hydrogen cells. The latter was made of several layers of expensive "gold beater's skin"—the outer membrane of cattle intestines, thin but with great tensile strength and used as an interleaf in the making of gold leaf—bonded to a light cotton fabric.

To defend against attack, *LZ38* was carrying nine-millimeter Maxim machine guns, some in the front and rear gondolas, others mounted on external gun platforms. On occasion commanders chose to fly without them because of their weight and because they believed a zeppelin's best defense against enemy fire was to rise out of range by jettisoning some of the water ballast stored in cloth-backed rubber bags.

To survive the subzero temperatures—sometimes as low as −30 degrees Celsius—Linnarz and his men were wearing two sets of thick woolen underclothes, leather overalls and helmets, fur-lined coats, scarves, and gloves. Their fur-lined shoes had straw or rubber soles since the metal nails of ordinary shoes could raise dangerous sparks from the ship's struts. They carried bottles of liquid oxygen round their necks in case of altitude sickness. To sustain them they had supplies of strong coffee and "a swallow of cognac"—the latter only permitted once a certain altitude had been reached—and bread, sausage, and chocolate. Proximity to so much flammable hydrogen put smoking out of the question.

Like submariners, Linnarz and his men had to cope with a cramped and isolated environment. Along the length of the airship's triangular keel—formed by the two bottom longitudinal girders of the hull and an apex girder—ran a narrow *langlauf* or catwalk connecting the various sections of the airship. From it ladders descended into the open air to the gondolas suspended beneath the keel. Climbing these ladders at altitude occasionally brought on vertigo, causing men to black out and tumble thousands of feet to their deaths. Along the catwalk were tanks of spare fuel for the engines, the bags of water ballast, the rudder-control cables, the speaking tubes through which the crew communicated, and the bombs hanging vertically in racks. Beneath them were shuttered hatches that could be opened either from the control hatch or by working control wires within the keel. On its mission to London *LZ38* was carrying thirty-five pear-shaped high-explosive bombs, weighing up to 220 pounds each, and ninety 20-pound incendiary bombs encased in tarred rope and packed with benzol, tar, and thermite—a substance that burns at a very high temperature.

Again like U-boatmen, airshipmen needed great skill to handle their fragile craft in difficult, often highly dangerous, conditions. An airman described the challenges of flying a zeppelin: "The aerial sea is in constant motion and in addition to variable currents flowing from different directions in the same horizontal plane . . . we have powerful up-draughts and down-draughts to allow for." As in a U-boat, the prospect of meeting a horrible end must have been hard to ignore. Peter Strasser, who ordered naval zeppelin crews not to carry parachutes because of their heavy weight—fifty-one pounds—provided his men with poison as "an unfailing preventive from the agonising death which results from being burnt alive." *LZ38*, as an army zeppelin, was carrying parachutes but the crew must have wondered whether they would in fact be of any use.

This was not Linnarz's first flight to England. Having taken delivery of *LZ38*, the German army had been probing London's eastern defenses.

On May 10—the day of the first mass burials of *Lusitania* victims in Queenstown—Linnarz had dropped incendiary bombs on the seaside town of Southend and also thrown out a large piece of cardboard upon which was written: "You English. We have come and will come again. Kill or cure. German." He had indeed returned, bombing Kent on May 17 and Southend for a second time on May 26, proving a raid on London was viable.

Now that the much-anticipated takeoff time had come, ground crew, holding the lines beneath the bow and stern, released them as Linnarz's mechanics kicked the engines into life. As darkness fell Linnarz set course for the English coast. He recalled how as it came in view "suddenly we had a queer feeling as if our nerves were tightening in an almost joyous anticipation. Would we succeed in breaking through the chain of coastal batteries and remain unobserved or at least undamaged?" He searched "for a cloud behind which we could slip through the English coastal defence. Under us, on the shimmering sea, cruised enemy patrol-boats; I prudently ordered the lights out. The airship became a ghostly apparition. In the control-car, the only light was on the dial of the machine telegraph. In his narrow cubicle the radio operator sat with his headset over his ears, listening to the confusion of signals and voices whispering in the infinity of space . . . The antenna followed the airship like the spawn of a mother fish."

Shortly before ten P.M., he was over the seaside resort of Margate where Petty Officer Edwin Oak-Rhind, stationed on lookout, logged *LZ38*'s height at some five thousand feet. Linnarz then piloted his ship through the darkness across the Thames estuary and headed westward toward London. "At high speed we steer for their city," he later wrote. Reaching northeast London an hour later he found "little effort to dim the city." Instead "London was all lit up and we enjoyed total surprise." Minutes later, he prepared to drop the bomb that would shatter forever the invulnerability of what was then not only the world's most populous city but its most important financial center and capital of a global empire.

Linnarz joined his bombardier who was already lying on his stomach on the catwalk by a bomb hatch, "ready to spill his murderous load overboard." Linnarz described the moment he gave the command. " 'Let go!' I cry. The first bomb is falling on London! . . . What a cursed long time it takes between release and impact while the bomb travels thousands of feet!

We fear that it has proved a dud—until the explosion reassures us. Already we have frightened them; away goes the second, an incendiary bomb, thrown out by hand, a pin being removed to make it 'live.' "

Linnarz's bombs tumbled on to unsuspecting Londoners thousands of feet below and unable to hear the rhythmic throbbing of the zeppelin's engines. An incendiary crashed through the roof of a Victorian terraced house, 16 Alkham Road, in Stoke Newington, a crowded, modestly prospering district of neat two- and three-storied houses, due north of the Tower of London. As the house's top floor immediately burst into flames, the occupants—clerk Albert Lovell, his wife, children, and two guests—scrambled out into the street unharmed. Meanwhile the *LZ38* dropped further incendiaries on nearby Dynevor Road, on an outbuilding behind a pub in Neville Road—though this bomb failed to ignite—and on 27 Neville Road, gutting the house.

The airship then passed over Stoke Newington High Street before heading south toward the working class district of Hoxton, described in a survey a few years earlier as "one of the worst parts of London, where poverty and overcrowding are characteristic of practically the whole district." The Smith family were in bed in their house in Cowper Road when they heard what sounded like "a terrible rushing of wind" and people shouting "Fire" and "The Germans are here." Running outside Mr. Smith saw that the second floor of the house of his neighbor, Samuel Leggatt, was on fire. Leggatt and his neighbors managed to reach the bedroom where his five children were sleeping and, despite being burned themselves, to rescue four. But in the confusion the youngest—three-year-old Elsie—was left behind in the mistaken belief that someone had already carried her to safety. A policeman later found her charred body huddled beneath a bed. That night, as a Russian night watchman fled the burning bamboo furniture warehouse he had been guarding, angry Hoxton residents, convinced he was German and must have started the fire, attacked him.

Meanwhile Linnarz took *LZ38* south dropping further incendiaries, including two that destroyed 187 Balls Pond Road, a three-story house belonging to builder Thomas Sharpling. A policeman heard "the sound of machinery in the air" then saw the house suddenly burst into flames. The Sharplings managed to get out and one of their lodgers leaped from a window into a blanket held out by rescuers, but two others—forty-six-year-old laborer Henry Good and Caroline his wife—burned to death.

Dazed citizens looked out of their windows to see roadways that had become "a mass of flames" and a sky "red with the light of flames." Arriving above Shoreditch—home in Elizabethan England to the country's first theater where Shakespeare's plays were first produced in London and in 1915 still a center of entertainment rivaling London's West End—Linnarz dropped three incendiaries on the Shoreditch Empire music hall, where a late-night performance was under way. Astonishingly no one was hurt and the orchestra played on while the audience was evacuated into the street. After setting a railway goods station alight, Linnarz headed southeast to bomb Spitalfields, long settled by refugees from persecution, from Protestant French Huguenot silk weavers in the 1680s to eastern European Jewish immigrants in the nineteenth century.

Next Linnarz steered for nearby Whitechapel, a poverty-stricken, densely packed area of slum lodgings and sweatshops described by Charles Booth, founder of the Salvation Army, as "the Eldorado of the east, a gathering together of poor fortune seekers; its streets full of buying and selling, the poor living on the poor." In 1888, the notorious Jack the Ripper had murdered his victims there. Linnarz's bombs hit a synagogue, a whiskey distillery, and a street still filled with people. One killed eight-year-old Samuel Reuben, on his way home after seeing a film at Greenberg's Picture Palace. His body was found with his entrails spilling out. Another injured a young woman so badly she died within a few hours.

Turning northeastward, Linnarz's explosive and incendiary bombs fell on Stepney, another area of overcrowded slums where east European Jews, Irish, Germans, Scandinavians, and Chinese lived side by side, many employed in the nearby docks. Reaching Stratford—home of the Eastern Counties Railway's main locomotive and rolling stock works and where many worked on the railways—at around eleven thirty P.M. he dropped an incendiary on 26 Colgrave Road. As it smashed through the house, it narrowly missed its occupants, Peter Gillies and his wife, lying in bed. A neighbor heard the droning of engines, then saw a dark object fall through the Gillies' roof. Linnarz dropped his final bombs on the nearby suburb of Leytonstone, then released water ballast to rise higher and turn away from the capital where his raid had lasted barely half an hour, and return safely to base at Evere.

The London Fire Brigade, whose fighters had been called to more than forty fires, counted the remains of ninety-one incendiary bombs and twenty-eight explosive bombs and estimated damage to property at £18,596. The human cost was seven dead, all civilians, including four children, and thirty-five civilians injured. Sylvia Pankhurst—daughter of suffragette leader Emmeline Pankhurst and friend of *Lusitania* survivor and fellow suffragette Margaret Mackworth—was nearly among the casualties. Having set up the East London Federation of Suffragettes, she had gone to live in the area and had been working at her desk when "huge reports smote the ear, shattering, deafening . . . An air raid! . . . The angry grinding . . . pulsated above us. Again that terrific burst of noise; those awful bangs, the roar of the falling buildings . . . What a burst of sound, tremendous; the very earth shook with it!"[*]

The raid had brutally exposed the difficulties of protecting civilian populations against aerial attack. Despite the highly colored accounts Linnarz subsequently gave to the press describing "searchlights reaching after us like gigantic spider's legs; right, left and all around," a "storm of shell and shrapnel" and sixty searchlights "still stabbing the darkness" as *LZ38* departed, not a single searchlight had caught the zeppelin in its beam, not a single gun had fired on it, and indeed in the dark scarcely anyone had caught even a glimpse of it. Of the British planes sent up to attack *LZ38*, only one sighted the zeppelin but engine trouble forced the pilot to turn back before he could attack.

A particular problem was that zeppelins raided by night and as a British observer put it, "Much as we loathe the Zeppelin raiders they must be given credit for their remarkable skill in making night journeys." The night-fighting skills of British pilots—and the development of suitable planes—were by contrast still rudimentary. To help prevent planes colliding in bad weather or at night, the Admiralty had ordered both the tips of

---

[*] In the first week of the war as a gesture toward national unity, the British government had remitted all suffragettes' sentences of imprisonment. However, Sylvia remained an advocate of peace unlike her mother and sister Christabel who both supported the war.

propeller blades and wing struts to be coated with luminous radium paint. To make landing in the dark less hazardous, flares were lit along the airstrips. To enable pilots to judge their distance above the ground they were provided with a makeshift device consisting of a length of weighted string to be dangled fifty feet beneath their plane when coming in to land. The theory was that the weight would strike the ground, triggering a signal in the cockpit. Sometimes the weight simply fell off or else hit an obstacle like a tree.

Matters were not helped by an ongoing debate over the responsibility for London's air defenses. In late May, following Churchill's departure from the Admiralty, his replacement as First Lord of the Admiralty, Arthur Balfour, had attempted to shift responsibility from the Admiralty—whose planes, he argued, were needed for anti-U-boat patrols—to the War Office. However, the latter had resisted, insisting it would not be in a fit position to take over the defense until sometime in 1916.

Londoners had been given some warning. On May 23, the *Guardian* and other papers reported advice from Scotland Yard on precautions to be taken "in case of an air raid on London" especially if zeppelins dropped bombs containing poison gas: "It would be well for persons . . . taking refuge (in houses) to keep all windows and doors on the lower floors closed, so as to prevent the admission of deleterious gases . . . The suspicion is quite justified that the Zeppelins, if they get to London, will use bombs containing poison gas. Germany has tried poisonous gas at the front." Zeppelins might drop poison gases of a yet more "insidious and perilous character" than seen on the western front.

Early on June 1, the Admiralty issued its first communiqué about the raid: "Zeppelins are reported to have been seen near Ramsgate and Brentford and in certain outlying parts of London. Many fires are reported, but these cannot absolutely be connected with the visit of airships. Further particulars will be issued as soon as they can be collected and collated." This brief and deliberately misleading statement reflected the Admiralty's concern that zeppelin raids would provoke panic on London's streets. A "guidance" note to editors, issued shortly afterward, effectively muzzled reporting of zeppelin attacks: "The press are especially reminded that no statement whatever must be published dealing with the places in the neighbourhood of London reached by aircraft, or the course proposed to be taken by them, or any statement or diagram that might indicate the ground or route covered by them. The Admiralty communiqué is all the news which can properly be published."

Across London rumor and confusion were rife. In the East End, which had borne the brunt of the attack, people assumed the entire city had been bombed. Elsewhere inhabitants had seen and heard nothing. They could learn little from the morning newspapers, which could only refer in the most general of terms to attacks "in parts of London." A further Admiralty communiqué later that day told people only a little more that was true, and quite a bit that was not:

In amplification of the information which appeared in this morning's papers, the following particulars of last night's Zeppelin raid in the Metropolitan area are now available for publication. Late last night about 90 bombs, mostly of an incendiary character, were dropped from hostile aircraft in various localities not far distant from each other. A number of fires (of which only three were large enough to require the services of fire-engines) broke out. All fires were promptly and effectively dealt with . . . No public building was injured, but a number of private premises were damaged by fire and water. The number of casualties is small. So far as at present ascertained, one infant, one boy, one man, and one woman were killed, and another woman is so seriously injured that her life is despaired of. A few other private citizens were seriously injured. The precise numbers are not yet ascertained. Adequate police arrangements, including the calling out of special constables, enabled the situation to be kept thoroughly in hand throughout.

The German authorities also issued a misleading statement, claiming: "We last night dropped bombs on the workshops and docks in London" and also that the raid was "by way of reprisal for the bombardment of the open town of Ludwigshafen." Reproducing the statement, the *Guardian* added that the raid on Ludwigshafen, carried out by eighteen French planes, had been on "the explosives factory there—one of the largest of the kind in Germany, and the chief source, it is believed, of the poisonous gas used by the Germans."

That same day—just as they had when news of the *Lusitania* sinking broke—angry crowds attacked shops thought to be owned by Germans. Victor McArdell, a child at the time, recalled how in Shoreditch "an angry mob gathered outside a house the occupants of which, according to rumour were German spies and furthermore someone had looked through the letter-box and had seen saucers of blood in the hall-way . . . No enormity, committed by a German, was too great for people to believe. In this case, the completely innocent occupants were eventually saved from a nasty mauling by the intervention of the police." As news spread of where the bombs had fallen, sightseers—"well-dressed people in motors, journalists, photographers, high military officials, Red Cross nurses . . . travelers from all over the world"—toured the areas of the East End damaged by those the press was now calling "the baby killers."

Though British journalists were constrained in describing the bombings in detail, they could cover the inquests on the various victims. On June 3, 1915, the *Guardian* reported the coroner's comments on the deaths of Henry and Caroline Good that "It is not desirable . . . to make much commotion about this matter. We do not want alarm to spread around the Metropolis, which has, up to the present, taken this act very quietly and coolly, although we all stand in danger" and that "the Government will not allow numerous details to be published in the Press." However, readers learned how a doctor called to the scene "found the dead couple in a back room on the first floor. Both were kneeling beside the bed and were naked. All the man's hair had been burnt off. The room was in ruins . . .The woman had a large piece of hair in her right hand . . . The man's arm was around the woman's waist."

The press also reported how the coroner in summing up said:

It was not so very long ago that the whole procedure of naval warfare had been disturbed by the advent of armed submarines. In this war armed submarines had attacked peaceable passengers . . . Recently we have experienced the first example of the results of aerial warfare. Aeroplanes and Zeppelin airships have created a new sphere for military genius to act in defence and attack. While armed airships [are] the proper means of attacking armies and navies, it [is] an entirely new and barbarous practice to use them as weapons of aggression against defenceless civilians in their beds in the undefended suburbs of our cities, seaside and health resorts and country villages.

Remains of some of Linnarz's bombs—described as "large metal instruments resembling stable lanterns . . . over one foot in length and very heavy"—were produced for the jury to examine. Their verdict, in line with the coroner's guidance, was that the Goods had died "from suffocation and burns, having been murdered by some agent of a hostile force." At the inquest into the death of three-year-old Elsie Leggatt held later that afternoon the jury learned that the incendiary bomb that killed her "bore the label of Krupps, Essen."

Britons already felt battered by bad news. A London woman wrote to her sister, "This last week we have had . . . more diabolical devilish horrors hurled at the nation—[I'm] bewildered with all the awful happenings . . . *Lusitania* being torpedoed . . . the news of the ghastly effects of that awful gas the wretches had sent out over the trenches . . . We went to St. Paul's on Monday night for the service held in memory of the Canadians who so gallantly fell at Ypres." A man wrote from Ayrshire to a friend: "What a terrible business this torpedoing of the *Lusitania* . . . That . . . and asphyxiating gases have just about 'put the lid on' and shown up these truculent Prussians in their true light. Pirates and murderers!"

Allied to news of other recent German "frightfulness," the raid on London encouraged people to join the Anti-German League formed that summer with the aim of enrolling one million members and achieving a total boycott of German goods—like the Rhenish wines taken off the *Lusitania*'s wine list and children's toys such as teddy bears and metal cars, and mouth organs then manufactured almost exclusively in Germany. The Trading with the Enemy Act of 1914 had already made conducting business with any person of "enemy character" an offense. However, plenty of German-made stock imported prewar remained. "When offered goods bearing the mark of the beast," a league leaflet appealed, "think of the vast army of phantom dead, of the poor breastless women, of the outraged girls . . . of our brave soldiers with their faces beaten to a pulp as they lay wounded, and of the sinking of . . . the *Lusitania* with hundreds of helpless victims sacrificed to the bloodlust of the Butcher of Berlin."

Just as the British government tried to downplay the raid, the German government naturally promoted reports of massive destruction in London and encouraged Linnarz's interviews with American and other neutral newspapers to feed them. The German public responded with enthusiasm to the raid on the city described in one paper as "the heart of the money world." The Leipzig *Neueste Nachrichten* declared:

> England [is] no longer an island. The City of London, the heart which pumps the life-blood into the arteries of the brutal huckster nation, has been sown with bombs by German airships, whose brave pilots had the satisfaction of seeing the dislocated fragments of docks, banks and many other buildings rise up to the dark skies in lurid tongues of flame. At last the longed-for punishment has fallen on England, this people of liars and hypocrites—the punishment for the overflowing measure of sins of ages past. It is neither blind hatred nor raging anger that inspires our airship heroes, but a solemn and religious awe at being the chosen instruments of the Divine wrath. In that moment when they saw London breaking up in smoke and fire they lived through a thousand lives of an immeasurable joy which all who remain at home must envy them.

Meanwhile, Londoners braced themselves for more attacks. A *Times* editorial of June 2 warned that "it is reasonably clear that the visits of the German airships have been in the main of an experimental character . . . They have not yet attacked in strength, but are still practising . . . Their principal object is extremely simple and thoroughly German. They wish to kill as many people and destroy as much property as they possibly can . . . Zeppelin attacks have become unpleasant realities and for technical reasons are exceedingly difficult to repel." People worried that German spies were in place in the capital, ready to direct incoming zeppelins to their targets with clandestine signals, even hanging out washing in a particular way as a coded message. They also worried that zeppelins would come on nights when the moon was full, though one woman assured her son that "the War

Office had produced a black searchlight that would 'black out' the moon." "It was useless," her son recalled, "saying that was an impossibility."

The next raid on London was intended for June 4, when the German navy dispatched its new zeppelin, *L10*, commanded by Kapitän-Leutnant Klaus Hirsch.° However, shortly after reaching the Thames estuary a shift in the wind led him to attack the naval base at Harwich in East Anglia rather than London. He later reported dropping thirty high-explosive and ninety incendiary bombs that "all exploded and all caused fires . . . Judging by an especially violent explosion, one of the hits must have been on some gasworks or an oil tank." In fact, he had mistakenly bombed the town of Gravesend on the Thames estuary, hitting a military hospital.

Two nights later the German army and navy sent airships in a combined operation. The three army airships—*LZ38*, again captained by Linnarz, *LZ37*, and *LZ39*—fared badly. Early engine problems forced Linnarz back to his base at Evere. The remaining two zeppelins sailed on but, meeting thick fog above the North Sea, were ordered to return to their base at Gontrode. A British listening post at the Hunstanton coast guard station on the Norfolk coast picked up the German signals to the airships and four RNAS pilots based at Furnes in Belgium were sent out. Flight Sublieutenants Reginald Warneford and John Rose, flying Morane-Saulnier Parasol monoplanes equipped with a Vickers machine gun and six twenty-pound bombs lashed beneath the fuselage, were ordered to try to intercept and destroy the returning zeppelins. Flight Lieutenant J. P. Wilson and Flight Sublieutenant J. S. Mills in Henry Farman biplanes, also armed with machine gun and bombs, were to attack the zeppelin sheds at Evere.

The ground crews had already run Linnarz's *LZ38* into its shed at Evere when Wilson arrived. Challenged in the darkness by a German searchlight he had the presence of mind to flash back with a pocket lamp. His signals deceived the Germans, enabling him to approach and drop three bombs on *LZ38*'s shed. Aware now what was happening German ground crew fired on Mills following behind, temporarily driving him off,

---

° Kapitän-Leutnant was the rank to which most naval airship captains were promoted. Army airship commanders usually had the rank of Hauptmann, "captain."

but he circled and came in again to drop four bombs on the same shed, which burst into flames destroying *LZ38*. Linnarz and his crew only just got out in time.

Pursuing the returning zeppelins, Rose crash-landed in a field. However twenty-three-year-old Warneford, who had only gained his wings three months earlier but already had a reputation for reckless bravado, caught up with *LZ37* near Ghent in Belgium. She was battling strong head-winds but her crew confidently expected to reach their base at Gontrode safely. In the control gondola Alfred Muhler recalled how "we breathed with relief because we thought we were out of danger. I was at my elevator rudder, when the observer on the upper platform reported through the speaking-tube: 'Airplane two thousand feet aft, above the ship.' We all knew what that meant; the enemy flier was already in the most suitable position for an attack, for we could not repulse him from the control-car. Without waiting for the command to do so the observer on the back of the airships sent a burst of machine-gun fire at the attacking flier."

Aware that his single Vickers machine gun was poor protection, Warneford coaxed his red-and-gray fighter, which had a maximum height ceiling of eleven thousand feet, directly above the airship, then dived. "When I was almost over the monster I descended to about 150 feet above it and released six bombs. The sixth struck the envelope of the ship fair and square in the middle. There was instantly a terrible explosion."

Alfred Muhler, huddled in the forward gondola, recalled feeling "a hit." Then,

> the ship quivered, and my helm turned loosely in the air. It found no more resistance—a sign that our steering mechanism had become use-less. The control-car swayed back and forth as if drunk, and I fell. While I was still trying to get to my feet, the entire crew either jumped or were thrown overboard; at any rate, I never saw them again. The whole immense hull above me was ablaze, instantly becoming a roaring, hissing inferno. Instinctively I threw myself flat on the floor of the car and clawed at the rails, desperately trying to avoid the merciless fire roasting down upon me. I wondered how long it took to fall 5,000 feet. I knew this was the end, but I actually welcomed it as preferable to the

slow torture of incineration. At last the gondola struck and everything went black.

In fact, *LZ37* had broken up and crashed in flames through the roof of the Convent of Saint Elisabeth in Ghent, setting it ablaze and killing two nuns, a man, and a child. Muhler himself landed on a nun's bed—the airship's sole survivor. Meanwhile, the pressure wave from the exploding zeppelin had flipped Warneford's plane over so that he suddenly found himself flying upside down in the darkness. "The aeroplane was out of control for a short period, but went into a nose dive, and the control was gained," his battle report described.

I then saw that the Zeppelin was on the ground in flames and also that there were pieces of something burning in the air all the way down. The joint on my petrol pipe and pump from the back tank was broken, and at about 2.40 am I was forced to land and repair my pump. I landed at the back of a forest close to a farmhouse; the district is unknown on account of the fog and the continuous changing of course. I made preparations to set the machine on fire but apparently was not observed, so was enabled to effect a repair, and continued at 3.15 am in a south westerly direction after considerable difficulty in starting my engine single handed. I tried several times to find my whereabouts by descending through the clouds, but was unable to do so. So eventually I landed and found out that I was at Cape Gris-Nez . . . As far as could be seen the colour of the airship was green on top and yellow below and there was no machine or gun platform on top.

I have the honour to be, Sir, Your obedient servant,
R.A.J. Warneford. Flt. Sub-Lieutenant.

That same evening, Kapitän-Leutnant Heinrich Mathy in the navy's *L9* was to "attack London if possible" with the army airships or else to select a coastal town "according to choice." Arriving over the Wash estuary in East Anglia and encountering strong headwinds and ground fog, he diverted to the northern England fishing port of Hull on which he dropped over fifty bombs, killed twenty-four, injured a further forty, and destroyed nearly fifty houses and shops before proceeding to the neighboring port of Grimsby and bombing that too. As in London, there were no air raid shelters yet and people had few places to hide. Many were hit as they fled through the streets or were trapped by wreckage. Two parents and their five children who had crouched against the kitchen wall of their house as the *L9* passed overhead emerged to find destruction all around and realized the wall could not have protected them. Luck alone had saved them.

The official British reaction to Mathy's raid—the most deadly so far—was guarded. An Admiralty communiqué stated only that an attack in the northeast [of England] had caused fires in "a drapery establishment, a timber yard and a terrace of small houses." However, anti-German rioting broke out in Hull and many of its inhabitants, convinced the authorities were powerless to stop the zeppelins coming and going as they pleased, sought places outside the city to sleep at night.

Naturally enough, the Admiralty made much of the destruction of the zeppelin shed and *LZ38* and in particular of Warneford's triumph as the first British pilot to destroy a zeppelin in the air. He was awarded the Victoria Cross within thirty-six hours but killed just a few days later when, on June 17, while taking American journalist Henry Needham on a flight from Paris, his plane went into a spin at two thousand feet. Warneford managed to pull out of the spin but in the process the plane's tail broke off and at seven hundred feet it turned upside down. Both men were thrown to the ground. Needham died instantly, Warneford an hour later.[*]

With the German army adjusting to the loss of two of its zeppelins, on June 16, Strasser sent two naval zeppelins—*L10* and *L11*—from Nordholz, headquarters of the German navy's Airship Service on bleak sandy flats near Cuxhaven at the mouth of the Elbe, to raid Tyneside, a center of coal, steel, and shipbuilding in northeast England. *L11* turned back because of engine problems leaving *L10* to continue alone. Warnings sounded by a naval

---

[*] After the war, nuns commemorated Warneford with a plaque on the wall of the Convent of Saint Elisabeth in Ghent, while a nearby street was named for him. A nun said, "There was in all our hearts a fierce joy for the intrepid daring and victory of Lieutenant Warneford."

patrol vessel that spotted her went unheeded in the Tyneside shipyards, where men in the workshops and blast furnaces were working at full stretch. Klaus Hirsch, *L10*'s commander, described how the "great number of lights and the glare of blast furnaces" perfectly illuminated the dreadnought *Resolution* under construction in Palmer's shipyard in Jarrow. He dropped seven high-explosive and five incendiary bombs, hitting Palmer's engine shop with devastating effect but leaving *Resolution* undamaged.

Total casualties for the raid were eighteen dead and seventy-two wounded of which all but one fatality were Palmer's workers.

CHAPTER SIXTEEN

"Order, Counter-Order, Disorder!"

ON JUNE 15, 1915, the same day that *L10* attacked Tyneside, the inquiry into the sinking of the *Lusitania* opened in Central Hall, Westminster, before Lord Mersey and four assessors—Admiral Sir Frederick Inglefield, another serving naval officer, and two Merchant Navy captains. Sir Edward Carson, KC, the attorney general, began proceedings for the government of which he was a member.[*] He said that the first torpedo had hit the ship between funnels three and four. Then, contrary to the information known to the Admiralty and the government through Room 40's decoded messages, but in line with the government's wish to explain away the second explosion reported by survivors and avoid any discussion that it might be due to munitions, he added that "there was a second and perhaps a third torpedo." He continued that the ship was only eight to ten miles from land when hit and although capable of twenty-one knots at the time was only doing eighteen. The court might consider, he said, whether the captain was correct in traveling at that speed, adding that Captain Turner had received "specific instructions and directions," and, again, the court should assess how far the captain had followed them.

Predictably most interest focused on how Captain Turner would

---

[*] Carson had successfully defended the criminal libel suit brought by Oscar Wilde against the Marquis of Queensberry which had led to Wilde's imprisonment in Reading Gaol for homosexual acts.

defend himself. He was probably suffering from posttraumatic shock, as just before the inquiry opened he wrote that he still could not bear "to think or speak" about the disaster. At his first appearance in open session, asked whether the *Lusitania*'s crew were proficient in handling lifeboats, he answered, "No, they were not." He later explained that they lacked practice and experience and admitted that he was "an old-fashioned sailor man" who did not think present standards matched those of his youth. Significantly, contrary to his evidence at the Kinsale inquest, he followed the Admiralty line and agreed that there had been not one but two torpedoes, the second "immediately after the first" which had struck between the third and fourth funnels. (In his only public interview about the sinking, which he gave to the *Daily Mail* in 1933, Turner reverted to there having been only one torpedo.)

Two sessions closed to the public considered the Admiralty's instructions to Captain Turner. Sir Edward Carson cross-examined him precisely and aggressively in a seeming attempt to confuse him into admissions of failure to follow Admiralty guidance. Carson described all the instructions Turner had received, including those relating to avoiding enemy surface vessels, which advised sticking to the coast and directly contradicted advice on how to avoid submarines—which was to stay out of sight of land. On all but one occasion Carson carefully quoted the date of each instruction and asked Turner "did you get that?" The exception was the guidance on zig-zagging. Carson read out all three paragraphs of the note of April 16, flagged by Webb and about which there was uncertainty as to whether Turner had received it. He did not give a date for it but simply asked Turner, "Did you *read* that?" Perhaps bemused, Turner replied, "I did." Carson then hopped back to another note dated March 22, 1915, about steering a mid-channel course. Resuming his previous mode of questioning, he gave the precise date and asked "Did you get this?"

Carson put it to Captain Turner that he had been eight to ten miles from land (and by implication not following the mid-channel guidance) at the time of the *U-20*'s attack. Turner replied he had been more like fifteen miles off. He had closed in to take a four-point bearing to establish his precise position. Carson suggested that he must already have known approximately. Turner snapped back, "I wanted to get my proper position off the land—I do not do my navigation by guess-work." The *Lusitania* had been doing only eighteen knots to allow him to time his arrival at the Mersey Bar so that he could cross it, as recommended, without delaying in known dangerous waters outside the harbor. Questioned closely on why he was not zigzagging at the time of the attack, Captain Turner replied that he thought he need only do so when he actually sighted a submarine. In any case the words about zigzagging that Carson had read to him seemed "different language" to what he recalled.

Throughout, Turner's answers tended to the monosyllabic. He seemed anxious and sometimes confused, Cunard's barrister once urging him "pull yourself together and think before you answer." The barrister also interpolated extra information helpful to Turner and thus to Cunard. Toward the end of the hearing, he apologized to Lord Mersey for Turner being "a bad witness" in the sense that "he was confused." Mersey responded: "In my opinion at present, he may have been a bad Master during that voyage, but I think he was telling the truth."

When the lawyers discussed evidence substantiating Turner's view about the hazards of delaying outside Liverpool harbor, Lord Mersey discovered that the Admiralty had supplied him with a less detailed memorandum, in particular about signals sent to the *Lusitania*, than provided to others. They were probably different drafts of Webb's submission. Plainly exasperated, Mersey was told that because of the confusion and possible uncertainty over which version Turner had thought they were referring to during cross-examination, it might be difficult to use some of the information in assessing Turner's actions.

In giving evidence on the number of torpedoes, most witnesses— among them Leslie Morton, the lookout who had seen the first torpedo—said there had been two. Two crewmen, both British naval reservists, said that in addition a third torpedo had been fired, perhaps by a second submarine from the port side. None said only one. Hugh Johnston, the quartermaster who was firm that there had been only one, was not questioned on the topic. Lord Mersey firmly deflected the Seamen's Union representative from discussing the nature and location of the alleged torpedo strikes and the attendant consequences for the watertight compartments of the ship. This was despite the representative's pleading that both he and Mersey had found bulkheads a relevant topic at the *Titanic* inquiry. Thus the effect of the torpedo on the *Lusitania's* vulnerable longitudinal bunkers and the consequence for the speed of both the list and the sinking were not debated.

On June 10, five days before the inquiry began, the government had broadened the Defence of the Realm Act to make it an offense "to collect, record, publish, or communicate or attempt to elicit information" on the nature, carriage, and use of His Majesty's "war materials" for any purpose. Previously the act had only prohibited the collection, recording, and so forth of such information if intended for communication to the enemy. Thus, in compliance with the new provision of the act, the inquiry did not discuss the *Lusitania's* cargo in detail. Sir Edward Carson merely read into the record the U.S. government's note to Germany refuting German allegations about the cargo, backed up with a note from the collector of customs in New York, Dudley Field Malone, to Cunard general manager Charles Sumner, confirming that the cargo did not violate American law on what passenger ships could carry.

When Lord Mersey and his assessors retired to contemplate their findings, his original intention was clearly to blame Captain Turner since he inquired through Admiral Inglefield whether the government would think it expedient that "blame should be very prominently laid upon the Captain" for disregarding Admiralty instructions. His concern was that if he did so Germany "might use it as another pretext for defending their action in sinking the vessel." Both the First Lord of the Admiralty, Arthur Balfour, and the Foreign Office were consulted before the Admiralty replied direct to Mersey that neither would object to a verdict "that the Master received suitable written instructions which he omitted to follow and that he was also fully informed of the presence of hostile submarines . . . If you should still have any doubts on the subject, Mr. Balfour would be glad to see you."

Whether Lord Mersey took up the invitation to meet is unknown. However, his short, two-paragraph-long report, published on July 17, did not blame Turner in any way. Instead, as Coroner Horgan had done, it placed responsibility for the disaster entirely on the captain and crew of the "submarine of German nationality" that carried out the attack, and on their superiors in Berlin. In a ten-page amplificatory annex, Lord Mersey stated that the attack was "murder" and "contrary to international law and the usages of war." Both Captain Turner and Staff Captain Anderson were "competent men and . . . did their duty . . . No doubt there were mishaps in handling the ropes of the boats and in other such matters but there was . . . no incompetence or neglect and I am satisfied that the crew behaved well throughout and worked with skill and judgement . . . They did their best in difficult and perilous circumstances and their best was good." The German warning demonstrated that the attack was premeditated and planned before the *Lusitania* sailed.

Lord Mersey concluded unequivocally that "two torpedoes" hit the *Lusitania* on the starboard side "almost simultaneously" but also gave some credence to the evidence of a second submarine firing from the port side, adding "there was no explosion of any part of the cargo." The Admiralty had devoted great care "to the questions arising out of the submarine peril" and the officials merited "the highest praise." The advice given to Captain Turner was not meant "to deprive him of the right to exercise his skilled judgement . . . His omission to follow the advice in all respects cannot fairly be attributed either to negligence or incompetence. He exercised judgement for the best . . . The whole blame for the cruel destruction of life in this catastrophe must rest solely with those who plotted and with those who committed the crime."

CONTINUING TENSIONS BETWEEN the civilian and naval factions within the German government, and the consequent arguments over the drafting of the reply to the second U.S. note, delayed its dispatch until July 8. Ignoring the American protests against sinking without warning, it reiterated complaints about the British blockade that forced Germany to defend "her national existence" with the submarine campaign. It offered to guarantee the safety of American ships and lives by introducing a safe-conduct scheme. Designated American ships flying the Stars and Stripes and painted in red, white, and blue would receive safe conduct through the submarine zone if they carried no contraband and gave reasonable advance notice.

The American press reaction was hostile. The suggestion that ships should be painted like "barber's poles" was an insult. The U.S. response sent on July 21 was the strongest yet, declaring that by offering special privileges to American vessels, Germany was setting international law aside; that by stating its submarine blockade was an act of reprisal the German government was admitting its illegality, reprisals being inherently illegal. The key issue was the "grave and unjustifiable violations of the rights of American citizens." The U.S. government would regard any further violations "as deliberately unfriendly." When he received the note, the kaiser scrawled on it, "immeasurably impertinent," "you don't say so!" and at the bottom "about the most impudent note which I have ever read . . . It ends with a direct threat!"

In the face of the continuing squabbles about the campaign Admirals Bachmann and von Tirpitz felt that the position of the U-boat service had become intolerable. "Order, counter-order, disorder!" von Tirpitz wrote.

Worse was to come for them. Fifty miles off the Old Head of Kinsale on August 19, the *U-24* sank without warning the sixteen-thousand-ton unarmed British White Star passenger liner *Arabic* which had avoided the *U-20* just before she had sunk the *Lusitania*. Forty-four passengers and crew including four Americans died. The U-boat commander claimed he had mistaken her for a freighter but had clearly contravened the orders issued in June not to fire if in doubt about the status of a vessel. Von Bethmann Hollweg now persuaded the kaiser to inform Washington that no unresisting passenger liners would be sunk without warning.

Bachmann complained that trying to distinguish a passenger liner could cause confusion. Von Tirpitz insisted that following these orders would endanger U-boats. His arguments were strengthened when, on the day of the *Arabic* sinking, the German U-boat service discovered in brutal fashion the existence of British "Q" or decoy ships. Originally the brainchild of Churchill and Fisher, these naval vessels were disguised to resemble ordinary tramp steamers but carried guns concealed behind collapsible screens. Q-ships aimed to entice U-boats to surface and approach, sometimes by pretending to be foundering, sometimes even by launching lifeboats full of apparently panic-stricken crews. Then at the last moment, they would hoist the Royal Navy's white ensign and attack.

On August 19, the Q-ship HMS *Baralong* approached the *U-27*, the submarine that had lain in wait in March for the *Lusitania*, while she was attacking another British freighter. The *Baralong* revealed her guns and fired on the *U-27*. As the submarine sank her crew abandoned her. The *Baralong*'s men shot some of the sailors in the water, then hunted down, killed, and threw overboard those who had sought refuge on the freighter. American muleteers aboard the freighter, which was carrying 250 mules to Britain, reported the incident.

Ambassador von Bernstorff protested to Lansing that the *Baralong* had been flying the Stars and Stripes just before revealing her guns and hoisting the white ensign. But Lansing did not protest to the British about either the use of the American flag or the merciless killing of the U-boat survivors, a crime the British tried lamely to defend on the grounds that the *Baralong*'s crew had thought the submariners were armed.

Von Tirpitz again submitted his resignation, which the kaiser again refused, trying to convince him of the need not to provoke the United States by resuming unrestricted submarine warfare. If America joined the Allies, he worried, it could provide "unlimited money for our foes." He told von Tirpitz, "First the war must be won, and that end necessitates absolute protection against a new enemy; how that is to be achieved . . . is My business. What I do with My navy is *My business only*." The kaiser did, however, accept Bachmann's resignation, telling Müller, "I must have a man who is personally devoted to me, not one who does what Tirpitz tells him to do." Bachmann's replacement was Admiral Henning von Holtzendorff, a friend of von Bethmann Hollweg and hostile to von Tirpitz.

On September 4, as dusk was falling, Walther Schwieger in the *U-20* sighted a ship eighty-five miles southwest of the Fastnet Rock. His war diary records that she was outside the usual shipping channels, zigzagging, and had dimmed her lights. He fired a single torpedo without warning and did not stay long enough to see his victim sink. She was the 10,920-ton British passenger liner *Hesperian*. Thirty-two lives were lost in the sinking.

On his return to port, Schwieger was ordered to Berlin to explain why he had attacked a passenger ship against orders. He claimed to have thought the *Hesperian* was "an auxiliary cruiser." He was not believed and ordered to acquiesce in the fiction already put about by the authorities, that the *Hesperian* had not been torpedoed but struck a mine, and to tell his men to say nothing about the sinking. Surprised by his hostile reception, Schwieger wrote a bitter six-page letter to Hermann Bauer complaining it was impossible to expect U-boatmen to distinguish between auxiliary cruisers, troop transports, and ordinary shipping.

CHAPTER SEVENTEEN

"A Gift of Love"

IN GERMANY, SENIOR commanders had been assessing the recent zeppelin raids as well as the submarine campaign. Just as with the gas attacks at Ypres, it was obvious that suitable weather was vital for the airships. Experts studied meteorological data on weather patterns in the North Sea and over England and as a result recommended that the best period for attacking London was late summer and autumn when the hours of darkness would be longer and weather conditions the most favorable. Raids would also no longer be undertaken on nights of bright moonlight. This, coupled with the fact that the German army had sent its two remaining operational airships to the eastern front, gave Britain's civilian population a temporary respite following the attacks of the first half of June.

When still in post as the chief of the naval staff Admiral Bachmann—a firm believer in unrestricted warfare in the air as well as at sea—wrote on June 18 to von Falkenhayn seeking his agreement to the lifting of all restrictions on bombing London. Von Falkenhayn agreed but proposed that since Germany as yet possessed too few zeppelins to inflict "maximum damage on the enemy" waiting until Germany had sufficient airships to launch a mass attack on London by both army and navy would be best. Bachmann, however, wished to deploy the navy's new zeppelins immediately.

On July 9, Bachmann secured von Bethmann Hollweg's support for unrestricted air attacks on central London though the chancellor requested these only be carried out on weekends to limit casualties. On July 20, Bachmann petitioned the kaiser, arguing that really effective attacks are possible only if the City, the heart of London commercial life, is bombed. The Chancellor has agreed . . . but requests on humanitarian grounds that these be made only on week-ends, from Saturday to Monday morning so that buildings in the City would be unoccupied. This limitation is unacceptable because of the dependence of the airships on the weather. Every night the City empties of people regardless of the weather, also the enemy shows no regard for human-itarian behaviour in attacks on Karlsruhe [by French pilots on June 15 killing twenty-nine civilians and wounding fifty-eight] and elsewhere. Therefore I request Your Majesty to withdraw this prohibition and . . . to designate the City of London as a target; monuments like St. Paul's Cathedral and the Tower will be spared as far as possible.

The kaiser agreed but insisted no historic buildings should be targeted. He also inclined toward the chancellor's view that raids should only take place on weekends until Bachmann finally convinced him that this would be unreasonable.

On August 9, with the nights beginning to lengthen, Strasser dis-patched four of the navy's newest zeppelins. Their orders were to "remain together until 8.45 p.m., then each airship will carry out an independent raid, first on the London dock, then the city." None reached their target because of mechanical difficulties and rainy, misty weather and either jet-tisoned their bombs in the sea or dropped them outside London. L12 attacked Dover in the mistaken belief that it was Harwich. Major Cuthbert Lawson, who had been in the Ypres Salient during the spring gas attacks, witnessed the raid and described it in a letter to his mother:

Our great excitement was a real live Zeppelin on Monday night—she arrived about 12.15 a.m. and stayed nearly half an hour dropping about ten enormous bombs—she was almost directly above the Admiralty pier which [was] set on fire with an incendiary bomb and she missed a hos-pital ship and a big boat full of petrol and ammunition literally by inches . . . It was a most wonderful sight, the searchlights on the hills round picked her up very quickly and concentrated on her and she looked exactly as if the sun was shining on her—and she was only about

4,500 feet up and looked enormous . . . The noise was tremendous while whenever she dropped a bomb the noise fairly shook the earth. She was hit three times by a 12 pdr. gun in the castle and hastily hopped it after the third time and was seen no more—but excitement was great next morning when we heard she was in the sea off Ostend and three destroyers from here went racing over to do her in but they found no trace of her.

In fact *L12* had crash-landed, frame broken, in the sea near Zeebrugge and been towed by a German torpedo boat to Ostend.

With the faint light of a new moon, on August 12, Strasser again dispatched four zeppelins to London. Strong headwinds and engine trouble prevented three even reaching England. Of these, *L11* was returning to base when she was caught in a thunderstorm. Her captain described how "lightning ran at intervals of five seconds from cloud to cloud and cloud to water and encompassed the airship, the points and wire stays of which emitted electric sparks. Bluish flames 3 centimetres long ran along the machine guns and even the crew on the top platform who were soaked with rain, were encircled in a ring of light. Had the airship been carried above her pressure weight by a squall, gas could have been given off and the airship would have perished by fire." However, she survived to regain her base at Nordholz. The only airship to cross the English coast that night— *L10*—merely got far enough to bomb the outskirts of Harwich.

On August 17, Strasser ordered yet another zeppelin raid. This time *L10*, commanded by Oberleutnant Friedrich Wenke, reached London. Approaching from the east at an altitude of 10,200 feet, he dropped incendiary bombs, according to his report, "between Blackfriars and London bridges." He was either confused about his location or trying to impress Strasser by exaggerating his achievements because his first bombs in fact fell near a railway station in the heavily populated and industrialized area of Walthamstow six and a half miles northeast of the City. Heading south he bombed houses and almshouses, and set a tram depot alight. He next passed over the working-class district of Leyton where his bombs killed two people, injured twenty more, and badly damaged several houses. He then arrived above the adjoining district of Leytonstone to bomb yet more houses and gut the recently built mission church of Saint Augustine of Hippo in Lincoln Street, close to where Linnarz's final bombs landed on May 31, before turning for home. Ironically Saint Augustine of Hippo was the earliest notable Christian thinker to ponder the question of "a just war," calling wars fought "with a malicious intent to destroy" a crime.

Wenke's raid, the second to hit the capital, killed ten civilians—seven men, two women, and a child—injured forty-eight, and did more than thirty thousand pounds of damage to property. Two RNAS pilots who had taken off earlier from Chelmsford, but too late to intercept *L10* on her westward flight, were waiting for her on her return but again failed to catch her. Both their planes crashed on landing, badly injuring the pilots. *L10* did not survive long either. Sixteen days later the airship exploded, possibly after being struck by lightning, and crashed into the sea off Cuxhaven, killing her entire crew.

Zeppelins next attacked London on the dark night of September 7. By now Londoners were growing knowledgeable about what was good "zeppelin weather" so that theaters reported smaller audiences on fine nights with little or no moon. During such periods, German airships were kept on standby for a quick departure, the huge rolling doors of their hangers open, the handling crew ready, the gas bags full of hydrogen, the outer skin tautened, and machine guns, ammunition, petrol, and bombs already aboard. This time the German army sent three airships.

LZ77 soon turned back; *SL2* and *LZ74* fared better. The former arrived above the Millwall Docks in London's Isle of Dogs just before midnight. Here its commander, Hauptmann von Wobeser, dropped eleven bombs, damaging the docks, destroying houses, and injuring several people. Next he took *SL2* south across the Thames toward Deptford, where Henry VIII's fleet once lay in the Royal Dock and his daughter Elizabeth I inspected Francis Drake's *Golden Hind*. Here he hit a British army depot, destroying supplies of tea and salt. Soon after, another of his bombs killed fifty-six-year-old William Beechey, his wife Elizabeth, and their three children in their nearby home. Continuing, *SL2* bombed Greenwich, home of the Royal Naval College, and finally Woolwich, where the antiaircraft battery managed to fire off four rounds at it only two minutes after being alerted to its approach. However, the gunners had no time to switch on their searchlight to pinpoint the airship, which they estimated was flying at around eight thousand feet between fifty and sixty miles per hour. It was soon beyond their range and heading home undamaged.

LZ74, commanded by Hauptmann Friedrich George, approached London from the north. To lighten his craft he dropped thirty-nine bombs on what he mistakenly thought was Leyton but was in fact the town of Cheshunt in Hertfordshire, fifteen miles from central London. George headed due south toward the City, bombing a warehouse in Fenchurch Street before sailing over the Tower of London and taking a southeasterly course, dropping bombs as he went.

The raid by the two airships killed eighteen civilians, including three children, injured twenty-eight, and caused ten thousand pounds worth of damage. A young nurse wrote to her mother:

> I have lived through an air raid . . . Fancy an air raid on London—an epoch making event . . . I flew out of bed . . . I saw the small luminous patch on which the searchlights were playing which was the Zeppelin . . . We saw the luminous cloud and the shrapnel bursting a good deal short of it . . . All this time our guns were firing like mad and the sirens were hooting, the whistles blowing and now we heard the fire engines racing to the scene . . . This is the nearest I have ever reached to being under fire and very exhilarating it was too. One of the patients said it was like being at the war again.

The next evening, September 8, with clear skies and a new moon, Strasser dispatched three naval airships to the capital. Engine trouble soon forced two back so L13 commanded by Kapitän-Leutnant Heinrich Mathy continued alone. Thirty-two-year-old Mathy, who boasted to the New York Times' Berlin correspondent that he would bomb London three times in succession or die in the attempt, had already made one hundred zeppelin flights. He dropped twelve bombs damaging three houses in Golders Green, a suburb northwest of the city, before, guided by the lights of Regent's Park's Inner Circle, which he described as "lit as in peacetime," heading toward central London at eighty-five hundred feet.

Here Mathy dropped an incendiary—the first bomb to fall on central

London—on Woburn Square in Bloomsbury near the British Museum. Nearby in Holborn, he dropped incendiary bombs and an explosive one. The latter struck a lamppost, detonated in midair, and dismembered a man standing outside the Dolphin Public House. After bombing Gray's Inn— one of London's four Inns of Court first established in the fourteenth century to enroll and teach lawyers—Mathy continued toward London's financial heart, the City. Still aboard *L13* was the largest bomb yet carried by a zeppelin—660 pounds. Its manufacturer had presented it to Mathy as a *Liebesgabe*, "Gift of Love," to London.

Mathy dropped his *Liebesgabe* close to London's oldest hospital, Saint Bartholomew's—founded eight centuries earlier by a monk who, taken ill while on pilgrimage to Rome, vowed to found a hospital in London on his return—and neighboring Smithfield, London's largest meat market. The bomb blew an eight-foot crater in the road, destroyed a printing works, and shattered windows for hundreds of yards around. Mathy reported: "The explosive effect of the 300-kg [660 lb] bomb must be very great, since a whole row of lights vanished in its crater." Two men who had just left the Admiral Carter pub spotted the airship and tried to run for cover but were "blown to pieces." Thirteen-year-old Violet Buckthorpe, who lived nearby, bravely scrambled up the stairs of her shattered home to rescue her two-year-old sister.

Passing the vast dome of Sir Christopher Wren's Saint Paul's Cathedral—though embargoed as a target by the kaiser it must have made a useful navigation aid—Mathy dropped bombs around the Guild Hall, where the City of London's Lord Mayors are elected, but failed to damage it. Others of his bombs landed close to the handsome eighteenth-century premises of the Bank of England—the most potent symbol of all of the "huckster nation" derided in the German press—which was also unscathed.

Many Londoners heard and saw the attack as it progressed. Elizabeth Tregellis and her family were just sitting down to supper when "suddenly there was a loud bang. My mother ran up to the door and saw the Zep, so did the others, but I stayed downstairs and turned the lights out. When all the commotion was over I found myself trembling and so were all the rest of us." A nurse lying in bed in Saint Thomas's Hospital, herself awaiting an operation, recalled how "the Zeppelin Raid sent nearly all the other patients into a panic. All day nurses . . . came down to the wards to soothe the patients." To a woman watching from her porch in hilly Hampstead, *L13* was "a wonderful sight . . . like a silver cigar and we could literally see our guns attacking it, for all the searchlights were concentrated on it, and it was something like looking at a magic lantern . . . One realises how helpless one is against a new horror of that sort and yet it did hold one fascinated to actually see that fight in the sky."

The Admiralty knew that zeppelins had set out for London because British listening stations had picked up signals from them and passed them to the Admiralty for the Room 40 team to decode. Over the city, twenty crisscrossing searchlights swept the sky while most of London's antiaircraft guns fired at the *L13*. American newspaperman William G. Shepherd saw one shell explode close to the airship and heard someone cry out, "Good God! It's staggering." However, the only damage the antiaircraft shells caused was on the ground from falling shrapnel. A message from the central control room told the gun crews: "All firing too low. All shells bursting underneath. All bursting short." A later official report stated, "Ideas both as to the height and size of the airship appear to have been somewhat wild."

Shepherd was one of many to capture the sense of unreality that night:

> Traffic is at a standstill. A million quiet cries make a subdued roar. Seven million people of the biggest city in the world stand gazing into the sky from the darkened streets. Here is the climax to the 20th century. Among the autumn stars floats a long, gaunt Zeppelin. It is a dull yellow—the colour of the harvest moon. The long fingers of searchlights reaching up from the roofs of the city are touching all sides of the death messenger with their white tips. Great booming sounds shake the city. They are Zeppelin bombs—falling—killing—burning. Lesser noises, of shooting, are nearer at hand, the noise of aerial guns sending shrapnel into the sky. "For God's sake don't do that," says one man to another who has just struck a match to light a cigarette. Whispers, low voices, run all through the streets. "There's a red light in the sky over there; our house may be burning," exclaims a woman, clutching at a man's coat. "There were a million houses in London; why ours particularly?" he responds. Suddenly you realise that the biggest city in the world has

become the night battlefield on which seven million harmless men, women and children live. Here is war at the very heart of civilization, threatening all the millions of things that human hearts and human minds have created in past centuries.

Such apocalyptic reactions were exactly what the German authorities hoped for in their bid to undermine the morale of British civilians.

L13 moved next toward London Wall—the street named for the Roman wall that once encircled "Londinium." Alfred Grosch, at work in a telephone exchange, looked through the window to see: "A streak of fire . . . shooting down straight at me . . . I stared at it hardly comprehending. The bomb struck the coping of a restaurant a few yards ahead, then fell into London Wall and lay burning in the roadway. I looked up, and at the last moment the searchlight caught the Zepp, full and clear. It was a beautiful but terrifying sight." Another eyewitness—watching from the roof of the *Morning Post* newspaper building—noted how "for a few minutes the Zepp seemed to float above us, as still as a becalmed yacht. It moved its way in and out of the searchlights as if they and the Zepp were playing a game. When the beams lit up the long, slender cigar shape, the scene might have been a set piece in a Crystal-Palace fireworks display, with the guns as theatrical noises off. It was all spectacularly beautiful, and then, like some silver ghost, she glided away northwards. Next morning I could hardly believe that it had been a murderer in the sky."

Near Liverpool Street Railway Station, Mathy released his final bombs. His report stated: "Manoeuvring and arriving directly over Liverpool Street Station I shouted, 'Rapid fire!' through the tube and bombs rained down. There was a succession of detonations and bursts of fire and I could see that I had hit well, and apparently done great damage." One of his bombs hit a No. 35 bus. Rescuers found the shocked driver staggering about the road with some of his fingers blown off. The conductor and many passengers were dead and others lay "shockingly injured" on the ground. Mathy's bombs also destroyed a No. 8 bus and ruptured water, electricity, and gas mains.

Shortly after eleven P.M. Mathy steered for home. He had killed twenty-two civilians, injured eighty-seven, and inflicted more than half a

million pounds worth of damage—a third of that the entire zeppelin campaign would cause. He had also left behind a memento. Next morning a
resident of Barnet in north London found a bag attached to a small para-
chute. Inside was a ham bone on which was inscribed ZUM ANDENKEN
AN DAS AUSGEHUNGERTE DEUTSCHLAND—"a memento from a fam-
ished Germany." Nevertheless, in an interview for the *New York World*
Mathy stated that he would "much rather stand on the bridge of a torpe-
do-boat, fighting ship against ship, than attack a city from the air . . . I want
to say that there's not an officer or man in the aerial fleet who doesn't feel
it deeply when he learns that women and children and other non-combatants have been killed."

The *Guardian*, reporting the interview to a British readership, was
skeptical:

> This is an interesting admission and . . . if the maker of it is an honest
> man he may be advised to go a little further and ask himself what sort
> of precautions any "officers or men in the aerial fleet" can take when
> dropping bombs from a great height and in the darkness on a crowded
> city, in order to ensure that their feelings shall not be "deeply" moved
> by the news that they have slain children in their beds . . . Obviously
> they can take no precautions; one of the blackest of the many crimes
> with which Germany has stained herself during this past year is that she
> has introduced this inevitably haphazard murder into warfare.

Londoners tried to come to terms with the bombing campaign.
Major Cuthbert Lawson, back in the capital, warned his mother, "I don't
think you'd better come to London—all the women are terrified of
Zeppelins and of course they're bound to come again!" People went to
inspect the damage. Five-year-old Leila Mackinley, who had been "lifted
up to see the Zeppelin fly over London," was taken by her mother to see
the bombed buildings. Newspapers called *L13*'s activities "Murder by
Zeppelin" and reported how children had been burned in their beds and
men blown to pieces in the streets. People asked why a clearly visible
airship had not been destroyed but allowed to travel where it pleased
above London. In fact, seven planes had been vainly seeking the

zeppelins that night. One pilot died when his plane crashed and exploded while landing in the dark.

Not only were British pilots still inexperienced at night fighting but their planes took far too long to reach the necessary altitude to attack a zeppelin effectively. Even the quickest—the BE2c fighters—took fifteen minutes merely to climb to thirty-five hundred feet and the zeppelins flew much higher. Mathy was absolutely correct in telling an American newspaper: "As to an aeroplane corps for the defence of London, it must be remembered that it takes some time for an aeroplane to screw itself up as high as a Zeppelin, and by the time it gets there the airship would be gone; then too, it is most difficult for an aeroplane to land at night, while a Zeppelin can stay up all night and longer if need be."

CHAPTER EIGHTEEN

"Do You Know Anything About Gas?"

WHILE THE NOVEL attacks at sea and from the air, with their long-term consequences for the conduct of warfare, had been taking place, fighting had continued on land. On the western front, German army gas attacks on Allied troops in the Ypres Salient persisted throughout May 1915. On May 2—the *Lusitania*'s first full day at sea—"Stinkpioneere" released chlorine against British troops in the trenches facing the German-held Mauser Ridge three miles due north of Ypres. Though British soldiers had been issued with basic gas "protectors," many took too long putting them on. They held the line but casualties were high. A British medical officer described how "all night in the trenches one heard groaning, not that of pain, but just the low muttering that is often heard in disease."

On May 6, the British withdrew from Hill 60 following a further gas attack. Methodist chaplain Owen Watkins, hurrying to a dressing station, passed "men lying all along the road gasping out their lives . . . The death cloud had swept down on them . . . These had run gasping until they fell, black in the face and dying." Watching the dressing station staff struggling to cope with twelve hundred casualties, Watkins thought "nothing seemed bad enough for the men who had done this thing." On May 24, in their final and greatest gas assault that late spring, the Stinkpioneere released chlorine along a two-mile front in an attack lasting four hours. Nearly three and a half thousand British soldiers needed treatment for gas poisoning.

In London, the request by Sir John French, commander in chief of the British Expeditionary Force, for Britain to produce and deploy gas was urgently debated. The effect on international opinion of Britain taking such a step weighed heavily. Well aware that neutrals had been quick to condemn the German use of gas, the British government did not wish to lose sympathy by being seen to descend to the same level as their less civilized enemy. However, French's arguments that his troops had to be provided with "similar means" of attack to the Germans prevailed.

On May 18 Lord Kitchener, minister of war, told Parliament that "His Majesty's Government, no less than the French Government felt our troops must be adequately protected by the employment of similar methods so as to remove the enormous and unjustifiable advantage which must exist for [the Germans] if we take no steps to meet on his own ground the enemy who is responsible for the introduction of this pernicious practice." In other words, the British would use gas when they could. An official record of the cabinet discussions states that "public opinion had compelled the Government to retaliate."

To his own surprise, Charles Foulkes, a forty-year-old major in the Royal Engineers—career soldier, big game hunter, and competitor in the 1908 Olympics—was put in charge of Britain's gas program. During a short interview with General William Robertson, French's chief of staff, on May 26 Robertson asked simply: "'Do you know anything about gas?' . . . to which I replied quite truthfully, 'Nothing at all.' 'Well, I don't think that matters,' he went on; 'I want you to take charge of our gas reprisals here in France. Something is going on in London, and you must cross over and find out all about it. Then come back here and tell me what you propose to do.'"

As the army's "Gas Advisor," Foulkes quickly grasped that his task was to enable Britain to use gases "which were as harmful, but not much more so, than those used by the enemy, though preparations and experiments might proceed for the employment of more deadly things." The immediate problem was how to produce enough poison gas—Britain's production capacity was tiny compared with that of Germany's chemical industry giants. Foulkes's tour of British factories revealed reasonable stockpiles of chlorine but only one plant capable of converting it into liquid form for transport and deployment. He urged British scientists and chemical companies to find ways of increasing the production of liquid chlorine and the manufacture of gas cylinders. He also began exploring possible methods of deploying gas on the battlefield.

Foulkes recommended the immediate establishment of a specialist gas warfare unit within the Royal Engineers whose first duty would be "the production of gas clouds." Civilian experts—science students and industrial chemists—and those already serving in the army with backgrounds in chemistry were recruited into the "Special Companies" (later the Special Gas Brigade), together with soldiers from infantry battalions "to supply experience of trench warfare." Lieutenant C. A. Ashley was suddenly informed that he had been transferred into the Royal Engineers and to report to Chatham next morning. On arrival, he and some other young men "were told only that we were a Special Company of the Royal Engineers . . . The only thing we could discover that we had in common was a knowledge of chemistry." They wondered whether their function would be "to test the water in wells as the army advanced."

By late July 1915, Ashley was one of two thousand men assembled near Saint-Omer in northern France. Here he learned that "an attack was being planned and that our part in it would be to let off poison gas." Foulkes later wrote that "I gave . . . every man the opportunity to return to England if he wished." Ashley did not recall being given the choice but wrote that his subsequent experience "did not lead me to suppose that gas was more objectionable on moral or any other grounds than high explosives." Soon the Special Companies were training in everything from meteorology to handling gas cylinders which, Ashley learned, "were to be placed in trenches in front of the infantry and the gas . . . let off through iron pipes to be attached to the cylinders and placed over the parapets. We practised with cylinders and pipes and thought that perhaps this was a job for plumbers but were gratified to hear that chemists were needed to give confidence to the infantry." Convinced that British success in using gas depended on preserving the element of surprise, Foulkes forbade his men ever to mention "gas" and told them to call the cylinders "accessories." They preferred "oojahs."

On July 29, 1915, the German army used another novel form of warfare against the British for the first time—the flamethrower. Many considered it inhumane, violating The Hague's prohibition on weapons that "caused unnecessary suffering." Lieutenant Carey, a British platoon commander, recalled that day: "I was quite incapable of any sort of consecutive thought. The first idea that sort of flitted through my mind was the end of the world had come and this was the Day of Judgement because suddenly the whole dawn had turned a ghastly crimson and red. Then as I began to come to my senses, I definitely saw four or five jets of flame passing across the trench I had been in one minute before . . . with a horrible hissing sound. At the edge of the flame there was a nasty sort of oily black smoke." Then he realized the German troops were attacking his trench and machine guns were opening up. Germans began to jump into the trench, bits of trees blew into the air, and he never saw four or five men of his platoon again. Although both sides would subsequently use flamethrowers (the German army had first deployed them without attracting attention against the French earlier in 1915), their utility beyond the initial terror was limited. This was particularly because the soldiers using them had canisters of flammable liquid strapped to their backs, making them highly vulnerable to being turned into human torches.

On August 22 Foulkes and his men demonstrated the principles of a gas attack to Sir Douglas Haig, commander of the British First Army, by letting off a small quantity of chlorine gas. By September 1915, with British factories having worked round the clock to produce them, fifty-five hundred chlorine-filled "oojahs" had been shipped across the Channel in unmarked wooden boxes, then carried by train to two railheads where Foulkes's men were waiting to unload them onto lorries and horse-drawn wagons that would carry them as far toward the front line "as the conditions of the road permitted." In an attempt to preserve secrecy, the wagons' wheels were muffled, the horse's hooves fitted with mini-sandbags, and they traveled by night.

The place chosen by Sir John French, in consultation with Haig, for Britain's first use of gas was Loos, a French mining village occupied by the German army some twenty miles south of Ypres. The attack at Loos was to begin a major Allied offensive agreed on with the French in July with the aim of breaking through the German lines before winter to restore a war of movement. These attacks would also relieve pressure on Russia on the eastern front by diverting German resources west. When they arrived at the British lines near Loos, Foulkes's men—distinguishable from other troops by their pink, white, and green armbands—began maneuvering the heavy iron "oojahs" and the connecting pipework through the network of muddy trenches up to the front. They were helped by the infantry who, Ashley recalled, "did a lot of the carrying." By September 20 they had dug in their fifty-five hundred cylinders which contained a total of around 150 tons of chlorine gas—close to the amount discharged by the Germans on April 22 at Ypres. While they waited for the attack, Foulkes's men "walked the trenches or sat on sand bags playing chess."

Haig scheduled the gas attack for the morning of September 25. The night before, Foulkes's men took up their positions. Forty of them, spread along the front trenches and specially trained in calculating wind speed and direction, telephoned in hourly weather reports. The night was wet and for a while the desired westerly wind blew, albeit not strongly. However, as the first light appeared in the east, in some places the wind began to drop and even to die away altogether. In others, it seemed to veer round from south to north meaning, as some of Foulkes's men warned, it would blow the chlorine back over the British lines.

At around five in the morning, Haig went outside his headquarters in a château near the lines to find only a slight breeze. His aide, Major Alan Fletcher, lit a cigarette. Haig noted the smoke was drifting "in puffs towards the N. E."—the appropriate direction. His diary records his decision to proceed with perhaps a hint of hindsight: "At one time, owing to the calm, I feared the gas might simply hang about our trenches. However, at 5.15 a.m. I said 'carry on.' I went to the top of *our* wooden look-out tower. The wind came gently from S. W. and by 5.40 had increased slightly. The leaves of the poplar trees gently rustled. This seemed satisfactory. But what a risk I must run of gas blowing back upon *our* own dense masses of troops!"

The exact time scheduled for the gas attack was five fifty A.M. "after the artillery bombardment had already started," as Lieutenant Ashley wrote. The plan was complicated. "We were given watches which were to be synchronised . . . and a printed sheet of instructions. Gas and smoke were to be let off alternately over a forty-minute period, with thick smoke only during the last two minutes so that the infantry could follow immediately behind it." The reason for supplementing the gas with smoke was that tests on masks found on captured German soldiers suggested they were only effective for about thirty minutes. Worried that he did not have enough chlorine gas to create a cloud that would last longer than that, and thus succeed in overcoming the defense provided by the masks, Foulkes had decided to use smoke to trick the German troops into keeping their masks on all the time. After forty minutes, with the German masks losing their effectiveness and the troops afflicted by the gas, the British infantry would charge from their trenches to attack the enemy lines.

At five fifty A.M. "the men of the Special Companies put on their gas helmets which consisted of a hood of grey flannel soaked in chemicals" and duly began releasing the chlorine. Some found that the spanners they had been issued did not fit the nuts on the cylinders. Writer and officer Robert Graves described how "the gas men rushed about shouting for the loan of an adjustable spanner." Lieutenant Ashley later heard how "one man was so frustrated . . . that he carried his cylinders some distance forward and then tried to burst them by firing at them." Lieutenant White found "great difficulty in letting off the gas owing to faulty connections and broken copper pipes causing leaks." Having done his best to release the gas he watched it first drift "slowly towards the German lines (it was plainly visible owing to the rain) but . . . at about 6.20 a.m. the wind changed and quantities of the gas came back over our own parapet, so I ordered all gas to be turned off and only smoke candles to be used." Elsewhere along the line chlorine engulfed some British soldiers either when the wind blew it back or when German shells ruptured the cylinders of gas before it had been released.

Nevertheless, in some places the gas was proving effective. Soon after six A.M., a report from aerial reconnaissance told Haig that "the gas cloud was rolling steadily over towards the German lines." German officers had anticipated the possibility of British gas attacks and instituted a system of warning by drums. Now these began to sound along the lines where soldiers, caught unprepared just as the French troops had been on April 22, panicked. Some never had time to find and put on their masks. In other cases, just as the British had hoped, the masks were ineffective. An advancing British sergeant reported twenty-three dead Germans, all wearing respirators. Within an hour of the first gas release British troops had penetrated a mile behind German lines. They included infantrymen of the King's Own Scottish Borderers. As gas had blown back over them while they waited beneath their scaling ladders in the trenches, ready to attack, their piper, Piper Laidlaw, had torn off his mask, leaped on the trench parapet, and played "Scotland the Brave" on his bagpipes.° As British troops advanced further they found German soldiers and officers lying in heaps, "blue in the face and undoubtedly gassed to death."

Reporting the outcome to London, Sir John French claimed the attack had "met with a marked success, and produced a demoralising effect in some opposing units." Foulkes had certainly succeeded in his aim of surprising the enemy. Gas had helped the British right wing capture Loos and take the German first line. Bernhard Kellermann, war correspondent of the *Berliner Tageblatt*, described how "behind the gas and smoke cloud there suddenly emerged Englishmen in thick lines and storming columns. They rose suddenly from the earth wearing smoke masks over their faces and looking not like soldiers but like devils."

However, as with the German gas attacks at Ypres, the British failed to capitalize on their success for reasons admitted by Lieutenant Ashley: "The artillery, with insufficient shells, had not cut the barbed wire defences effectively at many points and the infantry had been held up. Reserves had been held too far back to exploit the initial success." Within a week, and despite further use by the British of gas, the Germans had retaken all their lost ground. Furthermore, two thousand British troops were reported to have been gassed by their own chlorine. Fifty-five were in a serious condition and ten died. The casualties included men of the Special Companies. As the chlorine had blown back on the British trenches, a sergeant saw "a gas officer in the trench. He looked ghastly and all the buttons on his tunic were green as if they were mouldy."

° Though wounded, Piper Laidlaw played on. He was awarded the Victoria Cross.

CHAPTER NINETEEN

"Zepp and a Portion of Clouds"

FOLLOWING THE SEPTEMBER zeppelin raids, the British authorities had worked to improve London's artillery defenses, then consisting of eight three-inch guns, four six-pounders with inaccurate gun sights, and some superannuated one pounder "pom poms" from the Boer War. Two days after Mathy's September 8 raid, First Lord of the Admiralty Arthur Balfour appointed sixty-two-year-old Admiral Sir Percy Scott to take charge. Scott had served under Jacky Fisher and been one of the few to perceive the submarine's destructive potential. Revered as the "father of naval gunnery," his appointment reflected the Admiralty's view that guns, backed up by searchlights, were a better defense against airships than air patrols.

One of Scott's first acts was to obtain a modern French seventy-five-millimeter mobile gun—the "auto-cannon"—from France where it was being used in the defense of Paris and to order thirty more. The gun fired a high-explosive shell with a time fuse up to twenty-one thousand feet. Scott also acquired additional guns wherever he could and mounted them on lorry chassis for mobility, as well as setting up fixed gun positions linked to searchlight stations. He concentrated his greatest fire power on the coast, while positioning backup guns along the approaches to London and within the city itself. Their number and locations were kept secret so that some Londoners soon got a surprise. A man walking along Grosvenor Place reported: "I was almost blown off my feet by the gun which fired from just over the wall in the garden of Buckingham Palace."

On the night of October 13 zeppelins returned in strength. Strasser sent five—*L11*, *L13*, and *L14* together with two new airships, *L15* and *L16*, fitted with 240-horsepower engines rather than the 210-horsepower engines of their sisters, and capable of sixty miles an hour. The airships were to rendezvous over the North Sea and then proceed together. *L11* arrived too late to do more than follow, drop several bombs over rural Norfolk, and return home where her captain claimed he had bombed Woolwich. The remaining four, under the overall command of Heinrich Mathy again aboard *L13*, approached the Norfolk coast at around six twenty P.M. Naval lightships in the North Sea had already reported their presence and a zeppelin warning had gone out to airfields around London. Due to thick ground fog only five planes took off. Just one, that piloted by eighteen-year-old Second Lieutenant John Slessor, would even sight a zeppelin that night.

As the four airships continued inland, machine guns—part of the new first line of defense—opened up from the ground but to no effect. *L16* soon fell behind and after dropping some bombs on the town of Hertford returned home, though its commander claimed to have bombed east London. Meanwhile, the remaining three zeppelins split up. Kapitän-Leutnant Alois Bocker, aboard *L14*, veered away for the Thames estuary and a little later Mathy departed to circle round and approach London from the southwest, leaving Kapitän-Leutnant Joachim Breithaupt, commanding *L15*, to come in from the north.

As *L15* flew through clear starlit skies a thirteen-pounder antiaircraft gun attacked it. Breithaupt's response was to drop three bombs which he thought destroyed the gun. He then steered toward central London. Two searchlights pinpointed his airship and another antiaircraft gun opened fire. Many people ignored whistles and shouts from policemen to take cover to stare fascinated at what a reporter described as this "thing of silvery beauty sailing serenely through the night."

Arriving over Charing Cross, Breithaupt dropped further bombs. London's nearby music halls, theaters, and restaurants were doing good business. A Londoner recalled how "during this period no restaurant keeper would be surprised if you ordered 'Zepp and a portion of clouds' . . . He would serve you without question with sausage and mashed potatoes." *Tonight's the Night*, a popular American musical comedy, was being performed at the Gaiety Theatre while *Potash and Perlmutter in Society*—a comedy by Charles Frohman's friend Charles Klein, who had died with him on the *Lusitania*—was also being performed. Breithaupt's first bombs hit the corner of the Lyceum Theatre where *Between Two Women* was playing. It was the interval and people were strolling outside or having a quick drink at the nearby Old Bell pub.

A member of Lyceum staff recalled seeing the zeppelin "as pretty as a picture up there . . . even afterwards, when I saw the dead bodies and the terrible injuries and helped with the wounded, I could not believe somehow that she had done it." Seven people were killed, twenty-one injured, and a gas main fractured. The next bomb landed close to the Strand Theatre where people were watching *The Scarlet Pimpernel*. Breithaupt, in his control gondola high above, found the scene "indescribably beautiful—shrapnel bursting all around (though rather uncomfortably near us), our own bombs bursting, and the flashes from the anti-aircraft batteries below."

Continuing down the Strand to the Aldwych, Breithaupt dropped two more bombs, killing three more people and wounding fifteen. An army officer, on leave from the western front, was in a taxi when his driver suddenly halted, jumped out, and ran away. He also got out and saw "right overhead . . . an enormous Zeppelin. It was lighted up by searchlights and cruised along slowly and majestically, a marvellous sight. I stood gaping in the middle of the Strand, too fascinated to move. Then there was a terrific explosion, followed by another and another."

Breithaupt's next bombs hit the nineteenth-century Royal Courts of Justice and Lincoln's Inn—the oldest of London's four Inns of Court—destroying the seventeenth-century stained glass window in the Inn's chapel and damaging the walls of the late eighteenth-century Stone Buildings, the world's oldest purpose-built offices where shrapnel holes are still visible. They also hit Chancery Lane, Gray's Inn, and Hatton Garden, the latter two bombed in the raid a month before. Breithaupt headed next toward the financial center of the City. Meanwhile, Sir Percy Scott's deputy, Lieutenant Commander Alfred Rawlinson, had been rushing the new French seventy-five-millimeter auto-cannon across London to the City. He was just in time to have the gun set up, estimate the airship's height at eleven thousand feet, and give the order to fire as *L15* appeared. The high-explosive shell, detonating at seventy-two hundred feet, fell short but Breithaupt realized something more powerful than the usual antiaircraft guns was attacking him. Swiftly dropping two further bombs, he ordered his crew to jettison water ballast and ascended. When Rawlinson was ready to fire again, *L15* was already beyond his reach.

Having raided the heart of London with little opposition, Breithaupt set course for home. Apart from Rawlinson's mobile cannon, no guns had troubled him. Neither had any aircraft. Young pilot John Slessor recalled the frustration of spotting *L15* while being unable to attack her. He had just pulled off his boots to lie down on his camp bed at his airfield when told that zeppelins were heading for London. He was to take off and patrol at ten thousand feet for as long as his fuel lasted: "The lights of the capital presented a wonderful spectacle. They did more. They illuminated quite effectively the great silver shape of Zeppelin L15 . . . Long before I had reached my patrol height I saw above me its impressively vast bulk like a cod's eye view of a liner apparently stationary and clearly visible in the glow from the lights of London." He tried to climb above her but was still one thousand feet below when he saw "streams of sparks as [*L15's*] engines opened up. The great bulk swung round and then . . . cocked its nose up at an incredible angle and climbed away from me . . . The great shape diminished and grew . . . indistinct as she drew away from me and from the lights of London. Finally I lost her altogether in the cloud—and then I found that I had also lost myself."

Meanwhile, Heinrich Mathy's *L13*, carrying the heaviest bomb load of the night, had navigated westward around London, got lost, but then made for central London, in the process sighting Alois Bocker's *L14*. After crossing the Thames estuary Bocker too had missed his way. Finding himself almost out over the English Channel he had returned inland, dropping some of his bombs before spotting *L13* close by to his south. The two airships exchanged signals. Mathy then headed north to attack Woolwich in mistake for the Royal Victoria Dock while Bocker bombed the prosperous London suburb of Croydon twelve miles south of the capital and described in the late nineteenth century as a place where "handsome villas spring up on every side tenanted by city men whose portly persons crowd the trains."

The raid killed 71 people and injured 128 (47 of the fatalities and 102 of the injured were in the capital). Total damage was around eighty thousand pounds. Major Cuthbert Lawson wrote to his mother that the zeppelins "seem to have pretty well put the wind up the population." At a public meeting held the next day at the Cannon Street Hotel, speaker after speaker criticized London's defenses and accused the government of keeping the public in the dark. To loud cheers Lord Willoughby de Broke demanded that "the kind of thing that happened last night has got to stop." Member of Parliament William Joynson-Hicks said that "all knew now that the shores of England were not inviolate. Every man and woman cried aloud for vengeance." A resolution was carried overwhelmingly calling for "a declared policy of air reprisals for Zeppelin raids on London and other open cities." together with a demand for Britain to build "a fleet of large aeroplanes capable of offensive warfare." Three men who objected were "roughly handled and forcibly ejected" while a vicar told the meeting, "Let us have done with soft and silly presentiments of Christianity."

The German high command again assessed the raids. Der Feuerplan had not yet succeeded. London had been attacked but not yet significantly damaged. Its citizens, though angered and shocked, had not buckled under the psychological pressure of aerial attack. Many, including Strasser, believed the pressure must be intensified and that coordinated and concentrated zeppelin attacks would deliver the best results. However, there were obvious problems. In the latest raid two airships had nearly collided. Furthermore, communications were poor—Mathy's radio operator, crouching in the tiny wireless cubicle in the control gondola, had lost radio contact with the other airships as they crossed the English coast. Navigation was also imprecise. The airships' liquid magnetic compasses, despite the addition of alcohol, frequently froze at subzero temperatures. Instead, commanders relied on dead reckoning at sea and identifying landmarks on the ground, leading to frequent failures to attack the right target.

However, Strasser placed his faith in a new generation of six-engine "super-zeppelins" already under construction with the first to be delivered in mid-1916, still in time, he hoped, to strike a decisive blow while London's air defenses remained embryonic.

In Britain, the government knew through its agents that upgraded zeppelins were coming and debated how best to respond. Sir Percy Scott's measures had had only limited effect and in the Houses of Parliament MPs reflected public anger and disquiet, asking, "Have the military authorities permission to fire at hostile aircraft?" and "Is the Home Secretary aware that during the last raid many motor cars with powerful lamps were observed in the main streets?" Scott himself blamed insufficient resources and interference from a bureaucratic Admiralty, writing to Balfour: "I must have a free hand to procure what is wanted, and how best I can, and not be handicapped by Admiralty red-tapism." The War Office view, as opposed to the Admiralty's, remained that the best—indeed only—way to defeat the zeppelins was to attack them in the air with airplanes. Thus the priority was to build more and better night fighters.

But as winter drew on and London's repaired Lyceum Theatre reopened at the end of December with a production of *Robinson Crusoe*, Londoners enjoyed another respite from zeppelin attack.

CHAPTER TWENTY

"Remember the *Lusitania*"

On October 12, 1915, the German authorities had further outraged neutral as well as Allied public opinion by executing forty-nine-year-old British nurse Edith Cavell in occupied Brussels. As the Geneva Convention required, she had treated sick and wounded soldiers of any nationality in the nurse training hospital of which she was matron and of which *Lusitania* victim Marie de Page's husband, Antoine, was medical director. However she had also given assistance to fugitive Allied troops who wished to escape to neutral Holland. Although she had not communicated military intelligence to anyone, the Germans accused her of being a spy and sentenced her to death.

The U.S. embassy in Brussels looked after British interests, including prisoners, just as they did in Germany itself, and attempted to intervene. German officials initially fobbed them off, not telling them when the death sentence had been passed and subsequently being deaf to pleas for clemency. Edith Cavell was executed in the small hours of the morning. She had previously told the U.S. embassy chaplain, "I realise that patriotism is not enough. I must have no hatred or bitterness towards anyone." The secretary of the U.S. embassy in Brussels, Hugh Gibson, wrote, 'Her execution in the middle of the night at the conclusion of a course of trickery and deception was nothing short of an affront to civilisation." The *New York Herald* typified the American response, calling Germany "the moral leper of civilisation." The *New York Times* wrote, "The world at large prays that Germany's enemies may triumph."

The British press and that of its dominions were equally outraged. The

Cape Times in South Africa was only one of many associating "the murder—
no other term will meet the case" with the deaths on the *Lusitania*. The
Montreal Gazette suggested the Americans should now understand how
barbarous the Germans were.

According to James Gerard, the U.S. ambassador in Berlin, the
German government had been hoping "to keep the *Lusitania* matter 'jol-
lied along' until the American papers get excited about baseball or a news
scandal and forget." However, in early November, the *U-38* sank the
Ancona—an Italian passenger liner on her way to New York—killing one
hundred people, including twenty U.S. citizens. Even though the *U-38* had
been loaned to the Austro-Hungarian navy and that government took
responsibility for the sinking, the incident, together with the heightened
anti-German feelings raised by Edith Cavell's execution, prompted the
United States to press for a response to their as-yet-unanswered third protest note of July 21 on the *Lusitania*.

President Wilson married Edith Galt on December 18. Despite
detractors' comments that her clothes were too tight and her neckline too
low and a widely circulated joke by an indiscreet British diplomat—"What
did the new Mrs. Wilson do when the President proposed?" "She fell out
of bed with surprise"—Wilson was devoted to his second wife. She would
play an increasingly important part in his political as well as his domestic
life. While the happy couple were honeymooning at Hot Springs, Virginia,
the pro-British Lansing pushed the German authorities so hard that
Chancellor von Bethmann Hollweg believed Germany had a stark choice—
either admit the illegality of the *Lusitania* sinking or face war with the
United States.

However, after his return, in early 1916 Wilson reined Lansing in,
partly because he retained hopes in a presidential election year of a successful U.S. mediation in the war that remained stalemated. Throughout
the autumn and early winter of 1915 Colonel House had continued a dia-
logue with the belligerents about a brokered peace. Both sides had been
at best noncommittal. However, in discussing possible peace terms British
foreign secretary Sir Edward Grey had written to House: "Would the
President propose that there should be a League of Nations binding themselves to side against any Power which broke a treaty; which broke certain

rules of warfare on sea or land . . . or which refused, in case of dispute, to adopt some other method of settlement than that of war?" House had agreed with the idea and had showed the proposal to Wilson who approved it on November 11, 1915. The league would become a centerpiece of Wilson's peace proposals at the end of the war. Another reason for the softening in Wilson's attitude was that on a tour of the Midwestern states where many German immigrants lived, he had found the public mood in general rather less concerned about the *Lusitania* than in the east.

Understanding the president's wish at this stage not to push the issue to an open breach, Lansing worked with Ambassador von Bernstorff on ways to resolve or at least cool the dispute. As a result, on February 4 von Bernstorff presented Lansing informally with a draft German reply to the third U.S. note. It said that in deference to U.S. concerns, Germany had already limited the scope of U-boat warfare. It expressed "profound regret" for the American dead on the *Lusitania*, assumed liability for them, and offered "a suitable indemnity." It did not, however, specifically acknowledge any illegality on the German government's part. Von Bernstorff told Lansing that the wording went as far as his government could, given German public opinion. Lansing told Wilson that even if the word "illegality" was not used, the United States could interpret Germany's concessions as an indirect admission of wrongdoing. Wilson agreed. Thus the draft note was formalized and submitted on February 16. Theodore Roosevelt derided the protracted exchanges with Germany as responding to the sinking of the *Lusitania* by writing "note after note, each filled with lofty expressions, and each sterile in its utter futility, because it did not mean action and Germany knew it did not mean action."

Despite its government's conciliatory approach to the United States, the German public remained staunch supporters of unrestricted submarine warfare. So strong was anti-American feeling that Ambassador Gerard became convinced that the United States, not Britain, was now the true focus of popular hatred, agreeing with his defense attaché that "every German feels and believes that America has been unneutral and that America is aiding in a great measure the Allies. They feel that by sinking the *Lusitania* they have 'got back' at us in a small way for what we're doing."

Nevertheless, von Bethmann Hollweg continued to succeed, with the kaiser's backing, in restraining the persistent and vociferous naval submarine lobby. In March 1916, the chancellor even induced the kaiser to remove some of von Tirpitz's ministerial powers. Eighteen years after he had first been appointed, von Tirpitz offered his resignation again. The kaiser accepted. The two men never met again in the fourteen more years von Tirpitz lived. Von Tirpitz's rage was, according to a member of the German court, "indescribable . . . The authorities gave out as reason for his retirement that he had broken down and needed rest. So he walked with his wife up and down the Wilhelmstrasse for two hours to prove to the crowd that it was untrue and he was in the best of health. Next day he took off his uniform and appeared in tall hat and frock coat to show he had been deprived of his uniform."

Despite the war, Admiral Jacky Fisher, who perhaps saw some parallels with his own exit, quickly dispatched him a frank and consoling letter. It began, "Dear Old Tirps" and ended "Cheer up old chap! Say 'resurgam!' You're the one German sailor who understands War! Kill your enemy without being killed yourself. I don't blame you for the submarine business. I'd have done the same myself . . . Yours till hell freezes."

On March 24, within days of von Tirpitz's resignation, a German submarine, UB-29, torpedoed without warning the small, slow French cross-channel ferry Sussex en route to Dieppe from England, blowing off her bows. Although the stern section of the ship did not sink and was towed into harbor, eighty people were killed or injured. Four Americans were among the wounded. The attack again violated Germany's promise made seven months earlier following the Arabic's sinking not to attack unresisting passenger ships without warning. As in the case of the Hesperian Germany at first denied responsibility, but confronted with overwhelming evidence announced that the U-boat captain had mistaken the Sussex for a warship. A cartoon in the New York World depicted the kaiser clutching a wreath labeled "Lusitania" while behind him the stricken Sussex blew up. The caption read, "Of course I didn't do it— Didn't I promise I wouldn't?"

President Wilson issued an ultimatum—unrestricted submarine warfare was against what "the Government of the United States must consider the sacred and indisputable rules of international law and universally recognised dictates of humanity. The Government of the United States is at last forced to the conclusion that there is but one course it can pursue. Unless the Imperial Government should now immediately declare and effect an abandonment of its present methods of submarine warfare against passenger and freight-carrying vessels, the Government of the United States can have no choice but to sever diplomatic relations."

An editorial in the *New York Sun* explained some of the reasons why the American reaction to Germany's unrestricted submarine warfare was so much stronger than that to the British blockade: "There is no parallel between our differences with Germany . . . and with Great Britain . . . No question of life divides Great Britain from us and Sir Edward Grey has neither asserted the right of murder nor has he been asked by us to give assurance against murder. Our cases against Great Britain are purely civil." What's more, even the effect of the British blockade on Germany itself was gradual and reversible.

The kaiser was affronted by Wilson's "impertinence" and believed "there was no longer any international law." Nevertheless, under strong pressure from von Bethmann Hollweg and against the advice of von Falkenhayn who now favored unrestricted U-boat warfare to take the pressure off his armies, the kaiser at the end of April issued orders that the Cruiser Rules must again be followed and no unresisting merchant vessels sunk without warning. On April 27, having gone to sea in *U-20* before the orders were promulgated, Walther Schwieger sank without warning the 13,370-ton U.S.-bound liner *Cymric* off the coast of Ireland as he had the *Lusitania* and the *Hesperian*. She was the thirty-seventh passenger vessel to be sunk without warning after the *Lusitania*.

THOUGH POISON GAS had not proved a decisive weapon for either side, both made increasing use of it until the end of the war. Scientists strove not only to find new poison gases but also to find better ways to protect their soldiers. Fritz Haber and his institute worked with industrial companies like Bayer to produce more effective masks for the kaiser's troops. The simple gauze pads used by British troops after the first German gas attack in April were quickly succeeded by new designs, from "veil respirators" treated with sodium thiosulfate and held in place by black netting to chemically impregnated "P Helmets"—flannel hoods with celluloid eyeholes and a rubber exhaust tube, nine million of which were issued to British troops in December 1915—to ever more sophisticated box respirators. The latter, which became available from early 1916, consisted of a metal container packed with chemicals and carried in a satchel. A rubber tube connected the box with a mask that the soldier fitted over his nose and mouth. Air entered through a valve in the bottom of the satchel to be filtered as it passed through the chemicals before being breathed in through a metal mouthpiece. The user was also required to wear a nose clip in case gas had penetrated his mask, and separate goggles with eye pieces set in sponge rubber. It was effective but cumbersome.

The success of such masks depended on a soldier's willingness to wear one. Most detested fighting in them because of the stress they caused, both mental and physical. Twenty-four-year-old Second Lieutenant Wilfred Owen's iconic poem "Dulce et Decorum Est" described the sensation:

> Gas! Gas! Quick, boys!—An ecstasy of fumbling,
> Fitting the clumsy helmets just in time;
> But someone still was yelling out and stumbling.
> And flound'ring like a man in fire or lime . . .
> Dim, through the misty panes and thick green light.
> As under a green sea, I saw him drowning.
> In all my dreams, before my helpless sight,
> He plunges at me, guttering, choking, drowning.[*]

The P Helmets had been rushed to the front in late 1915 in the hope they would better protect British troops against a new chemical that intelligence reports suggested would soon be used against them—phosgene, described by Douglas Edwardes-Ker, the British assistant director of gas services on the western front, as "much nastier than what the Germans had started with." After German organic chemist Emil Fischer had first pointed out its potentially lethal qualities in early 1915 and industrialist Carl

---

[*] A bullet killed Wilfred Owen in November 1918, a week before the end of the war.

Duisberg had begun experimenting with it, Fritz Haber and his teams had developed it into a weapon. Haber believed that the longer the war went on, the greater the imperative to develop new poison gases: "A good army must change the gases it uses as often as possible in order to cause the enemy . . . anxiety and insecurity and the difficulties of devising fresh countermeasures."

In the summer of 1915 in Britain Foulkes had also realized phosgene's potential after having a sample tested in a laboratory. Having negotiated with a French factory owner for the rights to a formula for producing it, he had arranged for the United Alkali Company to manufacture quantities in great secrecy at a new plant at Lancaster in northern England. However, Germany was the first to use phosgene in battle.

At five thirty on the morning of December 19, 1915, again near Ypres, Haber's gas pioneers loosed fast-moving clouds not only of chlorine but also of phosgene. The chlorine had the familiar if horrific effects—some men died quite quickly, their skin discolored and spewing green froth. The effects of the colorless, odorless phosgene were quite different. Victims were unaware they had been poisoned until a terrible lethargy overtook them. A report by a British army doctor described how

> some 30 or 40 men left the trench to report sick. To get to the road the men . . . had to go across about 100 yards of very rough muddy ground. The exertion in heavy wet great-coats, and with all their equipment, caused great alteration in their condition, and by the time they reached the road they were exhausted and were quite unable to proceed any further . . . The history of the men who remained at duty in the trenches was still more striking. One man, feeling fairly well, was filling sandbags when he *collapsed and died suddenly*. Two more men died in the same way that evening.

Phosgene's delayed action made it seem especially frightening and sinister. A gassed man at first felt little except a slight prickling in the nose and throat that soon passed. For the next two days or so, he might even feel a little exuberant. However, all this time his lungs were filling with fluid. Victims could take forty-eight hours to die, coughing up four pints of yellow, blood-streaked liquid an hour. As a soldier recalled, "the victim virtually drowned." Phosgene also brought on heart attacks.

The French used phosgene in the defense of Verdun in February 1916. The British first used it at the Battle of the Somme in July 1916 when they released gas containing both chlorine and phosgene along a seventeen-mile front. The gas cloud rolled twelve miles behind German lines. The *Frankfurter Zeitung* described the hundreds of dead rodents left in its wake. In the first eighteen days of the Somme, Foulkes's men launched "more than fifty gas cloud attacks" and in the next nine months would release more than fifteen hundred tons of phosgene—"our main battle gas for the remainder of the war"—against the enemy lines. In Britain the *Daily Chronicle* reported jubilantly that "the effects of the new gases exper-imented with are terrible . . . Two hundred and fifty corpses were counted lying huddled together."

Foulkes himself took a sharp interest in any available information about the gas's effects, not "for ghoulish reasons" but because "we were really carrying out experiments on a gigantic scale and were in the same position as a chemist in a laboratory who, unless he can observe the reac-tions taking place in his test-tubes, is wasting his time." Despite reports of "immense numbers of corpses" the new gas gave the British army little lasting strategic advantage. When the Battle of the Somme ended in November 1916 the Allies had lost more than six hundred thousand men and advanced barely seven miles.

As gas warfare became routine, the belligerents sought more precise ways of delivering poison gas to the enemy than release from cylinders. In Britain, Captain F. H. Livens of the Special Gas Brigade—a former civil engineer with, according to Foulkes, a "strong personal feeling" against the Germans motivated by "the sinking of the *Lusitania*"— invented the Livens Projector. This was a three-to-four-foot-long, eight-inch-in-diameter steel tube that could be dug into the ground at an angle of forty-five degrees. When triggered, the projector could hurl a drum filled with thirty pounds of phosgene up to a mile toward enemy lines. The only warning to the enemy before the drum's TNT core exploded was the dull red flash of the firing mechanism. The Livens Projector was not only simple but cheap. Livens himself calculated that if manufactured "on a large scale the cost of killing Germans would be reduced to only sixteen shillings apiece."*

The British first used Livens Projectors at the Battle of Arras in April 1917. A captured German report described the horror of the exploding drums: "volcanic sheets of flame . . . thick black smoke clouds, powerful concussion, whistling . . . the noise [resembling] that of an exploding dump of hand-grenades." Soon British troops were using the projectors in batteries of thousands. Sometimes they simply filled the drums with noxious smelling substances to compel the enemy to endure the misery of wearing their gas masks. A German diary that fell into Allied hands described not only the "many casualties through gas poisoning" but the writer's feelings: "I can't think of anything worse; wherever one goes one must take one's gas mask with one, and it will soon be more necessary than a rifle. Things are dreadful here; one can't talk about them." German engineers attempted but failed to make an effective version of the projector themselves.

The British army also used in large numbers at Arras the Stokes mortar—a device invented by Wilfred Stokes that consisted of a steel tube capable of firing four-inch mortar bombs each holding two liters of gas up to one thousand yards. It was more accurate than the projector and an experienced crew could launch fifteen bombs before the first had hit its target. In addition, by 1917 the British, French, and German armies were all making extensive use of gas-filled artillery shells.

BY LATE 1916, the kaiser was again coming under pressure to authorize unrestricted submarine warfare. At the end of May, the British and German High Seas Fleets had clashed at Jutland. Although the British had lost more ships and at nearly sixty-eight hundred suffered twice the casualties, dead and wounded, than had the German fleet in what was the biggest naval battle of the war, after returning to base to replenish fuel and ammunition the British fleet commander Admiral John Jellicoe had signaled that his ships were ready to put to sea again at four hours' notice. In contrast, the German fleet was not. Many of the surviving German vessels were badly

---

* At this time the same sum would buy about four bottles of whisky.

damaged. Britain retained the crucial mastery of the sea, never again to be seriously challenged by the German surface fleet. In the mind of the German naval command, the only remaining way of reversing British supremacy and breaking the maritime blockade was unrestricted submarine warfare.

The blockade was proving increasingly effective. With many supplies reserved for the fighting troops, German civilians referred to the winter of 1916–17 as the "turnip winter" since turnips were the main component of their diet following a failure of the potato crop. At the beginning of the war Berlin abattoirs were killing twenty-five thousand pigs a week. Now the number was less than five hundred. Sugar and butter were scarce as well as potatoes and rationing had been introduced. Only one egg per person was allowed every fortnight. "We are all gaunt and bony now," a female member of the German court wrote. "We have dark shadows around our eyes and our thoughts are chiefly taken up with wondering what our next meal will be." The blockade was also diminishing the supply of raw materials for the war effort despite the work of German scientists and industrialists to find substitutes, while American-manufactured supplies flooded into Allied arsenals. In an effort to sustain output and replace workers now in the trenches, the German authorities had begun to transport Belgians forcibly to Germany to work in their industries.

On land the German army had repulsed the British army on the Somme and the Turks forced the British to evacuate Gallipoli and the Dardanelles. (The British authorities had not taken up a suggestion from Churchill that they should use gas against the Turkish forces. Churchill had argued that "the massacres by the Turks of Armenians and the fact that practically no British prisoners have been taken on the peninsula, though there are many thousands of missing, should surely remove all false sentiment on this point.")

However, elsewhere the war was not going as well as the German authorities might have wished. German forces had not broken through at Verdun despite inflicting massive casualties on the French. Portugal had joined the Allies in March 1916 followed by Rumania in August 1916. A Russian offensive had inflicted such severe setbacks on the Austro-Hungarians that Germany had had to transfer divisions to reinforce them.

Austro-Hungary's new emperor Karl—Franz Joseph had died in November at eighty-six—had told Berlin that Austria would not last another winter and hoped for a compromise peace. Paul Von Hindenburg, who had replaced von Falkenhayn as army commander in chief, and his chief of staff Erich Ludendorff, were arguing in support of their naval colleagues and claiming that if the flow of arms across the Atlantic to the Allies were not stopped, they might well give a decisive advantage to them.

An additional factor in German thinking was President Wilson's re-election in November 1916. Although he won by only a very narrow margin, his victory suggested to many in the German hierarchy that Americans preferred a "writing" to a "fighting" president and that his campaign slogan, "He Kept Us Out of War," symbolized American attitudes. Ambassador Gerard was convinced that the German administration believed "America could be insulted, flouted, and humiliated with impunity."

IN LATE DECEMBER 1916, Chief of the Naval Staff Admiral von Holtzendorff produced a two-hundred-page document advocating the resumption of unrestricted submarine warfare. In it he presented a multitude of statistics and details to substantiate his case. If the war was not to end badly for Germany, it had to be concluded before "the autumn of 1917." Britain was the strongest of Germany's enemies and the best way of weakening it would be to cut off its maritime trade using unrestricted submarine warfare. Germany's expanded submarine fleet, including many advanced vessels, would be able to sink six hundred thousand tons of shipping per month as well as frighten many neutral vessels from Britain's shores. If this figure was achieved, von Holtzendorff stated, "we may reckon that in five months shipping to and from England will be reduced by 39%. England would not be able to stand that. I do not hesitate to assert that . . . we can force England to make peace in five months."

At a meeting at the German supreme headquarters in the three-hundred-room white castle of Pless in early January 1917, von Bethmann Hollweg objected that unrestricted submarine warfare was likely to bring the United States into the war. Von Holtzendorff responded, "I pledge on my word as a naval officer that no American will set foot on continental soil." England would indeed be forced to capitulate. Both von Hindenburg and Ludendorff backed him up. Von Hindenburg asserted, "We are in a position to meet all eventualities against America . . . We need the most energetic and ruthless action possible. Therefore the U-boat war must begin not later than February 1, 1917." Ludendorff said unrestricted U-boat warfare would "improve the situation even of our armies . . . We must spare the troops a second Somme battle." Left without allies, von Bethmann Hollweg acquiesced in the decision to resume the submarine campaign although telling a colleague it was *"Finis Germaniae"* (the end of Germany).

The kaiser signed the authorization for the new campaign. "I order that unrestricted submarine warfare be launched with the utmost vigour on the 1st of February . . .Wilhelm I. R." All ships—enemy and neutral, armed and unarmed—would be attacked in the war zone. The decision would only be announced on the evening of January 31 within hours of the first potential attacks. The United States was to be offered a small concession—one specially marked American vessel a week would be allowed to enter and leave the English port of Falmouth.

When the announcement of the campaign was made, President Wilson responded on February 3 by severing diplomatic relations with Germany. The British naval attaché in Washington dispatched a jubilant telegram to Reginald Hall, the head of the British Admiralty's intelligence unit who was responsible for Room 40: "Bernstorff goes home. I get drunk tonight."

Wilson decided to see whether the Germans carried out their threat before taking the final step of declaring war. Hall, however, had in his London safe a document that would increase the pressure on the president. In case the declaration of Germany's new submarine campaign brought the United States into the war, the German administration had made plans to keep them occupied at home. On January 16, 1917, Arthur Zimmermann, the German foreign secretary, using facilities granted by the United States for diplomatic purposes, sent a telegram to von Bernstorff in Washington for onward transmission to the German embassy in Mexico. It baldly proposed an alliance between Germany and Mexico: "Make war together, make peace together, generous financial support, and an understanding on our part that Mexico is to reconquer the lost territory in Texas, New Mexico and Arizona." The message went on to suggest that Japan should be invited to switch sides and declare war against the United States.[*]

Room 40 had decoded the telegram and passed it to Hall. He waited until the middle of February when it was clear that the German announcement of its submarine campaign would not provoke the United States into an immediate declaration of war. Then Hall showed it to Edward Bell, an intelligence officer at the U.S. embassy in London and Hall's longtime associate, whom he used to get messages quickly and accurately to Washington.[†] Bell in turn showed Zimmermann's telegram to the American Ambassador to Britain Walter Hines Page. Together they passed it to Washington, ensuring that its source was not revealed so as not to let Germany know its code had been broken by Room 40. On receiving the document on February 24, Wilson and Lansing released it to the press, most of whom were outraged. However, a few staunchly anti-interventionist papers suggested it was a fake until Zimmermann, for reasons best known to himself, confirmed its authenticity. Then they too changed their minds. The *Omaha World Herald* wrote: "The issue shifts from Germany against Great Britain to Germany against the United States." The *Cleveland Plain Dealer* thought there was "neither virtue nor dignity" in not fighting now.

On March 18 U-boats sank three unarmed American freighters without warning and with the loss of fifteen men on one of them, the *Vigilance*. Wilson summoned a special session of Congress on April 4 and told them: "The present German submarine warfare against commerce is a warfare against mankind. There is one choice we cannot make, we are incapable of making: we will not choose the path of submission. The status of belligerent has been thrust upon us . . . It is a fearful thing to lead this great peaceful people into war. But the right is more precious than peace. The world must be made safe for democracy. The day has come when America is privileged to spend her blood . . . for the principles that gave her birth." By April 6 Congress had ratified the declaration of war.

---

[*] Japan had joined the Allies in August 1914, seizing several German North Pacific territories.

[†] Bell said of Hall, "No man could fill his place—a perfectly marvellous person but the coldest-blooded proposition that ever was—he'd eat a man's heart and hand it back to him."

Recruitment posters appeared headlined REMEMBER THE LUSI-TANIA. Another depicted a drowning woman, hair streaming out like seaweed in blue-green water and a baby clasped tight to her chest. A single bloodred word was superimposed over the image—ENLIST.

CHAPTER TWENTY-ONE

"Each One Must Fight On to the End"

DESPITE THE U.S. declaration of war, that year, 1917, was not a successful one for the Allies on land, at sea, or in the air. In March, revolution in Russia saw Alexander Kerensky's provisional government take power after the abdication of the czar. Although the provisional government kept Russia in the war, its allies knew that for the present little could be expected from the Russian armies wracked by desertions and turning in on themselves. Then in the summer of 1917 Russian armies suffered a series of heavy defeats resulting in the loss of much territory including cities such as Riga. In October 1917, nine Austro-Hungarian and six German divisions attacked and routed the Italian army at Caporetto in the Italian foothills in the Alps, pushing them back seventy miles. The Italian army suffered two hundred thousand casualties and in addition nearly four hundred thousand men deserted. The French authorities felt compelled to send six divisions to Italy to reinforce their allies, and the British sent five.

On the western front, French armies were exhausted after the attritional fighting around Verdun and their morale was weakening, leading to several mutinies. British attacks at Arras and around Ypres—among their aims to seize occupied Belgian ports being used as bases for the marauding U-boats and the airfields from which German planes took off to attack London—failed to gain significant ground. They finally petered out in the thick mud around the village of Passchendaele in mid-November. British casualties in the preceding six months had been 275,000, of whom 75,000 were dead.

British troops had become accustomed to protecting themselves from attacks by German phosgene and chlorine shells—their box respirators successfully kept these gases out. However, on the warm summer evening of July 12, 1917 near Ypres the British Fifteenth and Fifty-fifth Divisions faced for the first time another and even more hazardous substance. They had been subjected to a heavy barrage mixing high-explosive shells with those containing shrapnel or phosgene before shells containing a liquid that to some looked like sherry burst around them. It vaporized to give off a gas variously described as smelling like "mustard, rubber, vulcanite, dead horses, diseased vegetables, petrol, garlic and lamp oil," even "freshly chopped horseradish." Some soldiers thought it was a weak tear gas and did not put on their box respirators. A few hours later they woke with pain in their eyes and "blisters and painful burns" on their skin. The first deaths occurred two days later "after a period of excruciating agony." The new weapon was mustard gas developed and manufactured under Fritz Haber's supervision as the head of the German Ministry of War's chemistry department. He hailed it as an "amazing success."

Observing some of the gassed men, a medical officer described faces "congested and swollen," covered with small blisters, and "a few cases . . . had blisters on the backs of the thighs and buttocks and even on the scrotum with oedema of the scrotum and penis . . . probably due to men sitting on the ground contaminated with the toxic substance." Another doctor described entering a ward of gassed men and being struck by "the incessant and apparently useless coughing." A British nurse, Vera Brittain, wrote of soldiers with "great mustard-coloured suppurating blisters, blind eyes . . . all sticky and stuck together, and always fighting for breath, with voices a mere whisper, saying that their throats are closing and they know they will choke."

Because its vaporization point was high, the liquid mustard gas lingered in water, in shell craters, and elsewhere and contaminated the soil—to the extent that gas used in late 1917 vaporized on the return of warmth in spring 1918. Frank Richards of the Royal Welch Fusiliers recalled, "Our new box respirators were proof against [the gas]. It would burn through the clothes and nasty blisters would break out. If an area had been shelled with these shells it was never safe to use a shell hole as a latrine . . . The gas would hang around." Gas shells of which "mustard was the most deadly sort" fell with "no loud explosions . . . They struck the ground with a soft thud and it was difficult to tell them from duds."

Blindness caused by mustard gas was usually but not always temporary. A British corporal described his fears, "Was I going to be blind for life? What was I going to do? My trade, my employment gone. It hit me very, very hard." Even if like this soldier men gradually recovered their sight, those afflicted were away from the battlefield for long periods and caring for them used up considerable resources. Life in the trenches became even more difficult. Soldiers had to protect themselves at nearly all times, frequently donning gas masks and goggles, covering exposed skin—a particular problem for kilted Scottish and Canadian Highlanders—washing as best they could any suspected contaminated clothing and using bleach to clear a path across heavily contaminated soil. Lieutenant Safford of the U.S. Marine Corps recalled how before going into battle soldiers "would often grease their bodies with lard" to stop the gas coming into contact with their skin.

General Amos Fries, head of the United States Chemical Warfare Service, thought "the reduction in physical vigour and, therefore, in efficiency of an army forced at all times to wear masks would amount to at least twenty-five per cent, equivalent to disabling a quarter of a million men out of an army of a million." And all this was in a sea of mud. A British sergeant major, Richard Tobin, described the conditions: "There was no chance of being wounded . . . at Passchendaele. You could either get through or die, because if you were wounded and slipped off the duckboards you just sank into the mud . . . Each side was a sea of mud, and if you stumbled you would go in up to the waist, and literally every pool was full of the decomposed bodies of humans and mules."

THE GERMAN U-BOAT commanders fulfilled Admiral von Holtzendorff's promise to the kaiser about the tonnage they would sink. Between the beginning of February 1917 and the end of April that year they sank almost two million tons of shipping, more than 870,000 tons of that in April alone.

This did not, however, cause the British authorities to seek peace. Instead, in May they somewhat belatedly instituted a convoy system—naval officers having been unnecessarily concerned about their merchant equivalents' ability to keep station and follow instructions from their naval escorts. Destroyers were the ideal escort but were in short supply. Therefore, the British naval headquarters at Queenstown was more than grateful when six modern U.S. destroyers arrived in the port in early May to be followed before the end of the month by twelve more. They were quickly integrated into the British naval operations—the U.S. Navy unlike the U.S. Army under General John Pershing did not insist on retaining its own independent command structure—and were soon at work with their British counterparts protecting convoys, searching for submarines, and enforcing the blockade to which until very recently their government had been taking exception as contrary to America's long-cherished policy of "freedom of the seas." By the end of July, the combined naval force at Queenstown had thirty-four U.S. destroyers, mostly larger than the British ones and therefore perfect for the Atlantic convoy role.

The introduction of the convoy system reduced, even if it did not halt, the sinkings. Karl Dönitz, commander in chief of the German navy in the Second World War, was in 1917 a submarine commander and reported, "the oceans at once became bare." The concentration and protection of the merchant ships was the key factor in reducing losses, not the number of submarines destroyed. Nevertheless, more submarines were being sunk due in particular to scientific and engineering advances accelerated by wartime needs. In 1915, the only method of detecting a submerged submarine had been rudimentary hydrophones that only worked in a shore installation or on a ship that had its engines and machinery stopped. Even then, waves hitting the hull provoked serious interference. During the next two years hydrophones—though still by no means perfect—were sufficiently improved to detect submarines from moving ships.

Until the invention of the depth charge in 1916, attacks on fully submerged submarines had in any case been virtually impossible. Depth charges looked like metal dustbins and were rolled off the stern of a destroyer when the vessel's crew believed it to be above a submarine. They contained three hundred pounds of TNT with a pressure fuse set to the depth the submarine was thought to be at. They achieved their first kill in December 1916.

When von Holtzendorff's five-month timescale for British capitulation passed at the end of June, shipping losses for that month were 696,000 tons, compared to May's 616,000 and April's record of over 800,000, but thereafter they began to decline. In November 1917 they were 302,000 and reduced further to some 230,000 per month at the war's end. By April 1918 U.S. and British shipyards were producing more new merchant tonnage than was being sunk. Even more significantly, of the nearly two million U.S. troops crossing the Atlantic to the western front less than seven hundred died as a result of submarine action.

ZEPPELIN ATTACKS ON London had continued through the first part of 1916 but British air defenses had improved. New fighters like the De Havilland DH2—with a one-hundred-horsepower rotary engine capable of ninety-three miles per hour and of reaching fourteen thousand feet— flew faster and higher. Their guns now had explosive and incendiary bullets, fired alternately first to puncture the zeppelins' gas cells, then to ignite the hydrogen within. Germans airmen called the bullets "an invention of the devil. Had we caught the man who invented that bullet, we should gladly have incinerated him in a stream of burning hydrogen." Also, in April 1916 the British captured one of the new German fighters, the Fokker Eindecker, designed by Anthony Fokker, a Dutchman working in Germany, and learned the secrets of its synchronization gear which allowed a forward-facing machine gun to fire through a rotating propeller. This mechanism would soon be introduced into British planes. (The DH2 avoided this problem by being a "pusher" biplane with the propeller facing the rear.)

In early September 1916, twenty-one-year-old Second Lieutenant William Leefe Robinson coaxed his BE2c (an older model of plane) to nearly thirteen thousand feet and attacking from above became the first British pilot to shoot down an airship (the German army's SL11) over England. Another airship commander watched as "it caught fire at the stern, burned with an enormous flame and fell." It crashed near the village of Cuffley in Hertfordshire with no survivors. A female onlooker thought "poor devils" but Londoners cheered, danced, and sang in the streets. Robinson received the Victoria Cross five days later. The German army disbanded its Airship Service shortly afterward. Peter Strasser still believed his naval zeppelins could inflict decisive damage on London, but by the end of 1916 five of his airships had also been shot down. Heinrich Mathy, the first commander ever to bomb central London, died jumping from his burning zeppelin above Potters Bar, north of the city.

In February 1917 the German naval air service took delivery of a new lighter zeppelin, the "Height-Climber," that could reach twenty-one-thousand feet—higher than any British fighter plane—and that Strasser hoped would perform better. However, several Height-Climbers broke up in the strong winds encountered at high altitude. Their crews also struggled to cope in the thin air and bitter cold. Officer Otto Mieth recalled, "We shivered even in our heavy clothing and we breathed with such difficulty in spite of our oxygen flasks that several members of the crew became unconscious." Disappointed with the Height-Climbers' performance, the kaiser concluded that "the day of the airship is past for attacks on London." The last raid on the city was on October 19, 1917, when a 660-pound bomb hit Piccadilly Circus. Strasser himself died on the last airship raid of the war on Britain—shot down in August 1918 as his zeppelin approached the Norfolk coast.

SINCE THE FIRST attack at the end of May 1915, German airships had targeted London twenty-six times and on nine occasions bombed its center, killing nearly two hundred Londoners, injuring more than five hundred, and causing one million pounds of damage. Overall their raids on Britain had killed more than 550 and injured some 1,350. The attacks had both fascinated and frightened the population and forced the British authorities to commit scarce resources to home defense.

However, well before the zeppelin assault ended Londoners were subjected to another aerial threat. On November 28, 1916, a single German plane dropped six twenty-two-pound bombs on London—a harbinger of what was to come. Since the war started, German engineers had striven to develop heavy bombers capable of reaching London, while in occupied Belgium the German army had created an elite cadre of pilots to fly them, code-named the Brieftauben Abteilung (Carrier Pigeon Unit), to deceive enemy agents about its purpose.

By early 1916, the first long-range heavy bombers capable of reaching London from Belgium—Gothas IVs—were available to the German fliers. However, the first planes were deployed to the fighting around Verdun and on the Somme. At the year end, with continuing stalemate on the western front, the German high command decided that some of the Gothas should conduct large-scale bombing raids on London to create massive firestorms in pursuit of the Feuerplan which the zeppelins had left unrealized.

The German army assembled an "England Squadron" of Gothas and their crews. With their seventy-eight-foot wingspan and two six-cylinder 260-horsepower Mercedes engines, these white biplanes were the largest aircraft yet built in Germany. (Their wingspan exceeded that of any German airplane sent against Britain in the Second World War.) Their range was over four hundred miles; they could reach 16,500 feet; and, with a top speed of eighty-seven miles per hour, they were as fast as most British fighters. They could carry eleven hundred pounds of bombs of two types—28-pound *Splitterbomben*, fragmentation bombs, packed with phosphorous and TNT and 110-pound high-explosive bombs. The steel noses of the latter five-foot-seven-inch-long missiles were designed to punch through roofs, letting them tumble down through a building before exploding, thus creating maximum damage. The Gothas carried a three-man crew—the pilot; the observer who, sitting in the nose, commanded the plane and was responsible for navigating, bomb-aiming, and operating a 0.311-inch machine gun that fired armor-piercing Mauser ammunition; and a rear gunner manning two further machine guns.

At two o'clock on the afternoon of Friday, May 25, 1917—the Whitsun holiday weekend in Britain—Gothas of the England Squadron, led by Hauptmann Ernst Brandenburg, took off for London. However, encountering heavy cloud and mist coming up from the west, Brandenburg diverted to attack secondary targets on the Kent coast. In the port of Folkestone, filled with holidaymakers, the drone of the approaching Gothas made people look skyward. To many the white planes were like giant seagulls or snowflakes. Then the bombs fell—thirty *Splitterbomben* and twenty high-explosive bombs. They ripped two girls to pieces and blew a man across a street to be impaled on railings. A nine-year-old boy watched as another man's "head rolled . . . into a gutter." The civilian casualties were the worst of the war so far—ninety-five killed and 195 wounded. Just as with the *Lusitania* victims, mass burials were held.

The scale of the attack surprised the British authorities. Since the successful shooting down of zeppelins the previous year, they had reduced home defenses. Almost half the pilots serving in England had been redeployed to the western front and some antiaircraft guns reallocated to merchant ships for defense against U-boats. To protect against the new menace the government ordered more raids on German airfields in Belgium and stationed more antiaircraft observers in the Thames estuary and along the east coast. However, many thought the steps wholly inadequate, including Sir John French, now commander in chief of forces in Britain, who predicted "disastrous results" if more was not done.

By June 13 the weather was good enough for another attempt on London by the England Squadron. As the Gothas were readied, "the thundering roar of the wonderful Mercedes engines filled the air . . . Engineers hurried back and forth as everyone strove to solve even the smallest glitches in the planes to which we were entrusting our lives," an airman recalled. Pilots gave instructions to the mechanics, and observers tested their bomb-release levers and navigational instruments. Shortly before ten A.M., Brandenburg gave the order to take off. Half an hour later twenty Gothas approached the English coast. They overflew a convoy of merchant ships protected by naval torpedo boats and destroyers which, spotting the Gothas, began zigzagging. Three Gothas peeled off to conduct diversionary attacks but seventeen flew on until, as one airman described, "the green countryside faded and a dark expanse, black and grey," appeared which "as our nerves tensed . . . gradually increased in size until it filled the horizon. Houses rose up in their thousands, hundreds of streets, squares and parks— boundless . . . the colossal city of London."

As the Gothas reached London, antiaircraft guns opened fire: "The blasts of the explosions were so loud . . . that sometimes they drowned out the noise of our engines and forced our aircraft temporarily to scatter." The observers peered through the Gothas' bombsights trying to identify targets before releasing their bombs. Some of them landed on Barking and more on nearby East Ham. A commercial traveler warned by a policeman to take cover instead looked up to see "what looked like large white butterflies . . . Soon came the frequent dull boom, then a horrid crash . . . I ran across the road. Three people were laid out at my feet. The gutters were running red." In Stoke Newington—bombed by zeppelins in 1915—schoolchildren looked out to see "tongues of flame" leaping in the air while, as an onlooker recalled, "the continued crashes told of targets found—houses, schools, factories. Across the road lay a horse writhing in its death throes. Its driver was buried beneath the splintered wood debris of the cart. Screams of terrified children mingled with the moans of the wounded."

Over Liverpool Street Station the Gothas dropped seventy-three bombs. A crewman heard the "tremendous crash" as they struck "the heart of England." It was "a magnificently terrific spectacle . . . The earth seems to be rocking and houses are disappearing in craters and conflagrations in the light of the glaring sun." Bombs hit several trains and passengers trapped in them were burned alive. Officer and war poet Siegfried Sassoon who was in the station saw "an elderly man, shabbily dressed and apparently dead" laid out on a luggage trolley: "In a trench one was acclimatised to the notion of being exterminated. But here one was helpless; an invisible enemy sent destruction spinning down . . . Poor old men bought a railway ticket and were trundled away again dead on a barrow."

The Gothas attempted to attack the Tower of London but though a bomb landed in the dry moat it failed to detonate. Another bomb crashed through five floors of a nearby school but again did not explode. Pupils of the two-story Upper North Street School for children of the poor in the East India Dock Road were not so fortunate. At eleven forty A.M. all were at their desks when a 110-pound high-explosive bomb smashed, as it was designed to, through the roof of the building to the basement where sixty-four of the youngest children had been making paper lanterns. When the raid began, their teachers had encouraged them to sing but as one recalled, "the noise of the anti-aircraft guns and the detonations of the enemy's bombs became audible above even our shrill voices."

As the bomb came through the ceiling, teachers and children heard a metallic click just before it exploded, blasting a six-foot crater in the basement's concrete floor where the mangled remains of five-year-old Florence Wood were later found. A child saw two classmates "driven like stakes into the earth" while Ivy Major was the sole survivor out of a row of twelve children. A soldier who rushed into the bombed basement to help found "many of the little ones . . . lying across their desks, apparently dead, and with terrible wounds on heads and limbs, and scores of others were writhing with pain and moaning pitifully . . . We packed the little souls on the lorries as gently as we could." Sixteen children, nearly all five or younger, had been killed instantly; two more died later of their wounds; and thirty were badly injured.

To the Gotha airmen, three miles above the sunlit streets, the carnage was remote. "In the excitement we scarcely thought about the people living in this giant city—people just like us and of our blood," one wrote. "It was war, pitiless war, demanding our utmost strength." The first Gotha raid on London had lasted an hour and a half during which four tons of bombs had fallen, killing 162 civilians and injuring more than 400. Returning to their airfields in Belgium, the airmen "sated our hunger, not forgetting to quench our thirst with a bottle of wine, as we discussed our unique experiences on this first London flight" and celebrated "a great success."

Public reaction to the raid and in particular the "murders of the innocents" was immediate and bitter. Again people with German-sounding names were attacked and their houses and businesses looted. Member of Parliament William Joynson-Hicks once more demanded immediate reprisals, suggesting that for every raid on London British bombers should "blot out" a German town. The *Daily Mail* produced a "Reprisal Map" identifying suitable targets. Lord Derby, who had replaced Lord Kitchener as minister for war after the latter had drowned in 1916 on a mission to Russia when HMS *Hampshire* struck a free-floating German mine, argued that "it would be better to be defeated, retaining honour, chivalry and humanity, rather than obtain a victory by methods which have brought upon Germany universal execration." His views found little support among a public incensed by the "Hun baby-killers."

Prime Minister Lloyd George favored a reprisal attack on Mannheim where chemical factories using Fritz Haber's process were producing large amounts of nitrates as well as poison gases under his direction. However Sir Douglas Haig and others opposed retaliatory bombing because it would divert planes from the western front, and Britain had few long-range bombers. The authorities eventually agreed to relocate one fighter squadron temporarily to England to strengthen London's defenses, to launch more bombing raids on the Gothas' airfields, and to increase the size of the Royal Flying Corps.

In Germany, when the news of the attack on "fortress London" broke, the reaction was jubilant. One paper compared the commander of the England Squadron, Ernst Brandenburg, to Hannibal while the *Berliner Morgenpost* assured its readers that "the English government is seriously considering moving the seat of government from London." Brandenburg was awarded Germany's highest military honor, Pour le Mérite, also presented that summer to Walther Schwieger, former commander of the *U-20*, for his achievement in sinking 190,000 tons of Allied shipping including the *Lusitania*. Schwieger was killed two months later when his new U-boat, *U-88*, was lost at sea probably after hitting a British mine.[*]

THE GOTHA RAIDS on London continued throughout 1917, unnerving many of its inhabitants. The War Cabinet devised a five-minute warning system using sirens but until it was in place citizens relied on policemen on foot or on bicycles wearing placards on which was written in large red letters POLICE NOTICE—TAKE COVER. After the Upper North Street School tragedy, even a rumor of a raid was enough to send parents rushing to schools to retrieve their children. During attacks, people crammed into underground [subway] stations and cellars of public buildings or tried to protect themselves in their own homes. A Londoner described how his family took refuge in their dining room where his brother "had made a little dug out of his own" between a sofa and an armchair where he was "snugly ensconced with our pet hedgehog . . . The rest of us huddled underneath the big dining room table, which was padded round with mattresses and

---

[*] *U-20* had run aground off Denmark in November 1916. Some parts of it including its conning tower are preserved in a museum in Jutland.

had on top . . . some baths of water. The idea was that any bomb which hit the house would fall clean through the roof and top storey into the baths of water and so be put out!"

Londoners were shortly to face a new and even larger German bomber. At the start of the war Count von Zeppelin, aware of the limitations of his airships, had advocated the development of *Riesenflugzeugen*—"Giant" planes. The first of these gray-and-black-painted biplanes, constructed of wood, aluminum, and steel, were ready by the late summer of 1916. Its 138-foot wingspan was nearly double the Gotha's and only three feet shorter than that of the American B-29 Superfortresses that in 1945 dropped the atomic bombs on Hiroshima and Nagasaki. The new planes were fitted with up to six engines producing over one thousand horsepower and were the first planes equipped with a supercharger—an air compressor designed to increase oxygen flow to the engine and thus power—giving them the ability to reach nineteen thousand feet. They cost over half a million marks each and only eighteen were ever built, but they could carry nearly two tons of bombs.

The plan was that Giants and Gothas should conduct joint raids. At present, however, there were not enough planes. The first Giants had been deployed to the eastern front to back up the German forces' successful attempts to take advantage of the weakness of Kerensky's Russian government and of its armies. What's more, a shortage of raw materials like copper and rubber caused by the British blockade hampered production so that not until July 1917 did the England Squadron acquire even one. While the squadron waited for Giants and also for improved Gothas, the existing Gothas were painted gray and black and sent over London on night raids when the risk of being shot down was less but so was the chance of precision bombing. Just as Londoners had learned to fear zeppelin attacks on dark nights, so they grew to fear what moonlight—"aider and abettor" of the "more deadly aeroplane" according to a *Times* journalist—would bring.

The first Gotha night raid on September 4, 1917, killed nineteen and began a terror campaign that Londoners would call "the Blitz of the Harvest Moon." In six raids over eight days, Gothas dropped eleven thousand pounds of explosive and incendiary bombs, killing sixty-nine people and maiming hundreds more. The raids caused such panic that people were crushed to death in stampedes into the cellars of public buildings and underground stations. A Londoner thought it "pitiful to see the people trying to get into the already crowded station. There were brave mothers with their little children clinging to their skirts; sometimes a kiddy would be seen carrying a bird in a cage." Inside the stations, with no sanitation the stink of urine and feces was so strong that people fainted. Soldiers home on leave thought the conditions worse than the trenches. At night more than a million citizens routinely left their homes to find somewhere safer to sleep, even if it was only beneath railway arches or out in the open. A survey of the Woolwich arsenal in September 1917 showed only a third of the night shift turned up for work for fear of the bombs. Meanwhile rumors spread that the German forces were using poison gas in their bombs—even dropping poisoned sweets on the city. Rioting broke out and a British pilot believed the raids were coming close to "cracking the morale of London. The 'stop the war' cry was heard . . . frequently."

On December 6, 1917, in the thin light of a new moon, Giants first attacked London when two accompanied Gothas on a raid. Between them the planes dropped nearly four hundred incendiaries—the largest number in any raid so far—causing several serious fires and killing eight people. Twelve days later fifteen Gothas and a Giant tried again, bombing London while the House of Commons was in session and causing the greatest property damage so far. The House of Commons suspended its sitting though some MPs objected. A *Times* journalist heard one complain that they "had been put into the humiliating position of having to desert their posts of duty and retire in the face of the enemy to the cellars. In other countries, he said, "men are shot for leaving their posts." Once again, the bombers raised no firestorms in the city while for the first time a British fighter pilot—Captain Gilbert Murlis-Green, flying another new model of fighter, a Sopwith Camel—shot down a Gotha.

A further raid by Giants on London on January 29, 1918, again brought terror. One plane dropped a 660-pound bomb on the Odhams Press building near the famous fruit and vegetable garden at Covent Garden killing thirty-eight and wounding one hundred. A Mrs. McCluskey sheltering in the basement recalled "a flash, followed by an explosion . . . The force . . . blew my baby out of my arms and it was never found again. I had all the fingers blown off one hand, a leg taken off . . . and my body burnt all over. I am just a piece of the woman I was before the air raids came."

However, analyzing the results of the recent raids, the German authorities realized that many of the incendiary bombs had not detonated. Even when they had, they had failed to cause the desired massive fires. The development of more effective incendiaries accordingly became the priority and for the moment German bombers dropped only conventional bombs, though with sometimes devastating results. In mid-February 1918, a Giant released a twenty-two-hundred-pound high-explosive bomb on the Royal Hospital in Chelsea while five smaller bombs hit the Midland Grand Hotel by Saint Pancras Station. An eight-year-old girl who had taken refuge with her brother nearby recalled "a sound that, even now, in my memory, turns me sick. It was a whizzing, cutting sound, almost as if a huge knife was being sent through the air. A woman screamed, 'My God! They've got us!' There was a terrified rush to the doors . . . I struggled to get away, to run anywhere. The air was full of screams and children crying."

The Giants returned to London on March 7. Later that month the German high command diverted all the Giants and Gothas to support a planned new offensive on the western front. However, thirty-eight Gothas and three Giants again took off for London on the evening of May 19 and half of them reached the city. During the raid they dropped twenty-two thousand pounds of bombs—not all on the capital itself—killing forty-nine and injuring a further 177. Believing this was the start of a fresh series of raids, Londoners braced themselves for further attacks. However, the German bombers were again diverted to the western front. A new series of raids scheduled for July was called off at the last moment.

The reason was that German engineers and chemists were close to perfecting a new type of firebomb—the Elektron bomb—and the high command did not wish to risk its planes until sufficient quantities of the new weapon were ready. The bomb was named for its cylindrical casing of a substance called Elektron, consisting chiefly of magnesium and aluminum. This casing was as light and as flammable as the bomb's magnesium powder core. The intention was to drop the new bombs in their thousands to ignite on contact and burn at temperatures of up to 3,000 degrees

Celsius. The German command planned to use them in a continuous series of fire raids on London in September 1918 that would finally see the Feuerplan achieved. However, Ludendorff called off the raids at the last moment because, with the Allies advancing, he believed they were unlikely to make the enemy "more disposed to sue for peace." Thus, after May 19, London was not bombed again.

Between them Gothas and Giants had targeted the capital eighteen times. Their raids on Britain had killed more than eight hundred and injured nearly two thousand, bringing total civilian casualties inflicted by German aerial bombing of the British mainland in the First World War to some fourteen hundred dead and thirty-four hundred injured.

As EARLY AS January 1915, Winston Churchill while First Lord of the Admiralty had sanctioned the development of a British bomber aircraft by the Handley Page company. Progress had been extremely slow. The Admiralty superintendent of aircraft construction rejected the first design as inadequate, saying "What I want is a bloody paralyser not a toy." However, by the end of 1917 the British had forty Handley Page bombers. They could each carry a ton of bombs but were slow and vulnerable to attack. Nevertheless, on December 12, 1917, ten Royal Flying Corps bombers finally raided Mannheim's chemical works—the kaiser had left the city just half an hour earlier aboard his imperial train.

Thereafter, the British bombers would sporadically raid Germany. Targets were formally strategic ones, such as munitions manufacturing facilities, or communications, such as railways, although raids were also designed to damage enemy morale. A British intelligence report noted with approval "the panic created at Cologne" on one occasion. In fact, the effects of the raids were negligible. In May 1918, a British official wrote to one of his fellows that bombing had two possible purposes, "(a) a serious attempt to end the war, (b) merely to keep our own unenlightened populace quiet [by fulfilling the demand for reprisals against Germany]." He clearly considered that because of the limited effect the latter was intended.

Nevertheless, senior figures hankered to damage German morale. Lord Weir, secretary of state for air, on September 10, 1918, wrote to the chief of the Air Staff, "I would very much like it if you could start up a really big fire in one of the German towns. If I were you, I would not be too exacting as regards accuracy in bombing railway stations in the middle of towns. The German is susceptible to bloodiness and I would not mind a few accidents due to inaccuracy." He never got his wish of a major impact on morale.

IN SAINT PETERSBURG in November 1917, the Bolsheviks under Vladimir Lenin had seized power from Alexander Kerensky's provisional government and immediately asked Germany for an armistice. The peace treaty signed at Brest Litovsk in March 1918 formally removed Russia from the war and cost it a million square miles of territory including Poland and the Baltic states, ceded to its enemies. The area lost was three times the size of Germany and contained a quarter of Russia's population and industrial resources. In December 1917, battered into submission and having lost nearly all of its territory, just over a year after entering the war, Rumania too asked for an armistice. The removal of both Russia and Rumania, the Italian defeat at Caporetto, and the consequent reduction of pressure on Germany's enfeebled ally Austro-Hungary, allowed Germany to move forty-four divisions from the eastern to the western front between November 1917 and March 1918. These reinforcements permitted Ludendorff to launch a major offensive on the western front before, as he put it, "the Americans can throw strong forces into the scales." The first American troops had paraded in Paris on July 4, American Independence Day, 1917, and their numbers had been building since, with some quarter of a million in theater by March 1918. However, many were still training and equipping.

In their massive assault launched in late March, using up to six thousand artillery pieces, the German armies exploited their continuing monopoly of mustard gas, interspersing shells containing the substance with those filled with phosgene or chlorine and sometimes tear gas, the latter designed to penetrate the respirators of Allied troops and cause them to tear them off, exposing themselves to the other gases. The French forces only received supplies of mustard gas in June 1918, the British in September, and the U.S. troops a little later to supplement the phosgene and chlorine gases with which they were already equipped.

The German offensive, which was supported by Gotha and Giant bombers diverted from the Feuerplan against London, had considerable success, pushing the Allies back. German officer Rudolf Binding rejoiced to be in the British rear areas with their plentiful food supplies which he called "a land flowing with milk and honey" compared to the blockade-reduced rations of the German troops. The scale of the continuing German successes caused British commander in chief Douglas Haig to issue a famous order of the day: "There must be no retirement. With our backs to the wall and believing in the justice of our cause each one must fight on to the end." The Allies slowed and eventually stopped the German advance after being pushed back fifty miles in some places. Among the many dogged actions fought by Allied troops was a famous one by U.S. marines at Belleau Wood on June 4.

Despite the stalling of their advance in the west, by mid-July, the German forces controlled more land in both the east and the west than ever before, and with their Austro-Hungarian allies were again attacking on the Italian front. However, even if the kaiser was looking forward with renewed enthusiasm to when a British mission came to sue for peace and he could make it "kneel before the German imperial standard for this [would be] a victory of monarchy over democracy," this was, as many in the German high command were beginning to realize, a high watermark. Their offensive had cost the German armies eight hundred thousand men, many of them their best troops, with little prospect of significant reinforcements, whereas on the Allied side there were now over one million U.S. troops in France. The front line that the reduced number of German soldiers had to defend had extended in length by over seventy-five miles.

On July 18, the French armies drove the German troops back from the Marne River and Paris as they had in the first battles in 1914. On August 8 the British armies attacked at Amiens, smashing eight miles through the German lines and in doing so exploiting their superiority in tanks, deploying more than 450, and in the air where some nineteen hundred planes were used mainly for artillery spotting. Ludendorff called it "the black day of the German army" when it lost twenty-seven thousand

men. Worryingly for their commanders twelve thousand of them had surrendered. Ludendorff wrote, "Whole bodies . . . surrendered to single
troopers or isolated squadrons. Retiring troops, meeting a fresh division
going bravely into action, shouted out things like 'blackleg' and 'you're
prolonging the war.' The officers . . . lost their influence and allowed themselves to be swept along with the rest."

Many further Allied attacks followed and, with the help of American
divisions arriving in ever increasing numbers, succeeded in pushing the
German armies back toward Germany's original frontiers. A German soldier wrote of their retreat, "Their aeroplanes were flying very low and
seeing everything that we were doing and bombing us . . . We moved to a
new line far further back . . . Our losses were enormous and the gas attacks
fearsome. The gas stuck into the high grass so that even our horses had gas
masks. We realised it was the beginning of the end."

On September 12, the U.S. First Army under General Pershing's personal command undertook the first all-American offensive, taking fifteen
thousand prisoners and 460 guns at a cost of seven thousand casualties in
an action east of Verdun. Six days later, a British and Australian offensive
pushed German troops even further back. On September 29, Ludendorff
told his superiors that Germany must seek an immediate armistice. On that
same day Germany's ally Bulgaria actually signed one.

The German authorities realized that some appearance of democracy
might lessen Allied hostility to "militaristic," "autocratic" Germany in armistice negotiations. Prince Max of Baden, a liberal, was appointed chancellor
and the most "respectable" of the dreaded socialists—the Social
Democrats—were invited to join the government. On October 4, Prince
Max tentatively approached President Wilson about possible terms for an
armistice, choosing him as likely to be the most sympathetic of the Allies.
Wilson initially replied encouragingly and without consulting the other
Allied leaders. However, his attitude changed when a week or so later a
German submarine sank the *Leinster*, a passenger ferry en route between
Ireland and England. Four hundred and fifty lives were lost, several of
them American. This was the very sort of "barbaric" action that had brought
the United States into the war, and Wilson toughened his stance. Germany
must cease submarine warfare at once and produce convincing evidence

of its democratization. In any case, armistice—as distinct from peace terms—was a matter for military commanders.

All the time the Allied troops were advancing toward Germany. On October 17 the British took Lille. A week later, an Allied offensive in Italy threw the Austro-Hungarian army back in confusion. On October 30 Turkey signed an armistice. So too did the Austro-Hungarians on November 3 . Emperor Karl abdicated and several of the empire's component nations such as Hungary and Czechoslovakia proclaimed their independence. On November 3 too, the German navy mutinied at Kiel and socialist revolutionaries appeared on the streets of several German cities. On November 8, a Germany delegation met an Allied one to request an armistice. The next day, the kaiser went into exile at Amerongen in Holland where his first request was for "a cup of hot, good, real, English tea." He formally abdicated at the end of November. Nevertheless, when at eleven A.M. on November 11, the 1,586th day of the war, Germany signed an armistice, its armies still stood on foreign soil.

Among those who had survived was twenty-nine-year-old corporal Adolf Hitler, recently awarded the Iron Cross for gallantry on the recommendation of the Jewish adjutant of his Bavarian regiment. On October 12 during one of the final Allied pushes, he had been temporarily blinded by the contents of a British mustard gas shell near the village of Wervik in the Ypres Salient. On the day of the armistice, having been evacuated by hospital train he was recovering in a German military hospital in Pomerania. That same day a British sergeant major, Richard Tobin, who had fought through since 1914 wrote, "The armistice came, the day we had dreamed of. The guns stopped, the fighting stopped. Four years of noise and bangs ended in silence. The killings had stopped. We were stunned . . . I should have been happy. I was sad. I thought of the slaughter, the hardships, the waste and the friends I had lost."

CHAPTER TWENTY-TWO

"Weapons of Mass Destruction"

IN THE FIRST years of the conflict, Britain in particular had made many pronouncements about, and promises of, war crimes trials in response to German actions such as the razing of Louvain, the unrestricted U-boat campaign, the bombing of London, and the executions of Edith Cavell and merchant captain Charles Fryatt. These had, however, been headline-grabbing statements designed to secure a propaganda advantage with neutrals such as the United States and to bolster morale at home. The authorities had given little thought as to how, where, and under what legal framework any such trials would be carried out. Since no international arrangements had been agreed or even discussed at the Hague conferences to judge impartially cases brought against either side in a conflict for infringements of the laws of war, any trials were bound to be "victor's justice." Even so, no lawyers had been put to work drafting detailed legal mechanisms, no consultations carried out among the Allies on the processes involved.

In the late summer and early autumn of 1918, with the realization victory was close, Allied talk of the trial of German leaders for war crimes resumed with added impetus, having subsided during the difficult times in 1917 and early 1918 when all thoughts had been concentrated on how to win the war. Now public pressure in the Allied nations mounted for trials, and lists of suitable candidates were drawn up. They included Haber for the use of poison gas, von Tirpitz for the unrestricted submarine warfare campaign, and above all the kaiser for "having provoked or brought about an aggressive and unjust war."

Such talk of war crimes trials clearly reached and unsettled the

German imperial court. At the end of August 1918, the kaiser inquired of Admiral von Müller, the head of his naval cabinet, whether his [the kaiser's] February 1915 unrestricted submarine warfare orders had permitted the sinking of the *Lusitania* without warning. Von Muller was in turn told by his advisers that they had. However, he persisted on the kaiser's behalf, writing "His Majesty still expresses his doubts whether the wording of the orders of February 4 1915, legally allowed the *unwarned* [*sic*] sinking of the *Lusitania*" but to no avail. The kaiser seems to have been trying to shift the blame for the sinking on to the now dead Walther Schwieger for exceeding his instructions.

The kaiser's anxiety about war crimes at this time may also have led to the destruction of some of the documents one would have expected to find about the authorization of gas warfare. While this cannot be proved, what is undoubtedly true is that on some occasion, quite probably around this time, the surviving copy of Walther Schwieger's *U-20* war diary for the cruise on which the *Lusitania* was sunk was crudely doctored. Some of the alterations were designed to show that Schwieger had not known which ship he was attacking until he had seen the *Lusitania*'s name on her bow as she sank. These amendments undermined the German authorities' long-argued contention that the *Lusitania* was legitimately sunk as an armed ammunition and troop-carrying vessel. If Schwieger had not known which ship he was attacking, he could not have known her armament, cargo, or passenger list, thereby invalidating any justification for the torpedoing based on them. The tampering also introduced other inaccuracies, together with spurious and discursive comments intended to put the sinking in the best light possible from the German perspective.*

Just after the war ended, in December 1918, in the British general election won by the sitting prime minister, Lloyd George (who had taken over from Herbert Asquith in December 1916), one of the most popular slogans was "Hang the Kaiser." King George V regarded with equanimity the trial of his cousin: "I look upon him as the greatest criminal known for having plunged the world into this ghastly war . . . with all its misery."

---

* A fuller discussion of the evidence that the diary was doctored and of the nature of the doctoring is included in the appendix "The *Lusitania* Controversies."

Participants in the Paris Peace Conference in early 1919 hotly debated the issue of war crimes. The United States was averse to any mechanisms that might set a precedent for infringements of national sovereignty in such matters by the creation of international bodies before which Americans might be compelled to appear as a result of future conflicts. Additionally, as a historian, President Wilson worried about making a martyr of the kaiser: "Charles I [of England and Scotland] was a contemptible character and the greatest liar in history [but] he was celebrated by poetry and transformed into a martyr by his execution." France, although in favor of war crimes trials, saw them as a side issue, its greatest concerns being to retrieve its lost territories of Alsace and Lorraine and so to weaken Germany as to prevent any future aggression on its part for generations. None of the three powers wished to set precedents that might limit their troops' freedom of action in future wars.

Nevertheless, when the peace treaty with Germany was signed on June 28, 1919, it provided for suspected war criminals to be tried by military courts and for the kaiser to be brought before a tribunal of Allied judges if the Dutch permitted him to be extradited from his place of exile at Amerongen. Even at the time of the treaty's signature the Allies knew the latter would be unlikely. Subsequently with Germany increasingly stricken by social unrest—partly caused by the blockade that had been maintained in force albeit with growing slackness until the signature of the treaty to prevent any German renunciation of the armistice—the Allies began to fear that if the envisaged trials of the over one thousand alleged war criminals went ahead they might lead to further violence and thereafter to a full-scale revolution and the triumph of the Bolshevism they both feared and detested. This concern, combined with confirmation of the Dutch refusal to hand over the kaiser, whose trial would have caused the greatest upset of all, led the Allies eventually to settle for the German Supreme Court at Leipzig trying a small number of individuals, mostly for the severe ill-treatment of prisoners of war. In those cases—by no means all—when the Leipzig court convicted the defendants, the sentences were light. Although this outraged Allied public opinion, Allied governments were too preoccupied with other issues, either internal or external, to take further action.

One case, however, formed some precedent for future war crimes trials. Two U-boat officers were found guilty by the Leipzig court—even if they were given sentences of only four years and escaped after a few weeks, quite possibly with the connivance of the authorities, and were never recaptured—of murdering survivors from a British hospital ship, the *Llandovery Castle*. Their U-boat had sunk the vessel in June 1918 without warning and the submariners had killed some of those who had managed to get into the lifeboats. In total 283 out of the 303 people aboard died. The Leipzig judgment stated that the U-boatmen should not have followed the orders of their commander to kill the survivors which they knew to be illegal. Most important, it specified that international law in such matters overrode national law: "The firing on the boats was an offence against the Law of Nations. In war . . . at sea the killing of shipwrecked people, who have taken refuge in lifeboats, is forbidden. The killing of enemies in war is in accordance with the will of the state that makes war . . . only in so far as such killing is in accordance with the conditions and limitations imposed by the Law of Nations."

The Allies did not sign a formal peace treaty with Turkey until August 1920 at Sevres in France. It was neither ratified nor implemented because of revolution in Turkey and conflict between Greeks and Turks. The possibility of war crimes trials, both for the Turkish ill-treatment of Allied prisoners of war and the massacres of Armenians, which had at one time seemed highly likely, lapsed.*

Hitler would later ask, "Who remembers the Armenians today?" Coroner John Horgan, who had presided over the first *Lusitania* inquest at Kinsale, wrote after the Second World War about the failure to punish the crime of the *Lusitania* sinking: "Modern history might have taken a far different course had not legal scruples and political pusillanimity eventually combined to prevent the appropriate punishment being put into effect." Some historians and lawyers would later argue that the failure to prosecute German and Turkish First World War crimes and thus to establish both the nature of their crimes and their guilt for them were factors in future

---

* Even though the United States had never declared war on Turkey, a proposal favored at one stage by some delegates was a U.S. mandate over Armenia.

conflicts. It allowed Hitler and other German nationalist leaders to deny any "war guilt" for the First World War and proclaim that the army had been "stabbed in the back" by social revolutionaries at home while still fighting proudly on foreign soil; and to believe genocide would go unpunished as had the Armenian massacres. The victims of their crimes would simply disappear nameless and unavenged into "*Nacht und Nebel*" (Night and Fog), as Hitler would put it.*

An International Criminal Court was eventually established in 2002, with its base at The Hague, to try war crimes. However, several major nations are not party to the treaty founding the court, which therefore, has no jurisdiction over them or their citizens. The United States is among them, maintaining the view expressed by President Wilson at Versailles that the court would infringe U.S. sovereignty. Other states which are not a party to the treaty or have not ratified it include China, Israel, India, and Russia.

ALTHOUGH INTERNATIONAL LAW emerged from the First World War battered, bruised, and in some cases disregarded and broken, in its aftermath governments recognized international agreements as still their only hope to regulate warfare. Therefore, in the sidelines of the peace conferences, and subsequently in greater earnest, governments once more met to negotiate conventions designed to limit what weapons should be used in future conflicts and against whom, even if they could agree no mandatory mechanism for enforcement.

Poison gas was a particular concern. Although it had not proved the decisive war-winning weapon as Haber among others had hoped, by the end of the war it had become a prominent component of the arsenals of all the belligerents. Some 124,000 tons of poison gas had been used, half of it by Germany. At one time or another in the conflict sixty-three different kinds of poison gas had been deployed albeit not all successfully. By November 1918, the United States, for example, was working on sixty-five

---

* Under the "Nacht und Nebel" directive—issued by Hitler in December 1941 and deriving its name from a spell in Wagner's *Rheingold*—anti-Nazi activists and resistance fighters were to vanish without a trace. At the Nuremberg war crimes trials, disappearances under the "Nacht und Nebel" program were classed as war crimes.

gas projects including one gas that would leave soil barren for seven years and a few drops of which would cause a tree "to wither in an hour." Fort Edgewood Arsenal, Maryland—the center of the U.S. effort that employed forty-eight thousand people in total—had been completed in less than a year after construction began in November 1917, had cost around forty million dollars, had 218 manufacturing facilities, twenty-eight miles of railway, fifteen miles of road, and was capable of producing two hundred thousand chemical bombs and shells per day. Gas was a government scientific project unrivaled in size or cost until the Manhattan A-bomb project a quarter of a century later. The British in 1916 had established their own chemical research laboratories on three thousand acres at Porton Down.

Estimating the number of casualties caused by gas in the First World War is a difficult and imprecise art for various reasons. Many bodies were never recovered. Post mortems were infrequent and there were often several contributory causes of death. Statistics were even harder to acquire on the eastern front than in the west. Available figures suggest that perhaps 1.3 million men were wounded by gas and that gas caused perhaps 1 percent to 4 percent of the nine to ten million deaths in the war. Fatal British and British Empire gas casualties may have been less than twenty thousand, some 80 percent of which were due to mustard gas during the last seventeen months of the war.

Statistics, however, understate the actual impact of gas warfare, as American general Amos Fries described, in debilitating troops as well as in psychologically damaging them. The latter was a key aim of Haber's original proposal and one he believed had been achieved; he wrote, after the war, that gas's "psychological effect on humans and the sensations they create vary a thousand-fold. Every change of sensation in the nose and mouth disturbs the mind, making it imagine an unknown effect and saps the soldier's moral resistance." The psychological revulsion felt at the use of gas was compounded in the public mind because, just as would be the case with nuclear radiation, victims might not even know they were afflicted, since some gases were relatively odorless, and might not feel unwell for some time before suffering effects like lung disease, which persisted and worsened over the rest of their often shortened lives.

Another historian has produced calculations on the British army which show the effectiveness of gas units in terms of casualties inflicted compared to those received:

- British infantry suffered one casualty (wounded or dead) for every 0.5 it caused;
- British artillery suffered one casualty (wounded or dead) for every 10 it caused;
- The British Special Gas Brigade suffered one casualty (wounded or dead) for every 40 it caused.

In 1925 at Geneva, an intergovernmental conference agreed to a protocol banning both chemical and bacteriological weapons including all poisonous gases. The protocol, however, required ratification by national governments. Most states including Britain, France, Italy, Germany, and the USSR ratified but usually only after adding a rider that if another nation used such weapons they would be free to respond in kind. None saw the treaty as prohibiting them from research or from building up substantial stocks of gas to be used if attacked. The potential effect of biological weapons had been shown by the Spanish influenza pandemic raging at the end of the First World War which killed up to thirty million people worldwide. At the time of the armistice the flu was killing seven thousand people a week in Britain. Among those who died was William Leefe Robinson who had shot down the German airship over Cuffley. Half a million Americans died, a greater number than killed in battle in both world wars, the Korean War, Vietnam, and subsequent conflicts up till now put together.

The U.S. Senate had previously failed to ratify the treaty establishing the League of Nations—the body Woodrow Wilson, Sir Edward Grey, and Colonel House had championed to ensure peace after the war. When the Geneva protocol on chemical and biological weapons was put to the isolationist Senate there were again many objections, including that gas was more "humane" than "the old horrors of battle." To avoid the humiliation of another rejection, the State Department withdrew the ratification proposal. Not until 1970 was it submitted again to the Senate and not until 1975 did the United States formally ratify the protocol. Japan followed the U.S. example and also did not ratify it until after the Second World War.

The bombing of civilian targets remained outlawed, although at the end of the First World War British officials had opposed the trial as war criminals of German pilots who had bombed civilian areas, since "to do so would be placing a noose around the necks of our airmen in future wars." Indeed, in 1919 the British bombed Kabul, and the emir of Afghanistan complained, "It is a matter for great regret that the throwing of bombs by Zeppelins on London was denounced as a most savage act, and the bombardment of places of worship . . . was considered a most abominable operation while now we see with our own eyes that such operations are a habit which is prevalent among civilised people of the West."

Also at around this time, British planes bombed hill villages in Kurdish and other areas of Iraq to put down a rebellion against King Faisal, the Arab ruler the British government had installed at the end of the war. There is some evidence that bombs containing gas may have been used. Churchill, then secretary of state for war, had written at the time, "I do not understand this squeamishness about the use of gas. I am strongly in favour of using poison gas against uncivilised tribes." A few years later both Spanish and French forces used gas to subdue rebellions in their Moroccan colonies.

Enemy submarines had sunk some thirteen million tons of Allied and neutral shipping in the First World War and in its immediate aftermath the inhumanity of U-boat torpedoing of merchant shipping without warning was so vivid from the *Lusitania* sinking and elsewhere that the Washington Disarmament Conference of 1921–22 attempted to ban the use of the submarine completely. The French government, who saw the submarine as a cheap way of retaining naval power, objected and the proposal was dropped. However, the conference reconfirmed the validity of the old Cruiser Rules requiring stop and search of merchant shipping and prohibiting unrestricted submarine warfare. These rules were reaffirmed by subsequent conferences in 1930, 1935, and 1936. Adherents included Britain, the United States, France, and Germany—the latter in 1936.

THUS TO ALL intents and purposes the legal position on submarines, poison gas, and bombing remained the same as it had before the First World War. However, the 1930s saw the strength of these prohibitions challenged. In 1936, the Italians used mustard gas, sprayed from aircraft or dropped in bomb form, in their conquest of Abyssinia. Emperor Haile Selassie told the League of Nations, "Special sprayers were installed on board Italian aircraft so they could vaporise over vast areas of territory a fine, death-dealing rain. Groups of nine, fifteen or eighteen aircraft followed one another so that the fog ensuing from them formed a continuous sheet . . . Soldiers, women, children, cattle, rivers and lakes were drenched continually . . . These fearful tactics succeeded. The deadly rain that fell made all of whom it touched fly shrieking with pain. In tens of thousands the victims of Italian mustard gas fell." In that same year, 1936, Japan used gas in its invasion of China as well as the bombing of civilian targets and continued to do so in that country until Japan's 1945 surrender.

Worried that Germany, like Italy, might use gas in any future conflict despite having ratified the Geneva protocol, Britain and France began to build up their own stocks of gas to retaliate if required. They also began to consider countermeasures. By 1938 the British authorities had issued thirty million gas masks to the public including cot respirators for babies. Their greatest fear was that gas would be released by attacking bombers. The supremacy and destructive power of the bomber had again been shown a year earlier in April 1937 when German and Italian planes, flying on behalf of Franco's nationalists in the Spanish civil war, had destroyed the Basque city of Guernica in three hours during its weekly market, killing more than sixteen hundred people. The attack on Guernica led the British archbishop of Canterbury to coin the phrase "weapons of mass destruction" to describe their bombs.

The memory of the First World War German blitz on London and the panic caused, combined with the speed of aircraft development in the 1920s, led to a belief that bombers would always be able to penetrate defenses to devastating effect. British prime minister Stanley Baldwin gave expression to this view in 1932, writing, "The man in the street [must] realise there is no power on earth that can protect him from bombing, whatever people may tell him. The bomber will always get through."

Such was the fear of the effects of mass bombing and gas bombing in particular that when the Second World War broke out in September 1939, in Britain everyone was ordered to carry their gas mask with them at all times and children were evacuated from London away from any new blitz. A British government document estimated that in the first three weeks of a German bombing offensive on London a quarter of a million of the city's inhabitants would die, three to four million would flee to the countryside, and one million would become psychiatric cases while 50 percent of the city would be destroyed. Among other preparations the British Ministry of Health issued one million additional blank death certificates to local authorities.

Bombing—whether purportedly restricted to military targets or extended to civilian areas—was indeed used extensively by both sides in the Second World War. London suffered another blitz and later both Britain and the United States used mass area bombing to destroy Hamburg, Dresden, and Tokyo, combining conventional explosives and incendiaries to generate firestorms of the type first planned by German commanders for London in the First World War.[*]

The Allied commanders justified such bombing by the exculpation—used by Haber of gas—that it was no worse than other methods of warfare and that it would shorten the war and save many Allied lives. Air Chief Marshal Arthur Harris, the head of Britain's bomber force, wrote that "bombing proved a comparatively humane method. For one thing it saved the flower of the youth of this country and of our allies being mown down by the military in the field, as it was in Flanders in the war of 1914–18."

When the Second World War turned into a "physicists' war" (the First World War having been known as a "chemists' war"), nuclear bombs destroyed Hiroshima and Nagasaki. A prime justification by commanders of the A-bombings was again the saving of a quarter of a million Allied lives likely to have been lost in an invasion of the Japanese mainland. The U.S. targeting committee, however, also agreed "that psychological factors in the target's selection were of great importance. Two aspects of this are, (1) obtaining the greatest psychological effect against Japan and (2) making the initial use sufficiently spectacular for the importance of the weapon to

---

[*] The incendiaries used in these attacks were similar to the Elektron firebomb developed by German scientists at the end of the First World War.

be internationally recognised when publicity on it is released." Potential as well as actual enemies, including the USSR, were put on notice as to the new weapon's potency.

Bombing continued to be a part of all conflicts after the Second World War. Authorities claim with lesser and greater degrees of justification to be avoiding civilian targets, something which became easier with the development of more sophisticated guidance systems. Nevertheless, errors continue to be made and collateral damage accepted as an inevitable consequence of the preference, perhaps particularly prevalent among Western governments, to deploy air power rather than expose their own ground troops to greater hazards.

ON THE OPENING day of the Second World War for Britain, September 3, 1939, Winston Churchill, returned from the wilderness, was once again appointed First Lord of the British Admiralty. On that same day and in direct contravention of the 1936 treaty, a German submarine north of Ireland sank without warning the British liner *Athenia* with some fourteen hundred people aboard. Over one hundred were killed including twenty-eight citizens of the neutral United States. Hitler's propaganda minister Joseph Goebbels at once accused Churchill of having had a bomb detonated on board by wireless signal because he wished to create a new *Lusitania* for his own political advantage.

Subsequently, both sides resorted to unrestricted submarine warfare. On the day of the bombing of Pearl Harbor, December 7, 1941, the commander in chief of the U.S. Asiatic fleet dispatched a message to his commanders in the Pacific: "EXECUTE AGAINST JAPAN UNRESTRICTED AIR AND SUBMARINE WARFARE." Before the convoy system was introduced, in April 1917 the British First Sea Lord Admiral Jellicoe told an American admiral that unless the rate at which German U-boats were destroying British shipping was reduced Germany would win the war. A quarter of a century later in the Battle of the Atlantic the German submarines were successful even against convoyed Allied merchant shipping, leading Churchill to comment after the war that the only thing that ever really frightened him was the U-boat peril. In 1942 the U-boats sank eight million tons of Allied shipping while Allied shipyards could only build seven million. It took improvements in underwater detection of submarines, increased air cover provided by longer range and carrier-based aircraft, as well as the availability of greater numbers of naval escort vessels to bring victory to the Allies over the German U-boats.

After the Second World War, submarines became an increasingly important part of the navies of all nations, being designed not only for attacks on enemy shipping but also for the launch of nuclear ballistic rockets. The only ship destroyed by a submarine torpedo in the last half century was the Argentine heavy cruiser *Belgrano*, sunk by the British nuclear-powered submarine HMS *Conqueror* without warning in the 1982 Falklands War. More than 250 of its crew died. As the *Belgrano* was a naval ship the British action was legitimate even under the disregarded but never repealed or replaced Cruiser Rules. Nevertheless, in Britain and elsewhere the severe loss of life promoted much debate about the morality of the torpedoing, particularly as some alleged that the *Belgrano* was heading away rather than toward the Falklands. The submarine's captain claimed— as had others before him—that in the context of the war the torpedoing had saved lives.

EXCEPT FOR THE use of poison gas by Japan in China, neither the Axis nor Allied powers used gas militarily in the Second World War. (One of the reasons for Japan using gas against the Chinese but not against the other Allies was that, in an echo about the debate about whether warfare could be conducted on a different basis with a "barbarian" nation than with a "civilised" one, the Japanese considered the Chinese an "inferior race." Such racism may also have influenced the Italian attacks in Abyssinia.)

Immediately after the end of the First World War, Fritz Haber had fled to Switzerland, at one point using a beard as a disguise because he feared arrest as a war criminal. However, he soon returned to Germany and to the Kaiser Wilhelm Institute for Physical Chemistry. There he assisted continuing research on the military use of gas, despite this being prohibited to Germany by the Versailles Treaty. The research was ostensibly aimed at pest control. In 1919 he learned that he had been awarded the

Nobel Prize for Chemistry for his work on the synthesis of ammonia. The Nobel Committee for Chemistry—citizens of neutral Sweden—considered Haber's achievement so significant that they did not allow his wartime work on poison gas to influence their decision. However, the award was widely condemned outside Germany. Theodore Richards, a Quaker who in 1914 had been the first American winner of the Nobel chemistry prize, turned down his invitation to the ceremony to avoid coming into contact with Haber.

The same year, 1919, Haber's institute developed a cyanide-based gas, Zyklon-A, actually for use in pest control. In 1924, others would modify it to produce Zyklon-B, thereafter used extensively against insects. Ultimately, however, it was the main gas used in the holocaust gas chambers. Haber himself throughout the 1920s continued to defend the use of gas in warfare while often suffering bouts of near nervous collapse as he had done earlier in his life—frequently feeling he was living "under a great boulder." A second marriage ended in divorce at the end of 1927 after ten years and two children. When Hitler came to power, as he was Jewish by birth, Haber was forced to leave Germany. He settled in Britain where the nuclear scientist Ernest Rutherford, a tireless worker for Jewish academic refugees, defended his right to asylum but refused to shake his hand because of his First World War work on gas. Haber died on a visit to Switzerland at the end of January 1934.

Some three years after his death another German scientist, Dr. Gerhard Schrader, again researching insecticides for I. G. Farben, discovered tabun, the first nerve gas. Further research led in 1938 to the discovery of the nerve gas sarin, more toxic and odorless. The German authorities quickly realized the military potential of both these gases and set up production facilities that came into operation in 1942 after many difficulties in construction and commissioning. Germany could have used tabun or sarin as well as the modified forms of mustard gas it had developed, weaponized, and stored in large quantities, against the Allies. For example, there was enough tabun available to kill the whole population of London, and the Luftwaffe had nearly half a million gas bombs of various types. Later in the war German engineers even produced warheads capable of carrying the gases on the V1 and V2 rockets launched against Britain in 1944 and

1945. Given that the V2, the world's first ballistic missile, even with only a conventional payload, unnerved Londoners at least as much as the Blitz, how much greater would the effect of nerve gas-carrying rockets have been?

The German army could have also used gas to deadly effect against the D-day landings in France. U.S. General Omar Bradley wrote, "When D-Day finally ended I was vastly relieved. For even a light sprinkling of persistent gas on Omaha Beach would have cost us our footing there."

Both Churchill and later Roosevelt publicly warned that if the Axis used gas so would the Allies and that they had the means to do so. Churchill had plans drawn up in 1940 for the possible use of poison gas as a last resort against any German invasion of Britain. Later in the war he shot off a memo to his advisers which came to nothing: "I want you to think very seriously over the question of using poison gas. I would not use it unless it could be shown that (a) it was life or death for us, or (b) it would shorten the war by a year. It is absurd to consider morality on the topic . . . In the last war the bombing of open cities was regarded as forbidden. Now everybody does it as a matter of course. It is simply a question of fashion changing as she does between long and short skirts for women."

President Roosevelt resisted popular U.S. calls for the use of gas against the Japanese, expressed in press headlines such as WE SHOULD GAS JAPAN, YOU CAN COOK 'EM BETTER WITH GAS, and SHOULD WE GAS THE JAPS? However, when plans were being made for the invasion of Japan after Truman had succeeded Roosevelt, the U.S. Army Chemical Warfare Service made detailed proposals for the use of gas in the invasion of the island of Kyushu, scheduled for November 1, 1945, and against Tokyo during the invasion of Honshu planned for a little later. Japan surrendered well before any such plans could have been put into effect, even if President Truman had authorized them which he had not.

That no side used gas in the Second World War is perhaps the first example of the effectiveness of mutual deterrence. The German authorities erroneously believed the Allies like themselves had nerve gases. Neither they nor the Allies saw the benefits of their first use of the weapon as outweighing not only the consequences of the inevitable retaliation but also the massive international condemnation.

Even though neither Germany nor Japan used gas against the British and Americans, that is not to say that the latter two countries did not suffer casualties due to poisonous gas in the Second World War. The Allies always wanted to have gas stocks close at hand to retaliate against any Axis use. In December 1943, the SS *John Harvey* lay in Bari harbor in Italy with a cargo of U.S. mustard gas aboard—part of a provision designed to ensure that the Allies could wage gas warfare for a month and a half if required in their Italian campaign. That evening in the space of twenty minutes, one hundred German bombers attacked the harbor. The *John Harvey* was hit and much of its cargo of mustard gas released. Nearly two thousand people, both military and civilian, died in the raid, many as a result of the gas. The Allied governments unsuccessfully tried to cover up that gas had been involved. By their refusal to acknowledge this fact, some casualties died needlessly through lack of proper medical treatment.

The 1925 Geneva protocol prohibiting the use of chemical and bacteriological weapons including poison gas remains in force. One hundred thirty-eight states have now adhered to it, the last being El Salvador in 2010. Nevertheless, poison gas has been used since the Second World War—in the Yemen civil war in the mid- to late 1960s and by Iraq in the Iran-Iraq War in the 1980s, when according to some sources 5 percent of Iranian casualties were due to Iraqi gas. In both cases mustard gas was one of the main gases used. The most infamous use of gas by Iraq was against its own Iraqi Kurdish civilians at Halabjah on March 16, 1988, when five thousand of the town's population of fifty thousand were killed. A British reporter wrote, "Like figures unearthed in Pompeii the victims . . . were killed so quickly that their corpses remained in suspended animation. There was a plump baby whose face froze in a scream stuck out from under the protective arm of a man feet away from the open door of a house that he never reached." Iraq undoubtedly possessed poison gas during the 1991 Gulf War but did not use it. The Allied commander in chief General Norman Schwarzkopf suggested the Iraqis feared retaliation with nuclear weapons. After the war Iraq agreed to give up its "weapons of mass destruction" and many were destroyed. However, Allied suspicion that Iraq retained some was the key stated justification for the 2003 invasion of Iraq. After this second Gulf War, the only WMDs discovered were some five hundred old mustard gas shells.

In 1994 terrorists first used poison gas when Aum Shinrikyo, a Japanese sect, released sarin gas in Matsumoto, killing eight and injuring two hundred. A year later they released the same gas in the Tokyo subway, killing twelve and injuring up to five thousand.

In 1997, the United States, Russia, the United Kingdom, and other countries brought into force a chemical weapons convention prohibiting research on and the use of such weapons and mandating the gradual destruction of existing stocks. By 2012 some 90 percent of the U.S. stockpile had been destroyed.

With the recent outbreak of civil war in Syria, reports that government troops were firing rockets filled with sarin nerve gas on civilian populations focused international attention on that country's large stocks of chemical weapons. A team of UN chemical inspectors found proof of one such attack having taken place in an agricultural area outside Damascus on August 21, 2013. The number of dead was put at some 630. Addressing the UN Security Council, UN secretary general Ban Ki-Moon called it a war crime and said that, according to the inspectors' report, this was the most significant confirmed use of chemical weapons since Saddam Hussein's deployment of them in Halabjah in 1988.

Under intense international pressure, the following month the Syrian government agreed to a deal brokered by Syria's ally Russia with the United States under which all of its estimated thirteen hundred tonnes of chemical weapons, which include mustard gas, would be removed and destroyed by June 30, 2014. The Organization for the Prohibition of Chemical Weapons (OPCW), headquartered in The Hague, would oversee the removal and destruction of the stockpile—mostly chemicals stored in liquid form. At the time of writing, this process seemed on the way to completion.

Chlorine, the first gas used as a military weapon at Ypres in April 1915, has many legitimate industrial uses and it was not included in the list of toxic agents declared and handed over by the Syrian government. Although its use as a weapon is of course banned, in August 2014, the United Nations reported allegations of the use of bombs containing chlorine gas by the Syrian government against civilians on eight occasions in April and May 2014. OPCW are investigating.

Although attention has focused on Syrian use of chemical weapons, bombing with explosives has caused the greatest number of civilian deaths in the conflict. Barrel bombs—oil barrels or metal cylinders filled with petrol, nails or shrapnel, and explosives—have been reported to have been frequently rolled out of helicopters on to undefended civilian areas.

LOOKING BACK OVER the century since those six weeks in spring and early summer 1915, the first use of poison gas, the sinking of the *Lusitania*, and the first aerial bombing of London remain resonant milestones in the development of warfare and of attempts to constrain it within a legal framework. In 1918 American philosopher John Dewey presciently commented, "The one phase of Prussianism which is likely permanently to remain is systematic utilisation of the scientific expert." In spring 1915, high science put itself unequivocally at the service of the military—a fact only underlined by the Manhattan atomic bomb project during the Second World War and the potential today for the use of biological and genetic weapons.

Each of the three new weapons of 1915 was designed to have a psychological effect beyond the actual damage created and thus to cause panic and a loss of morale among both troops or civilians. Each would know that death could come without warning, at any time, however far they were from the battlefield. The anxiety of waiting for the next attack, uncertain of where and when it might occur, and the scale of the precautions and constant vigilance required, such as the need to carry gas masks and the use of blackouts on a daily basis, have echoes in the present age of terrorism, with airport and public building scanners and so forth ever present reminders of an unseen threat.

Gas inspired (and retains), as the world's horror at its use in Syria shows, a particular revulsion—as nuclear and biological weapons have come to—as the first weapon not all of whose effects were immediately apparent. Victims could appear healthy only to succumb hours, months, and sometimes even years afterward.

Bombing and the submarine in particular introduced a disconnect between the perpetrator of an action and its victim. The zeppelin commander would never see the result of his bombing. This clinical or dehumanizing effect is now more extreme when a ballistic missile or pilotless drone is deployed. Similarly, these weapons marked a step change even over the machine gun and artillery in the small number of military personnel required to kill a large number of the enemy, civilians or otherwise. Simultaneously, they placed a heavier moral burden on the individual warrior while leaving society more vulnerable to an individual's actions. One man, Raimund Weisbach, pressed a torpedo firing button on the *U-20* and as a consequence 1,198 people on the *Lusitania* died while another *U-20* submariner, Charles Voegele, refused to be involved in the attack.

The three events of 1915 combine with those of later years to suggest that in the continuing absence of globally accepted, effective, impartial enforcement measures, well-intentioned international conventions regulating warfare only have full impact when either there is an element of mutual deterrence or if adversaries perceive they have less to gain in either military or political terms than to lose by international condemnation or retaliation. In each case in 1915, the German authorities believed they would secure greater advantage by flouting international law than respecting it. The British in particular, and perhaps a little hypocritically, gained more in propaganda terms, especially in wooing the United States, by retaining the moral high ground.

The exculpation that actions, however inhumane, can be justified on the grounds of shortening conflicts or saving one's own side's lives (always perceived as more valuable than those of the enemy) is older than a century but the nature of the new weapons introduced in 1915 gave it a considerable added potency requiring the strongest moral conscience to resist. Albert Einstein was pessimistic, later commenting, "It has become appallingly obvious that our technology has exceeded our humanity." We can only hope that he was wrong.

APPENDIX

The *Lusitania* Controversies

IN APRIL 1918, a New York judge, Julius Mayer, heard claims for negligence against Cunard by survivors or relations of the *Lusitania*'s American victims. During preliminary discussions between lawyers the plaintiffs agreed to drop allegations that the ship had been armed and carrying clandestine ammunition and Canadian troops, all of which, if proven, would have considerably aided their case. Judge Mayer said simply, "That story is forever disposed of."

Statements were taken from, or evidence given by, many people, including Captain Turner. Several passengers confirmed portholes had remained open despite Captain Turner's instructions to close them. Much further evidence was given on the cargo. An expert from Remington stated that neither fire nor impact could have caused the rifle cartridges aboard to explode. A representative from Bethlehem Steel confirmed the shrapnel cases were unfilled and that the separate consignment of fuses did not contain any explosives. On torpedoes, witnesses said there had been from one to three, with most suggesting two. Wesley Frost, the U.S. consul in Queenstown whose report to the State Department had unambiguously stated that the *Lusitania* was sunk by one torpedo and had collected numerous statements from American survivors on which he based his view, was not called to give evidence. Nor did the State Department volunteer to make available the passengers' statements.

Judge Mayer's opinion, handed down on August 23, 1918, absolved Cunard and Captain Turner from blame: "The cause of the sinking of the *Lusitania* was the illegal act of the Imperial German Government, acting through its instrument, the submarine commander, and violating a cherished and humane rule observed, until this war, by even the bitterest antagonists." Mayer also ruled that no materials had been carried that "could be exploded by setting them on fire in mass or in bulk nor by subjecting them to impact." He agreed with Lord Mersey's erroneous conclusion that there were two torpedoes, declaring "the weight of the testimony (too voluminous to analyse) is in favour of the two torpedo contention" and that "as there were no explosives on board it is difficult to account for the second explosion except on the theory that it was caused by a second torpedo."

On Captain Turner's conduct Mayer concluded, "The fundamental principle in navigating a merchantman whether in times of peace or of war is that the commanding officer must be left free to exercise his judgement. Safe navigation denies the proposition that the judgement and sound discretion of the captain of a vessel must be confined in a mental straitjacket."

Despite Judge Mayer's conclusions that some issues were "forever disposed of," this did not prove to be the case. Controversies about the *Lusitania* have continued to this day, only partially resolved by dives on the wreck, in particular that by Bob Ballard and his Woods Hole team, backed by *National Geographic*, in 1993 using remotely controlled submersibles with modern video and lighting equipment.

Some writers have quoted Churchill's comments of February 1915 to Walter Runciman, president of the Board of Trade, that "it is most important to attract neutral shipping to our shores in the hope especially of embroiling the USA with Germany." They link these words with the limited efforts made to warn or protect the *Lusitania* to suggest that Churchill deliberately conspired to expose the *Lusitania* to bring the United States into the war. The kaiser on some occasions subscribed to this theory. Nearly a year after the sinking, he told U.S. ambassador Gerard that "England was really responsible as the English had made the *Lusitania* go slowly in English waters so that the Germans could torpedo it and so bring on trouble."

However, there is no evidence of any such conspiracy. The general consensus at the time in the British government was that it was better to maintain the United States as a friendly supplier of munitions, rather than have it enter the war and wish to have a large say in dictating the peace. Rather than conspiring, the Admiralty appears to have been complacent, almost to the point of negligence, in disregarding information that the *Lusitania* was a German target (including the New York newspaper warning) and trusting in the *Lusitania's* speed to get her through without taking any protective measures. Such complacency is partially explained by Churchill and Fisher being distracted by the foundering Dardanelles/ Gallipoli campaign over which they were at loggerheads.

There is, however, clear evidence that after the sinking the British government, concerned not to forfeit any part of the propaganda advantage, conspired first to place the blame on Captain Turner for putting his ship at risk, and then to explain away the widely reported second explosion by attributing it to a second torpedo when they knew definitely from the message intercepted by Room 40 that there had only been one. The U.S. administration, unsurprisingly at the time of the Mayer hearing when the United States was in the war, took no action to disturb this conclusion despite the considerable information it had to the contrary.

When he realized the damage world outrage was causing to his and Germany's reputation, the kaiser said that he would not have authorized the sinking with the resultant deaths of so many women and children had he known in advance. At the same time the German authorities continued illogically to justify the sinking on the grounds of *Lusitania's* alleged armament and carriage of Canadian troops and of munitions. They did not recognize the inconsistency that if Schwieger had not known which ship he was attacking he could hardly have known her armament, cargo, or passenger list, thereby invalidating any justification based on them. The reality is that the *Lusitania* was an acknowledged target for the German U-boat service. Her name appears the most frequently in the merchant shipping targets identified in the German telegrams decoded by Room 40. U-boat commander Bernhard Wegener did not doubt that she was an authorized target when he lay in wait for her in the *U-27* in Liverpool Bay in March 1915. He recorded his actions carefully in his war diary stating he was following guidance from "Half-Flotilla Commander Hermann Bauer." He signed off his war diary for each day of the cruise. It was circulated as normal and he was not rebuked or told he was wrong to target the *Lusitania*.

The *U-20*'s war diary for the voyage on which the *Lusitania* was sunk was doctored between 1915 and 1918. At the end of a mission U-boat commanders brought their war diaries on shore, handwritten in pencil. They were subsequently and invariably typed up, usually on a purpose-designed form using both sides of the paper. Sometimes a form was not used, although both sides of the paper were still covered. Also invariably U-boat commanders signed off each day's report. When copies were made the same format was followed and the position of the captain's signature on the original was faithfully recorded. The only surviving copy of the *U-20*'s war diary is preserved in the German military archive at Freiburg and does not follow the normal format, being neither on a printed form nor double sided. Some of it is in a discursive style entirely uncharacteristic of the war diaries for Schwieger's other voyages. Highly significantly, Schwieger's signature is recorded for every day of the cruise with one notable exception—May 7, the day he sank the *Lusitania*. The copy shows many signs of cutting, pasting, and rebinding. Entries are typed more closely together and ignore usual practices on the lining up of paragraphs.

Much of the *U-20* war diary's content is dubious, including, for example, Schwieger's reasoning about whether to continue to Liverpool or whether to remain in the southern Irish Sea. In particular several elements of the unsigned entry for the day of the sinking are inaccurate, inconsistent, or clearly later additions. According to Schwieger's war diary, when the *U-20* first sighted the target she was dead ahead (*"recht voraus"*), yet he also recorded that her four funnels were immediately visible, which would have been hard—indeed impossible—to distinguish if the ship were indeed approaching head-on from the horizon. The war diary incorrectly states that the *Lusitania* made the final fatal turn that brought her into range of the *U-20* toward Queenstown. In fact she turned away from the port.

The diary states Schwieger only identified the *Lusitania* by the name in gold letters on her bow as she sank. Impartial testimony states that the ship's name had been carefully painted over in black. A competent well-briefed U-boat commander like Schwieger, assisted by an experienced merchant mariner such as Pilot Lanz who, according to Schwieger, knew "all English ships by their build" would have known immediately which ship he was attacking. Only five British liners had four funnels and the activities of each were well known to the German authorities. Only the *Lusitania* could possibly have been inbound at the time.

Schwieger's diary reflects in detail on the sinking. He asks what was the nature of the second explosion—"boiler or coal or powder?" He states that "the ship stops immediately." She did not. She was still moving when she sank eighteen minutes later. He also incorrectly states the bridge was torn asunder. Neither the reliable witness, Quartermaster Hugh Johnston, who was at the wheel, nor Captain Turner mentioned any damage to the bridge.

Schwieger's personal comments, such as "it would have been impossible for me to fire a second torpedo into this crushing crowd of humanity trying to save their lives," are out of character and out of place. Personal remarks of any kind are rare in war diaries. So too are discursive observations such as "it is surprising that just today there is so much traffic here although yesterday two big steamers have been sunk south of the St. George's Channel. Also that the *Lusitania* was not sent through the north channel remains a mystery." Such disingenuous remarks smack of additions made later to display German conscience and suggest British incompetence. The additions and changes were most likely made in 1918 when a worried kaiser inquired about the possibility of war crimes charges. By then Schwieger was dead and could not have signed off a revised entry for May 7, 1915.

A key German justification for the sinking was that the *Lusitania* was armed. There is no evidence in surviving records that guns were ever mounted. The only preparations made for the possible use of the *Lusitania* as an auxiliary cruiser (which never materialized) were the emplacement in the deck of four six-inch gun rings in 1913, visible in some photographs of the ship. However, no one saw guns mounted on them or elsewhere in the ship despite many careful inspections, including by U.S. customs staff before departure. After the sinking U.S. consul Wesley Frost specifically asked all American survivors whether they had seen guns. None had. Those questioned included Michael Byrne, who wrote to the U.S. administration stating he had made a thorough search and found nothing. Equally, the movie film of the ship leaving New York for the last time showed nothing. Some writers have suggested that guns were stored secretly to be mounted if the need arose. If so, they were not reported by officials, passengers, or crew. More important, they would have taken at least twenty minutes to retrieve and mount at sea in an emergency. By then either any raider would have disappeared or the *Lusitania* would have been sunk. Conclusively, Bob Ballard and his team found no guns when they dived on the wreck.

Another charge made by the German government was that the *Lusitania* was carrying Canadian troops. If the troops were "organised and armed" their presence would under international law have made her a troop ship, which could legitimately have been sunk without warning. However, no survivors' accounts mention any organized body of troops. Dudley Malone and other U.S. customs officials testified on June 4, 1915, that "the *Lusitania* did not have Canadian troops or troops of any nationality on board," adding that since the war began she had never done so.

In 1973 the Canadian Ministry of Defence checked whether any unaccompanied male passengers of British nationality (there was no separate Canadian nationality until 1947) whose journeys began in Canada and who died in the sinking were listed in the Canadian Book of Remembrance for May 7, 1915, as servicemen dying on duty. There were none. Neither was there any evidence in the ministry's records of Canadian troops being on the *Lusitania*.

The German accusation that the *Lusitania* was carrying contraband was entirely correct. Her supplementary cargo manifest given out by the New York customs house after the sinking states that the *Lusitania* was carrying 4,200 cases of rifle bullets, 1,250 cases of unfused shrapnel shells, and 18 cases of percussion fuses. The rest of the cargo was, by the admission of both the British and U.S. administrations, "nearly all contraband" such as material for uniforms and leather belts. Nevertheless, the issue of contraband was, as the U.S. authorities later stated, irrelevant to the circumstances of the sinking. The presence of contraband would have justified a German vessel stopping and searching the *Lusitania* under the Cruiser Rules, impounding her cargo, and seizing the vessel as a prize or destroying her after making proper provision for the safety of the crew and passengers. It did not justify a "sink on sight" policy.

Two aspects of the *Lusitania's* cargo have been queried. First was whether the declared munitions were as described in the manifest or whether the shrapnel shells were filled and the fuses contained explosives—both charges denied by the Bethlehem Steel Company at the Mayer hearing. A recent researcher has shown that the individual shell weight of eighteen pounds derived from the manifest and other shipping documents was that of an unfilled shell—a filled one would have weighed twenty-two pounds. Divers have retrieved examples of the fuses. They contain no explosives. Second was whether the *Lusitania* was carrying additional munitions to those on her manifest, either undeclared or listed as something else to disguise them. Numerous attempts have been made to confirm this theory, not least by German agents in the United States after the sinking. None have succeeded. One of the main items suspected of concealing clandestine munitions was a large consignment of furs but there is plenty of evidence that these were indeed furs. Many were washed up on the Irish coast after the sinking, dried, and resold.

One of the key findings of Bob Ballard's exploration of the wreck was that there was no damage to the area of the ship around the cargo hold and that therefore whatever its contents, they had not exploded and contributed to the sinking as the British government had feared.

If munitions did not account for the second explosion and the speed of the sinking, then what did? An engineering report commissioned by this author for an earlier book suggests that where the torpedo hit—about 160–180 feet from the bows at the forward end of boiler room one near or at a main bulkhead—was one of the few places where the *Lusitania's* structural integrity could have been as badly damaged as it was. The initial hole punched by the torpedo would have been about twenty feet long and ten feet high. Water would have immediately begun to penetrate the vulnerable starboard coal bunker which ran the length of the vessel. Just as it had in the *Hogue*, *Aboukir*, and *Cressy*, with their similar designs, when they were torpedoed by *U-9*, it produced an immediate list and a speedy sinking.

Because the steering was disabled almost at once and the engines could neither be stopped nor reversed, the ship's forward momentum would have pushed more water into the hole and loosened further rivets over the eighteen minutes of life left to the *Lusitania*. On the very conservative assumption that the rate of seawater flow into the ship was only 10 percent of the potential, traveling at a speed of eighteen knots, the liner would have been taking in over eight hundred tons of water per minute. This is without the later effect of water flowing through open portholes of which witnesses attested there were many. The starboard list allied to the bows' downward position, and the forward momentum produced twisting and bending pressures, causing the stern to lift and rotate as described by Margaret Mackworth and others, further increasing the strains on the hull and internal structures and causing them to fail more quickly. Therefore, the main factor in the *Lusitania's* speed of sinking was where the torpedo hit and the effect it had on the structure, not the secondary explosion, which did, however, undoubtedly occur.

Apart from munitions, which can now be discounted, other theories for the cause of the second explosion have been a coal-dust explosion in the nearly empty coal bunkers or a similar particulate explosion in the aluminum powder being carried aboard. Certainly coal, like many types of dust including not only aluminum powder but also everyday substances such as flour, talcum powder, and sawdust, can ignite if subject to a spark or flame while in a uniform mixture with air. The torpedo's impact and explosion would have created the necessary ignition sources. However, suitable conditions for an explosion were unlikely. The bunkers were not insulated and separated from the cold sea only by the hull plating. Seepage of seawater into the hull was an inherent problem in all vessels. Moisture migrated toward the bottom of the ship to produce pools of bilge water. Also, warm moist air from the boiler rooms would have gotten into the cooler bunkers and condensed. The dampness of the bunker would have prevented the dust being shaken into the air to form an explosive aerosol. The location of the stored aluminum powder and its robust containment make an aluminum-dust explosion equally unlikely.

Reliable witness reports of dense moist steam following the second explosion and enveloping the decks strongly suggest that the liner's power plant was involved. No other suggested cause produces steam. The second explosion was reported as loudest by those on the decks, suggesting it occurred in a boiler room where sound could be transmitted to the deck via the funnels and vents. Some experts have suggested a boiler lost water as a result of the torpedo strike and consequently exploded. However, the second explosion does not seem to have been large enough nor does the amount of steam and smoke observed seem commensurate with such a big explosion.

Engineering calculations also show that a boiler explosion would have been equivalent to around five hundred pounds of TNT—a third more than the content of a torpedo warhead. Additionally, there were survivors from the first and second boiler rooms, something that would have been highly unlikely had a boiler exploded.

Therefore, the engineering study suggests the cause of the second explosion was indeed a steam explosion, not of a boiler but of one or more of the steam lines that carried steam from the boilers to the turbines. The probable cause was either thermal shock of cold seawater on hot metal or shock and vibration created when the torpedo detonated. Captain Turner certainly believed a steam line explosion occurred. He told the Mayer hearing: "The torpedo burst the steam pipe and put the engines out of commission."

ACKNOWLEDGMENTS

As ALWAYS I am grateful to Michael, my husband and coauthor, without whom this book would not have been written.

I would also especially like to thank the following for giving generously of their time and expertise: Dr. Tim Cook, Canadian War Museum; Dr. Janet Howarth, St. Hilda's College, Oxford; Kim Lewison, Neil Munro; Professor Holger Nehring, University of Stirling; Paddy O'Sullivan, Dirk Ullmann, the Archiv der Max-Planck-Gesellschaft; Donald Wallace FRCS, Dr. Ingrid Wallace, and Dr. Mike Wood.

In the United Kingdom the help of the staff of the British Library; the London Library; the Bodleian Library; Churchill College, Cambridge; the National Maritime Museum; the Merseyside Maritime Museum; the National Archives; the BBC Written Archives Centre; and the Cunard Archives was invaluable. I am also very grateful for the insights of *Lusitania* survivor Audrey Lawson-Johnson, née Pearl, and Joe Wynne for his recollections of George Wynne. In the United States I must thank the staff of the Library of Congress, the National Archives and Records Administration, the Hoover Institution, Stanford University, and the Mariners' Museum, Newport News, Virginia. In Canada, I am indebted to CBC for access to taped interviews with *Lusitania* survivors and to the staff of the Canadian War Museum. In Ireland I much valued the assistance of the Cobh Museum and the National Maritime Museum and in Germany the help of the archivists of the Militärarchiv, Freiburg, and of Bernd Hoffmann of the Archiv der Max-Planck-Gesellschaft, Berlin.

I would like to thank my mother, Florence Faith, for all her many years of encouragement.

I also much appreciate all the help, advice, and encouragement of my agents Bill Hamilton in London and Michael Carlisle in New York and of George Gibson and all his team at Bloomsbury.

NOTES AND SOURCES

To help simplify the notes, I used the following abbreviations and designations to identify some of the main sources:

ARCHIVES

- BBC. Interview transcripts in the production files for two programs—*Fifty Fathoms Deep* and *Who Sank the* Lusitania?—containing much unused material and a file about salvage operations between 1982 and 1987 which are in the British Broadcasting Corporation's Written Archives Centre, Caversham Park, UK.
- CBC. Lengthy taped interviews (around eight hours in total) with *Lusitania* survivors and a member of the *U-20*'s crew recorded by the Canadian Broadcasting Corporation for its 1965 program *Rendezvous with Death.*
- Churchill Archives, Churchill College, Cambridge University.
- Cunard archives. The archives of the Cunard Steamship Company, Liverpool University, Liverpool, UK.
- German Military Archive, Freiburg. The Bundesarchiv-Militärarchiv, Freiburg, Germany, which holds the German naval files for the period.
- Fisher Collection, Churchill College, Cambridge University.
- The Hoover Institution on War, Revolution, and Peace, Stanford University, Stanford, CA, which houses the extensive papers collected by Thomas A. Bailey and Paul B. Ryan for "The *Lusitania* Disaster."
- IWM. The archives of the Imperial War Museum in London include a large collection of recorded and written interviews and memoirs of those who experienced the events described in this book—British combatants, pacifists, other civilians, and German soldiers and sailors—and a large amount of correspondence with *Lusitania* survivors (the Prichard collection) as well as transcripts of the Kinsale inquest (Special Miscellaneous Collection V5). References are prefixed (IWM/R) for recorded interviews and (IWM/D) for written material.
- The Mariners' Museum, Newport News, VA, which holds a collection of letters from *Lusitania* survivors and their relations collected in the 1950s by A. A. Hoehling and M. Hoehling for their book *The Last Voyage of the* Lusitania.
- MPG—Archive zur Geschichte der Max-Planck-Gesellschaft, Dahlem, Berlin, which holds papers relating to Fritz Haber's career collected by his former student Johannes Jaenicke after the Second World War, including some of Haber's own letters and interviews with friends and colleagues.
- NARA. National Archives and Records Administration, Maryland, and New York, which holds many of the key political documents for the period, papers describing the German spy rings in America,

and the statements of American survivors given to Consul Frost. Unless otherwise specified, material quoted is from microfilms M 580 197, M 580 198, and M 973 187.

- For the UK National Archives, Kew, UK, individual file numbers are given with prefixes ADM, AIR, CAB, FO, DT, PREM, and WO to denote respectively the Admiralty, Air Ministry, Cabinet Office, Foreign Office, Department of Trade, Prime Minister, and War Office.

SPECIFIC DOCUMENTS

Mayer (O). Opinion of Judge Mayer.

Mayer (T). Transcript of Mayer Limit of Liability Hearings.

Mersey (R). Report of Mersey inquiry.

Mersey (TO). Transcripts of open sessions of Mersey inquiry.

Mersey (TC). Transcripts of closed sessions of Mersey inquiry.

Parliamentary Debates (Official Report) of the House of Commons (1914–18) published by HMSO.

Wynne (T). Transcripts of evidence given before Commissioner Wynne in London for the Mayer Limit of Liability Hearings in New York.

War Diary of the *U-20*. Daily diary kept by Walther Schwieger, commander of the *U-20*. All quotes for the voyage of April–May 1915 are from the version on file in the German Military Archive, Freiburg. My English translation is based on that in the Hoover Institution, with some modifications.

SPRING 1915—THE LEGACY

1   "During . . . country.": Quoted I. Novak, *Science: A Many Splendored Thing.*

1   "In . . . killing.": R. Harris and J. Paxman, *A Higher Form of Killing*, p. xv. (It is sometimes suggested that Haber made this comment in his Nobel Prize for Chemistry acceptance speech. However, he actually made these remarks later in 1923. (See "Killers in White Coats" by Efraim Karsh, King's College, London University, *Daily Telegraph*, March 12, 2002.)

1   "*Lusitania* . . . Queenstown.": NARA, Nora Bretherton.

2   "The principal . . . can.": *Times*, June 2, 1915.

3   "The humanising of war . . . violence!": Admiral Jacky Fisher, quoted Admiral R. Bacon, *The Life of Lord Fisher*, vol. 1, p. 121.

4   "a poison . . . frightfulness.": *Observer*, May 2, 1915.

4   "While . . . virulence.": Ibid., May 9, 1915.

4   "frightfulness . . . *Lusitania*": *Washington Herald.*

4   "a piece of 'frightfulness.' ": *Manchester Guardian*, June 1, 1915.

5   Syria's . . . civilization . . . it takes . . .

poison gas": Andrew Roberts, *Wall Street Journal*, August 25, 2013.

CHAPTER ONE—"A FLASH OF LIGHTNING FROM THE NORTH"

6–7   The quotes from the Old Testament Book of Deuteronomy are from chapters twenty and twenty-one.

7   Sun Tzu, *The Art of War*, chapter 2, e-book.

7   "mild . . . cruelty": Cicero, quoted A. C. Grayling, *Among the Dead Cities*, p. 220.

7   "with a . . . vengeance . . . in a just cause": Saint Augustine quoted C. Moorehead, *Dunant's Dream*, p. 23.

7   "the advancement . . . evil": Saint Thomas Aquinas, *Summa Theologica*, part 2, quoted Grayling, *Among the Dead Cities*, pp. 211–12.

7   "rules . . . battlefield . . . Do not . . . inhabited place.": *Al-Muwatta*, the first written collection of hadith compiled by the Imam Malik Ibn Anas, book 21 (p. 174 of edition in the bibliography).

7–8   The Koran reference is Sura Al-Baqara 2:190–93.

9   "that there . . . crimes.": H. Grotius,

Prolegomena to the Law of War and Peace, p. 21.

9 "people . . . impunity . . . becoming . . . character.": A. C. Grayling, *Among the Dead Cities*, p. 218 quoting Grotius, *De jure belli ac pacis*, book 3, chapter 1, section 4; chapter 4, section 2.

9–10 "The received . . . must be.": H. Lushington, *A Great Country's Little Wars in Afghanistan and Scinde*, p. 27.

10 "Corpses . . . ground.": H. Dunant, *A Memory of Solferino*, p. 41.

10–11 "some . . . wounded.": Quoted C. Moorehead, *Dunant's Dream*, p. 8.

11 "quite harmless . . . it with.": Ibid., p. 47.

12 "any act . . . difficult . . . Men . . . God.": F. Lieber quoted ibid., p. 38.

12 "in violation . . . war.": Transcripts of the trial and the judgment are available on many websites, including the BBC's and archive.org.

13 "a flash . . . north": *Le Temps*, August 30, 1898.

13–14 "the grave problem . . . military . . . unknown . . . The intellectual . . . themselves.": Count Muraviev, quoted Tuchman, *The Proud Tower*, p. 229.

14 "an omen . . . century . . . the most . . . history.": Quoted ibid., p. 230.

14 "some new . . . Tsar's head.": Frances, Countess of Warwick, *Life's Ebb and Flow*, p. 119.

14 "put a . . . democracy . . . what . . . workers with?": Quoted B. Tuchman, *The Proud Tower*, p. 241.

14 "he . . . stage.": quoted Prince B. von Bulow, *Memoirs*, vol. 1, p. 233.

15 "I'll go . . . the waltz.": M. Macmillan, *The War That Ended Peace*, p. 279.

CHAPTER TWO—"HUMANISING WAR"

16 "in a spirit . . . result.": A. White, *Autobiography*, vol. 2, p. 256.

16 "favour the . . . civilised.": Quoted Macmillan, *The War That Ended Peace*, p. 280.

16 "The conference . . . fanatics.": Quoted B. Tuchman, *The Proud Tower*, p. 257.

17 "suicide": Quoted Macmillan, *The War That Ended Peace*, p. 270.

17 "a condition . . . necessity.": Ibid., p. 269.

17 "the queer . . . indeed.": A. White, *Autobiography*, vol. 2, pp. 261–62, 271.

17 "for the . . . work.": Ibid., p. 347.

17–18 "deepened . . . nation?": Quoted A. J. Marder, *From the Dreadnought to Scapa Flow*, vol. 1, p. 17.

18 "The humanizing . . . clear of you.": Quoted Admiral Sir R. Bacon, *The Life of Lord Fisher of Kilverstone, vol. 1*, p. 121.

18–19 "Suppose that . . . still less.": *Review of Reviews*, February 1910.

19 "control of . . . nations.": Quoted L. E. Livezey, *Mahan on Sea Power*, p. 281.

19 "prevented . . . appears.": A. White, *Autobiography*, vol. 2, p. 347.

19 "the object . . . the sea": Quoted Livezey, *Mahan on Sea Power*, p. 274.

20 "that the . . . mankind.": G. Best, "Peace Conferences and the Century of Total War: The 1899 Hague Conference and What Came After," *International Affairs*, vol. 75, no. 3, July 1999, p. 631.

20 "not to . . . period": Quoted Tuchman, *The Proud Tower*, p. 261.

20 "the great danger . . . wrong.": Quoted Livezey, *Mahan on Sea Power*, p. 272.

20 "a hoax . . . I consented . . . decisions.": Quoted Tuchman, *The Proud Tower*, p. 266.

20–21 The conference . . . assault": All quotes in this paragraph are from *The Hague Convention Regarding the Laws and Customs of War.*

21 "under . . . conscience.": Quoted G. Best, "Peace Conferences and the Century of Total War," p. 627.

21 Alfred Nobel made his initial fortune from the oil fields of Baku, now in Azerbaijan, as did the Rockefellers.

22 "un-Christian weapons.": Quoted E. A. Roberts and R. Guelff, eds., *Documents on the Law of War*, p. 29.

22 "murderous . . . warfare.": Quoted Grayling, *Among the Dead Cities*, p. 226.

22 "you have . . . to play": Quoted G. Best, *Humanity in Warfare*, p. 137.

22–23 "The civilised . . .your head.": Ibid.

23 "a sad . . .miscreants.": Quoted K. Coleman, *A History of Chemical Warfare*, p. 7.

23 "every animal function.": Quoted D. T. Thomas, *Cochrane*, p. 194.

24 "accord . . . warfare": Ibid., p. 326.

24 "No conduct . . . inhuman . . . the most . . .at all.": Quoted J.F.C. Fuller, *Machine Warfare*, p. 232.

24 "so horrible . . . no honourable combatant": Quoted W. Moore, *Gas Attack!*, p. 5.

24 "Four or . . . coke . . . a couple . . . barrels . . . igniting . . . potassium.": Quoted Thomas, *Cochrane*, p. 338.

24 "smoked . . . blown up": Quoted Moore, *Gas Attack!*, p. 4.

24 "thousands of lives": Quoted Thomas, *Cochrane*, p. 337.

24 Palmerston wrote cynically to his secretary for war that provided Cochrane was prepared to go to the Crimea to oversee his scheme in person they should accept his offer: "If it succeeds, it will, as you say, save a great number of English and French lives; if it fails in his hands we shall be exempt from blame, and if we come in for a small share of the ridicule, we can bear it and the greater part will fall on him." (Thomas, *Cochrane*, p. 338.)

24–25 "such . . . guns.": Quoted W. D. Miles, "The Idea of Chemical Warfare in Modern Times," *Journal of the History of Ideas*, vol. 31. no. 2, p. 299.

25 "It is . . . incomprehensible.": Ibid.

25 "a scheme . . . destructive . . . such a . . . world.": Ibid. p. 303.

25 A geologist, Forrest Shepherd of Connecticut, urged President Lincoln to use hydrogen chloride to force Confederate troops from their entrench-ments: "By mingling strong sulphuric acid with strong hydrochloric . . . a dense white cloud is at once formed . . . When the cloud strikes a man it sets him to coughing, sneezing etc., but does not kill him, while it would effectually prevent him from firing a gun . . . It has occurred to me that Gen. Burnside, with his colored troops might, on a dark night, with a gentle breeze favorable, surprise and capture the strongholds of Petersburg or Fort Darling, perhaps, without loss or shedding of blood."

25 "Chlorine . . . gas.": "The Idea of Chemical Warfare," p. 300.

25 "genius . . . in inventing . . . war": Quoted A. A. Roberts, *The Poison War*, p. 20.

26 "What would . . . region": Dr. S. Johnson, *Rasselas, Prince of Abissinia*, chapter 6 (*A Dissertation on the Art of Flying*).

26 "Of what . . . baby?": Quoted E. Dudley, *Monsters of the Purple Twilight*, p.11.

26 "must have . . . engine.": Ibid.

26 "as the . . . life": Ibid., p. 12.

26 "dirigible balloons . . . a very . . . warfare": Dr. Hugo Eckener, Count Zeppelin's business partner, reporting the count's views, ibid., p. 13.

CHAPTER THREE—"THE LAW OF FACTS"

28 "A small . . . experience.": *Life Magazine*, November 15, 1900.

28 "agitation . . . notoriety": Quoted Moorehead, *Dunant's Dream*, p. 145.

28 "When . . . a war? . . . When . . . barbarism": Ibid.

29 The first defensive military use of barbed wire was during the Spanish-American War of 1898.

29 The kaiser had also coined the phrase "The Yellow Peril" for the Japanese five years previously after Japan's victory in another war against China.

30 "Every Chinaman . . . revolting.": R. Keyes, *Adventures Ashore and Afloat*, p. 296.

30 "the frequent . . . women" . . . It is . . . French soldier.": G. Lynch, *The War of the Civilisations*, p. 140.

32 By then . . . "further serious study.": Quotes are from B. Tuchman, *The Proud Tower*, pp. 278 and 285.

33 "a great government": Quoted S. Budiansky, *Air Power*, p. 24.

33 "wonderful . . . advance": Quoted H. G. Castle, *Fire over England*, p. 5.

34 Japan . . . compensation: The extracts from the convention on neutral rights are from Roberts and Guelff, eds., *Documents on the Law of War*, p. 63.

34 "by the . . . facts.": Quoted Tuchman, *The Proud Tower*, p. 284.

CHAPTER FOUR—"A SCRAP OF
PAPER"

36 "the battleships . . . future.": Quoted R.
K. Massie, *Castles of Steel*, p. 123.

37 "a mode . . . deprive us of it.": Quoted
H. C. Fyfe, *Submarine Warfare, Past,
Present and Future*, p. 14.

38 "As to . . . progress.": Quoted P. R.
Compton-Hall, *Submarine Boats*, p. 50.

38 "not our concern.": Quoted Fyfe,
Submarine Warfare, p. xiii.

38 "submarines . . . defensive.": Response
to parliamentary question asked on April
6, 1900, by Captain Norton, MP.
(*Hansard*). Lord Goschen was the eldest
brother of Sir Edward Goschen, British
ambassador to Berlin on the eve of the
First World War.

38 "The Admiralty . . . nation . . .
Underwater . . . crews.": Quoted D. van
der Vat, *Stealth at Sea*, p. 33.

39 "the immense . . . war": Letter from
Fisher to Admiral May, April 24, 1904, in
Marder, *Fear God and Dread Nought*,
vol. 1, p. 308.

39 "any maritime . . . defence": Quoted
Compton-Hall, *Submarine Boats*, p. 129.

39 "would . . . wars . . . the constant . . .
destruction": Quoted in R. Hough, *First
Sea Lord*, p. 5.

40 "an utterly . . . box . . . a coffin . . .
like . . . plaster . . . into . . . pot . . .
Read . . . perseveringly . . . Not . . . to
be.": Charles Dickens's comments are
from his *American Notes* (chapter 2, "The
Passage Out"), to be found, inter alia, on
the Internet at www. people.virginia.edu
(edited by J. L. Griffith, University of
Virginia).

40 "we must . . . these.": Quoted T.
Coleman, *The Liners*, p. 41.

41 "Morganization . . . Atlantic": Quoted
ibid., p. 48.

43 "restless . . . originality": Quoted R. K.
Massie, *Dreadnought*, p. 766.

44 "For Germany . . . possible.": The full
memorandum is quoted in J. Steinberg,
*Yesterday's Deterrent—Tirpitz and the
Birth of the German Battle Fleet*, pp.
209–21.

44 "I could . . . kaleidoscope.": Von Tirpitz,
My Memoirs, vol. 1, p. 99.

45 "already . . . Belgium . . . Our inva-
sion . . . reached.": The full text is in R.
H. Lutz, *Fall of the German Empire,
Documents 1914–18*, vol. 1.

45 "excited . . . very agitated . . . unthinkable . . . like . . . assailants . . . just . . .
nation.": These quotes are from the *"Blue
Book" of British Government*, no. 160,
Goschen to Grey.

45–46 "of quite . . . women . . . seemed . . .
treason.": The sources for these quotes
are Sir H. Rumbold, *The War Crisis in
Berlin, July–August 1914*, p. 323, and M.
Gilbert, *The First World War*, p. 33.

46 "My blood . . . war.": T. Bethmann
Hollweg, *Reflections*, p. 159.

46 "He is Satan . . . he is.": R. Zedlitz-
Trützschler, *Twelve Years at the Imperial
German Court*, p. 178.

46 "a very . . . foreigners.": Quoted Massie,
Castles of Steel, p. 7.

46 "I have . . . for me.": Von Tirpitz, *My
Memoirs*, vol. 1, p. 275.

46 "to think . . . allowed it . . . only . . .
Georgie.": Quoted Blücher, *An English
Wife in Berlin*, p. 14.

47 "the two Teutonic nations": Quoted G.
MacDonogh, *The Last Kaiser*, p. 252.

47 "with such . . . armaments.": Ibid.

47 "I have . . . liked by us.": Quoted Massie,
Dreadnought, p. 167.

47 "the English . . . Portugal.": Von Tirpitz,
My Memoirs, vol. II, p. 235.

48 "All is . . . lost.": Quoted M. Gilbert, *The
First World War*, p. 32.

48 "The army . . . the world.": J. Gerard, *My
Four Years in Germany*, p. 64.

48 "quite spontaneously . . . convoy.":
Quoted J. Keegan, *The First World War*,
p. 82.

48 "with flags . . . souls.": Quoted, ibid., p.
81.

48 "not ashamed . . . such times.": Quoted,
ibid.

48 The magnificent Moorish-style synagogue
in Oranienstrasse, inaugurated in 1866,
was attacked by the Nazis on Crystal
Night in 1938 and badly damaged by
Allied bombing raids but has been rebuilt
and restored.

49 "a holy . . . justice.": Quoted H. Strachan,
The First World War, vol. 1, p. 116.

49 "The Church . . . holy war.": Quoted
    ibid.
49 "I have . . . fond.": Elizabeth Owen,
    quoted M. Arthur, *Forgotten Voices of the
    Great War*, p. 15. (This is a compendium
    from taped interviews held in the
    Imperial War Museum.)
49 "We were . . . term].": Private Godfrey
    Buxton quoted ibid., p. 16.
49 "You will . . . trees.": Quoted Tuchman,
    August 1914, p. 123.

CHAPTER FIVE—"THE WORST OF
CONTRABANDS"
50–51 But . . . "Mitteleuropa.": The quotes
       about Germany's war aims are from
       Fischer, *Germany's Aims in the First
       World War*, p. 105.
51 "elimination . . . politics.": Ibid., p. 108.
    Historians continue to debate how far
    such views, most of which were almost
    impossible to reconcile with the
    requirement for waging a "just war," and
    in particular those of von Bethmann
    Hollweg, had underlain Germany's
    strategic maneuverings in the years
    leading up to the First World War and in
    particular during the Sarajevo crisis, and
    how far they were opportunistic,
    stemming from the sudden and joyous
    anticipation of winning the place in the
    European sun they craved and deserved.
    The balance of opinion is now, perhaps
    correctly, tending toward the war aims
    having been long held, even if Sarajevo
    provoked a European-wide conflict
    none were looking for at the time it
    broke out.
51 "Germany's . . . materials.": Ibid., p. 109.
52 "against . . . use them.": Quoted, C.
    Tansill, *America Goes to War*, p. 18.
52 "As if . . . flash . . . the issue . . . law.":
    Ibid., p. 24.
52 "republic . . . disputes.": Quoted J. Dos
    Passos, *Mr. Wilson's War*, p. 12.
53 "like writing on ice . . . a jellyfish . . .
    party politics.": Quoted R. Gregory,
    Walter Hines Page, p. 101.
53 "I can . . . suffering.": Quoted Dos
    Passos, *Mr. Wilson's War*, p. 98.
53 "My hope . . . purpose.": Wilson to Grey,

quoted R. S. Baker, *Woodrow Wilson—
Life and Letters*, vol. 5, pp. 55–56.
53 "reap . . . doing it.": Remarks to a press
    conference, given in full in A. S. Link,
    ed., *The Papers of Woodrow Wilson*, vol.
    30, p. 332.
53 "neutral . . . action . . . speak . . .
    peace . . . play . . . mediator.": These
    remarks are from President Wilson's
    address to the American people, ibid., p.
    394.
53 "interpreted . . . people.": Fischer,
    Germany's Aims in the First World War,
    p. 119.
54 "We shall . . . have done!": Quoted
    Gilbert, *The First World War*, p. 43.
55 "the greatest . . . vengeance.": Asquith,
    reported *Times*, September 5, 1914.
55 "We may . . . felons.' ": Dean of
    Peterborough, ibid., September 16, 1914.
55 "if it had . . . swept away.": Keegan, *The
    First World War*, p. 93.
55 "essential . . . operations.": The U.S.
    request for compliance with the
    Declaration of London and the UK
    response are in *US Foreign Relations
    1914*, pp. 215–16 and 281–20
    respectively.
57 "the maximum . . . United States":
    Viscount Grey, *Twenty-five Years*, vol. 2,
    p. 103.
58 "escaped disaster . . . pure good luck . . .
    necessary . . . waged.": Quoted Bailey
    and Ryan, *The Lusitania Disaster*, p. 29.
58 "the worst . . . things": Letter from Bryan
    to Wilson, August 10, 1914, Bryan
    Correspondence.
58 "inconsistent . . . neutrality.": Ibid.
58 "A greater . . . country.": Letter from J. P.
    Morgan to H. White, June 5, 1914, White
    Correspondence.
58 "meticulous, metallic and mousy.": J.
    Daniels, *The Wilson Era*, vol. 1, *The Years
    of Peace, 1910–1917*, p. 441.
59 "An arrangement . . . money . . . not . . .
    Government": "A Memorandum Written
    by R. Lansing at 9.30 p.m., October 23,
    1914 of a Conversation with President
    Wilson at 8.30 p.m. That Evening,"
    Lansing Papers and Link, *The Papers of
    Woodrow Wilson*, vol. 31, p. 219.
59 Figures on British imports from the

United States are from Strachan, *The First World War*, p. 963.

59 "I have . . . Germany.": Gerard, *My Four Years in Germany*, p. 155.

59 "contrary . . . arsenal.": Tirpitz's *Memoirs*, vol. 2, p. 392.

59 "The sabotage . . . matériel . . . suitable . . . sabotage.": Quoted in R. Doerries's foreword to Rintelen, *The Dark Invader*, p. xv. The consensus is that German agents caused the explosion that destroyed the Black Tom plant, although some suggest that Irish nationalists might have been involved.

59 "Lord Fisher . . . rug": Quoted in J. Morris, *Fisher's Face*, p. 202. Fisher succeeded Prince Louis of Battenberg, father of the future Lord Mountbatten, who had retired despite his royal connections, in part due to suspicion of his German name and antecedents. One critic had denounced him as "a German—he has German property and German servants and should not therefore occupy his present position."

60 "I'm exceeding busy . . . I've just . . . accordingly.": Letter from Fisher to Lord Remant, November 5, 1914, Fisher Collection, Churchill College, Cambridge.

60 "The Miraculous . . . Fishes": Quoted P. Beesley, *Room 40*, p. 22.

CHAPTER SIX—"ENGLAND WILL BURN"

61 "the greatest donkey" . . . "the greatest . . . century . . . the Conqueror . . . Air.": Quoted Dudley, *Monsters of the Purple Twilight*, pp. 15–16.

61 "disappointment . . . dismay . . . There . . . portend?": Quoted H. G. Castle, *Fire over England*, p. 18.

62 "imagine . . . Britain . . . afford . . . airships.": Kapitän von Pustau quoted Dudley, *Monsters*, p. 21.

62 "we could . . . cars . . . At . . . flames.": Future zeppelin commander von Buttlar quoted Dudley, *Monsters*, p. 70.

63 "within . . . Calais.": H. G. Wells, *Daily Mail*, June 27, 1909.

63 "the little . . . immunity": H. G. Wells, *Daily Mail*, July 25 1909.

63 "a useless . . . fad.": Quoted A. P. Hyde, *The First Blitz*, p. 19.

64 "There is . . . cavalry.": Ibid., p. 16.

64 Lurid . . . Knightsbridge.": Dr. Karl Graves, *The Secrets of the German War Office*, pp. 176–77.

64 "I believed . . . monsters . . . to restrict . . . airplanes.": Quoted Massie, *Castles of Steel*, pp. 362–63.

66 "As I . . . shed.": Quoted Dudley, *Monsters*, p. 28

66–67 "the English . . . reason . . . not . . . old woman . . . if one . . . sight of": Von Tirpitz, *My Memoirs*, vol. 2, p. 487 and p. 502.

67 "all that . . . city.": Ibid., p. 502.

67 "should leave . . . this end.": Quoted Dudley, *Monsters*, p. 34

67 "lukewarm flabbiness": Von Tirpitz, *My Memoirs*, vol. 2, p. 502.

67 "carrying . . . considerable.": W. S. Churchill, *World Crisis* 1915, pp. 62–63.

67 "London . . . bombed.": Quoted Dudley, *Monsters*, p. 34.

68 "two bright . . . apart": Quoted K. Poolman, *Zeppelins over England*, p. 39.

68 "the biggest . . . life . . . a church . . . sideways.": Ibid., p. 40.

69 "shattering . . . The anti-aircraft . . . invisible.": Quoted Dudley, *Monsters*, p, 37.

69 One of these remarkably tiny observation cars is in London's Imperial War Museum.

CHAPTER SEVEN—"A MOST EFFECTIVE WEAPON"

70 "at the summit . . . battle.": W. S. Churchill, *World Crisis*, p. 21.

71 "entirely . . . anticipated.": Quoted in L. Thomas, *Raiders of the Deep*, p. 34.

71 "From a . . . imports.": Quoted V. E. Tarrant, *U-Boat Offensive*, p. 12.

72 "most effective weapon.": Von Tirpitz, *My Memoirs*, vol. 2, p. 391.

72 "fought . . . warfare.": F. von Rintelen, *The Dark Invader*, p. 48.

72 "Now . . . traffic? . . . Why not? . . . blockade.": Quoted A. C. Bell, *A History*

of the Blockade of the Central Empires,
1914–1918, pp. 210–11.

72 "to get . . . nothing.": Von Tirpitz, *My*
Memoirs, vol. 2, p. 500. According to his
postwar memoirs, von Tirpitz had
personally favored a more limited
blockade of the Thames because
Germany did not yet have enough
submarines for an effective blockade of
all British ports.

73 "would be . . . neutral ships.": Quoted in
full in R. H. Gibson, *The German*
Submarine War, p. 27. Hermann Bauer
interpreted the announcement in
unequivocal terms, writing to his
submarine commanders on February 22,
1915, that henceforth "all English ships
and any which in spite of neutral flags and
markings could be taken for such" were to
be annihilated (RM 86/224, Freiburg
Military Archive).

73 "neutral . . . more ado . . . to avoid . . .
complications.": Message from Berlin to
German embassy, Washington, D.C.,
decoded by the British, file ADM
187/3962.

73 "Thinking . . . mistake . . . hoped . . .
about it.": From an interview with von
Bernstorff by an American newspaper
editor O. G. Villard recorded in his book
Fighting Years, pp. 268–69 and also in an
article published in the *American*
Mercury, May 1935.

74 fast steamer . . . 5th March: file ADM
137/4177.

74 American . . . spared: Decoded telegram
to U-boat commanders, February 19,
1915, ADM 137/3958. Another copy is on
ADM 137/1428.

74 "the *Lusitania* . . . her.": War Diary of
U-27, file RM/97-680, Freiburg Military
Archive.

75 "Mr. House . . . are one.": C. Seymour,
The Intimate Papers of Colonel House,
vol. 1, p. 118.

75 "Every newspaper . . . hearsay.": Colonel
House's diary, February 6, 1915.

75 "to a strict accountability . . . full
enjoyment . . . high seas.": *Foreign*
Relations of the U.S., 1915 supplement,
p. 99.

75 "magnificent . . . as exciting . . . as novels.":

Von Tirpitz, *My Memoirs,* vol. 2, p. 513.

76 "most important . . . better still.":
Gilbert, *Winston S. Churchill,* companion
vol. 3, p. 501. Churchill's February 10,
1915, instructions to merchant captains
are in file ADM 187/2958.

77 "terrorism . . . It is . . .of all.": Quoted J.
Willis, *Prologue to Nuremberg,* p. 31.

CHAPTER EIGHT—"SOMETHING
THAT MAKES PEOPLE PERMANENTLY
INCAPABLE OF FIGHTING"

78 "the ordinary weapons . . . gas.":
Falkenhayn, General HQ, 1914–16, p. 47.

79 "wasteland . . . fever . . . a splendid . . .
intelligence": Quoted D. Stoltzenberg,
Fritz Haber, pp. 28–29.

80 "his immediate . . . objective.": Lise
Meitner's recollections of Haber, 1954,
MPG, Va5/HC 1484.

80 "both . . . same time.": Quoted R. L.
Sime, *Lise Meitner—A Life in Physics,* p.
142.

81 "You have . . . pouring out.": Quoted
Stoltzenberg, *Fritz Haber,* p. 87.

81 "we should risk it.": Ibid, p. 88.

81 "splendid man . . . personal vanity.":
Quoted D. Charles, *Between Genius and*
Genocide, p. 136.

81 "hunger for power": James Franck's
memories of the Habers, April 1958,
MPG, Va5/1449.

82 "the relationship . . . war": R. Willstätter
quoted J. A. Johnson, *The Kaiser's*
Chemists, p. 185.

82 The full text of the "Proclamation to the
Civilised World" is readily available on
the Internet.

82 "much-praised . . . civilization . . . an
axe . . . criminal.": Quoted D. Charles,
Between Genius and Genocide, p. 151.

82–83 "developing shells . . . fight.": Quoted
Stoltzenberg, *Fritz Haber,* p. 134.

83 "imperious . . . life": Quoted Harris and
Paxman, *A Higher Form of Killing,* p. 9.

84 "something . . . fighting": Quoted M.
Szollosi-Janze, *Fritz Haber,* p. 324
(author's translation).

84 "all suitable . . . German Empire":
Quoted Johnson, *The Kaiser's Chemists,*
p. 190.

84 "even in . . . dilution": Ibid.

84 "the work . . . night.": Quoted Harris and Paxman, *A Higher Form of Killing*, p. 10.

84–85 "owing to . . . effect . . . the use . . . mortars.": Quoted Stoltzenberg, *Fritz Haber*, p. 135.

85 Otto Hahn helped Lise Meitner who was of Jewish extraction escape from Germany in 1938 at considerable personal risk to himself.

85 "lying . . . bed . . . how . . . frozen . . . the fronts . . . immobile . . . the war . . . of them.": O. Hahn, *My Life*, p. 137.

86 "by using . . . gas . . . it was . . . sooner.": Ibid., p. 118.

86 "in the . . . weapon": Ibid., p. 119.

87 "with outspoken . . . husband's": James Franck's memories of the Habers, April 1958, MPG, Va5/1449.

87 "when von Falkenhayn . . . sector . . . I must . . . soldier . . . using . . . exists.": B. von Deimling, *Aus der alten in die neue Zeit, Lebenserinnerungen*, p. 201.

88 "at times . . . enemy lines.": Hahn, *My Life*, p. 119.

88 "They suffered . . . devices.": Deimling, *Aus der alten in die neue Zeit*, p. 202.

88 "pale and exhausted . . . a charlatan . . . gas . . . extremely unhappy.": MPG, Va5/HC1480.

88 "at the first . . . opportunity": Duguid, *Official History*, appendix 706.

88 "alternate gas front": Quoted J. McWilliams and R. J. Steel, *Gas! The Battle for Ypres, 1915*, p. 25.

89 "An attack . . . without losses.": Ibid., p. 12

89 "to exercise . . . of gas.": Quoted D. Dancocks, *Welcome to Flanders Fields*, p. 154.

89 "to avoid . . . of war.": General E. Ferry, "Ce qui s'est passé sur l'Yser," *La Revue des Vivants*, pp. 889–900, Paris, July 1930.

89 "all this . . . seriously.": A. F. Duguid, *Official History of the Canadian Forces in the Great War, 1914–19*, vol. 1, appendix 318.

90 "at the first . . . wind.": Account published in *Daily Express*, January 1, 1933.

90 "cylinders in dozens . . . was passed . . . headquarters": Foulkes, *Gas! The Story of the Special Brigade*, p. 32.

90 "it has been . . . quickly.": *Times*, April 9, 1915.

90 "Passages . . . necessary.": Duguid, *Official History*, appendix 323.

90 "a rumour": War diary of Canadian assistant medical director, quoted McWilliams and Steel, *Gas!*, p. 15.

91 "Last night . . . normal.": *With the First Canadian Contingent*, p. 75.

91 "We were aware . . . uneasy.": British Report, WO 32/5183.

91 "shells . . . gas": German communiqué quoted Dancocks, *Welcome to Flanders Fields*, p. 154.

91 "the German mentality . . . were . . . in advance.": British Official History quoted Dancocks, *Welcome to Flanders Fields*, p. 154.

CHAPTER NINE—"OPERATION DISINFECTION"

94 The nickname "Les Joyeux" is connected to the words sung to their bugle call:

> *Joyeux fais ton fourbi*
> *Pas vu, pas pris,*
> *Mais vu, rousti*
> *Bat' d'Af!*

Slang and double entendres make translation difficult but roughly:

> *Joyeux tend your kit [or do your "scam"]*
> *Never seen, never caught,*
> *But if seen, "busted"*
> *Bat' d'Af!*

The "bugle song" is discussed in A. D. Lougheed, *Too Many Heroes*, vol. 1, (war diaries of 1er and 3e Bataillons de Marche d'Infanterie Legere d'Afrique), p. 16 (this author's translation).

94–95 "In certain . . . anyone": L. Botti, *Avec les Zouaves*, p. 99.

95 "looked like . . . unshaven": Fusilier V. Packer quoted Arthur, *Forgotten Voices of the Great War*, p. 83.

95 "if Jerry . . . someone there.": Ibid., p. 85.

95 "they would . . . things.": Ibid.

95–96 "the battlefield . . . old battlefield.":
R. Binding, *A Fatalist at War*, p. 64.

96 "a Frenchman . . . galore.": Quoted
Dancocks, *Welcome to Flanders Fields*, p.
143.

96 "It was not . . . King.": *Toronto Globe*,
ibid., p. 33.

97 Canada sends . . . fought: Ibid., p. 83.

97 "nothing . . . the Conqueror.": *Times*,
ibid., p. 83.

97 "enough . . . cry.": W. A. Quinton, IWM/
(D)4205.

97 "are the very deuce . . . chance": Quoted
Dancocks, *Welcome to Flanders Fields*, p.
124.

98 "Khaki" —a word found in Hindi and
Urdu but originally Persian in origin—
means literally "soil colored."

98 "a mere . . . behind": Quoted Dancocks,
Welcome to Flanders Fields, p. 145.

98 "The French . . . latrines . . . used . . .
hands with.": Quoted ibid., pp. 145–46.

98 "The position . . . the toe.": Major C. G.
Lawson, IWM/(D)/7834.

98 "we . . . biscuits.": Lieut. H. F. Maxwell-
Scott, IWM/(D)/7200.

98 "the very . . . spring . . . when the . . .
violets.": G. C. Nasmith, *Canada's Sons
and Great Britain in the Great War*, p.
178.

98 "a dark red pall . . . smoke": A. F.
Duguid, op. cit.

98–99 "in scattered . . . storm": Ibid.

99 "how extraordinary . . . living thing.":
Quoted *Times History of War*, vol. 5,
p. 56.

99 "the north wind . . . products": Quoted
A. D. Lougheed, *Too Many Heroes*, p.
123.

99–100 "this panic . . . the sky . . . cloud . . .
through green glasses . . . throat . . .
lost.": J. J. Mordacq, *Le drame de l'Yser*,
pp. 74–75.

100 "a heavy . . . lines . . . the French . . .
back . . . could . . . more.": Lieut. H. F.
Maxwell-Scott, IWM/(D)/7200.

100 "even before . . . waver.": German official
account Duguid, *Official History*,
appendix 706.

100 "an enormous . . . landscape . . . The
Joyeux . . . trench! . . . the . . . cloud . . .a
horrible . . . burning . . . refused . . . air":

Capitaine Tremsal, quoted A. D.
Lougheed, *Too Many Heroes*, p. 121.

101 "pouring . . . place.": Quoted McWilliams
and Steel, *Gas!*, p. 51.

101 "we distinctly . . . prisoner": J. J.
Mordacq, *Le drame de l'Yser*, pp. 68–69.

101–102 The first . . . suddenly turned
mad.": Colonel Mordacq's account in
these two paragraphs is from his *Le
drame sur l'Yser*, pp. 62–63.

102 "It produces . . . stare.": Quoted K.
Coleman, *A History of Chemical Warfare*,
p. 18.

102 "wriggling . . . throats . . . Look . . . for
them.": Private W. A. Quinton, IWM/
(D)/4205.

103 "absolutely in rout . . . ambulances . . .
away . . . tearing . . . agonies.": Lieut.
Col. Morrison, quoted Dancocks,
Welcome to Flanders Fields, p. 161–62.

103 "running . . . distressing.": Quoted,
McWilliams and Steel, *Gas!*, p. 55.

104 "what . . . bayonets made.": Quoted D.
Dancocks, *Welcome to Flanders Fields*, p.
177.

104 "like hailstones . . . roof.": *With the First
Canadian Contingent*, p. 87.

104–105 "dreadful . . . conflict . . . We
fought . . . rear.": *New York Times*, May
8, 1915.

106 "No ground . . . itself.": *British Official
History*, quoted Moore, *Gas Attack!*, p.
36.

106 "the infantry . . . losses.": War Diary,
German Twenty-third Reserve Corps
quoted ibid., p. 37.

CHAPTER TEN—"THIS FILTHY LOATHSOME PESTILENCE"

107 "in the ditch . . . trench.": Quoted A.
Iarocci, *Shoestring Soldiers: The 1st
Canadian Division at War, 1914–15*, p.
137.

107 "powerful . . . effect . . . as a temporary . . . handkerchiefs.": Quoted Moore,
Gas Attack!, p. 37.

107–108 "I don't mind . . . again!": A. J.
Bromfield, IWM/(D)/4038.

108 "men . . . parapet . . . much like . . .
green gas.": Quoted D. Dancocks,
Welcome to Flanders Fields, p. 223.

107 "red stars . . . quite . . . sight . . . our gaze . . . of us.": Lieut. H. F. Maxwell-Scott, IWM/(D)/7200.

108 "a heavy . . . came.": Quoted McWilliams and Steel, *Gas!*, p. 104.

108 "Captain McLaren . . . breath.": Lieut. H. F. Maxwell-Scott, IWM/(D)/7200.

108 "barely conscious . . . coaxed . . . pushed": Ibid.

108 "managed . . . rum . . . the enemy . . . concussion!": Lance Corporal J. Keddie, quoted Lyn Macdonald, *1915*, p. 222.

109 "all hell . . . high explosive . . . helped . . . strings . . . saliva . . . Some . . . lips.": Quoted, McWilliams and Steel, *Gas!*, pp 105–6.

109 "a fiery steed . . . difficulty.": Ibid., p. 111.

109 "started . . . of us.": Ibid., p. 122.

110 "with some . . . clothing.": War diary, Tenth Battalion quoted Dancocks, *Welcome to Flanders Fields*, p. 249.

110 "encountered . . . slowly.": official German account quoted Dancocks, *Welcome to Flanders Fields*, p. 282.

110 "adventure . . . The Cloth Hall . . . imagine.": Sergeant Cyril Lee quoted Arthur, *Forgotten Voices of the Great War*, p. 81.

110 "a whirling . . . flames.": Lieut. Bruce Bairnsfather quoted McWilliams and Steel, *Gas!*, p.159.

110 "that the men . . . heat . . . a terrible . . . desolation.": Trooper Stanley Down quoted Arthur, *Forgotten Voices of the Great War*, p. 86.

110 "Dante . . . Ypres.": Quoted A. Iarocci, *Shoestring Soldiers*, p. 136.

111 "a huge effort . . . rear.": P. Whitehouse, IWM/(D)/13108.

111–112 "the effects . . . yellow.": R. Binding, *A Fatalist at War*, p. 64.

112 "**Versuch**": F. L. Haber (son of Fritz Haber), *The Poisonous Cloud*, p. 34.

112 "Had we . . . Ypres.": Deimling, *Aus der alten in die neue Zeit*, p. 203.

112 "proudly . . . outfit.' ": Otto Lumitsch, *Memoir of Haber*, July/August 1955, MPG,Va5/HC/1480.

112 "the fact . . . suicide.": James Franck's memories of the Habers, April 1958, MPG, Va5 1449.

112 "despair . . . animals.": Quoted Charles, *Between Genius and Genocide*, p. 166.

112–113 "the words . . . I suffer.": Haber's letter of June 12, 1915, MPG,Va5/HC/856.

113 A lurid account of Clara Haber discovering her husband with Charlotte Nathan (who would become Haber's second wife) is on MPG, Va5/HC/260.

113 "to give . . . comrades.": Quoted Charles, *Between Genius and Genocide*, p. 171.

113 "to imagine defeat.": F. Haber, *Funf Vortraege*, p. 36.

113 "psychological imponderables . . . from being . . . people . . . more . . . destruction.": Ibid.

113–114 The Allies . . . asphyxiation.": Quotes in this paragraph are from Haldane's letter of April 27,1915, to Lord Kitchener reprinted in the *Guardian*, April 29, 1915.

114 "have prevented . . . line . . . the gaseous . . . warfare": *New York Tribune*, April 25, 1915.

114 "the terrors . . . gas . . . the seeming . . . battle . . . coldly . . . undismayed.": *Windsor Evening Record*.

114 "Prehistoric Methods.": *Bassano Mail*, June 1, 1915.

114–115 "burned down . . . warning . . . effects . . . murderous": *Le Matin*, April 27, 1915.

115 "the whole . . . combine . . . turned . . . barbarity . . . had the monopoly . . . respected . . . signed.": *La Croix*,

116 "The Germans . . . beforehand . . . atrocious . . . name.": *Times*, April 29, 1915.

116 "I had . . . murder.": trooper in the Fourth Dragoon Guards quoted L. James, *Warrior Race*, p. 478.

116–117 "The disapproval . . . weapons . . . smoke . . . acid": F. Haber, *Funf Vortraege*, p. 34.

117 "Apparently . . . troops.": Sir John French's report of April 23, 1915, WO 142/240.

117 "contrary . . . war . . . of the degraded Germans": Lord Kitchener, April 24, 1915, WO 142–240.

117 "on the recent . . . gases . . . As the . . . Convention.": CAB 37/127/40.

118 "A face . . . the pad": *Times*, April 28, 1915.

118 "You can't . . . retire . . . We'd had . . . towards Ypres.": Sergeant Jack Dorgan, Arthur, *Forgotten Voices of the Great War*, p. 82.

118 "make . . . push . . . the area . . . shell-fire.": Quoted A. J . Smithers, *The Man Who Disobeyed*, p. 253.

118 "had abundance . . . troops . . . vigorously . . . the French.": Quoted Dancocks, *Welcome to Flanders Fields*, p. 322.

118 "command . . . about Ypres": Quoted Smithers, *The Man Who Disobeyed* , p. 257.

118 "in . . . agreement . . . as to . . . done.": Quoted Moore, *Gas Attack!*, p. 49.

119 "what . . . death trap.": General Sir Douglas Haig's diary, April 30, 1915, given in Private Papers of Douglas Haig 1914–19, p. 92.

119 "Clean killing . . . comprehensible . . . but . . . the hill.": Quoted Moore, *Gas Attack!*, p. 51.

CHAPTER ELEVEN—"SOLOMON"S TEMPLE"

Because this book is for the general reader, I have not given sources for each individual quote from passengers and crew of the *Lusitania* and others in this and the three subsequent chapters—twelve, thirteen, and fourteen—except where it is unclear who is speaking or where the quote is significant for understanding what happened.

However, the main sources for those whose words are not always referenced are given below. Full details of the sources are in the bibliography.

Passengers:

Oliver Bernard: Account in his book *Cocksparrow*; articles in the *Royal Magazine*, September 1915 and *Current Opinion*; correspondence in the Imperial War Museum.

Charles Bowring: Mayer (T).

Norah Bretherton: NARA.

Avis Dolphin (married name Foley): BBC; Mariners' Museum, Newport News.

Elizabeth Duckworth: Imperial War Museum; Mariners' Museum, Newport News(personal account and letters from son-in-law).

Mabel Henshaw: CBC interview.

Ian Holbourn: Mariners' Museum, Newport News (letter from wife) and account in his book *The Isle of Foula*.

Charles Lauriat: Account in his book *The "Lusitania's" Last Voyage* and Mayer (T).

Ethel Lines: Mariners' Museum, Newport News.

Florence Padley: Mariners' Museum, Newport News.

Amy Pearl: NARA.

Audrey Pearl: Author's interview.

Major Warren Pearl: NARA.

Theodate Pope: Mariners' Museum, Newport News.

Charlotte Pye: CBC interview.

Viscountess Rhondda (Lady Mackworth): Mariners' Museum, Newport News; her article in the *Spectator*, May 5, 1928; account in her book *This Was My World*.

Crew:

R. Clark: BBC interview.

Ben Holton: BBC interview.

Hugh Johnston: BBC interview, Mersey (TO) and Mariners' Museum, Newport News.

Leslie Morton: BBC interview; Mariners' Museum, Newport News and Mersey (T); account in his book *The Long Wake*.

George Wynne: BBC interview.

121 "The fact is . . . can get near her.": *New York World*, May 2, 1915.

121 "mighty good care . . . nothing to fear.": *New York Times*, May 2, 1915.

"1 May . . . 8 May": information dated April 26, 1915, Germany Military Archive Freiburg, RM2/1962. (In German: "1. Mai: D. Lusitania, englisch, 30,396 R. T. nach Liverpool, an etwa 8 Mai.)

124 "Large English . . . warships.": War diary of H. Bauer, German Military Archive, Freiburg.

124–125 "When . . . to it.": J. Spiess quoted in L. Thomas, *Raiders of the Deep*, p. 89.

125 "enough to give you a headache . . . over.": J. Spiess quoted in ibid., p. 29.

125 "the real pirates of old days.": Quoted K.

Neureuther and C. Bergen, *U-Boat Stories*, p. 17.

125 "the moisture . . . sleeper.": J. Spiess quoted in Compton-Hall, *Submarine Boats*, p. 176.

125–126 **"In the dim glow . . . the commander.":** Quoted Neureuther and Bergen, *U-Boat Stories*, p. 12.

126 "foaming masses . . . more calm.": Ibid., p. 13.

126 "the magical green light": Ibid.

126 "stare . . . in the turret.": Forstner, *Journal*, p. 16.

126 "infernal . . . water.": Quoted Neureuther and Bergen, *U-Boat Stories*, p. 13.

126 "peculiar thrill and nervous sensation": Quoted Thomas, *Raiders of the Deep*, p. 12.

126 "a gigantic mouse-trap.": Quoted Neureuther and Bergen, *U-Boat Stories*, p. 55.

126–127 "A burst . . . witness.": Ibid., p. 145.

127 "death . . . conjure.": J. Spiess quoted in Thomas, *Raiders of the Deep*, p. 11.

128 "advisedly simpler.": *Engineering*, July 19, 1907.

129 "lavish . . . British.": The Cunard *Daily Bulletin* is in the Cunard archive.

130 "looked about . . . any incident.": Letter from O. Hanson to A. A. Hoehling, June 13, 1955, Mariners' Museum, Newport News.

131 A copy of the manifest and "Supplemental Manifest" are in the Franklin D. Roosevelt Presidential Library in New York.

131 "practically all . . . some kind": Letter from A. J. Peters, Treasury Department, to R. Lansing, May 8, 1915, NARA.

132 "the ship . . . sunk.": Evidence of A. Booth Wynne (T).

132 The quote from the *Times* about the warning is from the edition of May 3, 1915.

133 **"The reference . . . and fast as the *Lusitania*.":** Frost, *German Submarine Warfare*, p.186.

133 The rumor that the stowaways were German spies is included in the sworn statement of C. T. Hill made in Queenstown to Frost on May 10, 1915, NARA.

133–134 By May 5 . . . fired upon": The quotes in these two paragraphs are from the *U-20*'s war diary, German Military Archive, Freiburg.

134 The timing of the receipt of information about the sinking of the *Candidate* is in file ADM 187/1058, as are the signals sent to the *Lusitania.*

134–135 **The war diary . . . unobserved.** The quotes in this paragraph are from the *U-20*'s war diary, German Military Archive, Freiburg.

135 Vice Admiral Coke describes sending the messages in a report of 1915, in file ADM 137/113.

135 "To all . . . Fastnet.": file ADM 137/1058.

135 "bloody monkeys.": Letter from A. Bestic to A. A. Hoehling, June 10, 1955, Mariners' Museum, Newport News.

136 May Barwell's message is in file ADM 187/1058.

136 "on entering the war zone . . . Royal Navy": NARA.

136 "of course . . . alarm.": Quoted in Hickey and Smith, *Seven Days to Disaster*, p.155.

136 Smoking was still considered very much a male pleasure. It was only seven years since the O'Sullivan Ordinance had forbidden women in New York City to smoke in public.

CHAPTER TWELVE—"THEY GOT US THIS TIME, ALL RIGHT"

138 The QUESTOR/WESTRONA exchange and the other messages are in file ADM 137/1058.

138–139 The description of the precautions taken by Captain Turner are from his evidence to Lord Mersey in 1915 and to Commissioner Wynne in 1917.

139 "for ships . . . the water": Evidence of Neil Robertson to Wynne.

139 "You could catch . . . submarines around.": Interview given by Quartermaster Hugh Johnston to BBC.

139 The description of Sir Alfred Booth's thoughts and actions comes from his evidence to Wynne.

140 The description of Colonel House's activities on the morning of May 7, 1915,

comes from his diary, Yale University, New Haven, Connecticut.

140   "submarines . . . at ten a.m.": file ADM 187/1058.

141   The principles of the four-point bearing are well explained in a footnote to an article by P. B. Ryan in the *American Neptune* (vol. 35, 1975). He states that a "point" equals 11/4 degrees. A navigator can obtain his position by the four-point, or "bow and beam," method. When a particular landmark is four points (or forty-five degrees) on the bow, a navigator takes a bearing and plots it on his chart. The ship must then maintain a steady course and speed until the landmark is broad on the beam (eight points or ninety degrees). A second bearing is then taken and plotted, effectively forming an isosceles triangle. The ship's distance to the landmark is equal to the distance traveled by the ship between observations.

141   "unusually . . . beautiful weather.": From the *U-20*'s war diary, RM97/578, German Military Archive, Freiburg.

141–142   Hermann Lepper, on watch that day, described what happened in an interview with the *Bochumer Anzeiger* on February 21, 1985.

141   "forest of masts and stacks . . . over the horizon.": Schwieger, quoted Thomas, *Raiders of the Deep*, p. 97.

141–142   "When the steamer . . . attack her . . . at that . . . we waited.": Ibid.

143   "like the banging . . . day . . . a kind of a rumble": Turner's evidence to Wynne.

143   "we couldn't see . . . a while: Interview given by Quartermaster Hugh Johnston to BBC.

143   "hard-a-starboard the helm": Evidence of Hugh Johnston, Mersey (TO).

143   "keep her head into Kinsale.": Deposition of Hugh Johnston, May 12, 1915, file ADM 137/1058.

143   "hard-a-starboard": Evidence of Hugh Johnston, Mersey (TO).

143   "My God": Hugh Johnston's interview with the BBC.

143   come . . . Old Kinsale . . . 10 miles . . . Kinsale: Evidence of Radio Officer R. Leith, Mersey (TO).

144   "in a rocking motion . . . over and over and over": Evidence of Mr. Duncan, Senior Third Engineer, Mayer (T).

145–146   "Clean bow shot . . . by the bow.": From the *U-20*'s war diary, RM97/578, German Military Archive, Freiburg.

148   "trying . . . children everywhere.": Quoted by J. Lawrence in an article in the *Coronet*, March 1950.

148   "Find all the kiddies . . . boy . . . dashed . . . time.": Quoted A. Hurd, *Murder at Sea*, p. 10.

149   "Why fear . . . us.": Quoted F. D. Ellis, *The Tragedy of the Lusitania*, pp. 38–39.

149   Up in the wheelhouse . . . bridge: All the quotes in this paragraph are from Quartermaster H. Johnston's interview with the BBC or from his letter to A. A. Hoehling of September 25, 1955.

150   "was crowded . . . water": J. McFarquhar, NARA.

150   "agonising . . . afloat.": Bernard, *Current Opinion.*

150   "mighty . . . whisper": Interview given by bellboy Ben Holton to BBC.

CHAPTER THIRTEEN—"WILFUL AND WHOLESALE MURDER"

152   "swooped . . . eyes out.": Letter from N. Turner, Captain Turner's son to A. A. Hoehling, July 9, 1955, Mariners' Museum, Newport News.

152   "flung . . . arm": *New York Tribune*, May 9, 1915.

152   U.S. consul . . . survivors: The quotations in this paragraph are from Frost, *German Submarine Warfare*, p. 187 and from his report to the U.S. State Department, May 11, 1915, NARA.

153   "as hard . . . we're there.' ": *Cork Examiner*, May 18 1915.

153   "a perfectly blank expression": Lauriat, *The "Lusitania's" Last Voyage*, p. 34.

155   At the Cunard wharf . . . husband.: Frost, *German Submarine Warfare*, p. 211.

155   company . . . not accounted for: Note from U.S. State Department to W. Frost, NARA.

156   "We shall be at war . . . within a month.": B. J. Hendrick, *The Life and*

Letters of Walter Hines Page, vol. 2, p. 2.

156 "piles . . . wharves.": Frost, *German Submarine* Warfare, p. 212.

157 The account of the Kinsale inquest is taken from the transcript of the "Proceedings of Coroner John J. Horgan's Inquisition into the Death of Captain R. Matthews as a Result of the Sinking of R.M.S. Lusitania," May 1915, in the Imperial War Museum, supplemented by reports in the *Times* weekly edition of May 14, 1915, and in the *Cork Examiner* of May 10, 1915. Coroner Horgan later joined the Coast Patrol Service to help in "bringing the criminals to justice" for the sinking of the *Lusitania*.

158 The telegram requesting the stopping of the inquest was sent by Captain Webb and is in file ADM 137/113.

159 "as belated . . . against attack.": J. J. Horgan, *Parnell to Pearse*, p. 275.

CHAPTER FOURTEEN—"TOO PROUD TO FIGHT"

160 "extraordinary success": *Frankfurter Zeitung*.

160 "hundreds . . . lines.": *Neue Preussische Zeitung*, May 10, 1915.

160 "citizens . . . shield.": *Kolnische Volkszeitung*, May 8, 1915.

161 "great joy": Telegram of 9 May 1915, RM 5/2981. German Military Archive, Freiburg.

161 The decoded translations of the German signals are in file ADM 137/4353 and ADM 187/1859.

162 hunt . . . swine: P. Q. asked by J. King, MP. May 19, 1915.

162 "When . . . fists . . . a mad . . . stolen.": Mr. Greenwood, IWM/(S)/4118.

162 The story of the two Americans joining in the rioting in Liverpool is from the *New York Times*, May 25, 1915.

163 "the German's divorce . . . complete": *Chatillonais et Auxois*, May 13, 1915.

163 "Criminal . . . devilish": *Telegraaf*, quoted in the *Observer*, May 9, 1915.

163 "the news . . . hate.": *Morgenblad*, May 8, 1915, quoted in the *Times* of May 10, 1915.

163 The full text of the House of Commons

debate is given in *Hansard*, May 10, 1915, columns 1859–63.

163–165 Captain Webb's memorandum of May 12, 1915, and Fisher's and Churchill's comments are in file ADM 137/1058.

165 "greatly in excess": Quoted in Hough, *First Sea Lord*, p. 336.

165 "I am off . . . questionings.": Fisher to Churchill, May 15, 1915, Marder, *Fear God and Dread Nought*, vol. 3, p. 228.

165–166 "guarantee . . . menace . . . Mr. Winston . . . me . . . absolutely . . . sea forces whatsoever": Fisher to Asquith, May 19, 1915, ibid., p. 241.

166 "extraordinary ultimatum . . . mental aberration.": Quoted in Marder, *From the Dreadnought to Scapa Flow*, vol. 2, p. 285. Admiral "Jackie" Fisher's life continued to run along its eccentric groove. After his resignation, rather than live with his wife, he had moved in with the Duchess of Hamilton, to whom he was close, and her husband. He spent his remaining years writing peppery and disjointed memoirs, dying in 1920.

166–167 In line with . . . Vanderbilt.: The documents and quotations in these four paragraphs are all in ADM 116/1416.

167 Among the informal statements from the Ministry of Defence is one to P. Beesly, Imperial War Museum archives.

168 In addition to . . . "only one.": The few sworn crew statements that survive are in ADM 187/1058. The quotation from H. Johnston is from his BBC interview.

168 "I have . . . abaft the bridge.": Letter from O. Bernard to Mrs. Prichard, August 15, 1915, Imperial War Museum.

169 "tears in his eyes": J. P. Tumulty, *Woodrow Wilson as I Know Him*, p. 232.

169–170 "see red . . . horrible a thing?": Ibid.

170 "America . . . lives.": Colonel House to President Wilson, May 9, 1915, in Link, *The Papers of Woodrow Wilson*, vol. 33, p. 184.

170 "the sinking . . . European respect": R. Gregory, *Walter Hines Page*, p. 96. Link, *The Papers of Woodrow Wilson*, vol. 33, p 129.

170 "the greatest . . . history . . .

immediate . . . vigour": *Literary Digest*, May 22, 1915.

170 "as insincere . . . Presidency.": Quoted Macmillan, *Peacemakers*, p. 16.

170 "the ruthless . . . neutrals": Link, *The Papers of Woodrow Wilson*, vol. 33, p. 151.

170 "because . . . withdraw from it.": Tumulty, *Woodrow Wilson as I Know Him*, p. 233.

170 "It would be . . . in front of an Army": W. Bryan to President Wilson, May 9, 1915. Bryan Correspondence, Library of Congress.

171 "As our main interest . . . guarded": Telegram from C. Spring-Rice to Foreign Office. May 9, 1915, in FO 115/1998.

171 "when . . . *love you*.": President Wilson to Edith Bolling Galt, in Link, *The Papers of Woodrow Wilson*, vol. 33, pp. 146–47.

171 The quotation from President Wilson's Philadelphia speech is in ibid., vol. 33, p.149.

171 "President . . . infamy": Quoted Ricard, *A Companion to Theodore Roosevelt*, p, 475.

171 "expressing . . . special matter.": Link, *The Papers of Woodrow Wilson*, p.154.

171–172 "I just . . . whirl.": May 11, 1915, ibid., pp. 160–61.

172 "deepest sympathy . . . ram submarines": The text of the German note is in *Foreign Relations of the U.S. 1915 Supplement*, part 2, p. 389.

172 During . . . reoccurrence: The text of the first American note to Germany is in *Foreign Relations of the U.S. 1915 Supplement*, part 2, pp. 393–96.

173 "England's . . . humanity.": President Wilson to W. Bryan, June 2, 1915, quoted Tansill, *America Goes to War*, p. 238.

173 "all the red blood . . . ask": *Baltimore Sun*, May 15, 1915.

173–174 "In view of . . . massacres.": Quoted Willis, *Prologue to Nuremberg*, p. 26. (Armenians consider the genocide of their people began on the night of April 23–24, 1915, with the arrest of 235 leading members of their community in Constantinople.)

174 "the necessity . . . neutrals.": Müller's diary for May 27, 1915, quoted in his book *Regierte der Kaiser?*

174 The text of Germany's response, which was dated May 28, 1915, and arrived in Washington on May 31, is given in *Foreign Relations of the U.S. 1915 Supplement*, part 2, pp. 419–21.

175 "more neutral powers . . . war.": Official report of May 31, 1915, cited in Admiral A. Spindler's *Der Handelskrieg mit U-Booten*, vol. 2. p. 101.

175 "which would be . . . people.": Ibid.

175 "which would take . . . account": Ibid.

175 The text of the orders is in RM 2/1982, German Military Archive, Freiburg.

175–176 President Wilson . . . wrote out his resignation.: The quotations in these five paragraphs about the cabinet meeting and subsequent events are from Seymour, *The Intimate Papers of Colonel House*, vol. 2, pp. 5–6 and from W. G. McAdoo's *Crowded Years*, pp. 330–36. Wilson's comments to Edith Galt are quoted in K. Marton, *Hidden Power*, p. 18.

176 The text of the second American note to Germany is in *Foreign Relations of the U.S.1915 Supplement*, part 2, pp. 436–38.

177 "executioner . . . avoid 'em!": Quoted in Gregory, *Walter Hines Page*, pp. 102–3.

CHAPTER FIFTEEN—"THE VERY EARTH SHOOK"

178 "quaint . . . tacit understanding": Quoted Dudley, *Monsters of the Purple Twilight*, p. 42.

179 "a keen . . . carrier pigeons": Ibid., p. 72.

180 "to exist . . . nerves . . . the demands . . . propeller.": Ibid., p. 46.

181 "a swallow of cognac": Ibid., p. 45.

181 "The aerial sea . . . allow for.": Quoted R. P. Hearne, *Zeppelins and Super-Zeppelins*, p. 60.

181 "an unfailing . . . alive.": Quoted Dudley, *Monsters*, p. 77.

182 "You . . . German.": Poolman, *Zeppelins over England*, p. 42.

182 "suddenly . . . undamaged? . . . for a . . .fish.": Linnarz's briefing of American war correspondents in Germany, quoted Dudley, *Monsters*, pp. 44–46.

182 E. Oak-Rhind's observations are in IWM/ (D)/14972.

182 "At high . . . city": Quoted Dudley,
   Monsters, p. 47.
182 "little . . . city.": Quoted H. G. Castle,
   Fire over England, p. 59.
182 "London . . . surprise.": Quoted W.
   Cross, *Zeppelins of World War 1*, p. 27.
182–183 "ready . . . overboard . . . 'Let
   go! . . . 'live.' ": Quoted Dudley,
   Monsters, pp. 46–47.
183 "one of . . . district.": Quoted *The
   London Encyclopaedia*, p. 398.
183–184 "a terrible . . . wind . . . Fire . . .
   The Germans are here . . . the sound . . .
   air . . . a mass. . . flames": All quotes I.
   Castle, op. cit., p. 20.
184 "the Eldorado . . . poor.": *The London
   Encyclopaedia*, p. 955.
185 "huge . . . with it!": S. Pankhurst, *The
   Home Front*, pp. 191–92.
185 "searchlights . . . around . . . storm . . .
   shrapnel . . . still . . . darkness": Dudley,
   Monsters, p. 47.
185 "Much as . . . journeys.": Quoted R. P.
   Hearne, *Zeppelins and Super-Zeppelins*,
   p. 63.
186 "Zeppelins . . . collated.": Quoted H. G.
   Castle, *Fire over England*, p. 63.
187–187 "The press . . .published.":
   Admiralty communiqué, Quoted Dudley,
   Monsters, p. 53.
187 "In amplification . . .throughout.": *Times*,
   June 1, 1915.
187 "We last . . . Ludwigshafen: *Guardian*,
   June 2, 1915.
187–188 "the explosives . . . Germans": Ibid.
188 "an angry . . . police.": V. McArdell,
   IWM/(D)/15933.
188 "well-dressed . . . world": Pankhurst, *The
   Home Front*, p. 193.
188 "the baby killers.": Quoted H. G. Castle,
   Fire over England, p. 67.
188–189 "It was . . . villages . . . large . . .
   heavy . . . from suffocation . . . force . . .
   bore . . . Essen.": *Times*, June 3, 1915.
189 "This last week . . . Ypres.": Mrs. K.
   Moore, IWM/(D)/12869.
189 "What a terrible . . . murderers!": J. C.
   Kennedy, IWM/(D)/15070.
189–190 "When offered . . . Berlin.": P. M.
   Yearsley, IWM/(D)/12053.
190 "the heart . . . world.": Quoted Poolman,
   Zeppelins over England, p. 11.

190 "England . . . envy them.": Ibid., p. 42.
190–191 "the War Office . . . impossibility.":
   R. F. Harrison IWM/(D)/982.
191 "all exploded . . . tank.": Quoted Captain
   J. Roberts, *The German Air Raids on
   Great Britain*, 1914–18, p. 19.
191 Wilson was a gifted steeplechase jockey
   who would win the Grand National in
   1925.
192 "we breathed . . . flier.": Quoted Dudley,
   Monsters, p. 63.
192 "When I was . . . explosion.": Ibid.,
   p. 64.
192–193 "a hit . . . the ship . . . black.": Ibid.,
   p. 65.
193 Warneford's full battle report can be
   found on www.militarian.com.
193 "to attack . . . possible according to
   choice.": I. Castle, London 1915–17 p.
   25.
194 "a drapery . . . houses.": Quoted H. G.
   Castle, *Fire over England*, p. 75.
194 "There was . . . Warneford": Quoted
   Gilbert, *The First World War*, p. 171.
195 "great number . . . furnaces": Quoted
   Roberts, *The German Air Raids on Great
   Britain*, p. 42.

CHAPTER SIXTEEN—"ORDER,
COUNTER-ORDER, DISORDER!"
   All quotes in the section about the
   Mersey Inquiry sessions are from the
   transcripts of either the open or the
   closed hearings unless otherwise
   indicated below. The Mersey Report was
   published on July 17, 1915.
197 "to think or speak": Letter from Captain
   Turner to Miss Bryant, June 10, 1915,
   Cunard archives.
199 When Lord Mersey . . . "glad to see
   you.": All quotations in this paragraph
   come from file ADM 116/1416. The
   Admiralty reply to Lord Mersey making
   the offer of a meeting with Balfour is
   dated June 30, 1915.
199–200 Whether Lord Mersey . . .
   "committed the crime.": All quotations
   in these two paragraphs are from Lord
   Mersey's report.
200 The texts of the second German note and
   third American note are in FO/115 1998

and also given in *Foreign Relations of the U.S. 1915 Supplement*, part 2, pp. 480–82.

201 The kaiser's furious notes are quoted in Link, *Woodrow Wilson—The Struggle for Neutrality*, p. 449.

201 "Order . . . disorder!": Von Tirpitz, *My Memoirs*, vol. 2, p. 416.

201 Bachmann's inquiry about the definition of a passenger ship is in his note of September 3 to the kaiser, RM 2/1992, German Military Archive, Freiburg.

201 Tirpitz's complaint about instructions is in his telegram of September 2, 1915, RM 2/1992, German Military Archive, Freiburg.

202 "unlimited money . . . *My business only*": Quoted in Clark, *Kaiser Wilhelm II*, p. 232.

202 The copy of the war diary of the *U-20* for the patrol of August 29 to September 15, 1915, in the German Military Archive, Freiburg, records the sinking of the *Hesperian.*

203 Schwieger's letter to Bauer, dated September 21, 1915, is in RM 97/384, German Military Archive, Freiburg.

CHAPTER SEVENTEEN—"A GIFT OF LOVE"

204 "maximum . . . enemy": Quoted Roberts, *The German Air Raids on Great Britain*, p. 45.

205 "really effective . . . possible.": Quoted D. H. Robinson, *The Zeppelin in Combat, 1912–18*, pp. 95–96.

205 "remain . . . city.": Quoted Roberts, *The German Air Raids on Great Britain*, p. 46.

205–206 "Our great . . . of her.": C. G. Lawson, IWM/(D)/7834.

206 "lightning . . . by fire.": Quoted Roberts, *The German Air Raids on Great Britain*, pp. 48–49.

206 "between Blackfriars . . . bridges.": Quoted H. G. Castle, *Fire over England*, p. 82.

207 "with a malicious intent to destroy": Quoted C. Moorehead, *Dunant's Dream*, p. 23.

208 "I have lived . . . war again.": Miss K. Bannerman, IWM/(D)/10775.

208 "lit as in peacetime": Quoted Robinson, *The Zeppelin in Combat*, p. 107.

209 "The explosive effect . . . crater": Quoted H. G. Castle, *Fire over England*, p. 85.

209 "blown to pieces": Quoted I. Castle, *London 1914–17— The Zeppelin Menace*, p. 36.

209 "suddenly . . . rest of us.": E. Tregellis, IWM/(D)/16679.

209–210 "the Zeppelin . . . patients.": M. Rattray, IWM/(D)/8196.

210 "a wonderful . . . sky.": Name unknown, IWM/(D)/15933.

210 "Good God! It's staggering": Shepherd quoted I. Castle, *London 1914–17*, p. 37.

210 "All firing . . . short . . . Ideas . . . wild": Ibid., p. 36.

210–211 Shepherd . . . centuries": Quotes in this paragraph are from Poolman, *Zeppelins over England*, p. 65, and Dudley, *Monsters*, p. 83.

211 "A streak . . . sight.": Alfred Grosch, quoted I. Castle, *London 1914–17*, p. 37.

211 "For a few . . . the sky.": Quoted H. G. Castle, *Fire over England*, p. 85.

211 "Manoeuvring . . . damage.": Quoted Poolman, *Zeppelins over England*, p. 62.

212 "much rather . . . killed.": *New York World Magazine*, 1915.

212 "I don't . . . again!": C. G. Lawson, IWM/(D)/ 7834.

212 "lifted up . . . London": L. MacKinlay, IMW(D)/15933.

212 "Murder by Zeppelin": Quoted Poolman, *Zeppelins over England*, p. 66.

213 "As to . . . need be.": Ibid., pp. 49 and 111.

CHAPTER EIGHTEEN—"DO YOU KNOW ANYTHING ABOUT GAS?"

214 "All night . . . disease.": Lieut. P. W. James quoted W. Moore, *Gas Attack!*, p. 52.

214 "men lying . . . dying . . . nothing . . . thing.": Ibid., pp. 52–53.

215 "His Majesty's . . . practice.": Parliamentary Debates, Lords, vol. 18 (1915) cols. 1017–18.

215 "public opinion . . . retaliate.": War Cabinet Meeting, November 16, 1932, 14, CAB 23/73.

215 ""Do you . . . to do": C. Foulkes, *Gas!
The Story of the Special Brigade*, p. 17.
215 "which were . . . things.": C. Foulkes, op.
cit., p, 20.
216 "the production . . . clouds.": C. Foulkes,
op. cit., p. 39.
216 "were told . . . advanced.": Lieut. C. A.
Ashley, IWM/(D)/3609.
216 "an attack . . . gas.": Ibid.
216 "I gave . . . done it.": C. Foulkes, op. cit.,
p. 57.
216 "did not . . . explosives.": Lieut. C. A.
Ashley, IWM/(D)/3609.
216 "were to . . . infantry.": Ibid.
217 "I was . . . smoke.": Carey/ IWM/
(D)/4050.
217 "as the conditions . . . permitted.": C.
Foulkes, op. cit., p. 64.
218 "oojahs": Harris and Paxman, *A Higher
Form of Killing*, p. 11.
218 "did . . . carrying.": Lieut. C. A. Ashley,
IWM(D) 3609.
218 "walked . . . chess.": Ibid.
218 "At one . . . troops!": Haig's Diary,
Private Papers of Douglas Haig, p. 104.
218 "after the . . . started . . . We were . . .
behind it.": Ibid.
219 "the men . . . chemicals": Ibid.
219 "one man . . . at them.": Lieut. C. A.
Ashley, IWM/(D)/3609.
219 "great . . . leaks . . . slowly . . . rain) . . .
at about . . . used.": Lieut. A. B. White,
quoted Macdonald, *1915*, pp. 502–3.
219 "the gas . . . lines.": Quoted Harris and
Paxman, *A Higher Form of Killing*, p. 14.
220 "blue . . . death.": Ibid., p. 15.
220 "met with . . . units.": Quoted K.
Coleman, *A History of Chemical Warfare*,
p. 24.
220 "Behind . . . devils.": C. Foulkes, op. cit.,
p. 80.
220 "The artillery . . . success.": Lieut. C. A.
Ashley, IWM/(D)/3609.
220 "gas . . . mouldy.": Sgt. F. M. Packham
quoted Macdonald, *1915*, p. 507.

CHAPTER NINETEEN—"ZEPP AND
A PORTION OF CLOUDS"
221 "I was . . . Palace.": Quoted H. G. Castle,
Fire over England, p. 91.
222 "thing . . . night.": Quoted I. Castle,
London 1914–1917 , p. 42.
222 "during . . . potatoes.": G. Davies,
IWM/1(D)/15933 (Collection of letters).
223 "as pretty . . . done it.": Quoted H. G.
Castle, *Fire over England*, pp. 91–92.
223 "indescribably . . . below.": Breithaupt's
account, *Living Age*, January 1928.
quoted I. Castle, *London 1914–17*,
p. 44.
223 "right . . . another.": Quoted I. Castle,
London 1914–17, p. 42.
224 Slessor later became Marshal of the Royal
Air Force Sir John Slessor.
224 "The lights . . . London . . . streams . . .
myself.": J. Slessor, *The Central Blue*, pp.
12–13.
224 "handsome . . . trains.": *London Society*,
1882.
225 "seem to . . . population.": C. G. Lawson/
IWM/(D)/7834.
225 "The kind . . . stop . . . all knew . . .
vengeance . . . a declared . . . cities . . . a
fleet . . . warfare . . . roughly . . .
ejected . . . Let us . . . Christianity":
Guardian, October 15, 1915.
226 "Have . . . aircraft . . . Is the . . . streets?":
Hansard for these and related PQs.
226 "I must . . . red-tapism.": Scott's minute
of October 18, 1915, quoted H. G. Castle,
Fire over England, p. 95.

CHAPTER TWENTY—"REMEMBER
THE *LUSITANIA*"
227 "I realise . . . anyone.": Quoted M.
Gilbert, *The First World War*, p. 202.
227 "Her execution . . . civilisation.": Quoted
on www.heritage-history.com,
"Frightfulness."
228 "to keep . . . forget.": Quoted in Bailey
and Ryan, *The Lusitania Disaster*, p. 267.
228 "What did . . . surprise": Quoted
Macmillan, *Peacemakers*, p. 16.
228–229 "Would the . . . war?": Seymour,
The Intimate Papers of Colonel House,
vol. 2, p. 88.
229 "profound regret . . . a suitable

indemnity.": The third and final German note is contained in C. Savage, *Policy of the United States Toward Maritime Commerce in War*, pp. 458–59.

229 "note after note . . . action.": Quoted in Richard, *A Companion to Theodore Roosevelt*, p. 477.

229 "every German . . . doing.": Defense attaché's report of May 18, 1915, archives of the U.S. Naval War College.

230 "indescribable . . . uniform.": Blucher, *An English Wife in Berlin*, pp. 120–21.

230 "Dear Old Tirps . . . Cheer . . . freezes.": Fisher's consoling letter was written on March 29 ,1916, and is reprinted in his *Memories*, p. 31.

230–231   "the Government . . . relations.": Quoted Bell, *A History of the Blockade of the Central Empires*, p. 594.

231 "impertinence": Quoted Massie, *Castles of Steel*, p. 551.

231 "no longer . . . law.": Gerard, *My Four Years in Germany*, p. 246.

232 Wilfred Owen wrote *Dulce et Decorum Est* in 1917.

232 "much nastier . . . started with.": IWM/(R)/24874.

233 "A good . . . countermeasures.": MPG, Va5 522.

233 "Some 30 . . . evening.": WO 142/99 (folder DGS/M/2—Report by Captain W. J. Adie, Royal Army Medical Corps).

234 "the victim . . . drowned.": Account of Lieutenant Safford, U.S. Marine Corps, given to *Sausalito News*, 1919.

234 The *Frankfurter Zeitung* report is in Foulkes, op. cit., p. 109.

234 "more than . . . attacks . . . our main . . . war": Foulkes, op. cit., p. 109.

234 "the effects . . . together.": *Daily Chronicle*, quoted ibid., p.127.

234 "ghoulish reasons . . . We were . . . time.": Foulkes, op. cit., p. 129.

234 "strong personal feeling . . . the sinking . . . *Lusitania*": Foulkes, op. cit., p. 169.

235 "on a large . . . apiece.": Ibid.

235 "volcanic . . . grenades.": Ibid., p. 200.

235 "many . . . poisoning . . . I can't . . . them.": Ibid., p. 191.

236 "We are . . . now . . . We have . . . will be.": Blucher, *An English Wife in Berlin*, p. 158.

236 "the massacres . . . point.": War Committee Notes, October 20, 2015, CAB 42/4/14.

237 "America . . . impunity.": Gerard, *My Four Years in Germany*, p. 246.

237 "the autumn of 1917 . . .": Quoted Massie, *Castles of Steel*, pp. 703–4.

237–238 "I pledge . . . 1917.": Ibid., p. 705.

238 "improve . . . battle.": General E. Ludendorff, *The General Staff and Its Problems*, vol. 1, p. 305.

238 "*Finis Germaniae*": Quoted Tuchman, *The Zimmermann Telegram*, p. 141.

238 "I order . . . Wilhelm I. R.": *Official German Documents*, vol. 2, p. 1210.

238 "Bernstorff . . . tonight.": Quoted Tuchman, *The Zimmermann Telegram*, p. 151.

238 "Make war . . . Arizona.": The text of the Zimmermann telegram is in *Official German Documents*, vol. 2, p. 1337.

239 "The present . . . birth.": Baker, *Woodrow Wilson—Life and Letters*, vol. 6, pp. 510–514 for Wilson's speech.

239 "No man . . . to him": Note by Eddie Bell on Admiralty staff, undated, Hall Collection, Churchill College Archives.

CHAPTER TWENTY-ONE—"EACH ONE MUST FIGHT ON TO THE END"

242 "freshly . . . horseradish.": Account of Lieutenant Safford, U.S. Marine Corps, given to *Sausalito News*, 1919.

242 "blisters . . . burns": Ibid.

242 "amazing success.": Transcript of Haber's meeting with representatives of the German chemical industry, May 15, 1918, MPG, Va5/HC/522.

242 Today a derivative of mustard gas is a prime component of some forms of chemotherapy used to treat cancer.

242 "congested and swollen . . . a few . . . substance.": Quoted Harris and Paxman, *A Higher Form of Killing*, p. 24.

242 "the incessant . . . coughing.": WO 142/99 report dated 7/22/1917.

242 "great . . . choke.": V. Brittain, *Testament of Youth*, p. 395.

242–243 "Our new . . . duds.": The two quotes in this paragraph are from F.

Richards, *Old Soldiers Never Die*, pp. 240 and 292.

243 "Was I . . . hard.": Corporal Ivor Watkins quoted Arthur, *Forgotten Voices of the Great War*, p. 262.

243 "would often . . . lard": Account of Lieutenant Safford, U.S. Marine Corps, given to *Sausalito News*, 1919.

243 "the reduction . . . million.": Quoted Harris and Paxman, *A Higher Form of Killing*, p. 27.

243 "There was . . . mules.": Sergeant Major Richard Tobin quoted Arthur, *Forgotten Voices of the Great War*, p. 243.

243–244 The U.S. commander of the first six destroyers, when wounded as a midshipman in the 1900 Boxer Rebellion, had found himself in the bed next to a severely wounded British captain called John Jellicoe, later the victor of Jutland in 1916.

244 "the oceans . . . bare.": Massie, *Castles of Steel*, quoting Doenitz, p. 733.

245 "an invention . . . hydrogen.": Quoted Major R. Fredette, *The First Battle of Britain*, 1917–18, p. 4.

245 "it caught . . . fell.": Quoted I. Castle, *London 1914–1917*, p. 68.

246 "poor devils": Civilian pacifist and organizer of women's trade unions, Helen Bowen Pease, IWM/(S)/821 (reel15).

246 "We shivered . . . unconscious.": Quoted *Midnight Raiders*, airspacemag.com.

246 "the day . . . London.": Quoted I. Castle, *London 1914–1917*, p. 85.

248 "head . . . gutter": Easdown and Genth, *A Glint in the Sky*, p. 100.

248 "disastrous results": French's letter to the War Office of June 5, H. A. Jones, *The War in the Air*, vol. 5, p. 25.

248 "The thundering . . . our lives": W. Aschoff, *Londonfluge 1917*, p. 37.

248 "the green . . . London.": Ibid., pp. 41–42.

248 "the blasts . . . scatter.": Ibid., p. 42.

249 "what looked . . . red.": *Evening News*, February 2, 1935.

249 "tongues of flame": Ibid.

249 "the continued . . . wounded.": Ibid.

249 "tremendous crash . . . the heart of England . . . a magnificent . . . sun.": *New York Times*, July 2, 1917.

249 "an elderly . . . dead . . . In a trench . . . barrow.": Siegfried Sassoon, *Memoirs of an Infantry Officer*, p. 250.

249 "the noise . . . voices.": Ivy Major, *Evening News*, January 31, 1935.

250 "driven . . . earth": Quoted Hyde, *The First Blitz*, p. 138.

250 "many of . . . we could.": *New York Times*, June 14, 1917.

250 "In the . . . people . . . It was . . . utmost strength.": Aschoff, *Londonflüge 1917*, p. 43.

250 "sated . . . flight . . . a great success.": Ibid., p. 48.

250 "blot out": *Times*, June 18, 1917.

250 "it would . . . execration.": *Times*, June 15, 1917.

251 "the English . . . London.": Quoted Hanson *First Blitz.*, p. 114.

251 "had made . . . his own . . . snugly . . . put out.": *Evening News*, March 11, 1935.

252 "aider and abettor . . . more deadly aeroplane": M. Macdonagh, *In London During the Great War*, p. 219.

253 "pitiful . . . cage.": *Evening News*, February 4, 1935.

253 "cracking . . . frequently.": Sir M. Campbell and J. W. Day, *Speed: The Authentic Life of Sir Malcolm Campbell*, p, 42.

253 "had been . . . posts.' ": M. Macdonagh op. cit., p. 258.

253–254 "a flash . . . raids came.": *Evening News*, March 4, 1935.

254 "a sound . . . crying.": *Evening News*, February 27, 1935.

255 "more disposed . . . peace.": Quoted Hanson, op. cit., p. 333.

255 "What I want . . . toy.": Quoted Budiansky, *Air Power*, p. 100.

255 "the panic . . . Cologne": AIR 1/460/15/312/99. (Report of British Consul General, Rotterdam, June 11, 1918.)

256 "I would . . . inaccuracy.": Quoted Strachan, *First World War (A New Illustrated History)*, p. 305.

256 "the Americans . . . scales.": Ibid., p. 283.

257 "a land . . . honey": Binding, *A Fatalist at War*, p. 208.

257 "There must . . . to the end": Quoted C. Barnett, *The Great War*, p. 172.

257 "kneel . . . democracy": Quoted Massie, *Castles of Steel*, p. 765.

257 "the black . . . army": Quoted Strachan, *The First World War (A New Illustrated History)*, p. 309.

258 "Whole bodies . . . the rest.": Quoted Barnett, *The Great War*, p. 183.

258 "Their aeroplanes . . . end.": H. Sulzbach, Ninth Division, German Army, Arthur, *Forgotten Voices of the Great War*, p. 292.

259 "a cup of . . . English tea.": Quoted Mcdonagh, *The Last Kaiser*, p. 419.

259 "The armistice . . . lost.": Quoted Arthur, *Forgotten Voices of the Great War*, p. 313.

CHAPTER TWENTY-TWO—"WEAPONS OF MASS DESTRUCTION"

260 "having provoked . . . war.": British Commission, quoted Willis, *Prologue to Nuremberg*, p. 58.

261 "His Majesty . . . *Lusitania*": Quoted Bailey and Ryan, *The Lusitania Disaster*, p. 320.

261 "I look . . . misery.": Quoted MacMillan, *Peacemakers* p. 173.

262 "Charles I . . . execution.": Quoted ibid., p. 174.

263 "The firing . . . Nations.": Quoted Willis, *Prologue to Nuremberg*, p. 138.

263 "Who . . . today?": Quoted MacMillan, *Peacemakers*, p. 388.

263 "Modern history . . . effect.": Horgan, *Parnell to Pearse*, p. 276.

265 "to wither . . . hour.": J. Terraine, *White Heat*, p. 160.

265 "psychological . . . resistance.": F. Haber, *Funf Vortraege*, p. 37.

266 The calculations on relative losses are in Griffiths, *Battle Tactics of the Western Front*, p. 43.

267 "to do so . . . wars.": Quoted S. Lindqvist, *A History of Bombing*, item 96, London: Granta 2001.

267 "it is a matter . . . the West.": Quoted D. S. Richards, *The Savage Frontier*, p. 163.

267 "I do not . . . tribes.": Churchill Papers, Churchill Archive, Cambridge,

20/23/13-82 – Papers Relating to Gas Attack 1919–1920.

268 "Special sprayers . . . fell.": Quoted K. Coleman, *A History of Chemical Warfare*, p. 47.

268 "weapons of mass destruction": Archbishop of Canterbury Cosmo Gordon Lang. *The Times* (London) in an article headed "Archbishop's Appeal," December 28, 1937.

268 "The man . . . through.": Quoted Grayling, *Among the Dead Cities*, p. 148.

269 "bombing . . . 1914–18": Sir A. Harris, *Bomber Offensive*, p. 176.

269–270 "that psychological . . . released.": Meeting of the Target Committee for the atomic bomb, May 10–11, 1945, MED file 5D roll 1 M1109, NARA.

272 "under . . . boulder.": Quoted Charles, *Between Genius and Genocide*, p. 204.

273 "When D-Day . . . there.": Quoted Harris and Paxman, *A Higher Form of Killing*, p. 63.

273 "I want you . . . women.": PREM 3/89.

273 WE SHOULD GAS JAPAN: This and other newspaper headlines are quoted in Harris and Paxman, *A Higher Form of Killing*, p. 118.

277 "It has . . . humanity.": Attributed to Einstein, "The Quotable Einstein," ed. A. Calaprice.

APPENDIX—THE *LUSITANIA* CONTROVERSIES

279 "That story . . . disposed of.": Mayer (T). Judge Mayer's Opinion . . . straightjacket": The quotes in these two paragraphs are from Mayer (O).

280 "it is most important . . . USA with Germany.": Churchill to Runciman, February 12, 1915, Runciman papers and Gilbert, *Churchill,* companion volume 3, p. 501.

280 "England . . . bring on trouble.": The kaiser's comments are reported in Ambassador Gerard's telegram to the State Department, May 6, 1916, *Foreign Relations of the U.S. 1916 Supplement*, p. 260.

281 The *U-27*'s war diary is in file RM97-680, German military archive, Freiburg.

282 The *U-20*'s war diary is in file RM97-578 German military archive, Freiburg.

283 Michael Byrne's comments about his search of the ship are in his letter of June 1915 to Secretary of State Bryan, NARA.

284 The information about Canadian troops and about Robert Matthews is in a letter from P.A.O. Chaplin, Senior Research Officer, Directorate of History, Canadian Ministry of Defence to P. B. Ryan, 10 June 1974, Hoover Institution, supplemented by author"s own researches in the Cunard archives.

284 Dudley Field Malone's testimony is given in Savage, *Policy of the United States*, vol. 2, pp. 333-34.

284 The supplementary cargo manifest was given out at the New York Custom House and reported in the *New York Times,* June 3, 1915, although some have claimed it was kept secret for many years.

285 The calculations about shell weight are by P. O'Sullivan and are given in his book *The Lusitania, Unravelling the Mysteries,* p. 100.

BIBLIOGRAPHY

BOOKS, DISSERTATIONS, AND GOVERNMENT PUBLICATIONS

Afflerbach, H., ed. *Kaiser Wilhelm II als Oberster Kriegsherr im Ersten Weltkrieg: Quellen aus der militaerischen Umgebung des Kaisers 1914–1918*. Munich: R. Oldenbourg Verlag, 2005.

Afflerbach, H., and D. Stevenson, eds. *An Improbable War?* New York: Berghahn Books, 2007.

Al-Muwatta of Imam Malik ibn Anas (the first written collection of hadith compiled by the Imam Malik Ibn Anas). London: Kegan Paul International, 1989.

Arthur, M. *Forgotten Voices of the Great War*. St. Helen's, UK: The Book People, 2002.

Aschoff, W. *Londonfluge 1917*. Postdam: Ludwig Voggenreiter Verlag, 1940.

Bacon, Admiral Sir R. *From 1900 Onward*. London: Hutchinson, 1940.

———. *The Life of Lord Fisher of Kilverstone*. Vols. 1 and 2. London: Hodder and Stoughton, 1929.

Bailey, T. A., and P. B. Ryan. *The Lusitania Disaster*. New York: The Free Press, 1975.

Baker, R. S. *Woodrow Wilson—Life and Letters*. Vol. 5. New York: Doubleday, 1935.

Balfour, M. *The Kaiser and His Times*. London: The Cresset Press, 1964.

Ballard, R. D. *Exploring the Lusitania*. New York: Warner/Madison Press, 1995.

Barnett, C. *The Great War*. London: BBC Worldwide, 2003.

Bauer, H. *Reichsleitung und U-Bootseinsatz 1914 bis 1918*. Lippoldsberg, Germany: Klosterhaus Verlag, 1956.

Beesly, P. *Room 40*. London: Hamish Hamilton, 1982.

Bell, A. C. *A History of the Blockade of the Central Empires, 1914–1918*. London: HMSO, 1961.

Bernard, O. *Cocksparrow*, London: Jonathan Cape, 1936.

Bernstorff, Count J. von. *Memoirs*. London: William Heinemann, 1986.

———. *My Three Years in America*. New York: Charles Scribner's Sons, 1920.

Best, G. *Humanity in Warfare*. London: Weidenfeld and Nicolson, 1980.

Bethmann Hollweg, T. von. *Reflections on the World War*. London: Thornton Butterworth, 1920.

Binding, R. *A Fatalist at War*. Translated by I. F. D. Morrow. London: George Allen and Unwin, 1929.

Bismarck, O. *Autobiography*. London: Smith Elder, 1898.

———. *New Chapters of Autobiography*. London: Hodder and Stoughton, 1920.

Blake, R., ed. *Private Papers of Douglas Haig 1914–19*. London: Eyre and Spottiswoode, 1952.

Blücher, Princess E. *An English Wife in Berlin*. London: Constable, 1920.

"Blue Book" of UK Government. London: HMSO, 1914–16.

Blum, J. M. "Tumulty and the Wilson Era." Ph.D. diss., Harvard University, 1949.

Bobbitt, P. *The Shield of Achilles*. London: Penguin, 2003.

Botti, L. *Avec les Zouaves*. Paris: Berger-Levrault Editeurs, 1922.

Brittain, V. *Testament of Youth*. London: Virago 1992.

Bryan, W. J., and M. B. Bryan. *The Memoirs of William Jennings Bryan*. Chicago: John C. Winston, 1925.

Budiansky, S. *Air Power*. London: Viking, 2003.

Bulow, H. von. *Geschichte der Luftwaffe*. Frankfurt am Main, Germany: Verlag Moritz Diesterweg, 1937.

Bulow, Prince B. von. *Memoirs*. Vol. 1. London: Putnam 1931.

Burton, D. H. *Cecil Spring-Rice, a Diplomat's Life*. London: Fairleigh Dickinson University Press, 1960.

Calaprice, A., ed. *The Quotable Einstein*. Princeton, NJ: Princeton University Press: 1996.

Campbell, Sir M,. and J. W. Day. *Speed: The Authentic Life of Sir Malcolm Campbell*. London: Hutchinson, 1931.

Castle, H. G. *Fire over England*. London: Leo Cooper, 1982.

Castle, I. *London 1914–17: The Zeppelin Menace*. Oxford: Osprey Publishing, 2008.

Charles, D. *Between Genius and Genocide*. London: Pimlico, 2006.

Churchill, W. S. *The World Crisis 1911–14*. Vol. 1. London: Thornton Butterworth,1923.

———. *The World Crisis*. Rev. ed. London: Thornton Butterworth, 1981.

Clark, C. *Kaiser Wilhelm II*. London: Longman, 2000.

Coleman, K. *A History of Chemical Warfare*. Basingstoke, UK: Palgrave Macmillan, 2005.

Coleman, T. *The Liners*. London: Allen Lane, 1976.

Compton-Hall, R. *Submarine Boats*. London: Conway Maritime Press, 1983.

Crane, D. *Empires of the Dead*. Harper Collins, 2013.

Creveld, M. van. *Technology and War from 2000 BC to the Present*. London: Brasseys, 1991.

Cross, W. *Zeppelins of World War One*. London, Tauris, 1991.

Crow, D. *A Man of Push and Go: A Life of George Macaulay Booth*. London: Rupert Hart-Davis, 1965.

Dancocks, D. *Welcome to Flanders Fields*. Toronto: M and S Paperback, 1989.

Daniels, J. *The Wilson Era*. Vol. 1, *The Years of Peace, 1910–1917*. Chapel Hill: University of North Carolina Press, 1944–46.

Deimling, B. von. *Aus der alten in die neue Zeit, Lebenserinnerungen*. Berlin: Ullstein, 1930.

Dommett, W. E. *Aeroplanes and Airships*. London: Whittaker, 1915.

Dos Passos, J. *Mr. Wilson's War*. London: Hamish Hamilton, 1963.

Dudley, E. *Monsters of the Purple Twilight*. London: Harrap, 1960.

Duguid, A. F. *Official History of the Canadian Forces in the Great War, 1914–19*. Vols. 1 and 2. Ottawa: Kings Printer, 1938.

Dunant, H. *A Memory of Solferino*. London: Cassell, 1947.

Easdown, M., and T. Genth. *A Glint in the Sky*. Barnsley, UK: Pen and Sword, 2004.

Eckener, K. *My Zeppelins*. London: Putnam, 1958.

Ellis, F. D. *The Tragedy of the Lusitania*. Philadelphia: National Publishing Company, 1915.

Esposito, D. M. *The Legacy of Woodrow Wilson*. Westport, CT: Praeger, 1996.

Falkenhayn, E. von. *General Headquarters 1914–1916 and Its Critical Decisions*. London: Hutchinson, 1919.

Fegan T. *The Babykillers*. London: Leo Cooper, 2002.

Fischer, F. *From Kaiserreich to Third Reich*. London: Allen and Unwin, 1986.

———. *Germany's Aims in the First World War*. London: Chatto and Windus, 1967.

Fisher, Admiral Lord J. A. *Memories*. London: Hodder and Stoughton, 1919.

———. *Records*. London: Hodder and Stoughton, 1919.

Foreign Relations of the U.S., The Lansing Papers. Vols. 1 and 2. Washington, D.C., 1989.

Foreign Relations of the U.S., 1915 and 1916 Supplements .Washington, D.C.

Foulkes, Maj. Gen. C. H. *Gas! The Story of the Special Brigade*. Edinburgh: William Blackwood and Sons, 1934.

Fredette, R. H. *The First Battle of Britain*. London: Cassell, 1966.

Frost, W. *German Submarine Warfare*. London: D. Appleton, 1918.

Fuller, J.F.C. *The Foundation of the Science of War*. London: Hutchinson, 1926.

———. *Machine Warfare*. London: Hutchinson, 1942.

Fyfe, H. C. *Submarine Warfare, Past, Present, and Future* . London: Grant Richards, 1902.

Garrett, R. *Submarines*. London: Weidenfeld and Nicholson, 1977.

Gerard, J. W. *My First Eighty-three Years in America*. New York: Doubleday, 1951.

———. *My Four Years in Germany*. London: Hodder and Stoughton,1927.

Gibson, R. H. *The German Submarine War, 1914–1918*. London: Constable, 1981.

Gilbert, Sir M. *The First World War*. London: HarperCollins, 1995.

———. *Winston S. Churchill, 1914–16*. Vol. 3. London: Heinemann, 1971.

———. *Winston S. Churchill, 1914–16*. Companion vol. 3. London: Heinemann, 1978.

Girard, M. *A Strange and Formidable Weapon*. Lincoln: University of Nebraska Press, 2008.

Goran. M. *The Story of Fritz Haber*. Norman: University of Oklahoma Press, 1967.

Graves, Dr. A. K. *The Secrets of the German War Office*. London: T. Werner Laurie, 1914.

Graves, R. *Goodbye to All That*. London: Cape: 1929.

Grayling, A. C. *Among the Dead Cities*. New York: Walker, 2006.

Gregory, R. *Walter Hines Page*. Lexington: University Press of Kentucky, 1970.

Grey, Viscount. *Twenty-five Years*. Vol. 2. London: Hodder and Stoughton, 1925.

Griffiths, P. *Battle Tactics of the Western Front*. London: Yale University Press, 1994.

Griffith, P., ed. *British Fighting Methods in the Great War*. London: Frank Cass, 1996.

Groner, E. *Die deutschen Kriegsschiffe, 1815–1945*. Koblenz, Germany: Bernard and Graefe Verlag, 1985.

Groos, D. *Der Krieg in der Nordsee*. Vol. 4. Berlin: E. G. Mittler, 1924.

Grotius, H. *De jure belli ac pacis, The Law of War and Peace*. Translated by F. Kelsey. Washitngton,D.C.: Carnegie edition, 1925.

———. *Prolegomena to the Law of War and Peace*. Translated by F. Kelsey. New York: Library of Liberal Arts, Bobbs-Merrill, 1957.

Gwynn, S. *The Letters and Friendship of Sir Cecil Spring-Rice*. Boston: Houghton Mifflin,1929.

Haber, F. *Funf Vortraege aus den Jahren 1920–23*. Berlin: Julius Springer, 1924.

Haber, L. F. *The Poisonous Cloud—Chemical Warfare in the First World War*. Oxford: Clarendon Press, 1986.

Hahn, O. *My Life*. New York: Herder and Herder, 1970.

Hanson, N. *First Blitz*. London: Doubleday, 2008.

Harris, Sir A. *Bomber Offensive*. London: Collins, 1947.

Harris, R., and J. Paxman. *A Higher Form of Killing*. London: Triad, 1983.

Hart, P. *The Great War, 1914–18*. London: Profile, 2014.

Hastings, M. *Catastrophe 1914: Europe Goes to War*. London: HarperCollins, 2013.

Hartcup, G. *The War of Invention*. London: Brassey's Defence Publishers, 1988.

Hayes, P., ed. *Themes in Modern European History, 1890–1945*. London: Routledge, 1992.

Hearne, R. P. *Zeppelins and Super-Zeppelins*. London: John Lane, The Bodley Head, 1916.

Hendrick, B. J. *The Life and Letters of Walter Hines Page*. Vols. 2 and 3. New York: Doubleday, Page,1926.

Hickey, D., and G. Smith. *Seven Days to Disaster*. London: Collins, 1981.

Hobsbawm, E. *The Age of Empire 1875–1914* . London: Weidenfeld and Nicholson, 1987.

Hoehling, A. A., and M. Hoehling. *The Last Voyage of the Lusitania*. Lanham, MD: Madison Books, 1996.

Holbourn, Professor I.B.S. *The Isle of Foula*. Lerwick, Scotland: Johnson and Greig, 1988.

Home, C., and W. F. Austen. *Source Records of the Great War*. 7 vols. Indianapolis: National Alumni Press, 1928.

Horgan, J. J. *Parnell to Pearse*. Dublin: Brown and Nolan, 1948.

Hough, R. *First Sea Lord*. London: Allen and Unwin, 1969.

Hurd, A. *Murder at Sea*. London: T. Fisher Unwin, 1915.

Hyde, A. P. *The First Blitz*. London: Leo Cooper, 2002.

Iarocci, A. *Shoestring Soldiers: The 1st Canadian Division at War, 1914–15.* Toronto, Canada: University of Toronto Press, 2008.

James, L. *Warrior Race.* London: Abacus, 2002.

Johnson J. A., *The Kaiser's Chemists.* Chapel Hill: University of North Carolina Press, 1990.

Jones, H. A. *The War in the Air.* Vol. 5. Oxford: Clarendon Press, 1935.

Jones, J. P. *America Entangled.* New York: A. G. Laut, 1917.

Keegan, J. *The First World War.* London: Pimlico, 1999.

Keyes, Sir R. *Adventures Ashore and Afloat.* London: Harrap, 1939.

Konig, P. *Fahrten der U "Deutschland" im Weltkrieg.* Berlin: Ullstein, 1987.

La Motte, E. N. *The Backwash of War.* London: Conway Publishing, 2014.

Lansing, R. *War Memoirs.* London: Rich and Cowan, 1935.

Latham, R., and W. Matthews, eds. *The Diary of Samuel Pepys.* London: G. Bell, 1970.

Lauriat, C. E. *The Lusitania's Last Voyage.* Boston: Houghton Mifflin, 1915.

Liddle, P., J. Bourne, and I. Whitehead, eds. *The Great World War, 1914 –45.* Vols. 1 and 2. London: HarperCollins, 2000.

Lindqvist, S. *A History of Bombing,* item 96. London: Granta 2001.

Link, A. S., ed. *The Papers of Woodrow Wilson.* Vols. 30, 31, 32, and 33. Princeton, NJ: Princeton University Press, 1980.

———. *Woodrow Wilson—Revolution, War, and Peace.* Arlington Heights, IL: AHM Publishing, 1979.

———. *Woodrow Wilson—The Struggle for Neutrality.* Princeton, NJ: Princeton University Press, 1960.

Livezey, W. E. *Mahan on Sea Power.* Norman: University of Oklahoma Press, 1981.

Lougheed, A. D. *Too Many Heroes.* Vol. 1. Create Space Publishing Independent Platform, 2012.

Ludendorff, General E. *The General Staff and Its Problems.* Vol. 1. London: Hutchinson, 1920.

———. *My War Memories.* London: Hutchinson, 1919.

Luetzow, F. *Der "Lusitania" Fall.* Leipzig: Sueddeutsche Monatshefte, 1921.

Lushington, H. *A Great Country's Little Wars in England, Afghanistan and Scinde.* London: J. W. Parker, 1844.

Lutz, R. H. *Fall of the German Empire, Documents, 1914–18.* Vol. 1. Stanford, CA: 1982.

Lynch, G. *The War of the Civilisations.* London: Green, 1901.

MacDonagh, M. *In London During the Great War.* London: Eyre and Spottiswoode, 1935.

Macdonald, L. 1915, *The Death of Innocence.* London: Penguin, 1997.

MacDonogh, G. *The Last Kaiser.* London: Weidenfeld and Nicholson, 2000.

MacKay R. *Fisher of Kilverstone.* Oxford: Oxford University Press, 1978.

Macksey, K. *Technology in War: The Impact of Science on Weapon Development and Modern Battle.* London: Arms and Armour Press, 1986.

MacMillan, M. *Peacemakers.* London: John Murray, 2001.

———. *The War That Ended Peace.* London: Profile, 2013.

Marder, A. J. *Anatomy of British Sea Power.* New York: Octagon Books, 1976.

———, ed. *Fear God and Dread Nought: The Correspondence of Admiral of the Fleet, Lord Fisher.* Vols. 1, 2, and 3. London: Jonathan Cape, 1952–59.

———. *From the Dreadnought to Scapa Flow.* Vols. 1–4. Oxford: Oxford University Press, 1961–66.

Marshall, L., ed. *Horrors and Atrocities of the Great War Including the Tragic Destruction of the "Lusitania."* New York: L. T. Myers, 1915.

Marton, K. *Hidden Power: Presidential Marriages That Shaped Our History.* New York: Pantheon Books, 2001.

Massie, R. F. *Castles of Steel.* London: Pimlico, 2005.

———. *Dreadnought.* London: Jonathan Cape, 1992.

Maxtone- Graham, J. *The North Atlantic Run.* London: Gassell, 1972.

Mayer Hearings, United States District Court, Southern District of New York, Steamship Lusitania Petition of Cunard for Limitation of Liability Before Hon. J. M. Mayer (all in Federal Archives, New York):

a. *Opinion*

b. *Transcript of Oral Hearings*

c. *Evidence Taken Before Commissioner R. V Wynne in London*

d. *Brief on the Facts for the Petitioner*

McAdoo, W. G. *Crowded Years*. Boston: Houghton Mifflin, 1981.

McInnes, C., and G. D. Sheffield, eds. *Warfare in the Twentieth Century—Theory and Practice*. London: Routledge, 1988.

McWilliams, J., and R. J. Steel. *Gas! The Battle for Ypres, 1915*. Ontario: Vanwell Publishing, 1985.

Mielke, O. *Der Fall "Lusitania."* Schicksaal Deutscher Schiffe No. 78. Munich: Arthur Moewig Verlag, 1955.

Mixed Claims Commission—(U.S. and Germany) Administrative Decisions and Opinions of a General Nature and Opinions in Individual Lusitania Claims and Other Cases to June 30 1925. Washington, D.C., 1925.

Moore, W. *Gas Attack!*. London: Leo Cooper, 1987.

Moorehead, C. *Dunant's Dream*. London: HarperCollins, 1998.

Mordacq, J.J.H. *Le drame de l'Yser: La surprise des gaz, avril 1915*. Paris: Editions des Portiques, 1933.

Morgan, T. *Churchill, Young Man in a Hurry*. New York: Simon and Schuster, 1982.

Morris, J. *Fisher's Face*. London: Viking, 1995.

Morton D., and Pierre-R Desrosiers. *Billet pour le front: Histoire sociale des soldats canadiens 1914–1919*. Montreal: Athena Editions, 2005.

Morton, L. *The Long Wake*. London: Routledge, 1968.

Müller, Admiral G. A. von. *Regierte der Kaiser?* Edited by W. Gorlitz. Berlin: Musterschmidt-Verlag, 1959.

Nasmith, G. C. *Canada's Sons and Great Britain in the Great War*. Toronto: John C. Winston, 1919.

Neureuther, K., and C. Bergen, eds. *U-Boat Stories*. London: Constable, 1981.

Novak, I. *Science: A Many Splendored Thing*. E-book. World Scientific Publishing Company, 2011.

Official German Documents Relating to the World War. 2 vols. New York: Oxford University Press, 1928.

O'Sullivan, P. *The Lusitania, Unravelling the Mysteries*. Cork: Collins Press, 1998.

Pankhurst, E. S. *The Home Front*. London: Hutchinson, 1932.

Papen, F. von. *Memoirs*. London: Andre Deutsch, 1952.

Pogge von Strandmann, H., ed. *Walther Rathenau, Industrialist, Banker, Intellectual and Politician—Notes and Diaries*. Oxford: Clarendon Press, 1985.

Poolman, K. *Zeppelins over England*. London: Evans Brothers, 1960.

Preston, A. *Submarines*. London: Octopus, 1975.

Raleigh, Sir W., and H. A. Jones. *The War in the Air*. Vols, 1, 2, 3, and 5. Oxford: Oxford University Press, 1922–35.

Rappaport, A. *The British Press and Wilsonian Neutrality*. Gloucester, MA: Peter Smith (Stanford University Publications University Series), 1965.

Rhondda, Viscountess (Lady Mackworth). *This Was My World*. London: Macmillan,1933.

Ricard, S. *Companion to Theodore Roosevelt*. Chichester, UK: Blackwell, 2011

Richard, F. *Old Soldiers Never Die*. London: Faber and Faber, 1933.

Richards, D. S. *The Savage Frontier*. London: Macmillan, 1990.

Rintelen, Franz von (foreword by R. Doerries). *The Dark Invader*. London: Frank Cass Publishers, 1997.

Roberts, A. A. *The Poison War*. London: Heinemann, 1915.

Roberts, E. A., and R. Guelff, eds. *Documents on the Law of War*. Oxford: Oxford University Press: 1982.

Roberts, Captain J. R. *The German Air Raids on Great Britain 1914–18*. Stroud, UK: Nonsuch Publishing, 2007.

Robinson, Douglas H. *The Zeppelin in Combat, 1912–18*. Henley-on-Thames, Oxon, UK: Foulis, 1971.

Rumbold, Sir H. *The War Crisis in Berlin, July to August 1914*. London: Constable, 1940.

Sassoon, S. *Memoirs of an Infantry Officer*. Leipzig: Bernhard Tauchnitz, 1931.

Sauder, E., and K. Marschall. *R.M.S. "Lusitania," Triumph of the Edwardian Age*. Blandford Forum, UK: Waterfront Publications, 1993.

Savage, C. *Policy of the United States Toward Maritime Commerce in War*. 2 vols. Washington, D.C., 1936.

Scott, Admiral Sir P. *Fifty Years in the Royal Navy*. New York: George H. Doran, 1919.

Seymour, C., ed. *The Intimate Papers of Colonel House*. 2 vols. London: Ernest Benn, 1926.

Shipping Casualties (Loss of the Steamship "Lusitania"), Proceedings in Camera at the Formal Investigation into the Circumstances Attending the Foundering of the British Steamship "Lusitania," Command 381. London: HMSO, 1919 (known as *The Mersey In Camera Proceedings*).

Shipping Casualties (Loss of the Steamship "Lusitania"), Proceedings on a Formal Investigation into Loss of the Steamship "Lusitania." London: HMSO, 1915 (known as *The Mersey Proceedings*).

Shipping Casualties (Loss of the Steamship Lusitania"). Report of a Formal Investigation into the Circumstances Attending the Foundering of the British Steamship "Lusitania," Command 8022. London: HMSO, 1915 (known as *The Mersey Report*).

Sime, R. L. *Lise Meitner: A Life in Physics*. Berkeley: University of California Press, 1996.

Simpson, C. *The Lusitania*. New York: Little, Brown, 1972.

Slessor, Sir J. *The Central Blue*. London: Cassell, 1956.

Smith, D. M. *Robert Lansing and American Neutrality, 1914–1917*. New York: Da Capo Press, 1972.

Smithers, A. J. *The Man Who Disobeyed*. London: Leo Cooper, 1970.

Snyder, L. *The Military History of the "Lusitania."* New York: Franklin Watts, 1965.

Soames, M. *Speaking for Themselves, the Personal Letters of Winston and Clementine Churchill*. London: Doubleday, 1998.

Souhami, D. *Edith Cavell*. London: Quercus, 2010.

Spiers, E. M. *Chemical Warfare*. London: Macmillan, 1986.

Spindler, Admiral A. *Der Handelskrieg mit U-Booten*. Vols. 1 and 2. Berlin: E. S. Mittler, 1932 and 1933.

Steinberg, J. *Yesterday's Deterrent—Tirpitz and the Birth of the German Battle Fleet*. New York: Macmillan, 1965.

Stephenson, C., and I. Palmer. *Zeppelins: German Airships 1900–40*. Oxford, UK: Osprey Publishing, 2004.

Stevenson, D. *1914–1918: The History of the First World War*. London: Allen Lane, 2004.

Stone, N. *Europe Transformed 1878–1919*. Oxford, UK: Blackwell, 1999.

Stoltzenberg, D. *Fritz Haber*. Philadelphia: Chemical Heritage Press, 2004.

Strachan, H. *The First World War*. Vol. 1. Oxford: Oxford University Press, 2001.

———. *The First World War (A New Illustrated History)*. London: Simon and Schuster, 2003.

Strother, F. *Fighting Germany's Spies*. New York: Doubleday, 1918.

Szöllösi-Janze, M. *Fritz Haber 1868–1934*. Munich: Verlag C. H. Beck, 1998.

Tansill, C. *America Goes to War*. Boston: Little, Brown, 1988.

Tantum W., and C. L. Droste. *The "Lusitania" Case*. Riverside, CT: 7CS Press, 1972.

Tarrant, V. E. *U-Boat Offensive*. Annapolis, MD: The Naval Institute Press, 1989.

Terraine, J. *Business in Great Waters*. London: Leo Cooper, 1989.

———. *White Heat—The New Warfare 1914–18*. London: Leo Cooper, 1982.

Thomas, D. T. *Cochrane*. London: Cassell, 1999.

Thomas, L. *Raiders of the Deep*. London: William Heinemann, 1929.

Tirpitz, Grand Admiral A. von. *My Memoirs*. Vols. 1 and 2. London: Hurst and Blackett,1919.

Tuchman, B. *August 1914*. London: Papermac, 1980.

———. *The Proud Tower*. London: Papermac, 1985.

———. *The Zimmermann Telegram*. London: Constable, 1959.

Tumulty, J. P. *Woodrow Wilson as I Know Him*. New York: Doubleday, 1921.

Van der Vat, D. *Stealth at Sea*. London: Weidenfeld and Nicolson, 1994.

Viereck, G. S. *Spreading Germs of Hate*. London: Duckworth, 1981.

Villard, O. G. *Fighting Years.* New York: Harcourt Brace, 1989.

Voska, E. V, and W. Irwin. *Spy and Counterspy.* New York: Doubleday, 1940.

Wall, R. *Ocean Liners.* London: Collins, 1978.

Warren, M. D. *The Cunard Turbine-Driven Quadruple-Screw Atlantic Liner "Lusitania."* Wellingborough, UK: Patrick Stephens, 1986.

Warwick, Countess Frances. *Life's Ebb and Flow.* London: Hutchinson, 1928.

Weinreb, B., and C. Hibbert, eds. *The London Encyclopaedia.* London: Book Club Associates, 1983.

Wells, H. G. *Anticipations of the Reaction of Mechanical and Scientific Progress upon Human Life and Thought.* London: Chapman and Hall, 1902.

Werner, M. R. *Bryan.* New York: Harcourt Brace, 1929.

White, A. D. *Autobiography.* Vols. 1 and 2. New York: The Century Company, 1914.

Whittle, T. *The Last Kaiser.* London: Heinemann, 1977.

Williams, J. G. *Colonel House and Sir Edward Grey.* London: University Press of America, 1984

Willis, J. F. *Prologue to Nuremberg.* Westport, CT: Greenwood Press, 1982.

Winton, J. *The Submariners—Life in British Submarines, 1901–1999.* London: Constable,1999.

With the First Canadian Contingent. Toronto: Hodder and Stoughton, 1915.

Wynne, R. V. *Evidence Taken Before Commissioner R. V. Wynne in London.* See Mayer Hearings.

Zedlitz-Trützschler, R. *Twelve Years in the Imperial Court.* London: Nisbet, 1924.

Zwehl, H. V. *Erich von Falkenhayn, General der Infanterie.* Berlin: Mittler und Sohn, 1926.

JOURNALS AND MAGAZINES

Where no specific dates are given, the issues are contemporaneous with the events they describe.

American Historical Review (October 1985–July 1986 and June 1997 [N. F. Gullace, "Sexual Violence and Family Honor: British Propaganda and International Law during the First World War"])

American Mercury (May 1985)

American Neptune (1975)

Coronet (March 1950)

Current Events

Current Opinion

Engineering (July 1907 and March 1918) and *Lusitania* Supplement (August 1907)

Hansard (1914–18)

International Affairs (July 1999 [G. Best, "Peace Conferences and the Century of Total War, The 1899 Hague Conference and What Came After"])

Journal of American History (September 1990 [H. R. Slotten, "Humane Chemistry or Scientific Barbarism? American Responses to World War I Posion Gas, 1915–1930"])

Journal of Modern History (1986)

Journal of Military History (July 2006 [T. Cook, "The Politics of Surrender: Canadian Prisoners and the Killing of Prisoners in the Great War"])

Journal of Social History ([N. F. Gullace, "Aliens and Enemies: Fictive Communities and the Lusitania Riots of 1915"])

Journal of the History of Ideas (April–June 1970 [W. D. Miles, "The Idea of Chemical Warfare in Modern Times"])

Liberty (June 2, 1928 [W. J. Flynn, "Tapped Wires"])

Listener (1972)

Literary Digest

Living Age (1928 and 1955)

Marine Rundschaue (1978)

Marine Technology (October 1996 [W. H. Garzke Jr., D. K. Brown, A. D. Sandiford, J. Woodward, and P. K. Hsu, "The 'Titanic' and 'Lusitania'—a Final Forensic Analysis"])

Nation (1928)

National Geographic Magazine (April 1994)
New Statesman (1957)
New York Magazine
New York Shipping Illustrated (1907)
Politics and Life Sciences (September 1998 [L. A. Cole, "The Poison Weapons Taboo: Biology, Culture and Policy"])
Review of Reviews
La Revue des Vivants (Paris, Juillet, 1930)
Royal Society (2004 [W. Van Der Kloot, "April 1915: Five Future Nobel Prize Winners Inaugurate Weapons of Mass Destruction and the Academic-Industrial-Military Complex"])
Scientific American (May 29, 1915)
Sports Illustrated (1962)
Strand Magazine (July 1914)

NEWSPAPERS (MAIN SOURCES)

United Kingdom
Daily Chronicle
Daily Despatch
Daily Express
Daily Mail
Daily Mirror
Daily Telegraph
Evening News (January–April 1935)
Evening Standard
Guardian
Journal of Commerce
Liverpool Daily Post and Mercury
Liverpool Echo
News of the World
Observer (1967)
Times

United States
Baltimore Sun
Boston Globe
Boston Herald
Chicago Tribune
Minneapolis Journal
New York American
New York Evening Sun
New York Herald
New York Sun
New York Telegraph
New York Times
New York Times Book Review (September 1999)
New York Tribune
New York World
Philadelphia Record
Providence Journal

Richmond Times-Dispatch
Sausalito Times
Washington Post

Canada
Bassano Mail
Empress Express

Germany
Berliner Tagesblatt
BochumerAnzeiger (February 1985)
Frankfurter Zeitung
Kölnische Volkszeitung
Neue Preussiche Zeitung
NorddeutscherAllgemeine Zeitung
Der Spiegel
Völkischer Beobachter (May 1935)
Vorwärts
Die Welt

Ireland
Cork Examiner
Sunday Press (1995)

France
Chatillonais et Auxois
La Croix
Le Matin
Le Monde (November 3, 1972)

SPECIFIC COLLECTIONS CONSULTED

Archive zur Geschichte der Max-Planck-Gesellschaft, Dahlem, Berlin—the Fritz Haber collection. Main documents consulted: Va5 –260, –522, –856, –860, –1084, –1449, –1479, –1453, –1480, –1484, –1511, –1678.

Bailey, Thomas A., and Paul B. Ryan. Archive. Hoover Institution on War, Revolution and Peace, Stanford University, Stanford, CA.

Beesley, Patrick. Collection. Churchill College Archives, Cambridge University, Cambridge, UK.

Bundesarchiv-Militararchiv, Freiburg, Germany. Collection of key German naval files for the period (in particular RM2/127,157,1962,1982,1992; RM5/2981, 2982, 2988; RM8/525; RM97/578; and the Press Bureau files in the RM3 series [9771/10312]).

Bryan, William Jennings. Correspondence. Library of Congress, Washington, D.C.

Churchill, Winston. Collection. Churchill College Archives, Cambridge University, UK.

Cunard archives, Liverpool University, UK.

Fisher, Admiral John. Collection. Churchill College Archives, Cambridge University, UK.

Garrison, Lindley. Papers. Seeley G. Mudd Manuscript Library, Princeton University Library, Princeton, NJ.

Hall, Reginald. Papers. Churchill College Archives, Cambridge University, Cambridge, UK.

Hoehling, A. A., and Mary. Archive. Mariners' Museum, Newport News, VA.

Hobson, Richard. Papers. Library of Congress, Washington, D.C.

House, Colonel Edward. Diary. Yale University Library, New Haven, CT.

Imperial War Museum, London—principal written documents consulted: 556, 3728, 4038, 4095, 4118,
    4130, 4154, 4205, 6659, 6705, 7200, 7834, 8498, 8550, 8794, 9115, 9209, 9559, 9625, 10676,10775,
    12869, 11315, 12249, 13108, 14972, 15272, 15751, 15933; 04/37/1, 06/57/1,06/61/A, 08/37/1,
    09/135/1,71/11/2, 06/92/1, 09/59/1, 85/22/1, 88/11/1, 88/46/1, 98/24/1, Lawrence Binyon Special
    Miscellaneous K10 P/C; principal sound recordings:17, 303, 331, 716, 821, 3609, 4038, 4039,
    4118, 4130, 4135, 4205, 4232, 4247, 4273, 6838, 7363, 9146, 9365, 9559, 9883, 10012, 10917,14599,
    22627, 24867, 24869, 24874, 30610.
Lansing, Robert. Papers. Library of Congress, Washington, D.C..
National Archives, London. Main files are: Admiralty series (prefixed by ADM) 187/47,187/113,187/1
    057,187/1058,187/1428,187/2958, i37/3883,187/3912,187/3923,187/3956,187/3957,187/3958,187
    /3959,187/3960,187/3962,137/3963,137/4101,187/4152,137/4156,187/4161,187/4162,187/4168,1
    87/4177, 187/4353,116/1416; Foreign Office series (prefixed by FO):115/1805,115/1806,115/180
    8,115/1809,115/1843,115/1847,115/1936,115/1938,115/1943,115/1962, 115/1979,115/1998,
    371/2587. In the Ministry of Trade series (prefixed by MI) there is one major relevant file, MT
    9/1826. (Key folders are: M 1984, M 12666, M 15283, M 17227, M 198845.)
Root, Elihu. Papers. Library of Congress, Washington, D.C.
Runciman, Walter. Papers. University of Newcastle, UK.
Spring-Rice, Sir Cecil. Collection. Churchill College Archives, Cambridge University, UK.
White, Henry. Correspondence. Library of Congress, Washington, D.C.
Wilson, Woodrow. Papers. Library of Congress, Washington, D.C..

OTHER ARCHIVES CONSULTED

Amis du Vieux Strasbourg
BBC Written Archives Centre, Caversham, Berkshire, UK
Bundesarchiv, Zentralnachweisstelle, Aachen, Germany
Canadian Broadcasting Company radio archives, Ontario, Canada
Cobh Heritage Centre, Cobh, Ireland
Cobh Museum, Cobh, Ireland
Deutsche Dienststelle (WASt), Berlin, Germany
Franklin D. Roosevelt Library, New York, NY
Library of Lincoln's Inn, London
Merseyside Maritime Museum, Liverpool, UK
Merseyside Police, Liverpool, UK
MOD Naval Historian's Department, London
National Army Museum, London
National Maritime Museum, Greenwich, London
National Maritime Museum of Ireland, Dun Laoghaire, Ireland
Naval War College, Newport, RI
Strasbourg Municipal Archives
U-Boat Museum Archives, Cuxhaven, Germany
U.S. Government Records, National Archives and Records Administration (NARA), College Park,
    Maryland, and New York

INDEX

ABOUT THE AUTHOR

DIANA PRESTON is an acclaimed historian and author of the definitive *Lusitania: An Epic Tragedy*, *Before the Fallout: From Marie Curie to Hiroshima* (winner of the Los Angeles Times Book Prize for Science and Technology), *The Boxer Rebellion*, and *The Dark Defile: Britain's Catastrophic Invasion of Afghanistan, 1838–1842*, among other works of narrative history. She and her husband, Michael, live in London.